AI in Financial Decision Making

Written by experts who have trained global audiences in finance and designed real-life solutions, this book provides exactly what financial decision-makers need: a survival kit for disruptive times.

The increasing use of AI has posed challenges and brought benefits at organizational and individual levels. However, financial decision-makers are often not equipped with the necessary skills and may even feel threatened by the speed at which AI is automating the decision-making process. This book takes a balanced look at how AI and ML are applied across operations, finance, and risk management. It is not meant to turn finance professionals into coders; instead it shows clearly how these tools can be used to tackle real business problems. This will help financial decision-makers actively engage with projects involving the implementation of ML tools in their organizations. Beyond simple ML tool identification, the book goes one step further and provides representative codes that the reader can use by tweaking information to make it relevant to their own situation. To keep up with the rapid developments in AI and ML, this book is accompanied by a website where tools and codes will be regularly updated as standards change.

Anyone involved in financial decision-making will find this book to be an invaluable resource, whether a CFO, finance director, management accountant, budget officer, auditor, strategic planner, or early career professional.

Arif Ahmed is a chartered accountant from the UK and India, ACMA (CIMA), CGMA (CIMA-AICPA), UK. He holds an MBA and a Doctor in Finance. His professional certifications include one on artificial intelligence. Arif has served as a member of the Sustainability Reporting Standards Board and Expert Advisory Committee of the Institute of Chartered Accountants of India. He has over 35 years of consulting and training experience.

Veena Hingarh is a chartered accountant from the UK and India, ACMA (CIMA), CGMA (CIMA-AICPA), UK. She also holds an MSc and a professional certificate in artificial intelligence, and is a company secretary from India. She has served on the boards of listed companies as an independent director and has been on the Expert Advisory Committee of the Institute of Chartered Accountants of India. Veena has over 25 years of training and consulting experience.

Arnaaz Ahmed is an ACMA (CIMA), CGMA (CIMA-AICPA), UK. She also holds an MSc in international accounting and finance from Heriot-Watt University, Edinburgh. She also holds a professional certificate in IFRS and is currently pursuing her doctoral studies. Arnaaz enjoys creating codes to solve financial problems.

AI in Financial Decision Making

Arif Ahmed, Veena Hingarh, and
Arnaaz Ahmed

Routledge
Taylor & Francis Group
NEW YORK AND LONDON

Designed cover image: Getty

First published 2026
by Routledge
605 Third Avenue, New York, NY 10158

and by Routledge
4 Park Square, Milton Park, Abingdon, Oxon, OX14 4RN

Routledge is an imprint of the Taylor & Francis Group, an informa business

Library of Congress Cataloging-in-Publication Data
Names: Ahmed, Arif (Accountant) author | Hingarh, Veena author | Ahmed, Arnaaz author
Title: AI in financial decision making / Arif Ahmed, Veena Hingarh, and Arnaaz Ahmed.
Description: New York, NY : Routledge, 2026. | Includes bibliographical references and index.
Identifiers: LCCN 2025031200 (print) | LCCN 2025031201 (ebook) | ISBN 9781041025139 hardback | ISBN 9781041019763 paperback | ISBN 9781003619628 ebook
Subjects: LCSH: Artificial intelligence—Financial applications | Corporations—Finance—Data processing | Corporations—Finance—Decision making
Classification: LCC HG4515.5 .A34 2026 (print) | LCC HG4515.5 (ebook) | DDC 658.15—dc23/eng/20250829
LC record available at https://lccn.loc.gov/2025031200
LC ebook record available at https://lccn.loc.gov/2025031201

ISBN: 978-1-041-02513-9 (hbk)
ISBN: 978-1-041-01976-3 (pbk)
ISBN: 978-1-003-61962-8 (ebk)

DOI: 10.4324/9781003619628

Typeset in Sabon
by Apex CoVantage, LLC

Access the Github site: https://github.com/arifahmed-books/AI-in-financial-decision

Contents

Chapter 1

Introduction

Artificial Intelligence (AI) and Machine Learning (ML) are transforming financial decision-making. Join us as we demonstrate that advanced analytics no longer requires complex coding knowledge or high-end systems. With Lo-code tools and accessible Python libraries, finance professionals can now apply powerful techniques using just their laptops. This chapter sets the stage for the application of AI/ML in financial decision-making.

The convergence of financial decision-making, AI, and ML

Financial decision-making involves a structured process where financial resources controlled by an entity are utilized to maximize wealth. This wealth ultimately belongs to the shareholders. The decision-making process has evolved over the years, becoming quicker, more efficient, and broader in scope. Automation and the use of advanced analytics in the decision-making process have gained prominence in recent years.

AI and ML are two major developments that have influenced the financial decision-making process. AI broadly refers to the capability of systems to perform tasks that typically require human intelligence. These would include reasoning, problem-solving, understanding language, perceiving environments, and other similar tasks. ML, on the other hand, is a subset of AI that involves training algorithms to learn patterns from data and make predictions or decisions without being explicitly programmed for each task. This does not mean that there is no programming involved. The main computational complexities are built into system resources.

Coding is simply limited to invoking the resource and feeding it with data. The performance of these models improves over time as they process more and more data.

The integration of AI and ML with financial decision-making is transforming the industry. It allows faster, more informed, and often more accurate assessments of risk, opportunity, and market behavior. Lo-code

DOI: 10.4324/9781003619628-1

platforms are making these advanced analytical techniques accessible to finance professionals without programming expertise. They are lowering the knowledge barrier by providing intuitive drag-and-drop interfaces, pre-built models, and automated workflows. This has allowed finance professionals to move away from rigid, rule-based processes to more flexible, data-driven decision-making.

In this book, we will closely examine business issues that can be addressed by various AI and ML tools. Do not worry, you do not need to be an expert coder to use these tools, and as long as you have a thorough understanding of the domain, you are good to go.

AI and ML in the evolving landscape of financial decision-making

The finance industry has a lot to gain by adopting transformative technologies such as AI and ML. The more relevant data we analyze, the more refined our decision is. AI and ML can apply advanced analytical methods on large datasets, thereby improving decision-making. The fusion of traditional financial acumen and technological capabilities is making it possible for us to analyze large data sets and get better insights into trends, risks, and opportunities. AI is already providing more accurate strategic insights into the value-generation process, making it more efficient. It is reshaping the financial decision-making process.

Corporate finance is where most financial decisions are made. The financial decision-makers frequently make decisions involving forecasting, resource allocation, cost optimization, and allied matters. AI tools analyze historical patterns, seasonal trends, and economic data to provide real-time insights, perform complex scenario modeling, and predict future requirements in the company. They can perform continuous monitoring and identify red flags and variances to support a more proactive and dynamic decision-making process.

In addition to supporting standard financial decisions, AI and ML tools now allow financial decision-makers to include dimensions that were difficult to consider earlier. For example, financial decisions can now include a dimension of sentiment analysis, customer segmentation, or fraud analysis. Activities like credit scoring, which used to remain in the hands of select experts, can now be led by financial decision-makers. One can compute customer lifetime value (CLV) by integrating such tools with domain expertise. Capital budgeting decisions can now consider multiple scenarios before selecting an investment. The possibilities are almost unlimited.

The evolving landscape at the intersection of financial decision-making and AI/ML technologies is characterized by increased accuracy, efficiency, and strategic depth. By combining domain expertise with AI-driven insights, organizations can navigate complex financial environments more effectively. This transformation is not just about the adoption of technology but also about redefining the role of finance professionals. They now emerge as strategic enablers with an enhanced portfolio of data-driven tools at their disposal.

Technology-driven transformation of traditional financial decisions

Traditional financial decision-making shifts from being manual and reactive to a more strategic, proactive, and insight-driven process. Embracing technologies like AI and ML is leading to a frontier where the decision-maker can consider multiple dimensions that were not considered earlier. This elevates the role of finance professionals to strategic advisers. They interpret data insights and guide business decisions to make better use of resources. Let us have a look at some of the decisions where technologies are reshaping the financial decision-making process.

Enhanced financial forecasting and budgeting

AI and ML improve financial forecasting accuracy by analyzing vast amounts of historical and real-time data. Time series forecasting, automated variance analysis, and scenario planning are dramatically improving strategic decisions. Predictive analytics using ML models are enhancing revenue forecasting, cash flow projections, and market analysis. ML-driven simulations for scenario analysis allow professionals to assess the financial impact of different business scenarios. For example, a retail company may use ML models to predict seasonal demand trends, which optimizes inventory and budget planning.

Strengthened risk management

Traditionally focused on historical data analysis, AI has transformed risk management into a dynamic function interpreting real-time data. The use of ML models for credit risk, detection of fraud, and more has made the risk management process proactive. AI systems analyze thousands of variables simultaneously to assess creditworthiness, moving beyond traditional credit scores. ML models detect fraud patterns and flag suspicious transactions more effectively than manual review. AI models continuously monitor financial transactions and market conditions, identifying potential risks. Even expert functions like model validation, scenario planning, and handling complex cases that require human judgment can now be accomplished by ML tools. The decision-makers can now focus more on the interpretation of model output rather than on the computation.

Strategic insights and financial decisions

With AI and ML tools taking over data-heavy and repetitive tasks, finance professionals can focus on strategic decision-making. Tools like robotic process automation perform invoice processing, reconciliation, and data entry. AI-powered dashboards provide real-time support and instant insights. Finance professionals can get cross-functional information and collaborate with marketing, operations, human resources, and other departments to support enterprise-wide strategies. AI can be also used to provide real-time updates and scenario analysis during executive meetings, improving decision-making speed and quality.

Compliance and ethics

AI and ML also significantly impact compliance and ethical considerations. Finance professionals are required to be updated with regulations like GDPR, IFRS, ISO standards, local laws, and allied. AI systems can assist finance professionals by reviewing documentation for fairness, transparency, and bias to ensure compliance with internal and external policies and regulations.

Effective operations and management

Robotics, the Internet of Things, and AI have become integral to various internal processes. They provide real-time data that can be used for financial decisions. Cost management may be optimized by using ML to implement activity-based costing (ABC), identify cost drivers, and allocate resources optimally. Performance measurement tools such as interactive dashboards, balanced scorecards, and employee performance analytics can also utilize these techniques. AI and ML help to forecast demand, optimize supply networks, and classify inventory. Capital budgeting can also be furthered by automating financial calculations, valuing real options, and optimizing investment portfolios.

Client-centric solutions

Using AI and ML enables companies to offer more personalized and innovative solutions to customers. They help to predict CLV, segment customers effectively, reduce churn, and potentially increase customer profitability. A financial adviser can use AI-generated insights to propose customized investment strategies. AI can also help us innovate new financial products, such as dynamic pricing models or tailored investment portfolios.

Portfolio management and trading

ML algorithms now handle complex portfolio optimization, analyzing vast amounts of market data to identify patterns and opportunities that human traders might miss.

Automated trading systems execute transactions at speeds and frequencies impossible for humans, while AI monitors market conditions to adjust strategies in real time. This has shifted the role of portfolio managers from direct trading to strategy oversight and risk management.

We have seen above that AI and ML are bringing in a paradigm shift and transforming traditional financial decision-making roles into dynamic, strategic, and technology-driven functions. By automating routine tasks, enhancing decision-making accuracy, and enabling real-time insights, these technologies empower finance professionals to focus on strategic leadership and innovation. As these roles evolve, the ability to harness AI and ML effectively will become a cornerstone of financial expertise in the modern workplace.

Importance of embracing AI/ML for strategic decision-making

Organizations face increasingly complex challenges that demand precise, agile, and forward-looking financial strategies. By integrating AI and ML tools in the decision-making process, organizations can better adjust to the ever-changing environment. Some of the reasons why this technology should be leveraged for strategic decisions in finance are given here.

Transforming data into actionable insights

AI and ML tools can provide a clearer picture of trends, customer behavior, and operational performance from a large dataset. These can be fed forward to the strategic decision-making process. Data integration, pattern recognition, and predictive modeling are some of the tools that uncover hidden insights. Using these tools reduces the risk of decision-making based on anecdotal evidence or personal biases. For example, a company may predict seasonal demand fluctuations, enabling data-driven inventory management and pricing strategies.

Enhancing decision-making speed, agility, and adaptability

We can analyze data in real time and provide relevant insights into changing circumstances using AI and ML tools. Real-time analytics provide instant updates and forecasts, which enable leaders to make timely decisions and reduce the decision cycle. Most AI and ML models continuously learn and update themselves, which allows them to dynamically adjust as new data is available. For example, a manufacturing company may use AI to monitor supply chain disruptions and dynamically adjust sourcing strategies, minimizing downtime and costs.

Driving competitive advantage

Better data analysis results in more actionable insights, which eventually lead to businesses being able to anticipate and respond more effectively to changing market conditions. This will help in identifying opportunities and risks faster, and factor them into the decision-making process. Market differentiation, new product development, increased operational efficiency, optimized resource allocation, and streamlined processes, are some of the areas that will emerge stronger with the use of AI and ML tools. For example, banks employing AI-powered customer analytics are likely to spot cross-selling opportunities faster.

Strengthening risk management and resilience

Strategic decisions often hinge on understanding and mitigating risks. AI and ML tools, besides quantification of different types of risk, can also run simulations to have a better view of the exposure. For example, an investment company may evaluate portfolio risks under different economic conditions, optimizing returns while minimizing exposure.

Encouraging innovation

The use of AI and ML tools brings forth insights that encourage innovation. These innovative ideas can be tested using simulated scenarios before deciding on whether to implement them. These tools also promote cross-functional interaction to facilitate comprehensive evaluation of new ideas. For example, the finance and operational team of a logistics company can use AI-powered route optimization tools.

A strategic imperative

Embracing AI and ML is critical for organizations to enhance their strategic decision-making capabilities. By transforming data into insights, these technologies support leaders to make smarter, faster, and more effective decisions. This advantage will allow organizations to navigate the challenges of the present along with being prepared for the future.

Overview of Lo-code AI/ML tools in Python

Terms like "data analytics," "computing technologies," "programming," and "information technology" often create a perception of complexity. AI and ML are viewed as tools that require top-class programming skills and powerful computers. While that is partly correct, it does not do justice to the advancements in technology and better accessibility. Many tools are available that can run on standard laptops. Cloud-based services make computational power available without investing in expensive hardware. Let us explore this shifting landscape where finance professionals can access advanced data analytics for decision-making.

The first challenge is in accessing new technology. Finance professionals have always been comfortable using spreadsheets like MS Excel due to their simplicity. Excel has evolved significantly over time and now has advanced data analytic capabilities. At the same time, no-code and Lo-code platforms like Power BI, Tableau, and others have made it easier than ever to build dashboards and models to analyze trends and generate insights without requiring extensive coding skills.

Similarly, there are many user-friendly libraries in Python like `Pandas`, `NumPy`, `Scikit-learn`, `TensorFlow`, and others, which have made complex processes easy to use. We will discuss and use these libraries extensively in this book. In fact, Python now comes integrated with Excel allowing the user to access powerful libraries within a familiar environment.

The next challenge is the cost of computing power. The good news is that the computing power requirements for many of these tools are available even on a standard laptop. Wherever there is a need for larger power and capacity, it is addressed by various cloud computing platforms that provide affordable, scalable computing power. Users pay for only the resources they need, making advanced analytics accessible to small organizations and individuals.

Another challenge is the perceived skill gap. Though it is undeniable that finance professionals need to have some additional skills to be able to use these tools, those are far from being complex. This book leverages the domain expertise of finance professionals and leads them to a Lo-code environment where the amount of customization requirement is amazingly little. Many software libraries that provide solutions to finance professionals require little to no technical expertise. The challenge is to plug the values in and play with the results. That being said, the role that data science and coding teams play is undeniable, especially where complex solutions are involved. In those cases, the awareness of finance professionals about the capabilities of these advanced AI and ML tools would allow them to contribute positively to the solution design and building process.

Accountants and finance professionals do not need to become programmers! With the right tools and some basic skills, they can do a lot using their domain expertise. Data scientists have done a commendable job in making the tools accessible to non-coders.

Lo-code tools and financial decision-making

Many AI and ML tools use Lo-code-driven libraries to generate AI-based output to allow users to build and deploy applications with minimal to no coding capability. Custom applications and workflows are created using minimal coding. In this book, we have provided standard application-focused templates with customizable components that make financial analysis a plug-and-play exercise. In some cases, these processes can even run entirely on their own or include minimal human involvement. In a nutshell, Lo-code AI is an approach to building AI-powered applications and analyses that just require basic coding. It enables finance professionals to utilize the power and capabilities of AI-powered applications. Finance professionals can generate insights without writing complex algorithms. It enables them to independently explore data and build models, away from complete reliance on IT teams or data scientists.

This book would enable finance professionals to use Lo-code tools to generate real-time analytics and have predictive capabilities. These applications can be used in financial forecasting and budgeting, including variance analysis and scenario planning. There are tools that would help in implementing cost-optimization methods such as ABC, cost driver analysis, and resource optimization.

Issues of performance measurement and management can be addressed by developing smart KPI dashboards, balanced scorecards, and other analytics. Strategic financial decisions like investment appraisal involve an understanding of market trends and sentiments. Various tools are addressing these competencies. There are AI- and ML-based tools addressing inventory and supply chain management, such as demand forecasting, supply chain optimization, inventory classification, and management. Capital budgeting and investment analysis have always been important to financial professionals. AI and ML can be used to automate computing for capital budgeting and investment analysis even in uncertain environments. Valuation of real options and optimization of the portfolio are supported by specific tools. Finance professionals are always concerned with the bottom line being profitable. Revenue and cost optimization, customer profitability and segmentation tools, predictive analytics, and other applications help finance professionals address operational issues. Lo-code approach to risk modeling, fraud detection, and compliance monitoring models would facilitate finance professionals in enhancing their oversight and monitoring capabilities and enable real-time responses. We have discussed all these in this book, both through examples and case studies.

These Lo-code tools provide cost-effective pragmatic solutions with reduced involvement of specialized programming resources while utilizing the core capabilities of finance professionals.

Overview of Python libraries

Before we start discussing this module, let us be very clear. The purpose of this module is to help you understand the codes that we have provided across the book. The goal is not to become a coder but to have enough understanding to use the code effectively. We should be able to tweak the code to customize it to our input files and parameters.

Python is a high-level programming language known for its simplicity and readability. Python's popularity in AI and data science is largely due to its extensive ecosystem of libraries including `NumPy`, `Pandas`, `SciPy`, `Matplotlib`, and `TensorFlow`. These tools provide robust functionalities for numerical computation, data manipulation, visualization, and machine learning, making Python a great base for using AI and ML.

Table 1.1 gives an overview of how libraries help.

At the initiation of the code, we will import the necessary libraries from the environment. If the library is not installed in the environment, we will have to install the same. Note that library names and their import names in Python may differ.

Table 1.1 Overview of Python libraries

Area	*Libraries*	*Functions*
Data Handling	`Pandas, NumPy`	Loading, filtering, transforming, aggregating data
Visualization	`Matplotlib, Seaborn, Plotly`	Creating charts, plots, dashboards
Model Building	`Scikit-learn, TensorFlow, Keras, XGBoost`	Training machine learning and deep learning models with just a few lines of code
NLP	`NLTK, transformers`	Tokenization, stemming, language models
Model Evaluation	`sklearn.metrics, Yellowbrick`	Confusion matrix, ROC curve, feature importance
Deployment	`Joblib, Flask, Streamlit`	Saving/loading models, creating web apps or APIs

Refer to the official documentation or search online for the correct syntax for importing specific libraries. Traditionally we assign an alias to a library while importing. An alias is just a shorter name which makes it easier to reference the library later in the code. For example,

```
import numpy as np
```

Here we have given `numpy` an alias np. Whenever we need to refer to the numpy library we will use np.

A library is a collection of modules packaged together. For example, `numpy` is a library and it contains modules like `numpy.linalg` for linear algebra. This module provides functions, such as matrix multiplication, solving systems of linear equations, and so on.

Within the module are stored functions that do the actual computation. For example, within the linear algebra module, we have a function to compute the inverse of a matrix. It is denoted by inv. If we want to compute the inverse of an array named A, we will have the following code:

```
A_inv = np.linalg.inv(A)
```

Let us now understand the components summarized in Table 1.2.

So, the complete code means, *use NumPy's linear algebra module to compute the inverse of matrix A and store it in A_inv*. You can even import specific functions. Look at the following code:

```
from numpy.linalg import inv
```

Table 1.2 Components of a library function

Component	What It Is	Description
A	Variable	A 2D `NumPy` array (matrix) passed as input to the inv() function
A_inv	Variable	The result (inverse of matrix A) stored in this variable
np	Alias	Short for `numpy`, used as import `numpy` as np
linalg	Module	Stands for Linear Algebra, a submodule in `NumPy` (`numpy.linalg`) that contains functions for matrix operations
inv	Function	Stands for inverse, a function inside the linalg module that computes the inverse of a matrix

This code imports the inverse function without importing the complete numpy library or linalg module. In this case, you can compute the inverse of A, directly.

```
A_inv = inv(A)
```

You can also import a specific module like the following

```
from numpy import linalg
```

If you want to have an alias you can use

```
from numpy import linalg as la
```

In that case, you will compute the inverse with the following code:

```
A_inv = la.inv(A)
```

A word of caution here; the programming world is continuously evolving. Python versions and libraries keep getting updated. These updates may not be simultaneous or compatible, which may result in the code not working as it was. It is important to be aware of such potential changes.

Hopefully, you are now comfortable with how Python libraries, modules, and functions are used in the code. Let us now see how to create an environment in which we use these powerful libraries.

Setting up AI/ML tools

As mentioned earlier, Python and its various libraries have increased the accessibility of AI and ML to financial decision-makers. They can now implement sophisticated analytics and modeling tools directly on their laptops. Below, we discuss some key tools and how they can be effectively implemented on your laptop.

Python and its ecosystem

When financial decision-makers want to prototype AI/ML solutions on their laptops, without depending heavily on IT infrastructure, JupyterLab or Jupyter Notebook is an ideal starting point. Both of these are web-based platforms which allow you to write and run Python code. You can use any platform that runs Python code. However, JupyterLab and Notebook have some advantages over plain Python scripts. For example, they can run parts of code in cells, which is useful for debugging, have better inline documentation features, and have better visualization tools. JupyterLab can be installed as a part of a suite or individually. We will discuss the installation of JupyterLab using the Anaconda suite.

We can use Anaconda, which is a popular Python distribution that comes bundled with several data science tools. To get started, visit the Anaconda website (https://www.anaconda.com/) and follow the on-screen instructions to install the Anaconda Distribution. It comes with both JupyterLab and Notebook. Once installed, open Anaconda Navigator and click on JupyterLab or Notebook. It will open on your web browser using a local server.

JupyterLab offers an interactive computing environment where you can combine executable code, rich text, visualizations, equations, and other media in a single document. It is a powerful tool for data analysis, machine learning, and scientific research. Jupyter Notebook also performs the same functions, but JupyterLab is more user-friendly. We will be using JupyterLab in this book, but you can use Jupyter Notebook too using the same instructions.

Once JupyterLab opens in your browser, you will see a folder tree on the left for easy navigation. On the right side of your screen, you will find the "Launcher" tab, with options like Notebook, Console, Terminal, Python, and more. Select the "Notebook" option to open a new notebook. The notebook will be titled "Untitled" by default. You can rename it by right-clicking on the "Untitled" tab and selecting "Rename Notebook . . . ." The notebook will automatically be saved in the folder from which JupyterLab was launched. Note that both JupyterLab and Jupyter Notebook save code fields as .ipynb (notebooks). The notebook is composed of cells. Each cell can be one of three types: code, markdown text, or raw text. To add more cells, click the "+" sign. To execute a cell, either press Shift + Enter or click on the play (▶) sign on the notebook window. This will only execute the selected cell. On the toolbar, you will find options for saving the file, inserting or deleting cells, copying or pasting content, starting or interrupting execution, restarting the kernel, running all cells, and selecting cell type from a dropdown menu. You can read more about Anaconda, its installation, and various guides on how to navigate its interface on many websites.

Let us take a quick look at a few of the options.

- **Restart kernel**: A kernel is the computational engine that runs the code. When you write Python code in a cell and press Shift + Enter, the code is sent to the kernel, which executes it and returns the result. On the extreme right corner of the toolbar, you will see a circle. This is the kernel status. A black circle (●) indicates that the kernel is processing, and a white circle (O) indicates that the kernel is idle. Sometimes, the kernel becomes unresponsive, and you are required to restart the kernel. After restarting the kernel, you have to process the code from the beginning.

- **Restart kernel and run all cells**: This option restarts the kernel and processes all cells in the notebook.
- **Cell type**: You can specify what the cell contains. There are three options: Code, Markdown, and Raw. Code executes Python code, Markdown is used for formatted text, such as headings, or lists, which are used for in-line documentation, and Raw contains plain text that is not interpreted.

You might have already realized that the power of AI/ML tools comes from the libraries. Many libraries are already present at installation. However, at times we may find that a particular library is not present, or their version needs updates. You will get error messages that notify you. To install/reinstall a library, simply run the following command in the command line. You will find the command line under the Terminal option in the Launcher tab.

```
pip install "library name"
```

For example, if we want to install Pandas, we would write:

```
pip install pandas
```

You can also install any library from the code cell in the notebook. However, you will need to have only that code in the cell and precede the code with "!" sign.

```
!pip install pandas
```

Once we are ready with the libraries and of course the code, we need to know if the code is being executed. The kernel status will indicate this. We also need to know which cells have been processed. To the left of each cell, you will find a square bracket []. Whenever a cell is selected, a colored bar will appear on the left margin of the cell. When the cell is being processed, an asterisk will appear within the square brackets, as [*]. Once the cell has been processed, the asterisk will be replaced with a number that indicates the order in which the cell was executed. The colored bar will also move to the next cell. Remember, in Jupyter Notebook, cells are processed individually, unless specifically instructed.

If you want to clear all the output of a processing run, you can right-click anywhere on the notebook and click on "Clear Output of all Cells" to reset the code devoid of all output. You can also select "Clear Cell Output" to clear the output of only the selected cell.

Note that correct syntax is crucial. Just like grammar is important in language, syntax is important for coding, perhaps even more so. While the difference between "Let's eat grandma" and "Let's eat, grandma" is understood by humans, computers may end up doing something catastrophic! Even a small mistake like a missing colon, incorrect indentation, wrong capitalization, or unmatched parentheses and quotation marks can cause a logically perfect code to crash. For example, writing print as Print, or writing print ("Hello) instead of print ("Hello"). Do not worry, because if there is a mistake, Python will usually give you a helpful error message to guide you.

With this basic understanding and a prepped environment, we are now set to harness the power of AI and ML for financial decisions. By combining lightweight Python libraries and Lo-code tools, we can now perform advanced analytics, automate processes, and make data-driven decisions without requiring enterprise-level infrastructure. These tools democratize AI/ML capabilities, making them accessible to professionals with varying technical expertise.

Key Python libraries for AI/ML applications

Python-based libraries provide a robust framework for implementing AI and ML models. These libraries simplify complex processes like data analysis, visualization, and algorithm development, making them accessible for beginners and experts alike. Below, we introduce some fundamental Python libraries and real-world cases to increase familiarity. You will find practical use cases that you may use yourself for financial decision-making.

These have been provided under various chapters of the book. Codes, wherever needed, have been provided to you, and all you will need to do is to customize the input data file and run the codes provided.

Following is an overview of some key Python libraries that are particularly useful for finance professionals venturing into AI/ML.

- **`NumPy`**, which stands for Numerical Python, is essential for numerical and mathematical computations and serves as the foundation for many other libraries. Its array-oriented computing capabilities make it an essential tool for fields such as linear algebra, statistical analysis, and ML. It may be used to calculate portfolio returns and risks and perform matrix operations for quantitative finance models.
- **`Pandas`** are used for data manipulation, cleaning, and analysis. It has data frames, designed like spreadsheets, for structured data handling. It has various functions for merging, grouping, reshaping, and aggregating data. `Pandas` can be used for handling missing data and

time series analysis. It is a useful tool for preparing financial datasets for analysis, generating financial reports, and performing exploratory data analysis.

- **`Matplotlib`** and **`Seaborn`** are data visualization tools. `Matplotlib` is used for creating static, animated, and interactive visualizations. It can be used to create various charts and make plots for data analysis and presentation. `Seaborn` is a library built on `Matplotlib` that creates statistical graphics for high-level functions for complex visualizations like heatmaps and pair plots.
- **`Scikit-learn`** is a library for implementing ML algorithms. It is an ML library that provides tools for data mining and analysis. It includes lots of ML algorithms for different tasks. It consists of tools for both supervised learning, like regression, or classification, and unsupervised learning, like clustering. It has preprocessing, model evaluation, and validation capabilities. It can be used for building models for credit scoring, fraud detection, or churn prediction. It can also be used for forecasting models for revenue or expenses.
- **`TensorFlow`** is used for deploying deep learning models. They are particularly used for training and inference of deep neural networks. Models for financial forecasting and anomaly detection may deploy these libraries. It is used for financial analytics and training models for natural language processing (NLP) like sentiment analysis.

These are some of the common Python libraries above. We would be introducing others as we discuss different applications under various chapters in the book while illustrating specific financial decision applications.

Setting expectations for the use of Python tools in this book

We know that integrating AI and ML into financial workflows enables professionals to make more informed and efficient decisions. This book aims to empower financial decision-makers with the knowledge and skills to use Python libraries for AI and ML with rudimentary programming knowledge. The focus of the book is not to make financial decision-makers write codes but to get codes to assist financial decision- makers. Different AI and ML tools will be used to address real-world financial challenges introduced in the respective chapter.

No prior knowledge of Python programming or ML capabilities is required. The cases and codes wherever used are self-explanatory. As stated earlier, the focus of the book is to improve your financial decision-making skills and not to make you a coder or an ML expert. Our focus is to help you to get your job done using appropriate tools.

You may even be able to take on challenges that you had to avoid earlier because of a lack of available tools.

Some of the other useful features you will find in the book include the following:

- **Step-by-step guidance**: Each chapter provides easy-to-understand step-by-step instructions and guidance for using Python tools to make financial decisions. Hands-on real-world examples, such as forecasting revenues or identifying fraud, demonstrate the practical application of the tools described. It will be a gradual development keeping in mind that our focus audience excels in financial decision-making.
- **Application of tools to real-world scenarios**: The book connects Python libraries directly to real-world decision-making with chapters using examples and case studies that replicate real life. We will use `Pandas` and `NumPy` to clean, manipulate, and analyze financial datasets, such as balance sheets, transaction logs, and cash flow statements. `Scikit-learn` and XGBoost would be used to build predictive models for tasks like credit scoring, customer churn prediction, and risk classification. We will explore deep learning applications, such as time series forecasting for stock prices or sales data. You may find us using the same tool in multiple business cases. Our focus is to show how these tools can be used in different business cases and not merely how they work.
- **Lo-Code solutions:** For finance professionals with no or limited coding experience, the book provides highly customizable, ready-to-use code templates. You can easily adapt it by simply plugging in your data. This hands-on approach will help you understand, modify, and apply these tools directly to your business. While we do not claim it to be a turnkey software solution, the book is designed to show you the computational power of AI and ML.
- **Gradual introduction to advanced concepts:** The book is designed with a progressive learning structure in mind. Both the overall flow and each individual chapter move from easy concepts such as simple forecasting to more complex ML tools like neural networks, NLP, and ensemble learning. All along you will find clear explanations of what is being done.
- **Alternative approaches**: We have not stuck to a unique style or the same approach in solving similar problems. You will find us solving the same task in multiple ways. This is done deliberately to introduce you to alternative approaches. We have mostly followed a similar coding structure throughout the book to improve readability.

By the end of the book, you will understand the basics of Python tools and how they apply to financial decision-making. You will gain practical experience by customizing and running the code yourself. You will also be ready to use Python tools for tasks like forecasting, risk analysis, and fraud detection and feel confident in deploying AI/ML solutions to address real-world financial challenges.

Key areas covered by this book

The book covers a wide range of problems faced by finance professionals. Once you complete the book, we expect you to be able to use Python to do the following:

- **Financial forecasting and budgeting**: Improve accuracy and efficiency using time series forecasting, automated variance analysis, and scenario planning.
- **Cost management**: Implement ABC, identify cost drivers, and allocate resources optimally.
- **Performance measurement**: Develop interactive dashboards, implement balanced scorecards, and examine employee performance.
- **Strategic planning**: Analyze market trends, perform investment simulations, and evaluate strategic options with decision trees.
- **Inventory and supply chains**: Forecast demand, optimize supply networks, and classify inventory for better management.
- **Capital budgeting**: Automate financial calculations, value real options, and optimize investment portfolios.
- **Customer profitability**: Predict CLV, segment customers effectively, and reduce churn.
- **Risk management**: Model credit risks, detect fraud, and monitor compliance using advanced analytics.

Hope you are all set to start your journey into the exciting world of using AI and ML in financial decision-making!

Chapter 2

Financial forecasting and budgeting

In today's fast-paced financial environment, forecasting and budgeting have evolved from periodic planning tools into dynamic, data-driven processes. Finance teams can make better forecasts and budgets just by using simple ML tools. In this chapter, we refresh our knowledge on the basics of budgeting and forecasting and then use tools like `Prophet` for predicting revenues and expenses. We also automate budget variance analysis and run different financial scenarios using ML. In addition, this chapter introduces us to a few key concepts related to AI and ML that we need to know to navigate the rest of the book.

Introduction to forecasting and budgeting

In this segment, we will understand the importance of forecasting in financial decisions, including budgeting. We have already seen how ML and AI are changing the way we make financial decisions. Let us dive into their applications, starting with forecasting and budgeting. Though both are independent activities by themselves, budgeting uses forecasting as one of the critical building blocks. Despite these activities being closely linked, they are not the same. Let us have a quick look at some of the unique features of budgeting and forecasting.

The process of budgeting involves planning and allocating financial resources to meet an organization's strategic and operational goals over a defined period. Budgeting broadly means expressing in numerical measures the achievements that the entity is seeking to achieve. These achievements are mostly the key result areas, control areas, and line items on financial statements. Budgeting involves multiple focus areas. Thus, we can have profit budgets, sales budgets, personnel budgets, marketing budgets, and allied budgets.

Forecasting is a method, often statistical, deployed to make a reasonable estimate of the future value of an object of interest. This may include sales for the next year, inflation rates in the next five years, the number of

DOI: 10.4324/9781003619628-2

employees likely to retire in the next two years, and others. Often these forecasted values become the starting point of the budget.

Let us now move into the essential steps of budgeting and forecasting.

Basic process of budgeting

Budgeting is a structured, multi-layered system that follows a series of predefined steps. At the highest level or the outermost layer is the master budget, which aligns with the top-level goals of the organization. For example, the master budget outlines how much the entity plans to earn and spend during the budget period. To effectively communicate these plans, a standardized reporting format is essential. Most organizations use the structure of financial statements to present budgeted figures, resulting in a budgeted balance sheet, budgeted income statement, and budgeted cash flow statement. In addition to these core statements, organizations also prepare specialized budgets to support financial decision-making, such as capital expenditure budgets, investment budgets, and more.

The master budgets at the outer layer are supported by more detailed budgets at the inner layers. This means that detailed computations are not presented at the top level. Instead, the top layer forms part of the management dashboard, offering a high-level overview. The detailed calculations are carried out within the lower layers, which consist of supporting budgets that feed into the master budget. For example, the revenue figure in the master budget will reflect a consolidated value, while the inner layers will break this down, specifying the products or services included, along with the quantities and prices considered. The same applies to expenses, where supporting budgets will detail the expected volume and unit cost of raw materials consumed.

Surely, you have not missed that this is where assumptions have started playing a role. These are also precisely the values that forecasting techniques would help us arrive at. So instead of assumptions, we will have values supported by unbiased techniques based on past data. We will discuss this in the next section.

If the entity operates a single factory, the budgeting structure will typically consist of just these two layers. The inner layers may get more complicated as the budgeting entity increases the levels at which they control the budget. The budgeting entity may have multi-country operations with one production facility in each country. If the control is exercised at the country level, before being aggregated at the global level, we will have an additional layer. We will have the outer layer reporting the budgeted financials at the global level – the master budget. The immediate next layer will now have the top-level values of each country – the first point of aggregation. The next level will now have the detailed computation using quantities and prices for each country.

If we add multiple production facilities under a country, the layers will remain the same. However, if we add another level of aggregation, splitting each country into zones, we will add another level. We see how it looks in Table 2.1.

The detailed computations are being done at the lowest level. The intermediate levels are essentially aggregating points for management control. This is an important decision as budgetary control will be implemented at these levels. These are the levels where variances will be computed after the budget is made functional. We will talk about variance computation later in this chapter.

The lowest layer shows the breakup of each of the budgeted figures. As admitted earlier, these data are described in terms of budgeted units and budgeted costs. In addition to the role of assumptions and forecasts in determining these values, the inherent behavior of the items plays an important role here. For example, a cost can be variable or fixed. This will

Table 2.1 Number of layers in the budget

Top layer: Global	*Layer 1: Country*	*Layer 2: Zones*	*Layer 3: Factory*
Total sales: 10,000 This is the outermost layer where we are accumulating the budgets from all other budgeting units across the entity. This is the topmost level of controlling the budget.	USA Sales: 2,400 India Sales: 4,100 UK Sales: 2,500 UAE Sales: 1,000 Total Sales: 10,000 This is next highest level of budgetary control – in this example, the country level. Here we have aggregated budgets for each country.	India Zones East India: 750 North India: 850 South India: 1,200 West India: 1,300 Total India: 4,100 This level breaks up the country at the zonal level. This is also an aggregated control level.	This is the base level of budgetary control. This is the computing level data describing each figure into its unit cost and unit consumption. East India Factories Factory 1: P × Q 150 × 3: 450 Factory 2: P × Q 75 × 4: 300 Total East India: 750

influence the value at different levels of activity. The demand for a product or service may be price-sensitive. Consequently, we may need to reduce the price if we wish to achieve a higher sale. All these business rules are reflected at the lowest level.

Forecasting techniques for financial decision-making

We have recognized the critical role that forecasting plays in budgeting. But the role of forecasting is not limited to budgeting alone. Many financial decisions require the support of forecasting. All decision-making involving uncertainty uses forecasting as a starting point. Forecasting would provide the decision-maker with choices, and the decision-maker may select one of the options or may even use a range of options.

For example, we are making a financial decision that requires the value of expected sales in the next three years. We can use a forecasting tool and assess this value. The tool may provide us with a singular or a range of values, viz. sales under an optimist view, under a pessimist view, and a most-likely view. We may, depending on our objective, use either the singular value or suggest a range of possibilities.

How do we know whether we will get a single value or a range of values? This would depend on various factors such as our needs, the nature of the data, the forecasting technique used, among others. Let us make an overview of some of the common forecasting techniques that we may use for financial decision-making. The techniques include the following:

- Expert judgment (qualitative forecasting)
- Time series analysis
- Regression analysis
- Neural networks and Random Forests

Expert judgment (qualitative forecasting)

This is a qualitative technique where we gather opinions from experts in the field to make predictions. This approach is very useful when there is little or no historical data or during forecasting under highly uncertain environments.

Two popular techniques under expert judgment-based forecasting includes Delphi method and market research. Let us have a quick look at these two techniques.

- **Delphi method:** A group of experts is consulted, and they provide their forecasts anonymously. These responses are then shared, and the experts provide another round of forecasts based on the new information provided. This loop continues till a consensus is reached.

- **Market research**: Under this method, surveys are conducted and focus groups help to gather qualitative and quantitative data. These collected data may be used forecast estimates or may be used as inputs to forecasts.

Time series analysis

This method uses historical data to predict future values. Time series data is specifically used when the data is dependent on time. The data points are collected or observed at regular intervals, viz., daily, monthly, or yearly. The key characteristic of time series data is that each data point has a time component associated with it, and the value at each point is usually influenced by previous values in the series.

Time series data can be decomposed into different components – trend, seasonal pattern, cyclicality, and random noise. We will explore these in detail when we use ML tools to perform the decomposition. For now, let us have a quick look at them:

- **Trend:** This is the long-term direction or pattern in a time series of data. It shows whether the data is generally increasing, decreasing, staying constant over time, or behaving in any different way. It is a component of the time series and is typically a smooth curve or line that reflects the underlying growth or decline. Trend analysis assumes that past trends will continue, making it useful for financial planning and budgeting. Trends can be linear or non-linear. Various techniques can be used to predict future trends.
- **Seasonal patterns**: These are the regular and predictable fluctuations that occur at regular intervals within a year, month, week, or day. These fluctuations are usually tied to external factors like weather, holidays, or societal events that repeat at the same time each period. For example, retail sales usually peak during the holiday season, or demand for icy drinks tends to be higher during the summer months.
- **Cyclic patterns:** These are long-term fluctuations that are not fixed to specific intervals like seasonal patterns but occur over irregular, often multi-year, cycles. These patterns are typically driven by broader economic or market forces. Cycles usually last longer and do not have a fixed, predictable period like seasonal patterns.
- **Random noise**: These represent the unpredictable and unexplained variations in a time series that cannot be specifically attributed to a specific trend, seasonality, or cyclic patterns. Once we have accounted for these components, it is the residual variability in the data. Random noises are irregular fluctuations that are not systematic or predictable. They cannot be explained by any identified pattern or external factor.

A time series analysis may use different techniques for forecasting. It may use the singular time-linked data or moving averages for forecasting. The moving averages seek to smooth the movement of base data using some kind of average. These may be simple moving average (SMA), weighted (WMA), or exponential (EMA). There are more complex models like Autoregressive Integrated Moving Average (ARIMA), but we usually do not have many applications of the same in financial decision-making. Since we may need to specify these when we do a time series analysis, let us first understand these terms.

- **Simple moving average (SMA):** This is one of the most basic types of moving averages used in time series analysis. It is calculated by taking the arithmetic mean of a set of data points over a specific period. Let us look at Table 2.2 with the price of crude futures and compute its four-day SMA. Each SMA is the average of the preceding four prices ending with the value of the day for which we are computing the SMA. So, the first value is (68.59 + 70.29 + 70.02 + 71.29) / 4 = 70.05.

Table 2.2 Computation of simple moving average

Day	*Dec-10*	*Dec-11*	*Dec-12*	*Dec-13*	*Dec-16*	*Dec-17*	*Dec-18*	*Dec-19*	*Dec-20*
USD	68.59	70.29	70.02	71.29	70.71	70.08	70.58	69.91	69.46
SMA	–	–	–	70.05	70.58	70.53	70.67	70.32	70.01

- **Weighted moving average (WMA):** A WMA is similar to the SMA, but instead of giving equal weight to all values, more weight is given to recent data points. The weights are specified by the user. Let us consider that in the same example, we give a weight of 4 to the latest data and a weight of 1 to the earliest data (Table 2.3). The last WMA has been computed as [(69.46 × 4) + (69.91 × 3) + (70.58 × 2) + (70.08 × 1)] / (4 + 3 + 2 + 1) = 69.88.

Table 2.3 Computation of weighted moving average

Day	*Dec-10*	*Dec-11*	*Dec-12*	*Dec-13*	*Dec-16*	*Dec-17*	*Dec-18*	*Dec-19*	*Dec-20*
USD	68.59	70.29	70.02	71.29	70.71	70.08	70.58	69.91	69.46
WMA	–	–	–	70.44	70.70	70.51	70.53	70.23	69.88

- **Exponential moving average (EMA):** This is a type of moving average that gives more weight to recent data points, like WMA. However, it does so in a smooth, exponentially decaying way.

  EMA is computed as $EMA_t = \alpha X_t + (1 - \alpha)EMA_{t-1}$

  where, $\alpha = 2 / (n + 1)$ is the smoothing factor (n is the period length),
  X_t is the current data point,
  EMA_{t-1} is the previous EMA value.

Let us use the same data set of the prices of crude futures on select dates and compute a four-day EMA. This will give us a smoothing factor *(α)* of 2 / (4 + 1) = 0.4. We will also need a value for the first day, and we take it as the SMA for the day, i.e., USD 70.05 on Dec-13. We can use other values also, like the actual price on that day. This is used for seeding the subsequent EMA.

EMA for the next day is computed as (0.4 × 70.71) + (1 – 0.4) × 70.05. You can see how the exponential works – it is giving a weight of 0.4 on the latest data and 0.6 on the moving average of all prior period data (Table 2.4).

- **Autoregressive Integrated Moving Average (ARIMA)**: ARIMA expresses the current value of a series as a linear combination of its previous values and a stochastic error term. Simply put, this model assumes that the current observation is influenced by a weighted sum of its past observations, with the error term accounting for randomness.

  The model explains a time series using three components:

  - Autoregressive (AR): In an AR model, the value of the time series at a given time depends linearly on its previous values (lags). The number of previous values used is denoted by p. Thus, an AR(p) model predicts a value based on a weighted sum of the previous p-values.
  - Integrated (I): Integrated refers to a differencing process used to make a time series stationary. Differencing is a transformation applied to the time series data to remove trends and seasonality, and this is what makes the series stationary. Simply put, this involves subtracting the previous observation from the current observation and continuing the process till the underlying trend is removed. Consider a time series with increasing values: 50, 55, 60, 65, 70. We can see a clear upward trend. To make it stationary, we apply first differencing: (55 – 50), (60 – 55), (65 – 60), (70 – 65) = 5, 5, 5, 5. Now we can see that this series does not have any trend; it is stationary.
  - Moving Average (MA): In an ARIMA model, the Moving Average component adjusts for any short-term dependencies in the data that are not captured by the AR part. This is critical when there are irregularities or sudden shocks in the data. Just to clarify, the AR component captures the relationship between the current observation and

Table 2.4 Computation of exponential moving average

Day	*Dec-10*	*Dec-11*	*Dec-12*	*Dec-13*	*Dec-16*	*Dec-17*	*Dec-18*	*Dec-19*	*Dec-20*
USD	68.59	70.29	70.02	71.29	70.71	70.08	70.58	69.91	69.46
EMA				70.05	70.31	70.22	70.36	70.18	69.89

its past values, while the MA component captures the relationship between the current observation and past errors. But do not worry, the software takes care of the same. We will show you how ML tools can be used for time series forecasting using various techniques.

Regression analysis

When we discussed time series forecasting in the last section, the underlying consideration was that the past value of an observation influences the future value. We did not have any other consideration. But what happens if other factors influence the future value? This is where regression analysis steps in.

To use regression analysis, we need two kinds of variables – the variable whose value we wish to predict and the variable(s) that influence the predicted value. The former is known as the dependent variable, since it depends on other values. The latter is known as an independent variable since there are no dependencies for them in this instant application. Say, the cost of a hotel room depends on the number of tourists arriving, their average stay duration, and the outdoor temperature. In this case, the cost of a hotel room is the dependent variable, while others are independent variables.

The process of arriving at the values of these independent variables may involve another regression analysis, wherein these variables may be the dependent variables. Essentially, when we speak about dependent or independent variables, we are speaking about a specific application. In our example, the number of tourists arriving may depend on the cost of flights, the issuance of tourist visas, etc. That could be another regression analysis. Are you wondering why we do not include these variables in the original model instead of using the variable number of tourists arriving? Possibly, the decision may depend on how complex it could make a model, the level at which you are making the forecast, the availability of the data at your level, among others.

As we have noted, the choice of independent variables is up to us. However, this choice carries the risk of errors. While regression analysis includes tools to assess how well the selected variables explain the dependent variable, mistakes in variable selection can still occur even when guided by data-driven methods.

Regression analysis can be of various types. Here are the most common ones.

- **Linear regression**: This is used to predict the value of a dependent variable using a linear relationship with one or more independent variables. If it uses more than one independent variable, we call it multiple linear regression. Estimating hotel revenue based on the number of nights is an example of simple linear regression, and estimating hotel revenue based on the number of nights stayed, visits to the spa, and usage of the restaurant is an example of multiple linear regression. A linear regression relation, where Y is the dependent variable and X is the independent variable(s), will be described as

$$Y = a + b_1X_1 + b_2X_2 + \cdots + b_nX_n$$

where,
a: This is known as the intercept which is not influenced by any values of the independent variables. For example, the booking fee on a hotel booking website is the same irrespective of the number of nights booked.
b_n: The rate of change in value of Y for each unit of X, say room rate per night, unit cost of each spa visit, etc.
X_n: Units of independent variables consumed, say number of nights stayed, the number of spa visits, etc.

- **Multiple regression:** Different from multiple linear regression, multiple regression also uses multiple variables but does not assume a linear relation. For example, the price of a house may depend on the floor area and the age of the house. The price of the house will increase with the floor area, but with an increase in the floor area, the value will increase at a slower rate. Similarly, the value of the house will diminish with increased age of the house, but the rate of decrease will increase as the age increases. These are non-linear relations, and we often use exponential or lognormal values to express the non-linear relations. A multiple non-linear regression may be expressed as

$$Y = a + b_1 \log(X_1) - b_2X_2^2$$

where,
a: Value of the house irrespective of any factor, may be the base value of the land on which it is built
b_n: The rate of change in value of the house for the floor area and the age of the house
X_1: The floor area of the house
X_2: The age of the house

You can see here that we have used a log value of floor area to reduce the rate of increase in price with an increase in floor area. Similarly, we have used an exponential of age to cause an accelerated rate of decrease in the price of the house as the age of the house increases. We generally do not see much use of non-linear regression in financial decision-making, except in cases of valuation.

- **Logistic regression:** Often in financial decision-making, our dependent variable is not a value but a classification. For example, if we are trying to predict whether a borrower will repay based on age and amount outstanding, logistic regression would be used. This statistical method models a relationship between one or more independent variables and a binary dependent variable. Simply put, it helps to predict the probability of an event happening, where the outcome is one of two possible categories, often conveniently described as 0 or 1. Let us consider our example. We will have records of payments or defaults of a borrower, along with the corresponding age and amount outstanding. In the model, we may designate 0 to express default and 1 for repayment. A logistics regression model, will give an output, say "p" where:

  $$p = 1/(1 + e^{-(b_0+b_1X_1+b_2X_2)})$$

  where,
  p: Probability that the borrower will repay the loan (Y = 1).
  b_0: The intercept (bias term) represents the baseline or starting point of the prediction when all independent variables are set to zero.
  b_1: How the repayment probability is influenced by the age of the outstanding.
  b_2: How the repayment probability is influenced by the loan amount.
  X_1: The age of the borrower.
  X_2: The amount of the outstanding loan.

  Based on the probability, we categorize the borrower as likely to pay or likely to default. We decide on a cutoff value for the probability, and any observation above the value will be categorized as "likely to default."

While using an ML tool, we will just identify the dependent and independent variables, and the software will take care of the rest.

Neural networks and Random Forest

Neural networks and Random Forest are two ML tools that are used for financial forecasting. They are powerful tools for decision-making in dynamic and complex environments. These techniques use algorithms to model complex, non-linear relationships and patterns found in large datasets. ML and AI algorithms "learn" from historical data and adapt to changing patterns over time.

Neural networks, particularly deep learning models, are designed to recognize complex patterns in large datasets. They consist of layers of nodes (neurons) simulating the way the human brain processes information. Neural networks are often used for prediction of stock prices, fraud detection, credit scoring, and others. Random Forest algorithms are used for both classification and regression tasks. It belongs to a family of models known as ensemble learning methods, which combine multiple models to improve prediction accuracy and reduce overfitting.

ML methods can be classified into supervised, unsupervised, and reinforcement learning, each having specific applications in financial decision-making. Let us understand these terms:

- **Supervised learning:** This is used for predicting outcomes based on labeled historical data, meaning the input data is paired with corresponding output labels. Supervised learning learns a mapping from inputs to outputs, enabling the model to make predictions or classifications on new, unseen data. In finance, supervised learning algorithms can forecast stock prices, economic indicators, or credit risk by learning from historical trends and patterns. Regressions and classifications are tools used under supervised learning.
- **Unsupervised learning:** This is a type of ML method where the model is trained using unlabeled data. Unlike supervised learning, there are no predefined output labels associated with the input data. Unsupervised learning tries to find hidden patterns, structures, or relationships within the data, which can then be used to make financial decisions. For example, it can be used to identify groups of similar financial assets or transactions, assisting in portfolio management and anomaly detection. Clustering, associations, and principal component analysis are some techniques used under unsupervised learning.
- **Reinforcement learning:** This type of ML involves training a model to make a sequence of decisions by rewarding it for taking actions that lead to desirable outcomes like profitable trades. Unlike supervised or unsupervised learning, reinforcement learning learns through trial and error. The model takes actions, receives feedback in the form of rewards or penalties, and adjusts its behavior to optimize performance over time.

Let us now review neural networks and Random Forests further.

- **Artificial neural networks (ANNs):** ANNs are computational models inspired by the human brain. These networks can learn complex relationships between inputs and outputs, making them effective for tasks like forecasting financial time series. They simulate the way the human brain processes information to make predictions, which is especially useful for complex financial markets and customer behavior forecasting. ANNs have three layers – input layer, hidden layer, and output layer. Let us have a quick look at them.

- **Input layer:** This is the first layer of the network that receives the input data. Each node in the input layer represents a feature of the data, for example, a variable in a dataset.
- **Hidden layers:** These are intermediate layers between the input and output layers. Each hidden layer consists of neurons that perform computations on the input data and pass the results to the next layer till these are ready to be sent to the output layer. There can be one or more hidden layers, depending on the complexity of the model.
- **Output layer:** The final layer produces the output, which could be a prediction or classification result. For example, in a binary classification problem, the output could be a value of 0 or 1 (for false or true).

  Once the data is fed into the input layer, it passes through the hidden layers to the output layer. This process is called forward propagation. After the data passes through the network, the predicted output is compared to the actual target value, and the difference is the error or loss. The loss function measures the difference between the network's prediction and the actual value. To minimize the error, the network backpropagates the data, i.e., from the output layer to the input layer, to adjust the weights and biases. As the ANN undergoes multiple iterations of forward propagation, error calculation, and backpropagation, the weights and biases get fine-tuned. This allows the network to make more accurate predictions. The learning process continues until the loss function converges to a minimum value or reaches a predefined stopping criterion.

- **Random Forests:** Random Forest is an ensemble learning technique that creates multiple decision trees and then combines their predictions to improve accuracy and robustness. Ensemble learning is an ML technique that combines the predictions from multiple models. These are often referred to as learners or base models, and they help to improve overall performance, typically by reducing errors and increasing accuracy. Random Forest models are primarily used for classification and regression tasks. The main idea behind Random Forest is to build a collection (or "forest") of decision trees, where each tree is trained on a random subset of the data. Multiple subsets of data are created by randomly sampling the original dataset with replacement. This means some data points may appear multiple times in a subset, while others may be omitted.

To understand how Random Forests work, we need to understand how the decision tree works. A decision tree splits the data into branches based on feature values. Nodes represent decision points where the data is split. The root node is the first node in the decision tree representing the entire dataset. The first decision about how to split the data is made here. At each node, the data is split into subsets based on a feature, for example, age, income, etc.

This process continues recursively until the data points are assigned to a leaf node. The leaf nodes are the final nodes in the decision tree where the final prediction is made. Predictions are made by following the path from the root to the leaves. Internal nodes are the decision points that lie between the root node and leaf nodes. The decision tree is built to minimize impurity, which is a measure of how mixed the data is at each node. We will discuss impurity when we start working on the models. Consider that you are building a decision tree for loan approval. Here is how it may go.

- **Root Node**: The root node might split the data based on credit score. For example, a branch for customers with a credit score exceeding 700 and another branch for others.
- **Internal Node 1**: This is the branch where the credit score is greater than 700. Now we split them based on a threshold income of say $50,000. Those with a credit score of more than 700 and income of more than $50,000 will proceed further, others will be excluded at this stage.
- **Internal Node 2**: In the branch where the credit score is less than 700, we may have a criterion based on the debt-to-income ratio. If the ratio is below 20%, they may proceed to the next stage, while others will be rejected.
- **Leaf Node**: Eventually, the data would reach a leaf node where the final decision is made, that is, either the loan is approved or denied.

Now, let us understand the concept of bootstrapping, a key concept in Random Forests. In bootstrapping, random subsets of the training data are created by sampling with replacement. This means that the data used in the first subset is available for selection in the second subset. This would ensure that each tree is trained on a slightly different set of data, with some data points appearing multiple times in a subset, while others may not appear at all. Since not all features will be present in all subsets, there is expected to be a low correlation between the subsets. Each tree is trained independently on a different bootstrapped subset of the training data, and each tree makes predictions based on a random subset of features at each node.

We are going to see these techniques in greater detail when we discuss the related ML tools used. The challenge now is how to select a forecasting tool, and after the selection, how to know that the model is working satisfactorily.

Use cases for various forecasting techniques

Let us have a quick look at the most common appropriate use for the techniques discussed earlier.

Use cases for expert judgment-based forecasting

This tool is best used when:

- Historical data is unavailable or insufficient, for example, in the case of new product launches or emerging trends.
- The available data is qualitative, subjective, or difficult to model numerically.

The advantage of this technique is that it is quick to implement, cost-effective, and based on real-world domain expertise. However, subjectivity and individual biases can influence the forecasts derived using this technique.

Use case for time series-based forecasting

We have various approaches under this technique, and their best use cases are stated here:

- Simple Moving Average (SMA) is best used for stable data without trends or seasonal patterns. This technique is simple and easy to implement and interpret. However, this cannot handle trends or seasonal variations effectively.
- Weighted Moving Average (WMA) is best used when recent observations are more important than older ones. This technique is more responsive to recent changes than SMA, but is exposed to the risk of the choice of the weights being subjective.
- Exponential Moving Average (EMA) is best used on data with trends, especially when more recent observations should be given a higher weight as compared with the earlier data. This method reduces lag compared to SMA. At the same time, this model can be sensitive to the choice of the smoothing parameter.
- Autoregressive Integrated Moving Average (ARIMA): This is best used for time series data that exhibit trends and/or seasonality. This technique can handle both trends and seasonality with appropriate adjustments. However, it requires stationary data and can be complex to implement and tune.

Use case for regression analysis-based forecasting

We have discussed three types of regression analyses. Their best use scenarios are stated here.

- Simple Linear Regression is best used when the relation between the dependent and independent variable(s) can be reasonably approximated linearly. This is easy to understand and interpret, though the assumption of a linear relationship may not always hold in real-world data.
- Non-Linear Regression, as the name suggests, is best for data with a non-linear relationship between independent and dependent variables. This model can fit more complex data patterns but are computationally intensive and harder to interpret.
- Logistic Regression is used when the dependent variable is categorical – binary or multinomial. In binomial, there will be only two choices, while in multinomial, there will be more than two choices. The model can handle binary or multinomial classification problems effectively, something that the other regression models cannot. However, the model assumes linearity in the log-odds of the dependent variable.

Use case for neural network- and Random Forest-based forecasting

Let us now discuss when we should use the two ML techniques described earlier.

- ANN are used for complex, non-linear data patterns that traditional methods cannot handle. This technique can capture intricate patterns in data but requires large datasets and computational resources. However, it can be too tailored or overfitted to the training data and lose its ability to generalize to other datasets.
- Random Forest is ideal for high-dimensional datasets with numerous variables and non-linear interactions. It is robust, and can handle large datasets, and is less prone to overfitting through ensemble learning. At the same time, this is less transparent and harder to interpret compared to linear models.

Selecting a forecasting tool and assessing its quality

Forecasting is a critical aspect of decision-making for various purposes. Selecting the appropriate forecasting technique and assessing its quality is essential for making informed decisions. We must however remember that forecasting is a technique that will process a set of data and generate an output, irrespective of the quality of data and fitness for the purpose.

Whether the input and the output are appropriate for the purpose would require a separate assessment methodology.

Assessing the quality of the forecasting model

A forecasting tool will use a set of inputs and generate a set of outputs. As users, we need to assess the performance and quality of the forecast. This assessment ensures that the model's predictions are reliable and valid. We use different approaches to make this assessment. Some of those approaches are discussed here. We have not discussed the computational framework of the measures as they will be computed by the software.

- Forecast Accuracy Metrics: To evaluate the performance of a forecasting model, several accuracy metrics are commonly used:
  - Mean Absolute Error (MAE): This measures the average of the absolute errors between forecasted and actual values.
  - Mean Squared Error (MSE): This measures the average of the squared errors, penalizing large errors more than MAE.
  - Root Mean Squared Error (RMSE): This is the square root of MSE, which brings the error metric back to the original units of the data.
  - Mean Absolute Percentage Error (MAPE): This metric measures the error as a percentage, providing a scale-independent measure.
  - R-squared (R^2): Measures the proportion of variance in the dependent variable that is predictable from the independent variables.
- Cross-Validation and Training/Testing Split: To evaluate how good the training and testing process was when the model was being designed.
  - Cross-Validation: Dividing the dataset into multiple subsets to test the model on different parts of the data to ensure robustness. A good model will perform efficiently across different parts of the data.
  - Training/Testing Split: Splitting the data into a training set and a testing set to avoid overfitting and ensure that the model generalizes well to unseen data. An improper split can make the model susceptible to overfitting.
- Residual Analysis: Residuals are the differences between the actual and forecasted values. If residuals show patterns like trends, it suggests the model has not captured all the information in the data, and calibration may be necessary. The residuals should ideally resemble white noise that is random and uncorrelated.
- Out-of-Sample Testing: The model should be tested on unseen data to assess how well it generalizes to future data.

- Model Comparison: This can be achieved through benchmarking. We can compare the performance of the chosen model with simpler models like moving averages to ensure that the model provides a genuine improvement over a simple approach.
- Overfitting versus Underfitting: We must check that the model is not overfitting or underfitting. Overfitting arises when a model fits the training data too well, capturing noise rather than the underlying pattern. This leads to poor performance of the model on new, unseen data. Underfitting arises with models that are too simple to capture the underlying patterns in the data.

Every time a model is designed, we must check, using an appropriate technique, whether the model is fit for the purpose. It is not only the correct computation that matters here. The model must be conceptually appropriate to use. We will revisit this issue when we discuss specific techniques for forecasting.

Time series forecasting with ML tools

In this section, we will learn how to use ML tools to forecast revenues and expenses with high accuracy using historical data.

Challenge of accurate financial forecasting in a dynamic environment

Any forecasting tool bases its application on a set of assumptions. Under a dynamic environment, these assumptions face a continuous threat of being outdated.

Consequently, the model is also threatened with the risk of being unfit for the purpose it was designed. We need to take note of these challenges and, wherever possible, seek to mitigate them. However, it may not be possible to mitigate the risk exposure arising from all these challenges. In such circumstances, we should use the model output with additional caution. We should preferably seek confirmation of the output by using alternative models or approaches. We have listed some of the aspects that we should be wary of to face the challenge arising from a dynamic environment.

- **Market volatility**: Markets, in general, and financial markets specifically, are subject to changes due to various factors that may include geopolitical events, economic shifts, and market sentiment. This volatility poses a challenge for ML models to provide consistent and accurate forecasts. Under a dynamic scenario, past patterns may no longer hold true beyond the short term. Consequently, models trained on historical data may fail to account for significant external shocks, leading to poor predictions. We may need to use approaches that would give greater weightage to data from the recent past over earlier data. We may also need to explore more deeply to assess if we can identify the indicators of such change and incorporate them in our modeling. At the least, we should disclose the limitations of the model to the user.

- **Data quality and availability**: The accuracy of ML models depends heavily on the quality and completeness of data. The data may be noisy, incomplete, or biased. Some data, like news items, may need preprocessing before being used. Unless we are careful about the data, we may end up overfitting, where the model would capture irrelevant patterns that are not features of real-world scenarios.
- **Feature selection**: The performance of a model depends greatly on the right selection of the input variables or attributes that will be used to make a prediction. In ML terms, these are called features. A dynamic environment will require models that can adapt to changing conditions, which means selecting the right variables that would reflect the changing scenario every time the model is run. Use of inputs that do not contribute to prediction quality is unnecessary, and at the same time, selection of wrong inputs or missing a right input can degrade model performance.
- **Overfitting and underfitting**: Overfitting is common when an ML model captures too many details from historical data, including noise. This makes the model too dependent on the past data, making it inefficient to generalize to future conditions. On the other hand, when the model is too simplistic and fails to capture essential patterns in the data, we have a chance of underfitting. Striking the right balance between these two extremes is necessary. Under a dynamic scenario, this becomes more challenging as the nature of the data keeps changing, making it difficult to separate the trend from noise.
- **Model interpretability**: Many ML models, such as deep learning, offer high predictive power. However, they often operate as "black boxes," where it is difficult to understand the reasoning behind the predictions. This lack of transparency can not only be a barrier to trust and acceptance but also make it difficult for model validation. Under a dynamic environment, it becomes difficult to guess the marginal impact of the changes in the environment on the model output. We therefore need a comprehensive model literature to avoid any interpretation error.
- **Training and retraining**: As the environment changes, a model that performs well today may not continue to be effective. This problem is addressed by frequently retraining the model. We also need to ensure that the model is adapting to the new data and emerging trends.
- **Behavioral impact**: Human behavior often influences market values. Behavioral biases like overconfidence, loss aversion, herd mentality, and like, often cause erratic market movements. ML models rely primarily on historical data and mathematical relationships rather than on the

underlying emotive decision-making processes. Models find it difficult to account for these behavioral factors.

- **Regulatory changes**: A forecasting model can be subject to regulatory frameworks. If we are developing or using the same, we need to ensure that the models comply with these regulations. As regulations change, we must be vigilant that the models developed earlier remain compliant with the altered regulations.
- **Market structure**: Markets are often complex systems with interconnected players operating under different operating and regulatory structures. Each of these players may have different motivations, risk appetites, and strategies. ML models must account for these complexities, which may be difficult due to the diverse and sometimes conflicting behaviors of market participants.

This discussion not only holds good for forecasting using time series but is also useful while designing models developed for various purposes using different techniques in this book and in real life.

ML tools library for time series forecasting

There are various ML libraries that are useful in time series forecasting. Let us learn about one of the most popular libraries for time series forecasting – `Prophet`.

`Prophet` is an open-source time series forecasting tool developed by Facebook. It works on time series data including those that exhibit strong seasonal patterns, holiday effects, and potential missing values. It requires minimal data preprocessing, and it is robust to outliers and missing data. `Prophet` automatically detects seasonal trends and allows users to include custom holiday effects for more accurate predictions.

In the next section, we will see the application of this library for forecasting revenue, expenses, or cash flows. The detailed code can be found in the code repository. This library may not be installed in your development framework, and you may have to install the same by running the following command:

```
pip install prophet
```

We can also do basic forecasting by using standard functions in `Pandas` and `NumPy`. Libraries like `sklearn` and `statsmodels` can be used for regression analysis and ARIMA-based models. We will show you their use in the next section. We must note that new libraries keep coming up, and existing ones get updated. So please feel free to experiment with other libraries too, keeping in mind the cautions and the purposes of use that we have discussed earlier.

Forecasting revenue, expenses, and cash flows

Three of the most common candidates for forecasting are revenue, expenses, and cash flows. However, for any forecasting tool these are mere numbers. Change of the label of the number like revenue, expenses, or cash flows does not affect the program methodology and its output. Forecasting them also forms an important pillar for budgeting. We will now discuss how `Prophet` and other library functions can be used for financial forecasting.

Forecasting using `Prophet`

This code (prefix 0201) can be used to forecast revenue using the `Prophet` model. You can download the code from the repository and customize it without rewriting any code. However, to be able to customize and use the code, we need to understand the code structure. Please note that the minimum requirement of data is that it must have a date and corresponding values.

The code is split into the following six sections:

- **Import libraries**: In this section, the required libraries are being loaded. You will find we are loading `pandas`, `Prophet`, `matplotlib`, `sklearn`, and `NumPy` libraries. `Prophet` is the forecasting model, `matplotlib` has been used to plot forecast values, and `sklearn` has been used for computing model validation metrics. `Pandas` is used for data management, while `NumPy` is used for numerical operations.
- **Customize**: In this section, we will specify our customization details. We will provide the following:
  - Name of our data file in CSV format.
  - Names of the columns that contain the date and values that we will forecast.
  - Value for the uncertainty interval. A `Prophet` forecasts a range within which the forecast values are likely to lie. This suggests that, given the data and the model, 95% of the future forecast values (across many samples) are likely to lie within the interval. The higher the value, the wider the range will be.
  - Name of the file under which we will save the forecast values.
  - Name of the JPG file to save the plot.

  Apart from this, there is another customization option available under the section where we prepare data for `Prophet`. The relevant lines from the code are given here with the values we need to provide italicized.

```
# Customize your application

#name of the file where you have historical data
myfile = '0201 Revenue_day.csv'

#Identify the columns in the data file which has the date
and values

date_column = 'Date'
value_column = 'Revenue'

# Specify the uncertainty interval
my_interval = 0.95

#Name the file where you want to store the forecast values
forecast_file = '0201 forecasted_revenue.csv'

#Name the jpg file where you want to save the plot
myplot = '0201 forecast_plot.jpg'
```

- **Load data and preprocess:** This section loads the data for further processing. At this stage the code also converts the date format used in the spreadsheet to `datetime` format used by Python. The date field in the historical data is in DD-MM-YYYY format. Any changes in this date format may require modification of the code.
- **Prepare data for `Prophet`:** The date and value columns are renamed to ds (date) and y (value), which are the required column names for `Prophet`. The `Prophet` model is then initialized, model fitted, and a forecast made. In this section, you will find an option to specify the number of days you want the forecast. We have kept a default value. You may change as per your requirement. Please note that the duration of the forecast will depend on the volume and quality of the historical data provided. If the data is highly volatile, it is better to choose a shorter duration for forecasting.

```
# Create a future dataframe for predictions
(e.g., next 50 days)

future = model.make_future_dataframe(periods=50)
```

- **Plot the forecast:** This section plots the forecast and historical values, clearly demarking the date from which the forecast starts. It shows the historical values, forecast values, and uncertainty interval. If you want, you can change the legends that appear on the chart by replacing them in the code with the ones you prefer.
- **Evaluate the model:** Here, we compute two metrics to measure the model's performance, which are MAE and RMSE.

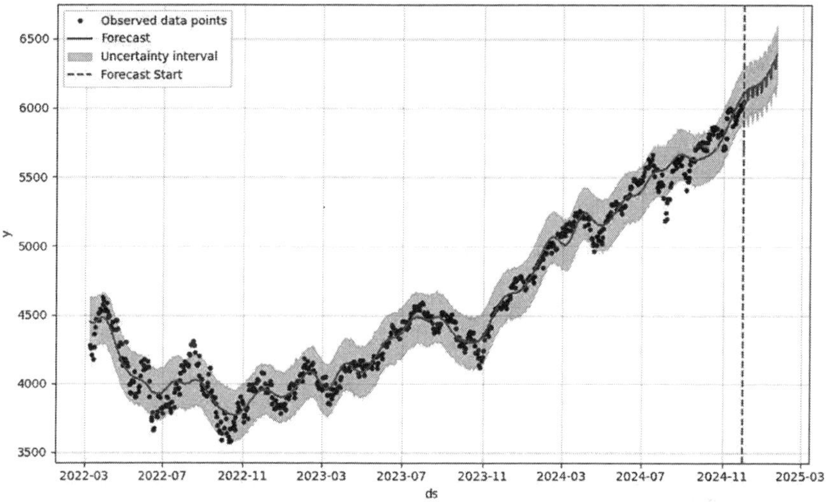

Figure 2.1 Plot of historical and forecast values generated by `Prophet`

Once you run the model, you will have two outputs. One is a spreadsheet containing the forecasted values, and the other is a graphics image of the plot. The spreadsheet will have four columns: ds – the date, yhat – the forecasted values, yhat_lower and yhat_upper – the lower and upper bounds of forecasted values.

The forecast plot is a visual representation of these data along with the historical values till wherever available (Figure 2.1).

Please note that Prophet has different functionalities for addressing non-linear trends, seasonality, and cyclicality. In this book, we have used a different tool to measure them.

Forecasting using moving average

This code (prefix 0202) will use different moving averages to forecast values of revenue. Let us understand the code and see what the customization requirements are. There are eight sections in this code. Let us have a look at the sections and understand their functions. The complete code is available in the code repository.

- **Import libraries:** This section will load the necessary libraries. The library that we have not used earlier is `statsmodels`. This model is used to estimate different statistical models, as well as for conducting statistical tests, and statistical data exploration.

- **Customize:** In this section, we will specify our customization details. We will provide the following:
    - o Name of our data file in CSV format.
    - o Values/periods of two moving averages we plan to compute. We have used default values, which you can change.
    - o Name of the file where the forecast will be saved in CSV format.
    - o Name of the JPG file where you want to save the plot.

  The relevant lines from the code are given here with the values we need to provide italicized.

```
#name of the file where you have historical data
myfile = '0201 Revenue_day.csv'

#days in first moving average ma1_day = 30

#days in second moving average ma2_day = 90

#Name the file where you want to store the forecast values
forecast_file = '0202 forecasted_revenue_ma.csv'

#Name the jpg file where you want to save the MA plot
myplot = '0202 ma_plot.jpg'

#Name the jpg file where you want to save the plot of the
forecast and actual

predplot = '0202 pred_plot.jpg'
```

  If your historical data set is very large and you want to use only a portion of it, you can specify it under the "Load data and preprocess" section. You can also specify the type of moving average you want to compute in the "Calculate moving average" section. Another customization option is available in the section "Forecast using moving averages," where we can specify how many days of historical data we should use to forecast.
- **Load data and preprocess:** This section loads the specified data for processing. The code ensures that the date format is in line with the requirements of Python. In addition, it sets up the date as an index field. This chronologically organizes the data, a necessary condition for computing moving averages. If we want to use a part of the data to compute the moving averages, we can specify it in this section. Look out for the following code:

```
#If we want to use some limited number of days
#df=df.tail(200)
```

We will remove the hash {#} sign from the code line and specify the latest number of days we want to use in the model. If we want to use the latest 200 days, the code will look like

```
df=df.tail(200)
```

If we want to use the complete data set, please ensure that the # sign is not removed from the beginning of the line of code.

- **Calculate moving averages:** This section computes moving averages, and we can specify if we want to compute a SMA or an EMA. In the code, you have three sections, A, B, and C, for computing simple averages, exponential moving averages, and weighted moving averages. Let us have a look at the structure of the code. The arrow signs are not a part of the code.

```
# Calculate moving averages

#Section A: Simple moving average
#'''
# Computing two simple moving averages
df['MA_1'] = df['Revenue'].rolling(window=ma1_day).mean()
df['MA_2'] = df['Revenue'].rolling(window=ma1_day).mean()
#'''
# End of section A

#Section B: Weighted moving average
'''
<Detailed code>
'''
# End of section B

#Section C: Exponential moving average
'''
<Detailed code>
'''
# End of section C
```

You must have noticed that there are three sections – A, B, and C. Each section is marked by a heading "*#Section*" and a footer "*#End of section.*" Just following the header and preceding the footer, there are three single quotes ('''), identified by the arrow sign. Naturally, these arrow signs are not part of the code. You will find that in the first section, these three single quotes at the beginning and end of the section are preceded by a # sign. This means that this section will be processed. The sections where these single quote series are not preceded by the # sign will not be processed. All you need to do is put the # sign in front of the header and footer single quote sequences of the section you want to process. Please ensure that the sections you do not want to process are without the # sign in front of the header and footer sequence of single quotes. A common error is not having the # sign in both the header and footer, so be careful.

- **Plot moving averages:** This section will plot the moving averages along with the plot of the original data. You will be able to visualize the extent to which the moving averages could smooth the original data. If you want to change any legend that appears on the plot, you can simply replace it in the code. This plot is also saved in a graphics file.
- **Forecast using moving averages:** This is an interesting section where we train a selected model using past data and make forecasts. The first step here is defining the data we plan to use. If we are fine with the entire data set, we do nothing here, we specify the number of days of data we intend to use. This is common when the entire data set is not representative of the current situation. The relevant code here is

```
# Use only the last specified days of data
df_pred = df.tail(100)
```

We will provide a numerical value representing the amount of the latest data we will use. If we want to use the entire data set, replace this line with

```
df_pred = df
```

Now we need to specify what part of the data will be the basis for training the forecasting model. Before we come to the code, let us understand what training means. This is the process where an ML model learns patterns from a dataset. During training, the model is provided with input data (features) and corresponding output data (target or labels). Once the model is ready, we predict the values using the balance part of the data, that is, the historical data that was not used for training. The model has not seen this data before.

However, this is also historical data, and we know the real values. The model would predict the values, and we will compare those with the actual values to see how good the model is working. This is called testing. If the model performs well on the training data but poorly on the test data, that may be a case of overfitting, memorizing the training data but failing to generalize. Let us look at the code now.

```
# Split the data into training and testing sets
X_train, X_test, y_train, y_test = train_test_split(X, y,
test_size=0.2, random_state=42)
```

You can see the parameter "*test_size=0.2.*" This means that 20% of the historical data will not be used for training and is reserved for testing. Inquisitive about the next component – random_state=42? Well, providing a value here means that the split will be consistent any time you run the code.

The split randomly shuffles and splits the dataset into training and test data. We have provided the random number generator with a seed value of 42. This would ensure that every time the code runs, we will get the same split of the training and test data. This is necessary as we want the model to be replicable. However, you can use any integer value instead of 42. We will come across this "train and test" approach in some of the other applications.

This code uses a linear regression model for forecasting. We can also use other models. In that case, we will have to ensure that the appropriate model library is loaded, and the code is changed to use that model. Here are some examples:

Using decision tree to capture non-linear relationships.

```
from sklearn.tree import DecisionTreeRegressor
model = DecisionTreeRegressor()
model.fit(X_train, y_train)
```

Using Random Forest, a more robust model, averages results from individual trees to reduce overfitting.

```
from sklearn.ensemble import RandomForestRegressor
model = RandomForestRegressor()
model.fit(X_train, y_train)
```

Using K-nearest neighbors (KNN), a non-parametric method that uses the average of the nearest data points to make predictions.

```
from sklearn.neighbors import KNeighborsRegressor
model = KNeighborsRegressor()
model.fit(X_train, y_train)
```

Using Prophet for forecasting with daily or seasonal data.

```
from fbprophet import Prophet
model = Prophet()
model.fit(df_train)
```

- **Plot actual and predicted:** In this section, we are plotting the actual values with the values predicted by the model. The plot is also saved to the file named in the "Customize" section. You are free to change the legends appearing on the chart by replacing them in the code.
- **Evaluate the model:** This section computes two performance metrics for the model – MSE and R^2. We will be discussing these metrics in a later section.

The model computes moving averages and generates plots for the actual value of revenue and the moving averages.

Surely, you can observe that the plot has become smoother as the number of days used to compute the moving average increases (Figure 2.2). However, smoothing does not always mean the prediction based on these moving averages will be more accurate. Moving averages can be very useful where the data is stationary or we are looking at short-term trends. Note that moving averages are lagging indicators; they are slow to respond to recent changes.

You might have observed that the predicted value is different from the actual value (Figure 2.3). It is extremely unlikely that these values will coincide. Prediction models seek to reduce the gap, but in reality, cannot remove the same. The model performance metric gives us an idea about how good the model is for use.

Decomposing time series into trend, seasonality, cyclicality, and others

This code (prefix 0203) can be used to decompose time series data into trend, seasonality, cyclicality, and random noise. The code has sections performing different functions.

- **Import libraries:** We have loaded the necessary libraries in this section. The new libraries used here are `warnings`, `datetime`, and `SciPy`. The warnings module issues warning messages in Python, `datetime` allows the code to handle date and time functions in different formats and perform mathematical operations, while `SciPy` is used for scientific and technical computing.

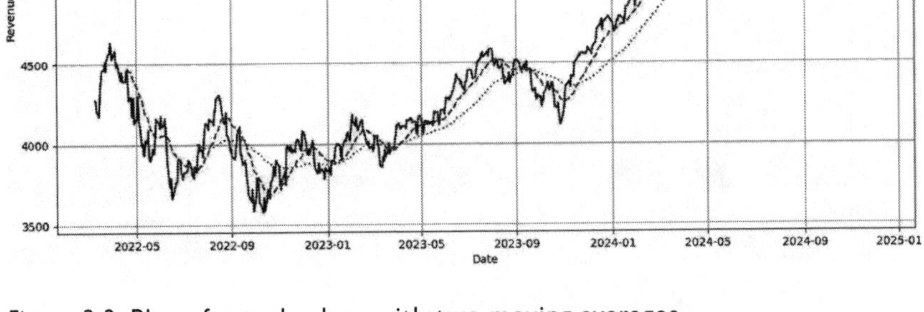

Figure 2.2 Plot of actual values with two moving averages

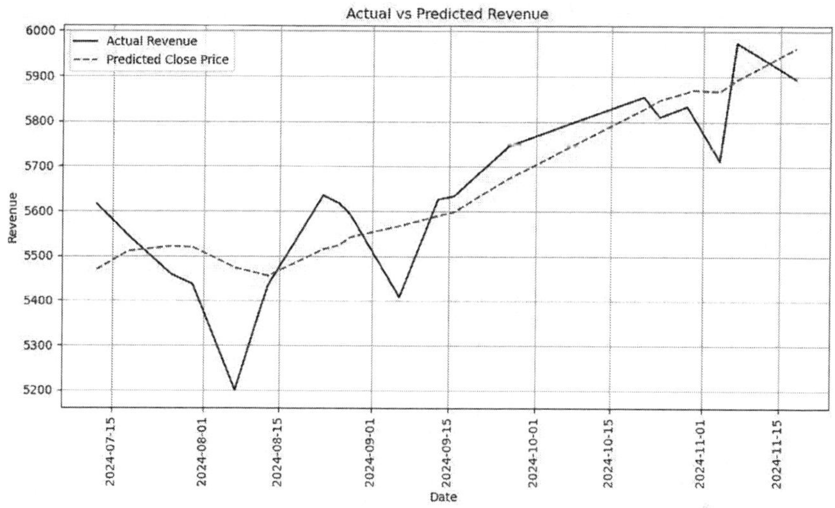

Figure 2.3 View of the plot of actual values with values predicted based on moving averages

- **Customize:** As earlier, we will be providing the customization parameters here. We will be customizing the following:
  - o Name of our data file in CSV format.
  - o Names of graphics files for saving the plots of decomposition, trend, seasonality, cyclicality, and residuals.

  Here are the relevant codes with the parameter values italicized.

```
#customize your application

#name of the file where you have historical data
myfile = '0203 Revenue_month.csv'

#Name the jpg file where you want to save the
decomposition plot

my_decomp_plot = '0203 decomp_plot.jpg'

#Name the jpg file where you want to save the trend plot
my_trend_plot = '0203 trend_plot.jpg'

#Name the jpg file where you want to save the seasonality
plot
my_season_plot = '0203 season_plot.jpg'
```

```
#Name the jpg file where you want to save the cyclicality
plot
my_cycle_plot = '0203 cycle_plot.jpg'

#Name the jpg file where you want to save the residual
plot
my_residue_plot = '0203 residue_plot.jpg'
```

- **Load data and preprocess**: In this section, we have loaded the data. We have also ensured that the date is in a Python-compliant format and indexed on the date column. In case you do not want to use the full dataset, you can use a portion of the same by tweaking this code here.

```
#If we want to use some limited number of days
#df=df.tail(200)
```

  You must remove the hash (#) sign from the beginning of the second line and provide the numerical value of the latest number of data points you want to use. The revised code will look like

```
df=df.tail(200)
```

  Please remember to restore the # sign if you want to use the full dataset.
- **Time series decomposition**: This section decomposes the time series into trend, seasonality, cyclicality, and residual, and presents a comprehensive plot of those. The plot is also saved for your use. The dataset may have annual data, but not all days may be working days. Considering 365 or 366 days in the dataset to make a year would be erroneous. In this code, you can provide the number of working days in a year or simply put approximately how many consecutive records make up one year.

```
# Decomposing to find seasonality with a yearly
periodicity (Annual working days)
result = seasonal_decompose(base_values,
model='additive', period=252)
```

  Provide the number of days to denote an annual dataset against the period parameter.
- **Plot and understand trend**: In this section, we are separating the trend element from the time series data. It gives us the direction of the data points over time. The trend is visually represented, and the plot is saved in a graphics file for future use.
- **Plot and understand seasonality**: The seasonality component of the time series data is separated and plotted in this section. The plot is also saved

as a graphics file. The plot helps in identifying the regular seasonal behavior in the data, which is important for forecasting, making decisions related to market trends, or developing predictive models. The seasonal component represents the recurring cycle, and it can be averaged or normalized to show the periodic pattern across years.

- **Plot and understand cyclicality**: Cyclicality is also a component of time series. This section computes cyclicality from the data, plots the same, and saves it for future use. We have used the Fourier transform to assess cyclicality (or periodicity) in time series data. It transforms the data from the time domain to the frequency domain, thus helping identify dominant periodic patterns, trends, or cycles that may not be immediately apparent. The plot uses frequency and amplitude as two axes. The horizontal axis represents frequency, indicating how often certain cycles or periodic movements occur in the data. The higher the frequency, the more rapidly the changes are repeated in the time series. The vertical axis shows the amplitude or strength of each frequency. The larger the amplitude, the more significant that frequency component is in the time series. A strong low-frequency component would mean that values are largely driven by long-term trends rather than short-term fluctuations.
- **Plot and understand residuals**: The final component of time series is the residuals. This section computes residuals, then plots and saves them as a graphics file. Residuals are the differences between the model's predicted values and the actual observed data. Positive residuals (above zero) indicate that the model's prediction is lower than the actual observed value, signifying that the model underestimated the value. Negative residuals (below zero) indicate that the model's prediction is higher than the actual observed value, a case of overestimation. The vertical axis measures the magnitude and direction of prediction errors (residuals) over time. Ideally, the residuals should resemble white noise, which is characterized by random fluctuations with no discernible pattern. This would happen when the model captured the underlying patterns in the data. A pattern or non-random fluctuations or the presence of large outliers or clustering would indicate that the fit of the model is not optimal. This may call for a review of the model and the consideration of the use of other explanatory variables.

Interpreting forecast outputs and linking with budgeting processes

Now we have various models that we can use to forecast. We have also seen how to decompose time series data to better understand the underlying trends, seasonality, cyclicality, and residuals. The question now arises on how to interpret the output and put it to use.

We have seen visual representations of the forecast using `Prophet` and moving averages. These plots are easy to understand and give us a better grasp of the nature of the underlying data. Let us discuss some of the outputs and how they can be used to improve the budgeting process.

- **Forecast plot**: The plot of forecasted and actual values gives us an idea about how well the model is performing, which will be useful in the context of using forecasted data. If the differences between forecasts and actuals are too wide, it may not be useful for budgeting. This would mean we will have to look for alternative models for forecasting.
- **Trend and seasonality**: While trend is a long-term phenomenon, seasonal components in the data may require us to adjust the budget based on anticipated fluctuations within the budget period. Trends will bring out the inherent direction, while seasonal elements will allow us precision within the period.
- **Uncertainty interval**: For a financial decision-maker, the uncertainty interval represents the area where most of the forecast is likely to lie. This can be used for scenario planning or defining what could be treated as extreme events. Please do not confuse this with probability. An uncertainty interval of 0.95 means that 95% of the values that may be drawn from various samples of forecast values are likely to lie within that boundary. Probability, in this case, is related to uncertainty about the model parameters, which is confirmed by past values; here we are using predicted values to define the range. If you have heard the term confidence interval, it typically refers to the probability that the true value of a forecast (or parameter) will fall within a given range based on repeated sampling.
- **Moving averages**: They help in smoothing out short-term volatilities, making them useful for long-term prediction. Moving averages can help us in forecasting trends, but they would not give us values to base our budget on. This trend would be useful for guiding future spending allocation.
- **Model performance metrics**: We have used the following model performance metrics in our code.

  - **Mean Absolute Error (MAE)**: Measures the average magnitude of errors between predicted values and actual values, providing insight into the accuracy of the model. It calculates the average of the absolute differences between predicted and observed values. For example, if the MAE is 7, it means that on average, the predictions are off by 7 units from the actual values. But note that MAE is scale-dependent. Hence, before you comment on two different MAEs, please consider the scale, or you may even normalize it by dividing it by the range or mean of the target. This turns MAE into a relative error, making it easier to compare across different problems or scales.

- **Mean Squared Error** (MSE): It measures the average of the squared differences between the actual and predicted values. MSE penalizes larger errors more heavily than smaller ones because the errors are squared. While squaring solves the problem of positive and negative deviations being set off against each other, it also makes MSE very sensitive to large discrepancies in predictions. Larger errors get more weightage, which makes it sensitive to outliers. If you have a cost forecast and the price was extremely high in one period because of scarcity, MSE will give that a higher weight. MSE is also scale-dependent, and the squaring makes it difficult to relate the value to the base figures. To interpret MSE in the same unit as the original data, you can use RMSE, which is the square root of MSE.
- **R-squared**: This is also known as the coefficient of determination. R-squared is a widely used model performance metric, especially for regression models. It provides a measure of how well independent variables explain the variation in the dependent (the target) variable. The value may range from 0 to 1. $R^2 = 1$ means a perfect fit – the model explains 100% of the variance in the target variable. A zero value means that the model explains none of the variance in the target variable. R^2 can be negative if the model is worse than even a simple mean model. No fixed cutoff value of R^2 can be used for model acceptance. It will depend on the nature of the data. For example, R^2 in social science may be low, while in business forecasting, it could be higher.
- **Mean Absolute Percentage Error** (MAPE): This is a widely used metric for evaluating the accuracy of a predictive model, including forecasting. It measures the average absolute percentage difference between the actual values and the predicted values. Unlike MAE or MSE, which are expressed in the same units as the target variable. MAPE expresses errors as a percentage of the actual values. It directly indicates how much off the predictions are in terms of percentage.

  This makes it easier to understand and compare across different datasets or models.

The quality of forecasting models will decide whether we can use the predicted values as the basis of our budgeting. We should remember that the use of forecasting tools is not limited to budgeting. There are forecasting models that focus on states – for example, will the borrower repay, will the customer buy, customer churn, extreme weather events, fraud detection, and so many more. We will introduce some of these tools later in this book.

Automated budget variance analysis

Budgets are often known as a tool for both planning and control. We have seen the planning component in the earlier section. Let us now review the control aspect.

Once a budget is accepted and implementation starts, the budgeted figure becomes a benchmark for control. One of the great tools of budgetary control is variance analysis – the difference between the budgeted values and actual values for the same level of activity and environmental characteristics. We need to remember that the budgets are based on some sets of assumptions. If those assumptions change, the performance values will not be the same as the budget. At this stage, we must be clear about one thing. Budget variance does not necessarily mean someone is accountable. The changes may be because of macroeconomic events, changes in customer preference, and many other factors that are often beyond the control of those involved in developing the budget. We need to identify and analyze the budget variance.

To compute budget variance, we will need to decompose the accounted values into two components – quantity and unit values. Thus, in the case of revenue, we need unit price and units sold; in the case of cost of power, we need units consumed and cost per unit, and similar.

Traditionally, financial control is mostly made at the level of total cost or total revenue, that is, at the highest aggregated level. While at this level, we may be able to detect variance; there can be situations where this may go undetected.

Consider the following situation faced by a small pizzeria in New York:

Budgeted revenue: $11,000, comprising 1,000 units to be sold at $11 each
Actual revenue: $11,000, comprising 1,100 units to be sold at $10 each

You can see that at the aggregated level, there is no variance – budgeted value has been achieved. But a closer look shows there are variances at the component level. If the pizzeria could have sold at a budgeted price of $11, it would have earned $12,100. But before we proceed to discussing budget variance, let us take a quick look at some other major concepts and terminology in the budgeting process:

- **Standard:** These are the base figures on which the budget is developed. The process of variance analysis is built around these values. Different organizations adopt different measures to decide on the standard. Some adopt what has been achieved in the past as standard, others regard the engineering standard as the base, while some may even base the standards on the advice of experts. The core focus should be a basis which is optimal for the circumstances and does not entertain underperformance.
- **Tolerance:** Budgets are financial estimates, while actuals are business performances. These two values would rarely match, and there will

always be some variance. These variations are only normal and do not signify any excellence or failure in performance. In some cases, normal deviation may be 5%, and, in some cases, it may be 0.1%. This depends on the nature of the industry. For example, in the case of the jewelry business, the deviation must be the minimum possible, considering the high cost of the material. The same may not be true for an ice cream parlor, where a variation of two scoops may not be material. In most cases, normal deviation will be factored into the price, and hence, reporting the same would not perform any control function. Thus, in decision-making, variance will be defined as only those beyond the tolerance limit.

- **Standard for actuals:** This is an important component of variance analysis. This is where we convert the budget or the standard for estimates to the standard for actuals. We use the quantity achieved and the standard prices to arrive at the standard for actuals. This signifies what could have been the revenue or cost if we had the budgeted price or cost at the actual volume achieved. This allows us to have the first sub-level of variance analysis. Let us use the earlier example of the pizzeria and compute variances.

A: Budgeted revenue: $11,000, comprising 1,000 units to be sold at $11 each
B: Actual revenue: $11,000, comprising 1,100 units to be sold at $10 each
C: Standard for actual: $12,100 – actual quantity (1,100) × standard price ($11)

Budget variance (The outer layer): A – B = 0; No variance
Now we break this into price and quantity variance, the first sublayer.
Price variance: B – C: (11,000 – 12,100): (1,100) Adverse
Quantity variance: C – A: (12,100 – 11,000): 1,100 Favorable

At this level, we can see that the sales team did a good job by selling more than expected. But the pricing team did not get the price correct. If we want to reconcile this method with a detailed formula approach, here we are.

Price variance:

= (Actual Price – Standard Price) × Actual Quantity
= (Actual Price × Actual Quantity) – (Standard Price × Actual Quantity)
= Actual Revenue – Standard for actuals

Quantity Variance:

= (Actual Quantity – Standard Quantity) × Standard Price
= (Actual Quantity × Standard Price) – (Standard Quantity × Standard Price)
= Standard for actuals – Budgeted

Total variance:

= Price Variance + Quantity Variance
= (Actual – Standard for actuals) + (Standard for actuals – Budgeted)
= Actual – Budgeted

So, there we are! Both formula-based and rule-based approaches lead to the same values for budget, price, and quantity variances. Computationally, the standard for actual value allows us to classify total budget into price variance and quantity variance.

Inefficiencies in manual variance analysis

When performing a variance analysis manually, we restrict ourselves to the top level and in the earlier example, we have seen a serious limitation of it. However, as we go down to the next level, the computations become complex. Every layer we add, the computations will become more complex.

In the example used, we considered one product that contributed to the total revenue. In any business, we are likely to have multiple products that will add up to the total revenue. Let us consider a café selling coffee and cookies in Edinburgh.

The budgeted revenue of the café is £70,000, comprising:

Coffee: 10,000 cups at £4: £40,000
Cookies: 10,000 pieces at £3: £30,000
If we compute the unit revenue, it will be £70,000 / 20,000 = £3.5

Let us consider the actual sales were £71,000, comprising:

Coffee: 11,000 cups at £4: £44,000
Cookies: 9,000 pieces at £3: £27,000
If we compute the unit revenue, it will now be £71,000 / 20,000 = £3.55

Note that the unit price and total volume have not changed; what has changed is the mix. The budgeted mix of coffee and cookies was equal; the actual mix was 11:9.

This mix has caused the difference. In this case, we can argue that we will compute the variance separately for coffee and cookies. That is possible because both are independent products, and we can add the product-wise price and quantity variance to show the total product and total quantity variance.

The price variance is zero for both coffee and cookies, as the prices have remained the same. We will only have quantity variance.

Quantity Variance (Coffee): (11,000 – 10,000) × £4 = £4,000
Quantity Variance (Cookie): (9,000 – 10,000) × £3 = (–) £3,000

Total budget variance of £1,000 (£71,000 – £70,000) is explained by favorable price variance of £4,000 and adverse quantity variance of (–) £3,000.

Let us now look at an example where the mix variance computation becomes complex. Consider an ice cream parlor in Dubai selling sundaes, with the following cost estimate:

The Dubai ice cream parlor expects to sell 10,000 sundae cups. To make them, they need 20,000 scoops of ice cream costing AED 6 per scoop and 10,000 spoonsful of nuts costing AED 3 per spoon. So, the total budgeted cost is = (20,000 × 6) + (10,000 × 3) = AED 150,000.

The parlor sold 12,000 cups of sundae in the budgeted period. It records that they have used 23,500 ice cream scoops costing AED 152,750 and 12,200 spoonsful of nuts costing AED 35,380. The total cost of making those 12,000 cups of sundae was AED 188,130.

We can now see that the computation is becoming more complex because the standard quantity is also linked to the mix.

This situation becomes more complex as the number of items increases. Manual computation, using tools like spreadsheet, becomes arduous. It becomes difficult to compute the detailed level. Let us see the computational steps.

Step 1: Collect the budgeted and actual values (Table 2.5).

Step 2: We will now compute the standard cost for actuals and the standard mix for actuals (Table 2.6). Standard cost for actuals is computed by multiplying the actual quantity by the standard price. Standard mix is obtained by distributing the actual total quantity across all materials in the ratio that each raw material enjoys with the total raw material quantity in the budgeted cost. The standard mix for actuals for ice cream is given by (12,000/18,000) × 35,700 = 23,800. In both tables, we will be using the budgeted unit cost.

Table 2.5 Budgeted and actual costs for producing 12,000 sundaes

Costs in AED	*A: Budgeted Cost*			*B: Actual Cost*		
	Units	*Cost/Unit*	*Total Cost*	*Units*	*Cost/Unit*	*Total Cost*
Ice-cream	24,000	6	144,000	23,500	6.5	152,750
Nuts	12,000	3	36,000	12,200	2.9	35,380
	36,000		180,000	35,700		188,130

Table 2.6 Computation of standard for actuals and standard mix for actuals

Costs in AED	*A: Standard for actuals*			*B: Standard mix for actuals*		
	Units	*Cost/Unit*	*Total Cost*	*Units*	*Cost/Unit*	*Total Cost*
Ice-cream	23,500	6	141,000	23,800	6	142,800
Nuts	12,200	3	36,600	11,900	3	35,700
	35,700		177,600	35,700		178,500

Step 3: At this stage, we have enough information to compute the variance for the top and the next immediate layer. Here they are:

- Budget Variance: Budgeted cost (Table 2.5 A) – Actual cost (Table 2.5 B) = AED 180,000 – AED 188,130 = AED 8,130.
- Material Price Variance: Standard for actual cost (Table 2.6 A) – Actual cost (Table 2.5 B) = AED 177,600 – AED 188,130 = AED (–) 10,530
- Material Usage Variance: Budgeted cost (Table 2.5 A) – Standard for actual cost (Table 2.6 A) = AED 180,000 – AED 177,600 = AED 2,400

Step 4: We will now go down one further layer and compute material mix and yield variance (Table 2.7). This is a segmentation of material usage variance. Material mix variance is computed by multiplying the unit consumption under the standard mix for actuals (Table 2.6 B) less the unit consumption under the standard for actuals (Table 2.6 A) by the standard price. The yield variance is computed by multiplying the unit consumption under the Budget (Table 2.5 A) less units consumed under the standard mix for actual (Table 2.6 B) by the standard price.

The material mix variance is AED 900; the material yield variance is AED 1,500, adding up to the total material usage variance of AED 2,400 computed in Step 4.

We can see how challenging it may be to compute the third level manually. One would need some extent of automation, be it by using a spreadsheet or by coding the same. A copy of the spreadsheet is available in the code repository.

ML tools to automate data manipulation and variance calculations

Application of ML in variance analysis can be made in a few ways:

Table 2.7 Computation of material mix and yield variance

Costs in AED	*A: Material Mix Variance*			*B: Material Yield Variance*		
	Units	*Cost/ Unit*	*Total Cost*	*Units*	*Cost/ Unit*	*Total Cost*
Ice-cream	300	6	1,800	200	6	1200
Nuts	–300	3	–900	100	3	300
	0		900	300		1500

Computing variance

This would involve using a Python code to automate the variance computation process. We do not need any major libraries for the computation. This would naturally be a post-mortem activity, as we will need data on actual performance. Depending on the number of elements of variance analysis, we may find it convenient to compute variance using the spreadsheet provided in the code repository. We may need to insert rows for additional components in the spreadsheet. We have also provided sample Python code in the code repository (prefix 0204). The code and the spreadsheet use the same data. Let us discuss various sections of the Python code:

- **Import libraries:** In this section, we are loading the necessary libraries. You will notice that the libraries are standard ones that we have used earlier.
- **Customize:** In this section, we will provide the values for customizable parameters. We have considered two types of material here. The code needs to be amended slightly if you have more than two materials. Customization includes the basic information about budget and actual performance, and the following other parameters.
  - The currency of transactions
  - Names of the files to save variance reports, stacked bars, and pie charts of computed variances
  - Names of the materials
  - Cost information, often known as a cost sheet
  - Production unit that is the unit produced under the standard cost sheet and the actual units produced
  - Budgeted and actual values of usage and costs

  The relevant lines from the code are given here with the values we need to provide italicized.

```
# Define the variables for budgeted and actual data

# Which currency are you using
mycurrency = 'AED'

# name the file to save the variance report
myfile= '0204 variance_report.csv'

# name the file to save the stacked bar chart
mybarchart = '0204 variance_stacked.jpg'

# name the file to save the pie chart
mypiechart = '0204 variance_pie.jpg'
```

```
# Provide the names of the materials
material_1 = 'Ice-cream'
material_2 = 'Nuts'

# Provide standard cost information
base_production_unit = 10000
base_material_1_usage = 20000
base_material_2_usage = 10000

# Provide budgeted usage and cost information about the
materials
budgeted_production_unit = 12000
budgeted_material_1_cost_per_unit = 6
budgeted_material_2_cost_per_unit = 3

# Provide actual usage and cost information about
the materials
actual_material_1_units = 23500
actual_material_1_cost_per_unit = 6.5
actual_material_2_units = 12200
actual_material_2_cost_per_unit = 2.9
```

- **Compute base data for variance analysis:** This is the initial computation section. Here we compute the necessary values for the budget and actual performance using the data provided.
- **Compute additional data for variance analysis:** In this section, we are computing the standard values for actual capacity along with the standard material mix for the actual production level. That information will allow us to go deeper than the top layer of variance analysis in the next step.
- **Compute variances at the top and first layer:** The top-level variance, that is the budget variance, is computed at this level. Then it goes ahead to split into price and usage variance.
- **Compute variances at detailed layers:** This section decomposes the usage variance into mix and yield variance. Mix variance focuses on the proportion of materials used compared to the standard material mix. Yield variance focuses on the input–output ratio and compares the actual material productivity against the budgeted output expected from those inputs.

Forecast variance

We can also use forecasting techniques to predict variance. We can identify variables which we feel can influence the variance and then forecast future variance. If we can observe from past variances a pattern matching time series, we can use time series forecasting tools to predict variance. We have discussed these techniques in the earlier section of this chapter.

Creating scenarios

We can also try to forecast a range of values of components of variance analysis like price and quantity. Various scenarios can be created, and we can use those values to predict a range for likely variances. We have discussed scenario creation in a subsequent section of this chapter.

Generate variance reports and visualizations

The final three sections of the code (prefix 0204) generate the variance report and visualize the same. These sections are:

- **Saving the variance values in a CSV file:** In this section, we save the variances computed at the top layer and inner layers in a specified file in CSV format. We store the values of budget variance, price variance, usage variance, material mix variance, and material yield variance for all materials.
- **Visualize variance – Stacked bar:** We design stacked bar chart for each material as well as aggregate material. The bars are stacked with values of price variance, mix variance, and yield variance. The plot is also saved in a specified graphics file for use with other reports.
- **Visualize variance – Pie chart:** This section plots the total variance as a pie chart to understand the relative importance of the three variances – price, mix, and yield. We need to note that the pie chart is drawn using absolute values of the variances. The negative values are denoted in red. In case there is more than one negative value, all will be in red. The actual values are stated in the legend. This plot is also saved in a specified graphics file for use in various reports.

The charts and the spreadsheet file would act as a base for variance reports and visualization requirements. The variance values can be drawn from the spreadsheet and incorporated into management reports. One can even automate the management report for variance analysis, but that may not be a great value addition since the variance report would also contain management action points. These action points need not necessarily have a standard format.

The format in which the spreadsheet stores the variance reports is shown in Figure 2.4.

	A	B	C	D
1	Particulars	Ice-cream	Nuts	Total
2	Budget variance	-8750	620	-8130
3	Price Variance	-11750	1220	-10530
4	Usage variance	3000	-600	2400
5	Mix Variance	1800	-900	900
6	Yield variance	1200	300	1500

Figure 2.4 Spreadsheet report of variance analysis

Enhanced real-time monitoring of financial performance

Use of the ML-based techniques discussed in the context of forecasting, budgeting, and variance analysis would allow modern businesses to achieve more accurate and quicker reports. It will assist in dynamic monitoring of financial performance, providing real-time insights into financial health and aiding the decision-making processes. ML algorithms can process vast amounts of historical financial data, identify patterns, and generate accurate predictions for future financial performance. This enables forecasting revenue, expenses, and cash flows objectively and accurately. Normalization of data and continuous learning ability of ML models are extremely useful under changing market conditions. This ability improves forecasting reliability over time using relevant past data.

In case of the budgeting process, ML tools can automate the allocation of resources based on predictive analytics. These tools use historical financial data, market trends, and other relevant inputs to provide more accurate and flexible budgeting outcomes. It can also incorporate the influence of relevant factors while predicting financial performance and developing budgets. Real-time monitoring also allows businesses to adjust their budgets dynamically, making them more responsive to changes in the business environment. ML-based tools can conduct variance analysis in real time, comparing actual financial performance against forecasted or budgeted figures. Early identification of variances allows organizations to address issues promptly, leading to better financial control. Detailed variance analysis can also assist in determining the root causes of variances. In addition, these tools allow forecasting of variance after factoring in the influences of relevant market variables.

We must note that ML-based tools are not the only way to achieve these betterments, but they are indeed a fast, adaptable, proactive, data-driven and user-friendly approach.

Scenario planning using ML tools

Scenario planning involves considering different future states of the base assumptions. These may include demand, price, inflation, non-recovery of dues, and many more. Scenario planning is based on various uncertainties, helping organizations prepare for potential outcomes.

ML tools can be used to improve the efficacy of scenario planning. These tools can potentially enhance this process by analyzing large volumes of historical data, identifying patterns in them, and generating predictive models. These outputs can then be grouped in combinations to simulate different scenarios.

In addition to creating inputs to define scenarios, ML models can keep learning from new data and adjust the scenarios accordingly. This dynamic scenario adjustment capability is very useful in a volatile environment when conditions change rapidly.

Simulation capability of ML tools can create multiple scenarios which can improve awareness of potential pitfalls.

Let us now see how scenario planning can be used in conjunction with ML tools.

Scenario planning in uncertain business environments

Businesses are always exposed to uncertainty, and most business organizations prepare for it. Scenario planning enables organizations to anticipate and prepare for plausible futures, strengthening their readiness for scenarios they understand best. If there are potential scenarios that the organizations may not be able to sustain, they need to take a call on whether to continue their operations in that sector. Scenario planning assists the business in several other ways.

- **Identifying risks and opportunities**: Multiple scenarios allow organizations to identify risks and opportunities that they might not have faced in their regular operations. Creation of scenarios involves experimentation with different possible values of inputs, and ML tools come in useful for it.
- **Strategic flexibility**: Without comprehensive understanding of the range of possibilities, strategies are most likely to be biased to known possibilities. Once the management is exposed to a wider range of possibilities, the strategies are expected to be flexible to a larger range of scenarios.
- **Resource allocation**: Knowledge of what may happen promotes pragmatic allocation of resources, including capital, human resources, and time. A review of scenarios would lead us to the common elements

across different scenarios. This will promote better resource allocation in areas that are likely to yield benefits across most scenarios. It would also allow us to set aside reserves for unexpected downturns.

- **Encourage long-term thinking**: When the management is exposed to a range of possibilities, the decision-making process tends to gravitate toward a long-term perspective. The various scenarios make the management appreciate what is more likely in the long run, rather than focusing on the short run. If you toss a coin ten times, it is not unlikely that the coin will turn out seven heads and three tails. But as you keep on tossing, this gap will start reducing, and the number of instances of heads and tails will be on a path of convergence. This is exactly what ML tools do to scenario planning. With a larger number of scenarios, the pattern that emerges would mostly converge to the one that has the highest likelihood.
- **Improved resilience**: The real challenge arises when a business is unaware of potential scenarios that could threaten its survival. Knowledge of a range of possibilities would allow an organization to be better prepared for improbable but possible scenarios. Mitigation decisions may take various forms, but awareness of potential scenarios and their risks ensures the organization is not caught off guard.
- **Mitigate cognitive bias**: Scenario analysis challenges static assumptions, and the study of multiple outcomes helps to mitigate cognitive biases like overconfidence or status quo bias. This is likely to lead to more objective strategic planning rather than having a subjective opinion on future possibilities.

Consider budgeting decisions. This involves assumptions relating to the price of raw material and finished goods, volume of raw material and finished goods, yield of raw material, possible mixes of raw material as well as finished goods, and similar. If we have even three possible values of each of these eight parameters, we can have 3^8 or 6,561 possible combinations. If the number of possible values increases to four for each of those eight parameters, the number of possible combinations will increase to $4^8 = 65{,}536$. ML makes it easy for us to enhance the range of scenarios.

Using ML models to simulate various financial scenarios

Let us continue with the last example of variance analysis and apply an ML-based tool for conducting scenario planning on the same. The relevant code (prefix 0205) is available in the repository. The code has the following sections:

- **Import libraries**: As earlier, we load the libraries in this section. You will find a new library named "random" that has been used here. As the name suggests, this library is used to generate random numbers.

- **Customize:** In this section, we provide value for the following parameters.
  - o Name of the currency
  - o Names of files to save the scenarios, frequency distribution table, and tornado chart
  - o Names of the two materials
  - o Total number of scenarios to be generated and bin size for the frequency distribution table
  - o The original budgeted total cost
  - o The upper and lower quantity range of the materials
  - o The upper and lower price range of the materials

  The relevant lines of code are reproduced here with the parameter values italicized.

```
#Customize

mycurrency = 'AED'
mysavedfile = '0205 scenarios.csv'
myfrequencyfile = '0205 frequency_dist.csv'
mytornado = '0205 tornado_plot.jpg'

material_1_name = 'Icecream'
material_2_name = 'Nuts'

num_scenarios= 10000
bin_size = 5000
budgeted_total_cost = 180000

material_1_use_lower    = 20000
material_1_use_upper    = 25000
material_2_use_lower    = 15000
material_2_use_upper    = 10000
material_1_price_lower  =     5
material_1_price_upper  =     8
material_2_price_lower  =     2
material_2_price_upper  =     3
```

- **Define random number generator:** This section of the code generates random numbers for the parameters for which we provided the lower and upper values. We will call this function to generate random values for each parameter when we develop scenarios.
- **Generate random numbers and scenarios:** We have provided the number of scenarios we will develop. Random values will be generated for each specified parameter for every scenario. The code generates random values for each parameter independently. We will end up having several scenarios comprising randomly generated values for each parameter.

- **Compute total cost and variance in the dataframe:** Now we have the scenarios and values for each parameter. Though generated randomly, these values are all possible and, being generated independently, are likely to create unique combinations. We compute the total costs and variance from the budget for each scenario and store them alongside each scenario.
- **Change column names and save scenarios in CSV:** We change the column names in the data set to recognize them easily with each material and then save the entire data set in **CSV** format. This file can now be used externally for further processing. We have used this file for creating reports that are useful for strategic decisions.

Impact of changes in key variables on financial outcomes

Assessing the impact of changes in key variables on financial outcomes is a critical area of concern in financial decision-making. Understanding how different values of key variables influence financial results would help in anticipating potential risks and making more informed decisions. These key variables would include interest rates, exchange rates, inflation, economic growth, consumer confidence, government policies, geopolitical events, and a host of other factors.

In our case, we will find these critical inputs in the values we provide for parameters. In addition, the underlying assumptions would also influence financial performance. Scenario analysis allows us to assess the impact of changes in key variables on financial outcome. As seen in the example, we can simulate a number of possible scenarios based on real-life observations and compute their impact on financial performance measures.

The impact of the changes can be measured in two ways, either individually or collectively as part of a scenario. We have already discussed the latter. When we change one parameter and observe the outcome, we can also measure the sensitivity of that input on the key financial performance. This is essentially done by dividing the percentage change in the value of the performance indicator by the percentage change in the value of the input. The inputs with the highest sensitivity are monitored closely, as a little change in their cost or consumption is likely to have a significant impact on the performance. ML tools can be used to automate this exercise, besides generating a series of values for each input.

Strategic planning with data-driven insights

The purpose of using ML is not merely to have better data processing capability. We need to use the data for our decisions, particularly strategic decisions. The actionable insights provided by ML tools facilitate seamless integration with the strategic decision-making process.

Let us continue with our example of creating scenarios for the variance analysis and see how this integration happens. The last three sections of the code are devoted to this purpose. They are essentially reports on various aspects of scenario planning and use the scenarios generated earlier.

- **Frequency distribution of variance scenarios:** You may remember that we have simulated several scenarios, each distinguished by a combination of values of parameters generated randomly. We have computed the total cost and variances for each of these scenarios. In this section, we take the lower and upper values of variance observed across scenarios. We have specified the bin size, which will be the size of each bin for creating a frequency distribution table. Please note that the best way to decide the bin size is to decide the number of bins you want to create. Then divide the difference between the upper and lower values of simulated variances by this number. The result will be the bin size, which you may round off. This frequency table is also saved under a specified name for future use. This is how the table is saved (Figure 2.5).
  We can see that each bin has specified the lower and upper bound enveloping 5,000 values between them. The frequency values show the number of observations that come within the range. The total of all frequencies would add up to the number of scenarios we had specified.
- **Tornado chart of variance scenarios:** The frequency distribution data can be presented in the form of a tornado chart, as shown here (Figure 2.6). The Y-axis shows the upper and lower limits of each bin, while the X-axis shows the frequency values. This gives a visual representation of

	A	B
1	Variance Bin	Frequency
2	(-58545, -53545]	10
3	(-53545, -48545]	31
4	(-48545, -43545]	92
5	(-43545, -38545]	174
6	(-38545, -33545]	249
7	(-33545, -28545]	371
8	(-28545, -23545]	430
9	(-23545, -18545]	550

Figure 2.5 Excerpt of the frequency distribution table

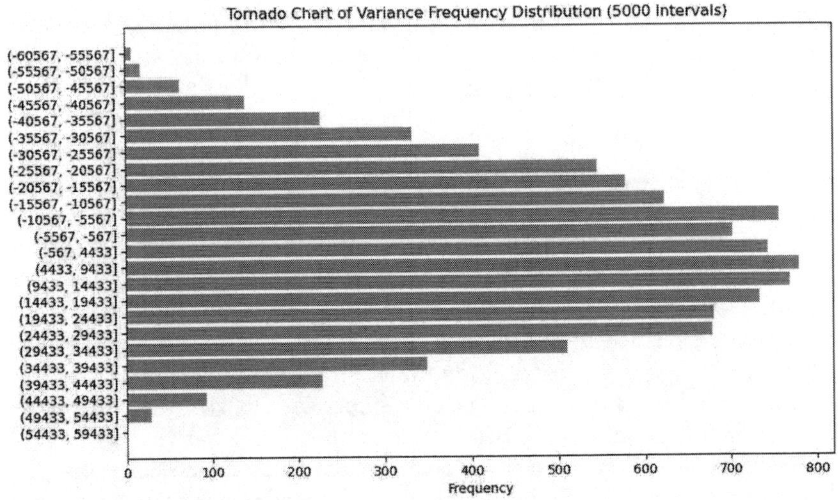

Figure 2.6 Tornado chart of frequency distribution generated from scenarios

the frequency distribution, and the decision-makers would get a better idea of how likely a specific variance is.

- **Positive and negative variance scenario**: Variance is computed as the difference between actual and budgeted. Hence, for cost analysis, negative values are unfavorable and positive values are favorable. This will be the opposite for revenue. This report finds out the highest and lowest variances from the variance scenarios created. The report states the variance value along with the corresponding values of units and unit prices that have led to the value of the variance. Please note that all these are simulated scenarios and not the actual performance.
- **Percentile analysis and report**: Once we have simulated various scenarios and computed the values for variance in each case, we can now make a percentile analysis of the same. In a percentile analysis, we find the percentage of total observations that are either above or below a certain value. This gives us an intuitive understanding of the probability of a value showing up in real life. This report shows the variance values at various percentile levels – 1%, 5%, 10%, 90%, 95%, and 99%. The value corresponding to the 1st percentile suggests that there is less than 1% chance that the variance will be lower than the corresponding value. Similarly, the 99th percentile suggests that there is less than 1% probability that the variance will exceed the corresponding value.

We can see how these reports add the strategy dimension to the decision-making process. Not only can we simulate the number of scenarios, but we can also use those to assess the probability of a variance value coming up in real life. This will allow the management to keep different plans ready to face different levels of variance. This will allow variance analysis to elevate from a reactive exercise to a proactive management function.

Key takeaways

We have seen that forecasting and budgeting are essential for financial planning, each playing a distinct but complementary role in decision-making. While budgeting translates organizational goals into financial terms for planning and control, forecasting provides the forward-looking insight necessary to build those budgets on a realistic and data-driven basis. We have explored how traditional statistical methods and emerging ML tools can be applied to enhance forecasting accuracy.

We also saw how forecasts can be integrated into the budgeting processes and used to support proactive variance analysis and performance monitoring. We will be using some of these tools in many places in the book and will refrain from giving a detailed description each time we use them. The value of any of these tools depends not just on technical implementation but also on thoughtful model selection, validation, and an understanding of their limitations. Ultimately, these tools empower financial professionals to make better-informed, quicker, and accountable decisions. The focus of the book is to use the tools to make our expertise in finance more effective.

Chapter 3

Cost management and optimization

Managing costs wisely is at the heart of every strong financial strategy. In this chapter, we explore how finance professionals can go beyond traditional methods to gain deeper insights into cost behaviors and how to control them. You will be introduced to using ML tools to perform ABC, cost driver analysis, and resource optimization. Whether you are pricing a product, analyzing overheads, or planning under tight budgets, this chapter will guide you in making smarter, data-driven decisions.

Understanding and using activity-based costing

The sustainability of an organization hinges significantly on, among others, cost management and resource optimization practices. Cost management is not only about reducing expenses by identifying cost-saving opportunities. It also entails aligning resource allocations with the overall business priorities. Inaccuracy in matching costs with the products may lead to distorted profitability analyses and inappropriate strategic decisions. Similarly, poor resource allocation may lead to the failed implementation of strategic planning and the failure to capitalize on opportunities.

Over the years, the faculty of cost management has developed tools and techniques to allow managers to make better decisions. These include techniques that optimize profitability under business constraints, allocate resources to support strategy, and adopt an activity-driven approach for better cost management. Of these, ABC has caught the fancy of practitioners and has been found useful. In this chapter, we explore what ABC is and how it can guide finance professionals to allocate costs more accurately. This would lead to better resource allocation and financial planning. We will also look at how to apply ML tools to make the ABC process faster with enhanced scope of application.

Businesses have innovated and modified the way they operate. Customers have also changed their preferences and look for variety. All this has

DOI: 10.4324/9781003619628-3

led to the emergence of a complex product process. Engineers have put in their efforts trying to develop common processes for varied projects, to the extent that it is technically possible.

These common processes perform specific activities, but not all products go through all activities. The question follows: How do we fairly allocate these costs to products? We should not charge products with unrelated costs.

ABC provides a framework to solve this problem. It lays out a methodology to charge products only with relevant overheads. Please note that this problem arises only with overheads since direct costs are charged based on the direct consumption of resources. The objective is that products that use a resource, whether shared or not, should seek to recover the related cost. One may argue, what is the harm if another product, which is in a better position to recover the cost, recovers a higher share?

Absolutely no harm, if that is a management decision after understanding the full picture. ABC provides the information that financial managers may utilize while making strategic decisions. A decision without a proper basis may end up in a high-performing product appearing unprofitable as it subsidizes a lower-performing product.

To appreciate how ABC improves our decision-making process, let us review why traditional costing systems often fail to allocate costs properly. This problem is accentuated in a multi-product or multi-process environment.

Limitations of traditional costing methods

Costs are broadly classified as direct and indirect. Direct costs are clearly linked to producing a specific product or service. Indirect costs are shared across multiple areas of the business. Direct costs are easy to charge as they can be traced back to the product. The challenge arises with indirect costs. Businesses have historically relied on absorption costing, also known as full costing, to allocate indirect costs.

They are allocated based on a predetermined overhead recovery rate. However, this often leads to severe distortion in reported costs and, consequently, profitability. This may eventually lead to designing a poor competitive strategy.

Consider two companies that produce bottled water. Both have factories of the same size and use similar machinery. One produces only mineral water, while the other has a product portfolio composed of 70% mineral water, 20% low-sodium water, and 10% vitamin-enriched water. The annual output in units of bottled water is 200,000 for both companies, and they both require the same direct labor hours and machine hours.

A bird's eye view of the production process looks like this: source water, purify it, and package it. The process for mineral water is identical for both companies. However, in the second company, further processing is required, such as assessment of sodium content, separate labeling, compliance with the regulatory norms for low-sodium water, and others. Similarly, additional processes are required for the vitamin-enriched water, including research, vitamin enrichment, testing, labeling, branding, advertisement, and compliance with regulatory norms.

Let us now look at the overhead cost distribution for both companies. Note, we have not considered any direct costs here, however, they would form part of the total cost of the product.

The total production volume is 200,000 units. Since the first company has only one product line, all the costs are allocated to it (Table 3.1).

Let us now look at the overheads calculated for the second company which has a larger and more complex operation (Table 3.2).

Since this is a company with multiple product lines, we need to allocate overheads. For this, we calculate the overhead absorption rate per unit. Let us consider that it uses labor hours as the base for allocating overheads (Table 3.3).

We find the overhead absorption rate of 4.53 by dividing the total overheads of 560,000 by the total labor hours of 123,500. It is then allocated to each of the production lines by multiplying the total volume of that line with the overhead absorption rate.

Let us compare the profit per unit of mineral water with that of vitamin-enriched water. The profit is much higher (Table 3.4). Now let us contrast the overheads per unit with the first company. The first company shows a higher profit margin on mineral water and a lower overhead

Table 3.1 Overhead costs for the first company

Overhead costs for the company producing mineral water only	*Amount*
Machine Setup and Maintenance	30,000.00
Secondary Packaging	15,000.00
Marketing and Advertising	50,000.00
IT Systems	60,000.00
Distribution and Delivery	25,000.00
Labor Recreation	100,000.00
Total overheads	***280,000.00***
Profit Before Overhead Recovery	1,000,000.00
Net profit	**720,000.00**
Overhead/unit	1.40
Profit/unit	3.60

Table 3.2 Overhead costs for the second company

Overhead costs for the second company producing mineral water, low-sodium water, and vitamin-enriched water	*Amount*
Machine Setup and Maintenance	60,000.00
Secondary Packaging	34,000.00
Marketing and Advertising	200,000.00
IT Systems	85,000.00
Distribution and Delivery	60,000.00
Labor Recreation	121,000.00
Total overheads	***560,000.00***

Table 3.3 Production volume and labor hours

Items	*Mineral water*	*Low–sodium water*	*Vitamin-enriched water*	*Total*
Production volume (units)	150,000	30,000	20,000	200,000
Indirect labor hours/unit	0.35	1.20	1.75	–
Total indirect labor hours	52,500	36,000	35,000	123,500

Table 3.4 Overhead and profit allocation for the three product lines

	Mineral water	*Low–sodium water*	*Vitamin-enriched water*	*Total*
Overhead allocation	238,056.68	163,238.87	158,704.45	560,000.00
Profit before overheads	750,000.00	210,000.00	240,000.00	1,200,000.00
Profit	511,943.32	46,761.13	81,295.55	640,000.00
Profit/unit	3.41	1.56	4.06	–
Overhead/unit	1.59	5.44	7.94	–

per unit. Consequently, it may reduce its price but remain competitive. In this scenario, the second company may decide to invest more in vitamin-enriched water and less in mineral water to remain competitive. However, this decision is based on an incomplete understanding of the cost behavior. While absorption costing does assign overheads in a structured way, it does not consider how resources are consumed across product lines. While this may work well for single-product production environments, it struggles to handle business complexities. The key limitations of absorption costing are:

- **Overhead misallocation:** Absorption costing assumes that overheads are primarily driven by a singular factor like labor hours or machine hours, and allocates the costs based on that. However, many overhead costs arise from batch-level, product-level, or facility-level activities. These are unrelated to any unique factor like labor hours or machine hours. For example, in our case, the advertising and marketing costs are not related to the labor hours.

- **Inaccurate product costing:** Products consuming disproportionate resources may receive incorrect cost allocations. For example, vitamin-enriched water with low volume and higher complexity may be under-costed under absorption costing.
- **Poor decision-making:** Naturally, if costs are incorrectly allocated, businesses may adopt ineffective strategies. They may even end up discontinuing profitable products or overinvesting in unprofitable ones.
- **Unsuitable for multi-product business:** Absorption costing works best for high-volume and standardized production systems, where the entire overhead cost is allocated to one product base. Introducing a more complicated method is unlikely to improve the quality of decision-making. However, for a multi-product company, absorption costing may be too simplistic and end up giving an unfair product cost.

So how can a multi-product company allocate its costs to get better quality information? ABC is one such approach.

Use of ABC in financial decision-making

ABC is a way of assigning overhead costs based on the activities that directly contribute to such costs. An activity can be anything in the production process required to produce each unit, even where it is not directly traceable to the final product. ABC was introduced in the late 1980s by Kaplan, Cooper, and Johnson. It is a modern alternative to absorption costing. It provides a better way of assigning costs by identifying the activities that trigger costs and assigning them to the products based on their consumption of the activities. Under ABC, managers would be able to make more informed decisions because of a thorough understanding of each cost.

Activities in ABC are related to overheads and indirect costs. Direct costs, like direct materials or direct labor, can be traced back to a product and charged. In our example, activities like machine setup and maintenance, advertising, research, and similar are candidates for ABC-based allocation. To produce one bottle of mineral water, the direct costs of the bottle, label, and water can be traced to the final product, but not costs like office rent or administrative staff salaries. How do we know what percentage of the money spent on quality and assurance pertains to mineral water, and what percentage pertains to vitamin-enriched water?

Such overheads cannot be traced to a specific product, and ABC comes into play here.

Understanding ABC follows a sequence akin to ABC in the alphabet! It is a series of continuous steps, like the sequential letters in the alphabet as described here:

- **Identify activities and assign cost pools:** The first step is to identify the activities involved in the production process. These include machine setup, office rent, advertising, research, and allied. The next step is to identify the overhead costs relating to each activity. These are known as cost pools.
- **Determine cost drivers:** A cost driver is what triggers the cost. For example, in the cost pool of advertising and marketing, the cost driver may be the number of advertisement campaigns run per product line.
- **Calculate the cost per unit of the cost driver:** Once we have the cost pools and cost drivers, we will divide the cost pool by the total number of cost drivers.
- **Allocate the costs to the individual products:** In this step, we will multiply the cost per unit of the cost driver found in the previous step by the cost driver usage per product. Once we add all the figures up, we get the allocation based on ABC.

This process is illustrated below. The cost pools and the cost drivers have been detailed in Table 3.5.

Table 3.5 Cost pools and drivers

Cost pools	*Amount*	*Cost driver*	*Mineral water*	*Low–sodium water*	*Vitamin-enriched water*	*Total*
Machine Setup and Maintenance	60,000.00	Number of Production Runs	700	400	250	1,350
Secondary Packaging	34,000.00	Units packaged	150,000	30,000	20,000	200,000
Marketing and Advertising	200,000.00	Number of marketing campaigns run	20	60	90	170
IT Systems	85,000.00	System usage hours	650	500	350	1,500
Distribution and Delivery	60,000.00	Number of deliveries	450	300	200	950
Labor Recreation	121,000.00	Total indirect labor hours	52,500	36,000	35,000	123,500

We now calculate the recovery rate of each cost pool (Table 3.6).

In the final step, we allocate the overheads to each product (Table 3.7).

It is important to note that while the method of allocation has changed, the total overhead remained the same. Therefore, the total overheads and profit would remain the same in both absorption costing and ABC. The differences arise in how much of the cost has been allocated to each product. ABC allocates the costs based on the actual consumption of each activity, rather than on a single basis, like machine hours or labor hours. Thus, ABC can trace individual costs back to the product in a better way than absorption costing. The key differences in both these methods are summarized in Table 3.8.

Table 3.6 Recovery rate

Recovery rate of cost pool	*Amount*
Cost per machine set up	44.44
Cost per indirect labor hour	36,667.67
Cost per unit packaged	0.17
Cost per marketing campaign	1,176.47
Cost per system usage hour	56.67
Cost per delivery	63.16

Table 3.7 Overhead and profit allocation for the three product lines

Cost Pool	*Mineral water*	*Low–sodium water*	*Vitamin-enriched water*	*Total*
Machine Setup and Maintenance	31,111.11	17,777.78	11,111.11	60,000.00
Secondary Packaging	25,500.00	5,100.00	3,400.00	34,000.00
Marketing and Advertising	23,529.41	70,588.24	105,882.35	200,000.00
IT Systems	36,833.33	28,333.33	19,833.33	85,000.00
Distribution and Delivery	28,421.05	18,947.37	12,631.58	60,000.00
Labor Recreation	51,437.25	35,271.26	34,291.50	121,000.00
Overhead allocation	196,832.16	176,017.97	187,149.87	560,000.00
Profit before overheads	750,000.00	210,000.00	240,000.00	1,200,000.00
Profit	553,167.84	33,982.03	52,850.13	640,000.00
Profit/unit	3.69	1.13	2.64	–
Overhead/unit	1.31	5.87	9.36	–

Table 3.8 Differences between ABC and absorption costing

Metric	*Type of water*	*Absorption costing*	*ABC*	*Takeaway*
Overhead allocation	Mineral	238,056.68	196,832.16	ABC assigns lower overheads to mineral water
	Low-sodium	163,238.87	176,017.97	ABC assigns higher overheads to low-sodium water
	Vitamin-enriched	158,704.45	187,149.87	ABC assigns significantly higher overheads to vitamin-enriched water
Profit/unit	Mineral	3.41	3.69	Mineral water is more profitable under ABC due to lower overheads
	Low-sodium	1.56	1.13	Low-sodium water is the least profitable under ABC
	Vitamin-enriched	4.06	2.64	ABC significantly reduces the perceived profitability of vitamin-enriched water
Overhead/unit	Mineral	1.59	1.31	ABC assigns lower overheads to mineral water
	Low-sodium	5.44	5.87	Low-sodium water has a higher percentage of costs under ABC
	Vitamin-enriched	7.94	9.36	ABC assigns significantly greater overheads to vitamin-enriched water

As you can see, ABC is capturing the essence and complexity of the costs better than the absorption costing system. In the case of mineral water, ABC shows it as more profitable due to lower assigned overheads, possibly reflecting fewer or simpler resource-consuming activities. In the case of low-sodium water, overheads are higher under ABC, reducing profitability, indicating that this product uses more costly activities. In the case of vitamin-enriched water, ABC uncovers hidden costs, revealing that vitamin-enriched water is far less profitable than assumed under absorption costing. By using ABC costing, financial decision-makers get deeper and more realistic insights into the overhead cost allocation. It helps them to make informed decisions on pricing, product mix, and cost control.

Importance of cost drivers

A cost driver is a factor that causes or influences the cost of an activity. Any factor or event that causes a change in the cost is called a cost driver. It has a causal relationship with the total cost of an activity. As mentioned previously, any distinct part of the production process can be termed an activity. For example, for the electricity bill, electricity consumption is the activity, and the number of units of electricity consumed would be a cost driver.

Recognition of cost drivers came into existence only around the late twentieth century. Before that, the chosen basis of cost allocation criteria could have been non-causal. There might not have been any defined relation between the indirect or shared expenses to the activities or objects that triggered the cost. These cost drivers were broad factors such as units produced, labor hours, and similar. Any change in the quantity of these cost drivers was not necessarily reflected in the final cost. It was not until ABC was introduced by Kaplan, Cooper, and Johnson that cost drivers emerged as an important concept.

Although there are no standards that prescribe how to select a cost driver, there are a few criteria to keep in mind. The effectiveness of ABC is dependent on the correct recognition of the cost drivers:

- **Causal relationship**: There should be a demonstrable cause-and-effect relationship between the cost driver and the activity cost. For example, the marketing spend depends on the number of advertising campaigns run. It is important to note that there may not be a unique cost driver for an activity. If there are multiple drivers, it is up to us to decide which is the most appropriate. The cost driver for marketing spend could also have been the size of the target audience or the number of advertising media chosen. It may have also been the number of celebrity endorsements or the number of people involved in the advertising campaigns for each product.
- **Measurability**: The cost driver should be quantifiable. We must assign a number to it. For example, a cost driver for marketing expenses cannot be how much people liked it, or how cool or creative the advertisements were.
- **Behavioral consideration**: The cost driver should adequately reflect the way the cost behaves. For the marketing spend, although the number of

advertising media may serve as a cost driver, it may not best reflect the changes in the actual cost. Factors like the intensity of advertisement, types, and quality may also be contributing to the total cost. Using a flat count would ignore these factors.

- **Cost-benefit balance:** Last but not least, the benefits of using a perfect cost driver should not outweigh the costs of identifying and measuring it. For example, while the number of people involved in the advertising campaigns for each product could serve as a cost driver, tracking this may be costly and complex. It may be debatable as to what constitutes being involved in the campaign. Will it be the people who researched the demographics, the people who reached out to the celebrities, the people who created the campaign, or all of them? Sure, we can take all of them, but there is likely to be an overlap between each of these activities; the people who created the campaign may also be the ones who researched the demographics. Would we be double- counting them, or should we start calculating the hours spent on each activity? To do all this, a robust IT system is required for people to clock in and out and maintain an activity log. It is much more reasonable and fairer to use the total number of campaigns run for each product.

Recognition of cost drivers has many benefits for an organization. First and foremost, it improves decision-making. Insight into cost behavior helps develop better cost-optimization strategies. It can provide guidance on resource allocation. If resources are allocated optimally, it would lead to better performance (more on that later!). All these give businesses a competitive edge. If we know what costs go behind a product, we can not only make better pricing decisions but also make better cost management decisions. In our example, the second company will be able to sell mineral water at a lower price, thus benefiting from their strategic decisions that led to the cost leadership. It also increases understanding of costs throughout an organization. Both managers and executives will be aware of the impact that cost drivers have on costs and are likely to be more mindful of the activities.

However, that is not to say that ABC does not come with its challenges. Identifying cost drivers is a complex process, and for organizations with highly complex operations, pinpointing specific cost drivers may be difficult. Additionally, it requires detailed data collection, making the process costly. Adding to its complexity, such data may also not be readily available. Moreover, business processes are dynamic and evolve constantly, causing cost drivers to change, necessitating continuous updates and reviews.

Working under resource constraints

While identifying the right cost drivers leads to better cost allocation, that alone does not influence operational efficiency. It needs resource optimization. Optimization is the process of making the most efficient use of available resources to achieve strategic goals mostly under resource constraints. The strategic goal could be to maximize profitability, minimize costs, or even improve market presence. Businesses face resource constraints regularly. Resource constraints can be both internal and external. The most common types of constraints include workforce, time, budget, and material. These constraints can delay and disrupt project initiation, progress, and completion. These may ultimately lead to underperformance, missed deadlines, dissatisfied shareholders, and reputation loss, among others. One of the best techniques for resource optimization is linear programming (LP). It is a modeling technique in which a linear function, usually cost or profitability, is minimized or maximized, under various constraints. To remain competitive in the long term, a business needs to focus on resource optimization rather than cost reduction or profit maximization.

Cost reduction, or as it is informally known, cost-cutting, are strategies to reduce expenses directly. This is achieved often through layoffs, using cheaper raw materials, or by cutting non-essential activities. However, these often come out as shortsighted moves. Consider a company producing smartphones which is experiencing declining profit margins due to rising raw material and labor costs. Its primary concern is to improve profitability as the stock prices are going down and the shareholders are becoming discontent. However, they are undecided on what strategy to implement. On one hand, cost-cutting may lead to improved margins; while on the other hand, resource optimization could be a long-term solution. To cut costs, the company may lay off 20% of the production workforce to reduce labor costs, switch to lower-quality display panels for smartphones, and reduce the number of quality inspections to save on testing costs. While these would reduce costs in the short term, there may be unfavorable long-term consequences.

Production efficiency is likely to reduce due to smaller workforce. Warranty claims may rise due to using lower-quality display panels. This will harm the brand reputation, which in turn could lead to lower sales and higher customer complaints. Eventually, product reliability will be questioned, its competitive advantage will decline, and it will suffer revenue losses over the long term.

If we look at the second option, which is resource optimization, the company would attempt to efficiently allocate resources without compromising quality. The tools to achieve this could be a combination of ABC and LP. ABC will help identify which activities drive the highest costs, while LP will optimize the production schedules, reducing overtime and idle machine hours. The company may automate quality control checks, reducing labor costs but keeping the standards high. An annual purchase contract can get volume-based discounts and reduce input costs without lowering the quality. As a result, the production efficiency would improve while maintaining its standard, satisfying both customers and shareholders. Using resource optimization, the company may be able to improve its profit margins without harming its reputation and brand.

Cost reduction is primarily a reactive approach that ends up focusing on reducing expenses, but often at the cost of quality and sustainability. On the other hand, resource optimization is a proactive strategy that maximizes efficiency without lowering quality and profitability. We will see in later sections how ML tools allow us to apply these techniques.

ABC automation

With the growing availability of operational data and digital transformation in finance, automating ABC using Python has become both feasible and highly beneficial.

Python's powerful libraries for data manipulation, statistical analysis, and visualization make it an ideal tool for building efficient, scalable ABC models. These modules can be regularly updated and integrated into management dashboards.

Using Python to automate ABC

The entire code is available at the repository (prefix 0301), and you can download the same. The code is divided into the following four major sections:

- **Import libraries**: As you know by now, Python uses libraries to extend its functionality so that we do not have to write code from scratch. The libraries that we have used for automating an ABC report are `pandas`, `matplotlib`, and `openpyxl`. The `openpyxl library` is used to format Excel output, such as applying fonts, colors, and charts. `Matplotlib` is a visualization tool. If any library is not installed, you will get a `ModuleNotFoundError`. We can run the `! pip install` command to install the required library from the Jupyter notebook.
- **Customize**: This is the only section of the code you need to make changes to. Here we provide the name of the input file, output files, files to save the plot, and the names of columns in the input file. You will also enter the currency you are dealing with. Your input CSV must have a column for cost pools, total overheads, and cost drivers. You must also keep the production volume and profit before overheads cells as it is positioned in the CSV. Note that the column names are in lowercase. This is

required for the code to run correctly. The relevant part of the code with the customizable parameters in italics is shown below:

```
# Customize parameters
file_path = "0301 Raw data.csv"
my_allocation_pie="overhead_allocation_pie_chart.png"
my_cost_pool_allocation="overhead_allocation_bar_chart.
png"

# Provide the output file names
my_abc_report = "0301 ABC_Report"
my_cost_pool_info = "0301 cost_pool_info"
my_cost_driver = "0301 cost_driver_breakdown"

costpools = "cost pools"
totaloverheads = "total overheads"
costdrivers = "cost drivers"
productionvolume = "production volume"
profitbeforeoverheads = "profit before overheads"
currency_symbol = "USD"
```

- **Develop functions for ABC analysis:** In this section, we develop a function to load data, clean it, and run various validations. We read the CSV file into a dataframe and drop all empty rows. To ensure continuity, we have converted all column heads to lowercase and trimmed whitespaces. We validated the columns, ensuring that essential columns "cost pools," "total overheads," and "cost drivers" are present. If any is not present, an error alert is displayed. The necessary columns are identified to the system in the code `required_columns = {costpools, totaloverheads, costdrivers}`. We search for the row labeled "`productionvolume`" and extract the values for each product that is Mineral, Low-sodium, and Vitamin from that row. We look for the row labeled "`profit before overheads.`" These values are adjusted later by deducting the overheads to get the final profitability. We proceed to remove the special rows, "`productionvolume`" and "`profitbeforeoverheads`," from the main cost pool data so they do not interfere with cost allocation. We have finally created a dictionary where each cost pool is mapped to its total overheads and cost drivers. We move ahead and build a nested dictionary with product names as keys and the usage of each cost pool's activity as values.
- **Cost, allocation, and profit computation:** In this section, we begin by calculating the cost per unit of activity by dividing total overheads by the total activity across all products. We repeat this process for each cost pool. Next, for each product, we multiply its usage of each activity by the cost per unit of that activity. This provides us with the total overhead allocation per product. We subtract overheads from the pre-overhead

profit to determine the actual profit. Finally, we calculate each product's share of the total profit and profit per unit.

- **Allocation based on ABC methodology:** In this section, we create a final table showing overhead allocations and percentages, profitability analysis both in total and per unit, and related values. All values are rounded for readability. We add a total row at the bottom for overhead and profit. From the housekeeping angle, we capitalize product names for a clean presentation. A dataframe with cost pool information is created. This dataframe lists each cost pool, its corresponding cost driver, and the calculated recovery rate, which is the cost per unit of activity.
- **Use of the cost driver:** In this section, we display each product's use of every cost driver. This is transposed for readability and kept ready for export to various files. A pie chart showing the allocation of total overheads across the product line is displayed and saved here.
- **Display and save chart:** We have created a pie chart and a grouped bar chart to show different dimensions of allocation. The charts are displayed and then saved for future use. We save the ABC report, cost pool details, and product-wise use of cost driver in CSV format. This can be used for further analysis and reporting.
- **Save report in CSV format:** We save all the reports generated in the previous sections to the specified CSV files.
- **Save to a formatted Excel file (Optional):** In this section, we have ventured out to show you that these reports can be formatted and offered as a comprehensive Excel file. The file will have different worksheets, including all the reports we saved in CSV format. In addition, we have created and saved some output charts in another worksheet of the same workbook. The Excel file has been formatted for readability and presentation. The `openpyxl` library has been used to color headers and totals rows, align text, and format percentages and currency. We have included this to demonstrate the capability of the code to create a comprehensive report, though we have also created CSV files that can be used in the future for decision-making and audit. This section concludes by confirming that the results have been saved in various files.

The output of the code is essentially the CSV and Excel files that contain the report of the ABC analysis. The ABC report shows the overhead allocation under ABC against each product along with other values like share of overhead, total overhead per unit, profit before and after allocation of overhead, and allied. The cost driver breakdown shows the value of different overheads allocated to each product line.

The file with cost pool information shows for each cost pool the recovery rate against each cost driver.

Assigning costs based on activities and resource usage

Let us revisit our example. Under absorption costing in the second company, mineral water was allocated higher overhead costs, making it seem less profitable. ABC helped to assign overheads based on actual overhead consumption. It resulted in the reallocation of the overheads, and mineral water overhead allocation was reduced, resulting in unit profit increasing from 3.41 to 3.69. The adoption of ABC helped the company to remain competitive. Additionally, under ABC, the unit overhead cost for mineral water is 1.31, which is lower than the first company's unit overhead cost of 1.40. Thus, now the second company may potentially be able to charge less for mineral water, giving it a competitive edge. ABC also highlights the hidden costs of low-sodium and vitamin-enriched water. Both have higher marketing campaigns and more regulatory and quality control checks. Absorption costing is unable to identify these nuanced costs. For instance, vitamin water appeared very profitable under absorption costing, showing a unit profit of 4.06, as opposed to a lower 2.64 under ABC. This demonstrates that vitamin-enriched water is far less profitable than initially thought, and managers need to reevaluate the pricing and strategic efficiency.

Cost transparency and pricing strategies

The transparent cost information provided by ABC is not just an accounting improvement but a strategic necessity. The cost information has been aligned with the actual resource consumption. This detailed visibility enables better pricing strategies, product mix decisions, and resource allocation based on cost and benefits. This leads to a sustainable competitive advantage.

We saw that ABC traces overheads and indirect costs to the specific activities and products that consume them. It avoids allocating costs on simplistic metrics like labor hours or machine time. This leads to accurate product costing, especially in complex, multi-product environments. In addition, it brings out visibility into non-value-adding activities and helps to highlight areas for cost reduction and process improvement.

Understanding cost behavior keeps the financial decision-maker aware and exposed to fewer surprises, a more achievable budget, and data-driven justifications for cost management initiatives.

Pricing strategies often rely on understanding the true cost of a product or service. ABC enables this by identifying high-cost products that may not be profitable even if they generate significant revenue. It enables value-based pricing, where prices are aligned not only with market demand but also with resource costs and availability.

The cost break-ups support creating differentiated pricing models such as premium pricing for high-service products.

ABC reveals the true profitability of individual products and services. This helps with product portfolio strategies such as eliminating or repricing unprofitable offerings, reallocating resources toward high-margin or strategically critical products, and managing cross-subsidization risks.

ABC also strengthens scenario analysis by allowing "what-if" simulations. A financial decision-maker can model the cost impact of launching a new service line, outsourcing a non-core activity, changing batch sizes or delivery schedules, and so on. This leads to more resilient pricing and cost strategies, particularly important in volatile or highly competitive markets.

Cost driver analysis using regression models

Understanding what drives costs lies at the foundation of being able to manage them. The understanding would not be restricted to the identification of the drivers. It would also include an understanding of how these drivers influence cost. Commonly, we use our domain knowledge or even engineering design to explain the relation between the cost drivers and the cost without testing the validity of the same. This may be an acceptable approach in cases of direct costs, their relation being demonstrated by the production process. However, in the case of overheads, this approach may result in using assumptions that are far from reality.

ML provides tools to establish a relationship between cost drivers and overhead costs, regression being one of them. This is a powerful approach to uncovering these relationships by analyzing historical data and revealing patterns. These patterns are often overlooked in traditional methods because they rely on expert opinion. The use of algorithms to capture patterns from large datasets allows us to move away from an intuition-driven approach to an evidence-driven one. ML tools using regression and other analyses can be useful in identifying critical cost variables and building predictive models. We can interpret these models effectively and eventually optimize operations by using resources judiciously to significantly impact the bottom line.

Identification of significant cost drivers

Let us use a case study to better understand how we can use regression analysis to identify significant factors that can affect costs and profitability. Our example will focus on the identification of cost drivers, which can be useful in allocating costs under both absorption costing as well as ABC.

Consider a mid-sized precision component manufacturer. They have relied on traditional costing techniques, allocating overheads based on a fixed percentage of direct labor costs. However, management feels that this method no longer reflects the actual consumption of overhead resources because of the changed nature of the business. The company produces several complex components that require frequent machine setups and substantial material handling. These activities are not accurately captured in the labor-based allocation system. As overheads continue to rise, senior finance executives decide to adopt ABC. However, to do so, they need to identify the significant cost drivers contributing to overhead costs.

To support the management, the finance team proposes using multiple linear regression to analyze historical operational data. This will also uncover the relationship between overhead cost and possible cost drivers like labor hours, machine hours, number of setups, batch size, and material movements. The team believes that a regression model will better estimate overhead costs based on cost drivers. The use of statistical measures will provide better insight into which drivers significantly impact overheads. The recovery rates per cost driver derived using regression coefficients could be used in the ABC cost assignment.

Let us have a look at the important components of the code (prefix 0302).

- **Import libraries:** We have loaded all necessary libraries in this section. The `statsmodels` library is used for statistical analysis as well as data exploration and hypothesis testing. Regression analysis can also be done using this library. Earlier, we had shown how to do linear regression using a different library called `sklearn` in Chapter 2. The `Matplotlib` library is used to generate static, animated, and interactive visualizations. `Seaborn` is a high-level interface for statistical graphics built on top of `Matplotlib`. `Docx` library creates Word documents, including the formatting of the same. If you do not have any of these modules installed, please install them by using the `pip install` command.
- **Customize:** In this section, we have specified the input file containing the cost data and identified the dependent and independent variables. Please ensure you use the exact name of the columns in the code and use square brackets and quotes. In addition, we have specified the names of the spreadsheet, document, and graphics output files. The relevant part of the code with customizable parts in italics is shown here.

```
# Customization parameters
my_input_file = "0302 input_cost_data.csv"
#specify variables
dependent_var = 'Overhead_Cost'

independent_vars = ['Labor_Hours', 'Machine_Hours',
'Number_of_Setups', 'Batch_Size', 'Material_Movements']
```

```
#specify output files
my_residual_plot = "0302 residuals_vs_fitted.png"
my_actual_vs_predicted = "0302 actual_vs_predicted.png"
my_model_output = "0302 regression_results.csv"
my_word_output = "0302 Regression_Overhead_Cost_Report.
docx"
```

- **Load and prepare data**: In this section, we are loading the input file and preparing the data for regression analysis. We have introduced the dependent and independent variables defined in the earlier section to the regression model. We have also defined whether the regression model will have an intercept.
- **Fit and display regression equation:** Once we have loaded and prepared the data, we load the regression model. In this section, we run the regression model and print the regression equation and the model fit summary metrics. These include R-squared, Adjusted R-squared, and F-statistic. The equation shows us how the intercept and values of the independent variables influence the values of the dependent variable.
- **Diagnostic plots**: The code in this section creates and displays two plots. The first one is a plot of fitted and residual values, while the second one is a plot of actual versus the predicted cost. Let us have a quick overview of these plots:
    - In the case of the plot of residual versus fitted, the residuals should ideally be randomly scattered around zero, showing no pattern. The red line here is the Lowess (Locally Weighted Scatterplot Smoothing) curve. This helps visualize the trends in residuals across the range of fitted values. If the model is well-specified, the red Lowess curve should be close to horizontal at zero, meaning no pattern in residuals. If the Lowess line curves upward or downward or intermittently, it suggests potential non-linearity or heteroscedasticity. Non-linearity means the relationship between the predictors and the overhead cost might not be purely linear. The model might be missing some non-linear patterns. Heteroscedasticity refers to the non-constant variance of the residuals. This means that the spread of residuals increases or decreases as fitted values increase. A good model assumes homoscedasticity.
    - In the plot of actual versus fitted overhead costs, the blue dots are individual observations comparing actual and predicted costs. The red line is a hypothetical line that would have been plotted if the predicted values and fitted values were the same. If the blue dots are close to the red line, the model is predicting well. Points scattered widely from the red line indicate the model may not have much predictive capability.

- **Export results:** This part of the code starts by exporting the regression equation to a CSV file. The file contains three columns: variable name, coefficient, and P-value. A Word file is also prepared and saved, highlighting the major values of the model. The file contains distinct sections on regression equation, model fit statistics, variable significance, and business interpretation.
- **Confirm output generation:** This section of the code merely confirms on screen that the output files have been created and saved.

The output from the code includes a screen display of the regression equation and model fit metrics, which are saved in a file. The plots are also saved as specified file. The regression equation is saved in a CSV file, and it contains the names of the independent variables, their coefficients, and p-values.

Using regression to identify influencers of cost

Regression analysis can be used by finance professionals to model the relationship between overhead cost and cost drivers like labor hours, machine hours, number of setups, batch size, and material movements. Instead of relying on subjective rules or outdated allocation bases, regression uses historical data to objectively determine which activities drive cost behavior and by how much. Let us understand the results of the code from the regression example.

The equation in this context is a standard multiple linear regression equation. This means that multiple independent variables can explain the behavior of the dependent variable, the overhead cost. The equation takes the following form:

$$Overhead\ cost = \beta_0 + \beta_1 .\ X_1 + \beta_2 .\ X_2 + \cdots + \beta_n .\ X_n + \varepsilon$$

where,
β_0: Intercept – baseline overhead cost when all drivers are zero.
β_n: Coefficients – cost incurred per unit change in driver X_i.
ε (epsilon): Random error, capturing noise or unmeasured factors
The intercept represents the estimated overhead cost when all independent variables are zero. This has important business implications:
$\beta_0 > 0$ Indicates a fixed component of overhead incurred regardless of activity level.
$\beta_0 \approx 0$ Implies nearly all overheads are variable and driven by operational activity.
$\beta_0 < 0$ Unusual and rare. This may be caused by model misspecification, multicollinearity, or poor driver choice.

A large positive intercept alerts management that a fixed portion of overhead persists even when activity is low. This would usually push up the break-even point. Such an occurrence may force the management to think over alternative strategies, technical or financial, that can bring this component down.

A question follows: What if there are no fixed costs? There could be a scenario where no activity means no overhead. Even in those cases, the standard regression analysis will show an intercept. In such cases, we must force the regression not to have an intercept by modifying the code used in the earlier section. In the code, we have a line.

```
X = sm.add_constant(X)
```

We have to comment out this line to force a zero intercept. Please remember that forcing the intercept to zero can bias coefficients if a true fixed component exists. It can also reduce model accuracy if unjustified. Hence, only force a zero intercept when it is conceptually sound. Always test model fit and interpret residual plots for validation.

Regression analysis gives financial decision-makers strategic insights into the cost drivers and their influence on cost. Among others, regression will have the following usage.

- **Quantifies cost behavior**: It allows us to understand how much each activity contributes to total overhead.
- **Justifies allocation base**: The tool allows us to use statistically significant cost drivers instead of those based on arbitrary assumptions.
- **Predict costing**: We can use the regression equation to forecast overheads for budgeting and what-if analysis.

Another important addition to the analysis would be to understand the relation between the variables, that is, how they move in comparison with each other. This would give us a better insight into their behavior. We can visualize this by creating a heatmap. Let us quickly go through this code (prefix 0303). The main components of the code are the following:

- **Import library**: As with the earlier section, we will load the necessary libraries in this section. We have already been introduced to these libraries.
- **Customize**: We need to define the name of the input data file and the name of the file to save the heatmap and correlation result. The relevant part of the code with the customizable section italicized is shown here.

```
# Customize parameters
my_input = "0302 input_cost_data.csv"
my_correl = "0303 correlation.csv"
my_heatmap = "0303 correlation_heatmap.png"
```

- **Load data and select columns:** We read the input file in this section. Since a heatmap can be drawn only for numeric fields, we select the numeric fields from the input.
- **Create, plot, and save heatmap:** This section creates the heatmap, which is essentially the correlation matrix of the numeric fields selected from the input file.
- **Save correlation matrix and plot:** We save the heatmap and the correlation matrix using the specified file name for subsequent use.

The output of the code is the heatmap, which is the correlation matrix. You will find the same field names across the rows and columns. The diagonal of the matrix is the correlation of a variable with itself, which is 1. The cells to the right of the diagonal are a mirror image of the cells to the left. The heatmap is color-coded to provide visual guidance about the strength of the correlation. As we know, the value of the correlation will range between –1 and 1. The color code will visually signify the strength of the correlation.

This analysis serves an important purpose. Before fitting the regression model, it is useful to compute a correlation matrix among the independent variables. High correlations between drivers, for example, machine hours and labor hours, may introduce multicollinearity. Multicollinearity potentially inflates standard errors of coefficients, makes interpretation unreliable, and may even result in incorrect driver elimination. In such cases, a small change in data can cause a major shift in coefficients.

If two independent variables are highly correlated, we can safely drop anyone from the regression model. This is likely to add model stability without compromising the predictive power.

Interpret model results

When we run a regression model in Python, we get a detailed output containing model diagnostics, coefficients, and p-values. Let us see how to interpret these (Table 3.9):

Let us consider that a regression gave the output:

- R-squared: 0.94
- Adjusted R-squared: 0.93.
- F-statistic: 56.7 ($p < 0.001$)
- Machine_Hours: Coefficient = 20.5, *p*-value = 0.003

Table 3.9 Regression analysis metrics explained

Parameters	*Meaning*
R-square	It tells us how well the regression model explains the variation in the dependent variable. A value closer to 1 means that the model explains a high proportion of the variance in the dependent variable, while a value closer to 0 means the opposite.
Adjusted R-squared	Adjusted R^2 modifies R^2 to account for the number of independent variables in the model. It penalizes the addition of irrelevant predictors. This helps in model comparison: if you add a new variable and the adjusted R^2 increases, it likely improves the model. If adjusted R^2 decreases, the added variable is likely not helpful.
F-statistic	The F-statistic tests the joint significance of all the independent variables in the model. It checks whether our regression model is better than a model with no predictors. A higher F-value indicates that the model is statistically meaningful. The F-value itself is less important than its p-value.
p-value (F-stat)	The p-value associated with the F-statistic tests whether the model as a whole is statistically significant. It tests if at least one independent variable has a non-zero coefficient. A low value (< 0.05) means the model is statistically valid. The value 0.05 holds for a 95% confidence level and will change at other levels. For example, at a 90% confidence level, it will be 0.10, and for a 99% confidence level, it will be 0.01.
Coefficients (β)	Each coefficient shows the change in cost for a unit change in the driver, considering no other changes. Positive β indicates a direct relationship with cost, and a negative β indicates an inverse relationship.
p-value (Variable)	Indicates whether the individual variable is statistically significant. In other words, a p-value tests whether the specific coefficient is significantly different from zero. If the value is less than (1 – Confidence level), it will be considered statistically significant.

This means:

- The model explains 94% of the variation in overhead costs. It is a strong fit.
- Even after adjusting for the number of predictors, the model remains robust.
- The overall model is statistically significant (as shown by the F-statistic).

- Every additional machine hour increases overhead cost by 20.50, not considering other factors. Further, since $p < 0.05$, this is a statistically significant cost driver and can be confidently used as an allocation base in ABC.

As financial decision-makers, we can eliminate irrelevant drivers with insignificant p-values to simplify costing. Once significant drivers are identified, their coefficients can be used as cost recovery rates. Overhead can be assigned to cost objects based on their consumption of these drivers and the recovery rate ascertained.

Optimize operation by focusing on key cost drivers

Now that we have identified the main cost drivers, let us move ahead to optimization. Optimization with an objective of profit maximization or cost minimization has been covered in the next section. In this section, we will focus on understanding the impact of movements on the recovery rates given by coefficients in the regression equation. We will change these values, one cost driver at a time, and see what happens to the total cost. This study will allow us to understand the sensitivity of the cost to changes in recovery rates of each cost driver. Let us have a look at the business problem.

The company has developed a regression model to understand the behavior of overhead costs with respect to various operational cost drivers. These cost drivers include labor hours, machine hours, number of setups, batch size, and material movements. The company now wants to find out the impact of movement of operational variables like labor or material movements on total overhead cost. This will eventually affect recovery rate.

The finance team has decided to perform a sensitivity-driven simulation using the regression equation. The simulation involves movement by 5%, 10%, and 15% on either side. Unlike traditional optimization, this approach recognizes that operational variables are often correlated, and thus, changing one variable can affect others. We saw this on the heatmap. The change in predicted cost is compared to the base case (0% change) to compute potential cost savings or increases. To avoid circular reference, only one driver is changed at a time. The correlated drivers are adjusted but not re-propagated.

Let us have a look at the important components of the code (prefix 0304).

- **Import libraries:** As with earlier cases, we will load the necessary libraries here. We are familiar with the libraries that we are using here.
- **Customize:** In this section, we will initially specify the file with the input values. This is the same file we have used in the earlier section. We will also load the values of the regression equation that we have saved earlier.

If you want, you can run the code (prefix 0302) and get those values here again. We have moved on to define the levels of changes we want to test for. Please note the use of square brackets. You can define your range here. Finally, we have to define the name of the variable we want to work with. This is the variable whose values we will change by using the data provided and see how it influences the value of the dependent variable. The relevant section of the code with the customizable values in italics is given here.

```
# Customize parameters
my_input_file="0302 input_cost_data.csv"
my_regression="0302 regression_results.csv"

#Define % change levels
percent_changes = [-15, -10, -5, 0, 5, 10, 15]

# User-specified variable to analyze
selected_driver = 'Labor_Hours'
```

- **Load database and model:** The input file and the components of the regression equation will be loaded here. You will have the names and the values of the coefficients displayed on screen for you to verify if these are correct. You can also double-check the name of the variable you want to change the values of.
- **Build correlation matrix:** In this section, we first calculate the correlation matrix. This is the same as we have done in the earlier section. The names of all variables are loaded from the regression results file, except for the constant or the intercept designated as '`const`'. If the field is named differently, please use the name in the code segment `driver_vars = [k for k in coefficients.keys() if k != 'const']`. The average values of these variables are computed from the input data file.
- **Run sensitivity:** Now we come to the core computation engine. We have selected a variable to be modified, and we modify its value by the ranges provided. We have defined this as `selected_driver`. Other variables are modified based on their correlation with the selected driver. These values are available from the correlation matrix. These altered values are then used in the regression equation to compute the predicted overhead cost. The movement in the total overhead cost from the base scenario, the zero change, is also computed. It is important to note that the regression model is not being refitted with each simulation. The simulation uses the mean values of the input variables and changes the value of the selected driver. Values of other variables are adjusted according to their correlation with the selected variable.

- **Create output, plot data, save results:** We store the output of the modification in a dataframe. Remember, a dataframe is like a table in a spreadsheet with rows and columns. These are saved to the specified `csv` file. The code plots the percentage change in the driver against the change in predicted overhead cost. The plot is also saved in a file specified by you.

The output of the code includes the plot of changes in overhead cost against changes in the cost of a driver. This plot is displayed on the screen, besides being saved in a file. The slope and the intercept of the plotted line are also displayed on screen. You are likely to find the plot to be a straight line if the regression is a linear regression. The intercept need not necessarily be zero, but that cannot be ruled out. You may often see a value of zero being displayed with or without a positive or negative sign. If you want to see the underlying value which is causing the signage, increase the number of places displayed after the decimal by tweaking the code print `(f"Intercept of the plotted line: {intercept:.4f}")`. The value preceding "`f`" is the number of digits after the decimal point that will be displayed. The slope shows the change in output cost for every unit percentage change in the values of the selected driver. Hope you have noted that we are not plotting total overhead cost in the Y-axis, we are plotting the change in the overhead cost, a value that we have computed earlier.

We can compute this value for all independent variables, and that will give us their sensitivity to the changes in the total overhead cost. It will make it easier to decide where to focus to achieve better cost management.

Resource optimization with linear programming

Organizations constantly face the challenge of allocating limited resources like capital, labor, or inventory, over competing demands from internal stakeholders. This allocation is done while keeping in mind objectives like maximizing profit or minimizing cost. LP provides a powerful, structured approach to address these optimization problems. LP models formulate business objectives and constraints mathematically to determine the most effective resource allocation strategies under defined conditions. Integration of LP with predictive analytics, automation, and decision systems offers new dimensions of speed, scale, and adaptability. This section explores the principles of resource optimization through LP. It discusses how ML-based tools can provide better insight into cost behavior, an understanding critical for optimization.

Linear programming as a method for optimal resource allocation

Resources that an organization uses are finite, and that leads to the need for optimal allocation to support strategic objectives. LP is a powerful mathematical tool we can use to address this challenge. LP has become a preferred solution to resource optimization problems in many organizations because of its ease of use. A typical LP model has the following components:

- **Decision variables**: These are the unknown quantities that the model is designed to solve. For example, in the case of a company wanting to determine its production levels for the next operating cycle, the decision variable is the production level. The number of products or facilities is known; the quantity for each is unknown. You will mostly find decision variables as non-negative values, that is, they should be greater than or equal to zero. However, one can make these values unrestricted, and they can assume a negative value in those cases. For example, an incentive scheme with an inbuilt penalty system will have an unrestricted value; it can be positive or negative.
- **Objective functions**: This is a linear equation that defines what needs to be achieved, for example, cost minimization, profit maximization, or use of a specific quantity of resources.
- **Constraints**: Constraints are the business case limitations that need to be considered while solving a given problem. For example, constraints may be that only a certain number of labor hours are permitted in a day, or restricted availability of a raw material, or the maximum volume that can be exported, and likewise.

LP offers a clear advantage over cost allocation based on simple allocation models using either static assumptions or working out trial-and-error scenarios. It offers a scalable and replicable way of identifying the best resource optimization solution. It can be used in financial decision-making for a variety of purposes, including but not limited to the following:

- **Cost minimization**: Identifies the lowest possible cost structure to meet the predetermined decision variable.
- **Budget allocation**: Determines the optimal distribution of resources across departments or projects.
- **Product mix optimization**: Selects the optimal product mix that maximizes profit within the constraints.
- **Capacity planning**: Ensures finite resources such as labor, equipment, capital, raw material, and others are deployed optimally.

LP can be very easily applied using built-in libraries for Python. Let us now explore how a manufacturing company can use LP to determine the optimal mix of products to manufacture, given the constraints on labor hours, machine capacity, and material availability.

Utilizing `PuLP` for optimization

Let us consider a company that manufactures chairs, tables, and bookshelves. As part of a strategic restructuring, the management is trying to cut down on costs while protecting its profit. They want to determine the production levels for the next accounting period for each product to minimize their costs. However, they have the following constraints, summarized in Table 3.10.

Additionally, they only have 45,000 labor hours available throughout the year across the three product lines. The factory is operational 250 days a year, and the management is keen to ensure that a profit margin of $8,000,000 is maintained. The total available wood for use in production is 1,300,000 board feet. The labor hour rate is $12, and the raw material cost per board foot is $13. Other relevant information is provided in Table 3.11.

Using Python for LP is extremely simple with its open-source library called `PuLP`. While you can solve optimization problems in Excel through its Solver add-in, matters become complicated when dealing with complex models and dynamic inputs. `PuLP` allows users to use optimization models that can be easily maintained, replicated, and scaled across different scenarios.

Table 3.10 Constraints for furniture manufacturer

Constraints	*Chair*	*Table*	*Bookshelf*
Minimum demand	10,000	7,000	6,000
Maximum demand	17,000	13,000	11,000

Table 3.11 Other information about the furniture manufacturer

	Chair	*Table*	*Bookshelf*
Profit per unit ($)	228	306	482
Total cost per unit ($)	272	544	668
Labor hours required per unit	1	2	1.5
Wood required per unit in board feet	20	40	50

Let us move on to the code (prefix 0305). The entire code is available at the repository, and you can download the same. The code is divided into the following five major sections:

- **Import libraries**: The libraries that we have used for solving LP models are `pandas` and `pulp`. You know that if any library is not installed, you will get an error, and we must install it in the environment.
- **Customize**: This section enables you to customize your parameters, which includes the product attributes and constraints. We will provide values for products, profit per unit, cost per unit, minimum demand, maximum demand, labor hours, and wood used per unit for the production of each product. We will also provide value for total available labor hours, total available wood, and minimum profit required. Please note the use of square brackets while providing values. Make sure you write the information in the same order as you have written the name of the products. We will further specify the names of output files in CSV format. The relevant part of the code with the customizable parameters italicized is stated here.

```
products = ["Chair", "Table", "Bookshelf"]
profit_per_unit = [228, 306, 482]
cost_per_unit = [272, 544, 668]
min_demand = [10000, 7000, 6000]
max_demand = [17000, 13000, 11000]
labour_hours = [1, 2, 1.5]
wood_units = [20, 40, 50]
total_labour_available = 45000
total_wood_available = 1300000
minimum_profit = 8000000
my_output = "0305_optimal_production_plan.csv"
my_currency = "$"
```

In Python, we can use "_" as a thousand separator to improve readability for larger numbers. So, the minimum profit of 8000000 may also be written as 8_000_000; it makes no difference in the numerical value!
- **Define LP problem**: In this section, you need to define the LP problem.

```
model = pulp.LpProblem("Cost_Minimization",
pulp.LpMinimize)
```

This line is initializing the LP problem. "`Cost_Minimization`" is just the name of the model. It has no impact on the solution. However, you cannot have any space in the model's name and will get an error if you do. pulp.LpMinimize indicates the type of optimization to Python. In the event that you want to maximize something instead, you could use pulp.LpMaximize.

```
x = [pulp.LpVariable(f"x_{i}", lowBound=0, cat="Integer")
for i in range(n)]
```

This line defines the decision variables. Here, the decision variables are the production levels for each product. It ensures that the production quantity is a non-negative whole number, rounding off any decimals, as one cannot produce 21.3 chairs! You can play around with this in real life and can modify the code to support more complex scenarios as well.

```
model += pulp.lpSum([cost_per_unit[i] * x[i] for i in
range(n)])
```

This line defines the objective function of the LP model. From the initializing line, Python already knows that it is a minimization problem. This line indicates what to minimize, in this case, the total cost.

```
# Common constraints
model += pulp.lpSum([labour_hours[i] * x[i] for i in
range(n)]) <= total_labour_available
model += pulp.lpSum([wood_units[i] * x[i] for i in
range(n)]) <= total_wood_available
model += pulp.lpSum([profit_per_unit[i] * x[i] for i in
range(n)]) >= min_profit

#Demand constraint
for i in range(n):
  model += x[i] >= min_demand[i]
  model += x[i] <= max_demand[i]
```

For the demand constraints, this same expression has been looped since it must circle through each of the specific demand constraints for each product.

- **Solve LP problem**: In this section, the LP model is saved according to the instructions above. Note that this cell will give an output of 1. This means that the model has found an optimal solution to the problem. It may also return 0, –1, –2, or –3, which would mean that your model has not been solved, it is infeasible to solve it, it is unbounded, or undefined respectively. Naturally, the objective is to get a 1 here.
- **Prepare summary and save results**: After the LP program is solved, the output of the code is the optimized mix. This is displayed on screen and also saved in a CSV file for subsequent use.

Relevant model constraints and objectives

When implementing an LP model for resource optimization and allocation, it is imperative to recognize that constraints and objectives vary significantly from company to company and within different business contexts. As such, users must ensure a custom approach tailored to specific circumstances. The objective function usually focuses on the maximization or minimization of value. Maximization algorithms may be applied to profit, production levels, revenue, and similar, while minimization may be applied to cost, resource usage, labor hours used, and similar. The constraints must be consistent with the company's resources, which yields far better results than a one-size-fits-all solution. Constraints can normally incorporate the following components:

- Strategic financial constraints
  - Capital expenditure thresholds according to the approved annual budget.
  - Operating expense budget by department and cost center.
  - Liquidity requirements and cash flow timing considerations.
  - Debt covenant restrictions, which may limit certain financial ratios.
  - Working capital requirements across business units.
  - Contribution margins by product line or service offering.
  - Fixed and variable cost structures across different production or service volumes.
  - Depreciation schedules and asset utilization rates.
  - Tax implications of different resource allocation strategies.
  - Transfer pricing considerations for multi-divisional organizations.
- Operational constraints
  - Manufacturing capacity limits (equipment throughput).
  - Storage and warehouse capacity constraints.
  - Transportation and logistics limitations.
  - Lead time requirements for production or procurement.
  - Minimum batch sizes for efficient production.
  - Setup time considerations between product changeovers.
- Market and risk constraints.
  - Return on investment (ROI) requirements for new initiatives.
  - Risk-adjusted hurdle rates for different business segments.
  - Foreign exchange exposure limitations.
  - Commodity price hedging parameters.
  - Regulatory capital requirements for financial services.
  - Risk exposure limits across different scenarios.
- Human resource constraints
  - Skilled labor availability by department or function.
  - Training requirements for new processes.

  - Overtime limitations and cost thresholds.
  - Shift scheduling requirements and limitations.
  - Productivity rates and learning curves for new processes.
- Supply chain constraints
  - Raw material availability and procurement limitations.
  - Supplier capacity constraints and minimum order quantities.
  - Supply chain reliability factors and safety stock requirements.
  - Geographical sourcing restrictions or requirements.
  - Import/export limitations and tariff considerations.
- Environmental and regulatory constraints
  - Emissions limits and environmental compliance requirements.
  - Waste disposal limitations and costs.
  - Regulatory approval timelines for new products.
  - Industry-specific compliance requirements.
  - Environmental, Social, Governance (ESG) policy requirements.
- Time-based constraints
  - Project timeline requirements and milestones.
  - Seasonality factors affecting both supply and demand.
  - Product life cycle considerations.
  - Technology obsolescence timelines.
  - New product introduction schedules.

This is not an exhaustive list; however, it provides us with an idea of the type of constraints that may form part of the decision-making process.

Consider the furniture manufacturer. Their constraint on wood is not arbitrary; it stems from tangible business challenges like procurement difficulties or limited supplier capacity. Similarly, their labor hour limitations reflect real operational boundaries, probably shaped by workforce regulations in their jurisdiction. Their production boundaries, both minimum and maximum, are grounded in careful market analysis and historical sales data. Producing beyond market demand ties up capital in unsold inventory, while underproducing means forfeiting possible sales and their associated profits. The company also has a minimum profit constraint to ensure financial viability. This enables them to meet debt obligations, satisfy shareholders' expectations, and fund future investments. Each constraint in their model relates to a specific business reality, and their objective of cost minimization reflects their overall business objective.

Enhance efficiency by determining the best mix of resources

Financial implications of suboptimal resource allocation are often not very evident as it takes time for a small misallocation to compound over time and be significant. This may lead to costs that do not necessarily appear explicitly as a separate item on the financial statements. Over time, this compounding of small costs may result in compressed margins, reduced ROI, and diminished stakeholder returns. LP works by systematically evaluating all combinations based on the given inputs and instructions. Therefore, it can identify truly optimal solutions. Optimal resource mix may differ substantially from historical patterns, which eventually improve performance using the same resource base.

In our example, the final production levels were 13,009 chairs, 7,000 tables, and 6,000 bookshelves. You may notice that tables and bookshelves are produced just enough to satisfy minimum demand, while chairs comprise the majority of the output. This is because the chair has the lowest cost per unit. Therefore, despite bookshelves having the highest profit margin, the LP model decided that producing chairs would have the lowest costs while maintaining the given profit margin. The focus on optimization of the LP model is better revealed for this case study if you attempt to maximize profit. The code for that is available at the repository. For the profit maximization model, the production levels were 14,500 chairs, 7,000 tables, and 11,000 bookshelves. Bookshelves are being produced at their maximum demand limit, which is very simple due to it having the highest profit margin. However, notice something interesting here. Tables are still being produced to only satisfy the minimum demand, although the per-unit profit from them is higher than the profit from chairs. LP considers all constraints dynamically, something that is impossible to do manually.

While using LP, we should consider these four factors:

- **Comprehensive constraint mapping**: The accuracy of any LP model depends on how well it can reflect the actual constraints facing the organization. In addition to identification of the constrained resource, other factors may have to be articulated. This would include factors like nature of constraint (absolute or flexible), interdependencies between constraints, variability in constraint parameters, and allied.
- **Financial parameter calibration**: The financial parameters used in an LP model must be continually validated to reflect full economic costs and benefits. Recalibration of these parameters would lead to better resource allocations. Further, other techniques like ABC, contribution analysis, and others, can be used in parameter calibration.
- **Constraint relaxation valuation**: Shadow price is a very important concept in LP. It represents the marginal value of relaxing a constraint by one unit. For example, say raw material is a constrained resource and has a shadow price of $50. This means that having one additional unit would improve the objective function of maximizing profit or minimizing costs by $50.

- **Change management:** Successfully implementing LP for optimal resource allocation is not only a concern for strategic management. It requires the presence of a robust management culture throughout the organization.

LP can be applied across all industries, to any application of resource allocation. It can be used for financial portfolio optimization, marketing resource allocation, human capital optimization, and capital optimization, to name a few.

Key takeaways

Effective cost management and resource optimization are essential for strategic financial decision-making. Traditional costing methods often misrepresent product-level profitability in complex environments, whereas ABC offers more accurate insights by linking overheads to actual resource consumption. When combined with regression analysis, financial leaders can identify and quantify key cost drivers, leading to more informed budgeting and pricing decisions. Additionally, LP enables optimal allocation of constrained resources, supporting cost minimization or profit maximization goals. We have demonstrated in the examples, how to leverage these tools with ML. This integration enables financial decision-makers to implement data-driven, efficient, and sustainable solutions.

Chapter 4

Performance measurement and management

Measuring performance goes beyond just tracking numbers. It is about understanding how well the organization is moving toward its goals. In this chapter, we look at ways to define and monitor both financial and non-financial performance, with key performance indicators (KPIs) and balanced scorecards. We will see how ML can help build interactive dashboards, analyze employee performance, and turn complex data into actionable insights. We will also integrate real-time data to get the latest information. With the right tools and techniques, finance professionals can play a key role in guiding effective strategy across the organization.

Performance analysis and financial decisions

Performance measurement is an important component of financial decisions. It may precede as well as succeed a decision. Accurate and timely measurement is likely to create a competitive advantage through operational efficiency and resource optimization. Traditionally, we use various financial metrics like ROI, profit margins, or earnings per share. Though these are essential for financial management, they often fail to capture the full spectrum of influencing factors.

Organizations aim to adopt strategies that consider non-financial factors like customer satisfaction, operational excellence, innovation capacity, human capital development, and so on. These, along with financial measures, create a complete ecosystem that is necessary for the sustainable growth of an organization.

Management studies have responded to these requirements and have come up with different solutions. These include balanced scorecards, integrated reporting, and other tools that look beyond traditional financial reporting. Those reports also sensitize financial leadership on how non-financial activities can influence corporate growth and performance. That is the precise reason why these tools have been included in this book.

DOI: 10.4324/9781003619628-4

In this section, we will explore some financial and non-financial performance measures and how financial decision-makers can leverage them for better strategies. We will also see how financial decision-makers can create their dashboard, which they may choose to keep private or let others access.

Performance indicators for decision-making

Performance indicators allow financial decision-makers to evaluate the impact of their decisions. Computation of the measures is one aspect of the process; the other aspect involves defining the measure. Traditionally, we seek to measure performance by quantifying the impact of the decision on the resources used. For example, return on capital, inventory turnover, among others.

However, as the business works, the impact of the decision may not necessarily be driven by the resources we directly allot to the activity. ML tools allow us to determine more precisely what influences performance. This additional input is likely to lead to better decision-making.

Performance indicators can broadly be classified into two categories:

- **Lagging indicators:** These measures follow performance like profit, market share, and allied. They are great indicators of past performance but have limited predictive value.
- **Leading indicators:** These indicators try to predict performance. For example, a high customer satisfaction score indicates potentially higher sales. These often double up as an early warning sign. For example, slowing sales is likely to cause higher inventory.

ML tools take these indicators to another dimension. For instance, regression models can identify key drivers of profitability by analyzing historical sales, cost behavior, and customer data. Similarly, unsupervised learning techniques like clustering can help segment customers based on profitability patterns. This additional information would allow more informed decisions on cost management or resource allocation. They can broadly be classified into the following groups of performance indicators:

- **Correlation analysis:** ML algorithms can identify non-obvious relationships between operational metrics and financial outcomes. This will assist the management in prioritizing metrics with the strongest influence on outcomes.
- **Anomaly detection:** ML systems can automatically flag performance deviations and alert users. This can help organizations take early action to prevent loss or profit from an opportunity.

- **Dynamic thresholds:** ML enables dynamic performance thresholds that adjust to contextual factors. This takes care of performance measurement distortions arising from seasonality, market conditions, and others.

Let us consider an example. A mid-sized manufacturing firm wants to identify which operational indicators are most strongly associated with a profit margin over the last three years. We can use regression analysis to assess the impact of variables like machine downtime, supply chain delays, raw material prices, and labor efficiency.

The output helps management prioritize areas with the highest impact on financial outcomes.

Let us have a look at the Python code showcasing this application (prefix 0401).

- **Import libraries:** The necessary libraries are being imported in this section.
- **Customize:** In this section, we are specifying the names of the file with input data, the name by which plots will be saved, and the variables for the regression model. For the regression model, we are specifying the names of the independent and dependent variables. Ensure that these fields are in the input data. Here is the relevant code with the customizable parameters in italics.

```
# Customize parameters
my_input_file = '0401 my_input.csv'
my_plot_prefix = "0401 my_plot_file"
my_x_columns=['Machine_Downtime', 'Supply_Delays',
'Raw_Material_Cost_Index', 'Labor_Efficiency']
my_y_column=['Profit_Margin']
```

- **Load data, prepare, and run regression:** In this section, we load the input data and then define the input for the regression model. We have specified that there will be a constant, that is, the intercept term in the model. If you do not want an intercept, replace the code `X = sm.add_constant(X)` with `model = sm.OLS(y, X).fit()`.
- **Generate regression output, display, and save plot:** The code generates and displays various metrics of the regression model, regression equation, and scatter plot of the dependent variable with each independent variable. These plots are also saved individually for later use.

The output of the model is a detailed result of the regression model fit. This includes audit data containing the specification of the dependent variable, date of model run, method of fit, number of observations, and allied. It also gives the model fit metrics, including the oft-used R^2 and p-values. Values of the constant and coefficient of each independent variable are also stated. The code also displays the regression equation for better understanding. The scatter plots are very useful in visually understanding the nature of the relationship between the dependent and independent variables.

How the balanced scorecard works

The Balanced Scorecard (BSC) provides a structured framework for integrating financial and non-financial performance measures. The measurement is done across four key perspectives: financial, customer, internal processes, and learning and growth. By linking performance indicators to strategic objectives, it fosters alignment across all organizational levels. The core components of BSC are the following:

- **Strategic objectives:** These are clear, concise statements of what the organization aims to achieve within each perspective.
- **Performance measures:** These are metrics that track progress toward strategic objectives.
- **Targets:** These are specific performance levels to be achieved for each measure. Performance is measured against these targets.
- **Strategic initiatives:** These comprise projects and programs designed to help achieve targets.

A balanced scorecard recognizes the cause-and-effect relationship between perspectives. For example, improvement in employee skills is expected to result in improved internal processes. Identifying cause-and-effect relations makes balanced scorecards a powerful tool in the hands of decision-makers. ML is likely to enhance the effectiveness of BSC in many ways, including the following:

- **Causality validation:** Every management has its view on the cause-and-effect relation between metrics across perspectives. ML algorithms can analyze historical data to validate these hypothesized cause-and-effect relationships. This validation ensures that the root cause accurately reflects organizational realities.
- **Predictive performance modeling:** ML models are great tools to forecast changes in leading indicators. This, in turn, will influence lagging financial metrics, enabling more accurate financial planning.
- **Automated insight generation:** At another extreme, NLP can continuously analyze performance data. They can automatically generate narrative insights highlighting critical trends, correlations, and anomalies across the scorecard.

Let us have a look at an example. A financial services company uses a BSC to evaluate branch-level performance. It builds an ML dashboard that tracks KPIs like revenue growth, customer satisfaction score, average service time per customer, and training hours. ML models identify patterns in underperforming branches and predict future service delivery risks. This integration not only provides real-time visualization but also supports proactive interventions.

Let us have a look at the main components of the code (prefix 0402).

- **Import libraries:** We load the necessary libraries in this section. You will find three new libraries being used here. Let us have a quick look at these.
  - ***`Plotly`***: The `Plotly` library in Python is a powerful, interactive graphing library. This is used to create high-quality visualizations for data analysis and dashboards. It supports both static and interactive charts and is extremely useful for browser-based, zoomable, and clickable plots. You can download the plots, zoom, pan, select a part, and do much more with `Plotly`.
  - ***`Dash`***: The `Dash` library in Python is an open-source framework developed by Plotly for building interactive web applications in Python. It is commonly used to create data dashboards, visual analytics, and ML model interfaces. The library has interactive components like sliders, dropdowns, graphs, and allied. `Dash` runs a web server internally when we launch a `Dash` app. This server can be accessed by others who know the IP address of the server. Please note that external access is subject to network rules. It is always available on the local machine and by default on port 8050, that is, on 127.0.0.1:8050. This will make it accessible on your machine. 127.0.0.1 is also known as the localhost. Note that we have used localhost in multiple places in this chapter. If you have an IP address that has already been used, you will need to modify the "0.0.1" part of the address. For example, change "127.0.0.1" to "127.0.2.0" or to "127.0.0.5." You will also observe in the later sections that we have done the same. Your IT department can advise you on how to close a running server.

    However, if you restart your machine, these servers will get reset.
  - ***`Socket`***: The `socket` library provides a low-level interface for network communication. It allows Python programs to send and receive data over TCP/IP or UDP protocols. This enables communication between different devices or applications over a network. We have used this library to identify the IP address where the `Dash` dashboard can be accessed.

- **Customize:** This code uses two customizable parameters – name of the input file and a list of features that will be used for clustering. The relevant section of the code with the customizable sections italicized is given here. Please be careful about the syntax of providing the names of the feature fields, and ensure that all these fields are present in the input file. Strictly speaking, there are other areas of the code that you would need to change while using input with different fields. We have identified them at appropriate places.

```
# Customize parameters
my_input_file='0402 my_input.csv'
my_x_fields = ['Revenue_Growth', 'Customer_Satisfaction',
'Service_Time', 'Training_Hours']
```

- **Load data and run clustering:** In this section, the input data is loaded into the model after normalization. The StandardScaler is a data preprocessing tool that standardizes features by removing the mean and scaling to unit variance. This sets the mean to zero and the standard deviation to 1. It avoids features with larger scales dominating the model, like salary in thousands versus age in years. We have used the K-means clustering tool. This is an unsupervised ML algorithm that groups data into K distinct clusters based on similarity. Its goal is to organize data such that points within the same cluster are more similar to each other than to those in other clusters. It is known as unsupervised learning, as we do not provide any labels or predefined categories. The tool finds structure or patterns in the data on its own. The code snippet `n_clusters=3` asks the tool to group data into 3 clusters. The number of clusters can be an executive decision, but we have measures like the Elbow Plot or the Silhouette Score to decide on the number of clusters that best suit the data. Setting the `random_state` to a specific number ensures that the random choices made during the algorithm are reproducible. Consequently, we will get the same results every time you run the code.
- **Launch dashboard:** We launch the dashboard to display interactive results, which can also be viewed on a browser running on a local web server. We can view the results displayed on the screen by going to the IP address where the web server is running. In the layout section, we have defined the dropdown options and what values they would display. These are marked as `'label'` and `'value'`. The corresponding name of the field is provided against `'value'`. The function will be called later by the ID given in the code snippet id=`'metric'`. Here is part of the code with the customizable parts in italics.

```
dcc.Dropdown(
     id='metric',
     options=[
     {'label': 'Revenue Growth (%)', 'value':
     'Revenue_Growth'},
     {'label': 'Customer Satisfaction', 'value':
     'Customer_Satisfaction'},
     {'label': 'Service Time (min)', 'value':
     'Service_Time'},
     {'label': 'Training Hours', 'value':
     'Training_Hours'}
     ],
     value='Revenue_Growth',
     clearable=False
),
```

You can change the type of graph also, but that would not qualify as Lo-code, and so we have given it a pass. The function is called back by the `app.callback` section. The display gets updated depending on the selection made by the user.

If you want the dashboard to be accessible to the external world, use host 0.0.0.0 in the `app_run`. You will have `app.run(host='0.0.0.0', port=8050, debug=True)` as the code. However, this will create a problem when Jupyter Notebook processes the code, as 0.0.0.0 is not an accessible address. You will get a processing error, though the dashboard will be accessible from the network. We have both options provided in the code. Please note that these are dependent on how your network has been designed and what permissions you have. You may need to involve your IT department to help you out here.

The output of the code has two parts. The first part displays a bar chart depending on the selection made by the user. These charts are self-explanatory. The second part renders a cluster diagram. The code has defined the cluster to be made around the dimensions of revenue growth, customer satisfaction, and training hours. The clusters are represented by different colors and numbered 0, 1, and 2. If you hover your cursor on any cluster dot, the branch ID, values of the dimensions, and the cluster number are displayed at the mouse tip. If you hover your cursor anywhere over the image, a menu will appear in the top-right corner of the image box. You can view the image in many ways by using the menu options.

You need to remember that the web server is not terminated when you quit the code or finish running it. The server continues running in the background. That is why if you complete using a code with the `Dash` library and move to another code with the same library, you may not find the dashboard being populated. The web server is still running the last code, and the IP address is not free for the new code. Either you have to stop the server running or change the destination IP address in the later code.

We have used `Dash` in several other codes in this chapter and have not repeated these explanations. Whenever you need to remember how `Dash` works, please come back to this section.

Identify employees with better potential

An effective employee performance measurement system will look beyond metrics like output generated or sales made. These systems will generate data-driven insights to influence talent development investments and organizational structure issues. A comprehensive performance measurement framework should incorporate, among others, the following:

- **Objective output metrics**: These record the quantifiable results achieved, such as sales targets or production volumes.
- **Behavioral competencies**: These recognize observable workplace behaviors that contribute to organizational success. These include collaboration, innovation, adaptability, and so on.
- **Skills assessment**: These are the basic technical and soft skills that are relevant to current and future organizational needs.
- **Growth trajectory**: Another critical area of focus is the rate of performance improvement over time. These metrics indicate the learning agility and development potential of employees.

What are the aspects of employee performance measures where ML tools can contribute? Well, there are quite a few, including the following:

- **Performance pattern recognition**: ML algorithms can identify complex patterns in employee performance data. This ability can be useful in recognizing potential behavior. Traditional analysis may not be able to identify such patterns.
- **High-potential identification**: Analysis of multiple performance patterns would allow ML tools to recognize signatures of high-potential employees. This can be useful in succession planning.
- **Development path optimization**: Analysis of performance patterns would allow ML tools to recommend individualized development plans for different employees. These interventions will be based on identified skill gaps, growth opportunities, and potential.
- **Bias mitigation**: One of the major threats of traditional performance evaluation systems is the biased view of assessors. The situation is even worse if the bias is unconscious. A well-trained ML system can help reduce unconscious bias in performance evaluations.

Multiple ML tools and approaches can be useful in this case. Supervised classification algorithms like Random Forests, decision trees, and logistic regression can be trained on historical employee data. They can use variables such as project delivery times, training participation, feedback ratings, absenteeism, and other relevant variables to predict future performance. These tools can also help identify high-potential talent.

Let us see how such tools can be used in business. Let us take the case of a multinational company that wants to identify employees with above-average growth potential. It can compile data from internal HR systems and use a Random Forest Classifier. This classifier will predict high performers based on historical patterns.

This will help HR teams design focused mentorship and development plans for the right individuals. The underlying assumption is that we know which factors point to a person potentially being a high performer. Now you know this is a supervised model, as we know both features and target labels. Talent analytics will aid better strategic workforce decisions, which are likely to improve the retention of top performers.

Let us see the main components of the code that exemplify the business case. The main components of the code (prefix 0403) are the following:

- **Import libraries**: We are loading all libraries in this section. We have imported new modules like `train_test_split` and `RandomForestClassifier`, from `sklearn`. We will discuss these a little later.
- **Customize**: There are five parameters that we are customizing in this section. They are the name of the input file, the file to save the confusion matrix and feature plot, and a list of dependent and independent variables to be used in the model. The extract of the code with a customizable section in italics is given here. Ensure that these fields are present in the input.

```
# Customize parameters
my_input_file ='0403 my_input.csv'
my_x_values = ['Project_Score', 'Training_Hours',
'Absenteeism_Rate', 'Peer_Feedback']
my_y_value = 'High_Performer'
my_confusion_plot='0403 confusion_matrix.png'
my_feature_plot='0403 feature_plot.png'
```

- **Load data and fit classifier**: In this section, we load the data from the input file. We define the features and the target. After that, we split the input data into two sections. The first section will be used to train the model, and the second section will be used to test the trained model. For the model, the test section will be unknown. You can change the value of `test_size=0.3` to decide the percentage of total data that will be reserved for testing. 0.3 means 30% of the data will be used for testing. Once we have readied the input data, we will fit the Random Forest Classifier. As we have seen earlier, a Random Forest Classifier is an ensemble ML algorithm that builds multiple decision trees during training. The model identifies the class a data point belongs to. The model classifies the data point into the class that the majority of the decision trees have indicated. It improves accuracy and reduces overfitting as compared to a single decision tree. You can specify the number of decision trees you want to work with by providing the value in the code snippet `n_estimators=100`. A value in the `random_state` ensures that we get the same results in every run. Armed with these values, the code starts fitting the model to the data provided.

- **Predict, evaluate, and report:** In the final section, the model predicts the values using the data from the section reserved for testing. The confusion matrix to map the extent of correct prediction is created and displayed. The model computes the respective importance of each feature and plots the same. Both plots are also saved for future use. The code also shows the predicted performance status against each employee ID and indicates whether the employee was a high performer.

The output includes the classification report, plot of the confusion matrix, and feature importance. The classification report evaluates the quality of prediction and uses the following terms.

- **Precision and Recall (Sensitivity):** Precision is the proportion predicted to be positive that turned out to be positive for each classification, 1 or 0. Recall or sensitivity is the proportion of actual positives that were correctly predicted.
- **F1 Score:** This is the harmonic mean of precision and recall. This is used instead of the arithmetic mean because it gives more weight to lower values. This sensitizes users about models that perform well on one metric but poorly on another.
- **Support:** The number of true instances for each class in the dataset.
- **Accuracy:** Number of predictions that were correct overall.
- **Macro average:** Average of the metrics treating all classes equally.
- **Weighted average:** Average weighted by the number of instances in each class.

A confusion matrix is a summary table that evaluates the performance of a classification model (Table 4.1). It plots the predicted values with the actual values in the test data and presents the same in a 2×2 matrix.

There are no universal threshold values of these metrics for the model to be accepted. It would vary from case to case, as well as the behavior of the industry.

The feature importance plot shows how important each feature is. The relative importance of a feature is computed based on how much the feature contributes to reducing impurity across all trees in the forest. We have

Table 4.1 Confusion matrix

Actual		Predicted	
		Repaid	Defaulted
	Repaid	True Negative	False Positive
	Defaulted	False Negative	True Positive

four features in this case, and the relative importance of each of them is plotted here. This information will allow us to focus on the more critical features.

Developing KPI dashboards with ML tools

Dashboards are a popular way of communicating key performance results with the stakeholders. Often, finance professionals supply them to the data team, and they populate the dashboard either in an automated process or manually. The dashboard remains static till the next update. ML tools can convert static dashboards into dynamic ones by combining performance analysis with reporting. The best part is that the finance professionals can now create their mini dashboard, which can be used by a close team or even for a short duration. ML tools allow them to do that without being dependent on the data team.

There are visualization platforms in ML that can be integrated with the ML algorithms to create intelligent dashboards. These dashboards can not only display historical data but can also uncover trends, detect anomalies, and forecast likely future outcomes.

In this section, we will examine the possibilities of creating our dashboard.

Visualizing KPIs for quick insights

Visualization enables faster comprehension and more effective decision-making. Relationships like correlation, trends, and anomalies are more easily understood through a visual depiction rather than through text. ML tools are not only capable of identifying and highlighting significant trends, correlations, and outliers, but they can also identify important factors from multi-dimensional KPIs.

Visualization works in tandem with ML techniques. For example, dimensionality reduction or clustering techniques can group related KPIs or departments exhibiting similar performance behaviors. These insights are then fed into visualization libraries to generate easy-to-comprehend renderings.

Let us consider that a retail chain wants to visualize daily sales, profit margins, inventory turnover, and customer footfall across 20 stores. Using K-means, the system groups the stores with similar performance trends. The code can then visualize them using an interactive bar and scatter chart. Outliers can be flagged for review.

Let us have a look at the main components of the code (prefix 0404).

- **Import libraries:** Apart from the regular ones, we have imported a new library for this code. `mpl_toolkits.mplot3d` is a submodule of `Matplotlib`. It provides 3D plotting capabilities.
- **Customize:** There are four input parameters that we have customized here. These are the names of the input file, the features we will use for clustering, and the names of files to save the plots. Here is the relevant code with customizable values in italics.

```
# Customize parameters my_input_file='0404 my_input.csv'
my_features = ['Daily_Sales', 'Profit_Margin',
'Inventory_Turnover', 'Customer_Footfall']
my_scatter_plot="0404 cluster_3d_scatter.png"
my_bar_prefix ="0404 bar_chart"
```

- **Load and prepare data, apply K-means:** We proceed to load data from the input file. Note that the features that have been entered above are names of fields in the input file. We standardize the data and then fit a K-means clustering model. We have specified in the code `n_clusters=3`, which means we are instructing the code to have three clusters. Remember, this is an unsupervised learning model where we have not provided any cause-and-effect relation within the input data. We fit the model and then go ahead with generating the clusters.
- **Visualize and save cluster:** We have created clusters and rendered them in 3D. In addition, we have created bar charts of each feature against all stores. We have saved both plot files for future use.

This code shows an advanced visualization against a business case similar to the one used earlier. Let us understand the cluster output (Figure 4.1).

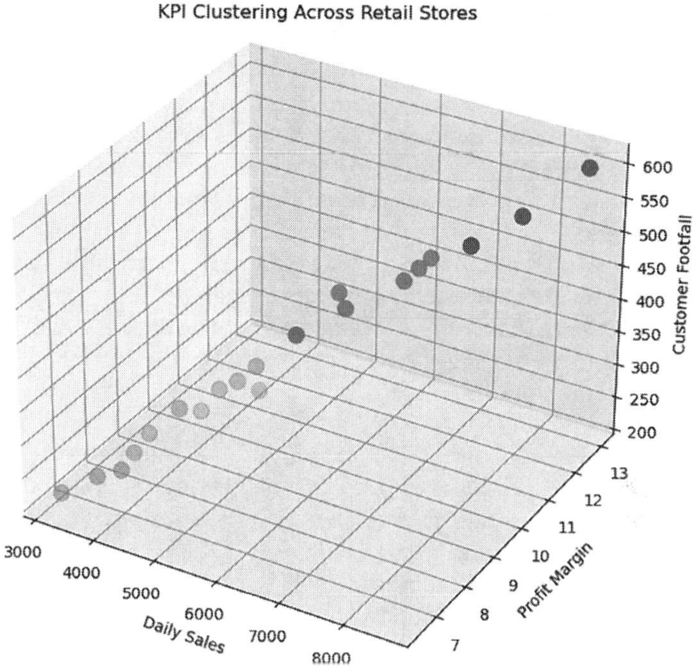

Figure 4.1 3D Clustering Output

The stores have been classified into 3 clusters as per our requirement. It had three features for clustering, and we have 3 axes. The features are daily sales, profit margin, and customer footfall. You can see that the 3 clusters are distinct, meaning they are not overlapping. Each shade represents a distinct group of stores that behave similarly across these three KPIs. The different shades represent clusters arising from the model fit.

This can help manage benchmark stores against similar peers within the same cluster. Underperforming stores in a high-performing cluster might warrant deeper investigation. There are other rendering tools like `Plotly`, which we have used earlier, that allow you to rotate the chart, of course, on the screen.

Interactive dashboards using ML tools

Interactive dashboards allow users to manipulate the display in real time, addressing their specific inquisitiveness. This is a major improvement over static dashboards that provide a snapshot. Most interactive dashboards would have some or all of the following features:

- **Dynamic filtering:** Allows users to instantaneously filter data across multiple dimensions to retrieve a visualization of their focus data.
- **Drill-down capabilities:** This feature enables navigation from high-level KPIs to granular details to support root cause analysis.
- **Scenario modeling:** Facilitates "what-if" analyses to explore potential outcomes of different decisions. This can be very useful during a meeting where various possible strategies are discussed.
- **Contextual recommendations:** ML can even go a step beyond mere visualization. It can even suggest relevant metrics and visualizations based on the user's exploration pattern.

There are multiple tools for visualization, and we will be using some of them here. You may break them into two categories: one that creates the visualization and the other that renders the visualization on the web or similar accessible platforms.

Consider a manufacturing company that wants an interactive dashboard to track equipment utilization, downtime, energy consumption, and quality defect rates. In a standard dashboard, these values can be easily visualized, even a standard spreadsheet would do a great job. An ML-powered dashboard can, in addition, use a regression model to forecast equipment failure risk. This can be displayed along with current operational KPIs in a real-time dashboard. The interactivity supported by ML-driven insights would help the operational teams take early preventive action. Let us have a look at the major components of the code (prefix 0405).

- **Import libraries:** We have loaded all necessary libraries. We have used these libraries in earlier codes too.
- **Customize:** We have specified the name of the input file, the features, the target, and additionally, the IP address to render the dashboard on a local web server. You may not specify the IP address, and the library will assign 127.0.0.1. However, as stated earlier, we have changed the IP address here under `my_host` as we have used 127.0.0.1 previously. By default, it runs on port 8050. Here is the relevant section of the code with the customizable parameters highlighted in italics.

```
my_input_file='0405 my_input.csv'
my_features = ['Utilization', 'Downtime',
'Energy_Consumption', 'Defect_Rate']
my_target='Failure_Risk'
my_host='127.0.0.7'
```

- **Read data and run regression:** In this section, we will first read the input data and then define the labels and target. We set the linear regression model and fit the data. We use the model to predict from past data. Please note that we are not doing a test-train split here and are using the same data to train and predict. We can also use the train and test method, which we have seen under other applications, if we want to do more detailed testing.
- **Build dashboard:** Armed with the predicted values, we move on to populate the dashboard. We have followed the same logic as earlier to use the `Dash` library.

The output dashboard has two sections. The top one has a dropdown menu, and you can display a chart depending on the option you have selected. The display below shows the predicted machine failure rate generated from the regression model. You can also use the dashboard from your local browser.

The purpose behind giving this example is not to establish the possibility of ML-driven better visualization, but to integrate ML-driven prediction.

Performance tracking using real-time data

Real-time KPI tracking is a significant leap from the periodic performance analysis done traditionally. This enables organizations to respond faster to changes in the environment and key assumptions. Integrating real-time feeds into KPI dashboards ensures that decision-makers do not rely on outdated or stale information.

The ability to integrate real-time data potentially reduces the lead time to make a decision. It can also enable early warning signals and facilitate continuous improvement in the process. A few advantages of using real-time data include the following:

- **Streaming analytics:** It facilitates processing continuous data flows and extracts meaningful patterns without human intervention.
- **Adaptive alerting:** The ability to adjust alert thresholds based on contextual factors is likely to reduce false positives. It will also let the user focus on significant alerts instead of facing a large number of inconsequential alerts.
- **Predictive monitoring:** ML tools can also forecast KPI trajectories, thus providing an early alert before a potential issue emerges.
- **Causal analysis:** At an advanced level, it is also possible to identify root causes of KPI changes in real-time. This will facilitate targeted interventions.

Though not described here, dashboards can connect with live data sources (IoT devices, ERP systems, or external APIs) using specialized ML tools. ML models can then process and analyze this data stream to generate alerts or recommendations as conditions change.

Consider a manufacturing company that streams live data from its factory into a real-time dashboard. These data could relate to machine utilization, downtime, energy consumption, defect rate, estimated failure risk, and others. An embedded ML model can flag failure risk based on other data being updated periodically. Since we do not have a system that will periodically update our data, we have created a routine to generate dummy data to show the performance of the model. In real life, this updated data will be available to you from external sources. Let us have a look at the main components of the code (prefix 0406).

- **Import libraries:** The libraries we are using for this code are all known to us from past usage.
- **Customize:** We have provided four parameters to run the code. The name of the input file, the names of the labels and target (the independent and dependent variables), and a refresh rate in seconds. While the first three are well known, the refresh rate is the time in seconds between every refresh of the dashboard. You can decide if you want 5 seconds, 10 seconds, 60 seconds, or whatever. Of course, you would have ensured that the labels and the target are all present in the input file. Here is the excerpt from the code with customizable parameters in italics.

```
# Customize parameters

my_input_file='0406 my_input.csv'
my_host='127.0.0.9'

# define regression paraneters
my_x_values = ['Utilization', 'Downtime',
'Energy_Consumption', 'Defect_Rate']
my_y_value = 'Failure_Risk'

# Seconds to refresh the dashboard
my_refresh=10
```

- **Load and train model on initial data:** In this section, we read the data from the input file and fit a linear regression using the labels and target. The regression creates a new set of data comprising predicted risk for every machine.
- **Function to create dummy data:** This is an interesting section, though it will be redundant in real-life applications. In this function, we are creating dummy data for every machine we have in the base input.

This dummy data is then used to refresh the dashboard. The generated dummy data is not saved. The first step we have taken here is to ascertain how many machines there are in the database input.

- **Set up the dashboard:** In this case, we have 30 machines, and we will generate dummy data for each of them whenever this function is called. Update frequency is also used here. The layout of the dashboard is also designed here.
- **Update dashboard using dummy data:** In this section, we display the KPIs, which are the machine utilization rate and the predicted failure rate. As the dummy data is generated at stipulated intervals, the dashboard is updated with new values. This will be very useful for monitoring dynamic data. You can select to make the dashboard available to others by publishing it on an IP address accessible to your target audience.

The output from the code is essentially two plots. One for machine utilization and the other for predicted machine failure. The first plot, apart from showing the machine utilization rate, is overlaid with a color depicting the predicted failure rate. Thus, it conveys two pieces of information to the user at the same time. The second chart is for the predicted failure risk. Both charts get updated at defined time intervals and show the latest dummy data.

In real-life applications, data will be fed into code from an external source. The external source just needs to adhere to the data structure of the host code.

Suiting different stakeholders' needs

A customizable dashboard would allow different stakeholders to populate the same with the data and visuals they need. Stakeholder-driven customization would require an understanding of the stakeholder characteristics. Though we are looking at the stakeholders developing their dashboard, let us still have a quick look at those characteristics.

- **Information scope**: The information requirement differs from the C-suite to functional experts. The information needed may be strategic, operational, or even specialized.
- **Decision timeframe**: The time impact of the decision may also differ from long-term strategic to immediate tactical. The dashboard will have to be populated to serve such a need.
- **Data aggregation**: The need for data aggregation would also differ from one user to another. A line manager may need a detailed analysis, while senior executives may need precise summaries.
- **Context awareness**: A report is to be populated and interpreted based on the context. The information being presented should also be tailored to specific business contexts and responsibilities.

In terms of designing the content for customizing dashboards, the ML tools may use different approaches. The tools can analyze, on their own, how users interact with dashboards and remember their preferences. This information is then used to populate the dashboard intuitively for different users. Another great tool is to enable a natural language interface. This allows non-technical users to request a custom view through a conversational process. Role-based generation of the dashboard is also a possibility. All this ensures that the displays are not only correct but are also relevant.

Let us look at an example. Consider a mid-sized enterprise implementing a dashboard. The dashboard adjusts its layout and KPIs based on the role of the logged-in user. Executives see strategic indicators, while team leaders see operational ones. An ML model monitors usage patterns to recommend layout changes and new KPI additions based on departmental focus. The code is very similar to the last one, except when it comes to visualization. Here, the user can select a profile, and the display will change to suit the defined needs of the role selected. In all cases, the data will get refreshed at the specified interval. Major components of the relevant code (prefix 0407) are the following:

- **Import libraries:** The necessary libraries are loaded, as usual.
- **Customize:** We can customize the name of the input file, specify the labels and the target, and provide the refresh rate. The relevant part of the code is given here, and as you can see, it is similar to the last example. The customizable parameters have been italicized.

```
# Customize parameters
my_input_file='0407 my_input.csv'
my_host='127.0.0.8'

# define regression parameters
my_x_values = ['Utilization', 'Downtime',
'Energy_Consumption', 'Defect_Rate']
my_y_value = 'Failure_Risk'

# Seconds to refresh the dashboard
my_refresh=10
```

- **Load and train model on initial data:** We load the input data and define the model and the parameters.
- **Function to create dummy data:** Similar to the last code, we have created a function to generate dummy data to be used to refresh the dashboard.
- **Set up dashboard app:** The dashboard application is also like the last example, except it allows users to select a role. For example, this code allows the user to select one of three roles of executive, operations

manager, or maintenance head. The content of the dashboard changes according to the selected role.

- **Callback with live data:** This section populates the dashboard with role-specific content, which is updated at a regular frequency.

As we stated earlier, the output from the model is role-specific. It also runs the regression model to predict failure risk and displays the same for the executives. The average utilization rate and the average predicted failure rate are also stated for the executive. The operations manager gets a view of real-life utilization and defect rate for each machine. The maintenance head gets a prioritized list of maintenance based on the predicted risk.

This tool allows a single dashboard serving different perspectives, allowing the users to select the view they want to have.

Balance scorecard implementation using ML tools

BSC is a strategic performance management framework. This framework enables organizations to translate their vision and strategy into a coherent set of financial and non-financial objectives. Traditional BSC implementations often struggle with data integration challenges, time lags in reporting, and limited analytical capabilities. ML tools can transform this dashboard into a data-driven application to monitor both financial and non-financial performance metrics.

Smart ML tools facilitate the development of web-based applications to communicate BSC metrics in real-time. They can integrate various data sources in real time and offer features like automated pattern recognition and predictive performance modeling. The stakeholders can get access to real-life data customized to their needs. The true power of ML-enhanced BSCs would lie in their ability to transform strategy from a concept to a measurable framework. This would facilitate the alignment of operations with organizational strategies. The data becomes accessible, understandable, and actionable across various levels of the organization.

A combination of BSC and ML would result in translating strategic objectives into measurable outcomes. Strategic clarity of BSC and analytical capabilities of ML, with interactivity of rendering tools, can build an intelligent performance tracking system. We will have a look at some of the potential in this module.

Align business activities and strategic objectives using BSC

An effective BSC implementation is a visual representation of causal relationships between objectives across different perspectives. Traditional strategy maps rely heavily on intuition and experience, which can lead to incorrect assumptions about cause-and-effect relationships. An ML algorithm-driven strategy map is highlighted by the following:

- **Empirical validation**: ML algorithms use historical performance data to validate hypothesized cause-and-effect relationships. This approach results in confirmation or refutation of these assumptions with evidence.
- **Relationship strength quantification**: ML tools, beyond establishing a binary connection, can determine the strength of relationships between metrics. This will help organizations in identifying initiatives with the highest strategic impact.
- **Time-lag analysis**: ML techniques can also identify the time delays between improvements in leading indicators (for example, employee training) and corresponding changes in lagging indicators. For example, how long after completing employee training can we expect customer satisfaction to improve?
- **Hidden relationship discovery**: Unsupervised learning techniques can uncover connections between metrics that are not obvious. These are often overlooked in traditional strategy mapping exercises. For example, some customers may avoid a restaurant because the images are not appealing on their social media profiles.

ML tools can augment the BSC by enabling data-driven alignment checks. For example, decision tree models can analyze historical BSC data to identify which non-financial indicators most influence financial outcomes. Organizations can use association rules or correlation mapping to evaluate how specific actions across departments contribute to strategic KPIs.

Let us look at an application. Consider a service-based company that tracks KPIs from each BSC perspective to determine which internal process indicators most influence customer satisfaction. They feel that innovation scores, process efficiency, employee training hours, issue resolution time, and customer satisfaction influence profit margin. The decision tree classifier may identify that service resolution time and support team training hours have the greatest influence. This insight would help realign operational targets with customer-focused strategic goals. Let us have a look at the code (prefix 0408).

- **Import libraries**: As usual, the necessary libraries are being loaded in this section. We will be using the `DecisionTreeRegresor` which we have installed.
- **Customize**: In this section, we are providing values for the names of the input file, files to save plots and predicted data, and features and targets to be used in the decision tree model. Here is the part of the code with the customizable parameters identified by italics. You will identify the

features you want to work with, ensuring that these are available on the input data.

```
# Customize parameters
my_input_file='0408 my_input.csv'
my_predicted_values="0408 predicted_kpi_data.csv"
my_features = [ 'Employee_Training_Hours',
'Customer_Satisfaction', 'Process_Efficiency',
'Issue_Resolution_Time', 'Innovation_Score']
my_target= 'Profit_Margin'
my_feature_plot = '0408 feature_plot.png'
my_decision_plot = '0408 decision_tree_visual.png'
```

- **Read data and fit model**: We have started the code by reading the input file. We moved on to loading the parameters for the decision tree, including the test-train split. Once defined, we used these parameters to fit the model. In the last few codes, we had simply predicted and did not follow this approach. This approach allows us to evaluate the fit of the model, and that is what the next part is about. It predicts the value for the target using the test part of the input data and then computes the MSE on the test set. This gives us an idea about whether the model is good to use.
- **Feature importance**: In this section, we have computed the relative importance of each of the labels in our model. The plot highlights the same, which is also saved for future use. If the model is good to use, this will give us insight into the importance of each label in influencing the target. This insight would be useful for management intervention.
- **Visual decision tree**: The decision tree model used here is a predictive model that learns if-then rules to predict a continuous numeric target variable. It recursively splits the dataset based on the values of the features and gives us a set of if-then gates to understand how the targets were achieved. We displayed the decision tree and saved it for future use.
- **Display predicted data**: This section displays the test data alongside the predicted target. In this case, the predicted target is the predicted profit margin. The actual profit margin is also displayed alongside to form an idea of how close or off the prediction was. Of course, the model fit metrics give us a comprehensive view based on the entire dataset. The entire dataset is also saved for subsequent use.

The output from the section includes a plot of feature importance, a decision tree, and a CSV file with predictions. Let us understand how to read the decision tree (Figure 4.2).

A decision tree, as the name suggests, spreads out as a tree from the top. It branches downwards, classifying observations till it reaches a point where further classification is not possible. The boxes show the question

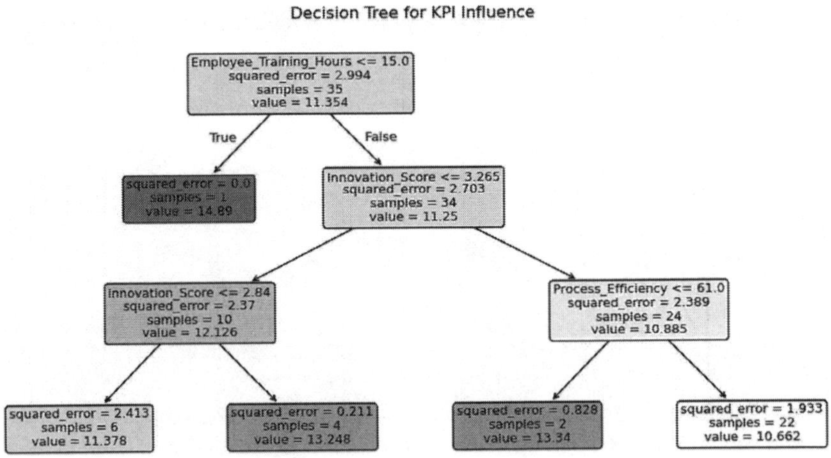

Figure 4.2 Understanding decision trees

being asked in the decision box, and answers branch out from there. They may also have additional information depending on the library being used. Let us look at a portion of the decision tree and try to understand the same.

The topmost box questions whether employee training hours were less than or equal to 15. The true branch consists of only one member and terminates there. If the response to the original question is false, there are 34 members in this classification. The model identifies the next factor contributing to further classification, that is, whether the innovation score is less than or equal to 3.265.

This again branches out into two groups with 10 and 24 members, and this process continues until the model determines that subsequent classification is meaningless. The boxes contain three parameters: squared error, value, and sample. The value refers to the mean value of the target variable, which is the predicted profit. This mean value is calculated at the node level over the members of the classification, as indicated by the value against the sample. At each level, the sum of samples at the branch level adds up to the immediately higher level. The squared error quantifies how far the predictions are from the actuals. A low squared error indicates that the data points are clustered closely around the mean, which signifies a good fit. For example, a squared error of 0.211 against a mean value of 13.248 suggests a very tight fit, indicating that most data points are situated close to the mean, forming a tight cluster. After the first split, we had a mean value of 11.25 and a squared error of 3.265. This suggests the possibility of a further split, which the tree proceeded to do. The splitting process will stop either when the sample size or the squared error figures reach a level at which any further meaningful classifiers are unavailable, or when additional classification does not improve the squared error. Although we have completed the analysis here, it is possible to specify the maximum depth of the tree and the minimum sample split threshold.

Web-based applications to track financial and non-financial metrics

A web-based application will be useful to give a multi-perspective performance monitoring report while remaining accessible to relevant stakeholders. As we have stated earlier, this could be very useful for meetings and closed group communication. The quality features of a web-based BSC application would include the following:

- **Unified view**: The application can present all four BSC perspectives in a coherent, integrated interface.
- **Multi-level drill-down**: As we have stated earlier, the application can enable a multifaceted view that can range between strategic objectives, tactical initiatives, and operational metrics.
- **Initiative tracking**: The dashboard, in addition to status reporting, can monitor the progress of strategic initiatives alongside related metrics.

Specific Python libraries can assist in the rapid development of applications that can develop interactive and web-based dynamic dashboards.

One of the applications of this can be in a bank. A bank may implement a web-based BSC dashboard that consolidates branch performance across four BSC categories. A built-in ML classification model can then segment branches based on their strategic alignment into high, medium, and low using their KPI scores. Management can interact with the dashboard to filter, rank, and drill into specific performance drivers. The bank has identified measures under each of the four perspectives. The details are shown below:

- Financial: Revenue growth, net profit margin, and predicted profit margin
- Customer: Customer satisfaction
- Internal Process: Service efficiency
- Learning and Growth: Employee training hours and innovation scores

Let us look at the major components of the code (prefix 0409).

- **Import libraries**: We have imported the libraries required to run the code. We have also used these libraries earlier.
- **Customize**: There are a few parameters that we need to provide. These are the names of the data input file, and list of features, and the target.

As always, ensure that the features and targets are available in the input file. We also need to provide the IP address for the localhost.

```
my_input_file='0409 my_input.csv'
my_host = '127.0.0.4'
my_features = ['Customer_Satisfaction',
'Service_Efficiency', 'Employee_Training_Hours',
'Innovation_Score']
my_target = 'Net_Profit_Margin'
```

- **Load data and train model:** In this section, we first load the data into the system. Then we specify the features and target to the model before fitting the model to the data. The model is then used to predict the values of the profit margin using the values of the features from the input file. Here also we have not split the data for training and testing purposes.
- **Setup dashboard app:** In this section, we have defined the KPIs under each of the four perspectives. We have also defined the layout of the dashboard. These perspectives are also included as components of the dropdown menu.
- **Display perspectives:** This section calls the data for display in the dashboard. The data content depends on the selected perspectives.

The output of the code is the KPI plots related to each of the four perspectives. The code populates the dashboard with the relevant KPIs, depending on the perspective that has been specified by the user.

Integration of various data sources

An effective BSC requires seamless integration of diverse data sources. This may include financial systems, customer relationship platforms, human resources databases, and so on. This integration will allow the creation of a comprehensive view of organizational performance without information silos.

Though data integration is possible and often achieved under traditional systems, there are a few challenges on the path. These include the following:

- **System fragmentation:** Performance data may be scattered across multiple disconnected systems. It would require a careful effort to create a BSC, taking input from diverse sources.
- **Manual aggregation:** The effort to aggregate data from various sources is usually time-consuming. In addition, manual data collection and consolidation are susceptible to human error, requiring greater investment in a control system.

- **Inconsistent definitions:** One of the major problems of getting data from diverse sources is the lack of consistent metric definitions. The same term may have different implications and at times different calculation methodologies across different systems. This feature often leads to inconsistent interpretation of KPIs between stakeholders.
- **Mismatch in update frequencies:** Different systems may refresh data at different intervals. This is likely to cause reported values of different KPIs reflecting different points in time. For example, sales data may be online while inventory values are updated periodically. Hence, there will be times when comparison between these two datasets involves two different points in time.

An ML-powered data integration solution should be able to integrate data. They would usually have an extract, transform, load (ETL) framework, which would normalize and integrate data from various sources. ML algorithms can also be used to reconcile definitional differences across various departments of the same entity. This will enable the system and the stakeholders to use a uniform definition of each KPI. ML tools can additionally treat missing values intelligently. These systems can either drop a missing value or use a proxy that will not change the interpretation but save the system from computational problems arising from missing values.

ML-based integration of data would facilitate analysis across domains. For example, it will be possible to see if a KPI of a domain, say, manpower churn, affects a KPI of another domain, say, quality-related complaints.

Let us have a look at a business case. Consider a retail chain that pulls data from various sources. For example, training hours from HR, conversion rates from sales, and customer complaints from CRM systems. All these are fed into its BSC dashboard. Using multi-source integration and correlation modeling, the retail chain may be able to identify features that were not apparent in the traditional system. It may be found that stores with high employee engagement tend to outperform others in both customer satisfaction and financial metrics. This would then validate the strategic importance of investment in training.

The major components of the code (prefix 0410) are discussed here.

- **Import libraries:** We have imported the libraries required to run the code.
- **Customize:** There are a few user-defined parameters that we will customize in this section. These are the names of the files with data from finance, HR, and CRM, besides the names to save the plots. In addition, the features and targets that will be used for analysis have also been specified here. In the code extract, these are marked in italics.

```
# Customize parameters
my_finance_data= "0410 finance_profitability_data.csv"
my_hr_data="0410 hr_employee_development.csv"
my_crm_data="0410 crm_customer_sentiment.csv"
my_correlation_plot="0410 correlation.png"
my_prediction_plot="0410 predict_and_actual.png"
my_features = ['Avg_Training_Hours',
'Employee_Turnover_Rate', 'Customer_Satisfaction',
'Complaints_Per_Month']
my_target = 'Profit_Margin'
```

- **Load and merge data:** In this section, we are combining the data input from three divisions into a combined database. The combination is being done based on the branch ID. This makes branch ID compulsory data in all input files. If you have a different linking field, replace the name with `Branch_ID`.
- **Compute correlation, display, and save plot:** This section of the code plots the correlation matrix across all numeric values in the combined database. The correlation values are displayed in each cell and overlaid with colors.
- **Fit model and evaluate:** We will now train the model using the integrated data. We will use a linear regression model and split the data for training and testing. We have made 70% of the data available for training by specifying `test_size=0.3`. After fitting the model, we used it to predict the test section of the input data. Finally, we compute the R-squared and MAE metrics for model performance. Though we will proceed with the next section of the code unless the model is a good fit, it is pointless to use the model output and move forward. If you change the split size, you may find a significant change in the model fit metrics. This may happen when the nature of the data is not homogeneous across the database.
- **Use model to predict on past data, show, and save plot:** This section plots the predicted profit against the actual profit in the integrated database. The plot gives a visual understanding of how good the prediction is.

The outputs of the code are primarily three. These are the correlation matrix, metrics of model fit, and comparison of actual and predicted profit. The correlation matrix helps the decision-makers understand how the features are related to each other. The diagonal of 1 is the correlation of the feature with itself. A high correlation is evidenced by the values inside the cell and color code, indicating that these two variables move together, either in the same direction or in the opposite direction. If two features ape each other, including only one of them in the model may be good enough to maintain the model's performance. Understanding the relation between two features will allow the decision-maker to foresee any domino effects.

R^2, as we have discussed earlier, is a popular metric of model performance. The closer the value is to 1, the better the model is. MAE is a widely used metric in regression tasks that tells you the average magnitude of errors between the predicted and the actual values. It does not consider the direction and treats all errors equally, whether positive or negative. There is no universal good MAE value, and it depends on the scale of the target variable, business context, and acceptable tolerance for error. If you divide MAE by the average of the profit margin, you will get an idea of relative error.

The predicted and actual plot shows how good the fit of the model is. This being a linear regression, the predicted line will be straight. The actual values are plotted as dots. The closer these dots are to the line, the better the predictive power of the model is.

Better communication of strategy

No matter how well-designed a dashboard is, unless it relates performance to strategy, it will not serve its purpose. Effective strategy communication is essential for translating measurements into action. However, there are some common barriers that an organization faces in communicating strategies effectively. Let us have a look at a few of them.

- **Implementation gap**: It is always difficult to connect high-level strategic objectives to day-to-day activities. They often have KPIs that range from being data-specific to abstract objectives.
- **Relevance filtering**: It is a challenge to ensure that each stakeholder receives information that is relevant to their role and responsibilities. Many times, data structure and report design aggregate or disaggregate the data in a manner that is not aligned with the expectations of each stakeholder.
- **Comprehension barriers**: Stakeholders often come from various backgrounds. It is a daunting task to be able to present complex strategic concepts in ways that are understood by all. The views of an engineer on capital budgeting will be quite different from those of a finance executive. One may be focused on reducing downtime and the other on increasing profit.
- **Feedback voids**: Often, the communication system is deficient in capturing and incorporating employee perspectives. Feedback from the employees may not find a way to contribute to the plan for strategy implementation.

ML tools can transform strategy communication from a top-down approach to an interactive, personalized engagement. The strategy presentation can be based on the user role, preference, and usage pattern of the stakeholder. Interactive tools can allow stakeholders to use predictive modeling to assess how certain developments can influence strategic objectives. Natural language interfaces can allow users to ask questions in everyday language.

Let us consider a manufacturing company that uses an ML-powered BSC application. This app can automatically generate monthly summaries for executives, managers, and staff. It can use a recommendation model to suggest priority actions to each team based on the latest performance trends. This can reduce strategic ambiguity and ensure that all levels of the organization are aligned and informed.

This code (prefix 0411) uses the earlier example of a role-driven dashboard and adds a strategic messaging feature to it. Here are the main components of the code described briefly.

- **Import libraries:** The required libraries are loaded here.
- **Customize:** The parameters the user will provide are the name of the input file, the list of features and the target, and the benchmarks. The relevant part of the code is given here with customizable parameters in italics and underlines.

```
my_input_file='0411 my_input.csv'
my_x_values=['Customer_Satisfaction', 'Training_Hours',
'Process_Efficiency']
my_y_value='Net_Profit_Margin'
my_target_profit=13
my_target_efficiency=70
my_target_training_hours=20
my_host = '127.0.0.2'
```

- **Load data and train model:** This section loads the data to fit the model and uses the fitted model to predict values for the target. We have not followed the train-test split method here.
- **Generate messages:** This is the section where messages are generated based on performance values and benchmarks. The rule to generate messages is given along with the role definition. Messages are generated for all three roles using role-specific KPIs.
- **Setup dashboard app:** The dashboard is in this section, with a dropdown option providing role selection.
- **Callback for messaging:** Once the user selects a role, the dashboard is populated with KPIs defined for the chosen role. In addition to the KPIs, the generated messages are displayed to the user.

The output of the code is a visualization of the KPI relevant to the role selected by the user. In addition, messages are generated pointing out to achievement or non-achievement of strategic goals.

Employee performance analysis with ML tools

Organizations need to evaluate the performance and potential of their employees to design development and succession plans. This task is a difficult one as it is prone to being subjective and consequently, exposed to bias. ML tools like advanced classification algorithms can objectively analyze complex patterns within employee performance data. They extract actionable insights that can be used in personnel planning. One of the most used classification tools is Random Forest.

Random Forest algorithms, as discussed earlier, can contribute greatly to employee performance analysis. Their ability to handle diverse input variables, manage missing data, and identify non-linear relationships between performance factors makes this a powerful tool. The use of ensemble learning methods combines multiple decision trees to produce robust predictions. At the same time, they provide transparent feature importance rankings identifying factors that influence performance outcomes.

Prudent use of the insights revealed by these tools can replace performance management with talent prediction. These data-driven approaches make the identification of high-potential employees more accurate. They also link specific factors that drive exceptional performance. Further, designing targeted interventions to develop talent across the organization becomes a lot more accurate and appropriate. As we explore in this section, ML transforms employee performance analysis from an administrative process into a strategic capability. This capability can directly contribute to competitive advantage and financial performance.

In this section, we will examine how ML tools can unearth hidden potential and get the best out of employees.

Analyze and predict employee performance

As stated earlier, ML tools can potentially transform organizations beyond reactive performance management to a proactive, data-driven approach. Traditional performance analysis usually relies on annual or semi-annual performance reviews, which are usually subjective assessments. These evaluations are also primarily reactive, and decisions based on them are more of a reward or a penalty.

ML-based approaches, in contrast, have the following advantages:

- **Continuous performance modeling**: ML tools can continuously analyze performance data instead of point-in-time assessments. This permits the identification of trends that are likely to indicate future success or challenges.

- **Multivariate analysis:** ML techniques can simultaneously process multiple performance variables. This is more likely to uncover complex relationships than what human analysts might be able to notice.
- **Adaptive benchmarking:** ML systems can be used to develop personalized performance benchmarks. These will be based on role characteristics, team context, and individual career stage. This will be in stark contrast to applying one-size-fits-all standards, as is common with traditional approaches.
- **Early signaling:** Predictive models can potentially identify performance trajectory changes. These changes are likely to signal potential issues ahead of when they may show up in traditional metrics.

Common ML techniques that can be used in performance analysis include regression (including logistic regression), time series, ensemble methods, and even neural networks. These are used for different purposes, including predicting performance metrics, identifying patterns and trends, and so on.

One of the great strengths of ML lies in its ability to uncover non-linear relationships and capture subtle performance drivers. This helps in continuously improving predictions over time. These models can be trained on known performance outcomes, like past appraisal scores, and used to predict the performance of an employee.

Let us look at the possible applications in a mid-sized IT firm. They may use a Random Forest model to predict performance ratings for employees. This could be based on their attendance records, project scores, peer ratings, skill development activity, and similar. The model would help HR identify potential high performers and underperformers early in their careers. We have used these tools on earlier occasions, and this code shows an application to a different domain.

The main components of the code (prefix 0412) are discussed here.

- **Import libraries:** We have loaded the libraries necessary for this code. The libraries are all known to us.
- **Customize:** The user will provide values for the name of the input file, features, and target, and names to save the plots. The relevant part of the code is shown here with the customizable parameters in italics.

```
# Customize parameters
my_input_file='0412 my_input.csv'
my_features = ['Project_Score', 'Training_Hours',
'Absenteeism_Rate', 'Peer_Feedback']
my_target = 'Performance_Level'
my_corr_plot = '0412 correl_plot.png'
my_feature_plot = '0412 feature_plot.png'
```

- **Load data and train classifier**: We have loaded the data at the beginning of the section. This is followed by defining the performance level. We have assigned three values for the performance level: 0 for low, 1 for average, and 2 for high. The conditions for the performance levels are also defined in this section. If you want to change them, this is where you can do that. The benchmark values for each KPI at each performance level are defined here. Here is the code excerpt.

```
conditions = [
    (data['Project_Score'] < 70) |
    (data['Peer_Feedback'] < 3.5),
    (data['Project_Score'].between(70, 85)) &
    (data['Peer_Feedback'] >= 3.5),
    (data['Project_Score'] > 85) &
    (data['Peer_Feedback'] >= 4.0)
]
```

  We have followed the split for the train and test routine here and have fitted the Random Forest Classifier model. We have linked the features and targets to fit the model. Once the model has been fit, we have used the same to predict values of the features from the test component of the input dataset.
- **Evaluate model**: We have generated a classification report and a confusion matrix to evaluate the model fit. Further, we have plotted the relative importance of features. These plots have also been saved for subsequent use. Often, the confusion matrix model may generate a warning if a lot of cells are not populated. Mind you that it is a situation that may have an impact on model performance, but it is not a mistake. Changing the split between train and test often resolves or creates this issue.

The output of the code is in three components: classification report, confusion matrix, and feature importance. We have discussed the interpretation of each of these earlier.

Identifying high-performing individuals and teams

Classification algorithms can be very useful to categorize employees into performance groups based on multi-dimensional data. This is likely to distinguish between employees with potential and those who are struggling with greater accuracy and objectivity.

There are multiple dimensions, including those below, over which a classification algorithm can categorize employees.

- **Performance level classification**: This approach would sort employees into performance tiers like those who exceeded, met, or remained below expectations. The categorization will be based on comprehensive data rather than the subjective discretion of the manager alone.

- **Performance direction classification:** This approach would identify employees with rising, stable, or declining performance trajectories. The current absolute performance level of the employees will not play any role here.
- **Potential classification:** This approach would distinguish between employees with high, moderate, or limited growth potential. The potential will be assessed based on their learning agility and adaptability indicators.
- **Fit classification:** Under this advanced approach, the tool will determine optimal role matches based on current performance patterns. Instead of reviewing the current role, the analysis will consider different types of assignments and responsibilities that the employee has gone through.

To achieve categorization using various dimensions, various classification techniques like Random Forests, support vector machines (SVM), KNN, gradient boosting classifiers, and ensemble methods, among others, can be used. These tools support various HR functions like performance benchmarking, resource allocation, leadership pipeline development, and so on. This is achieved by pinpointing not only who is currently performing well but also highlighting the conditions and the context of these performances.

Consider how a consulting firm can apply a decision tree classifier to categorize teams into high, moderate, and low-performance groups. The influencing variables, features as they are called, examined may include average project score, average training hours, collaboration score, and turnover rate. The resultant model can help senior leadership in allocating high-potential teams to strategic accounts. The code, apart from generating a classification report, confusion matrix, and feature importance, also identifies high-performance teams using a specified benchmark.

The code classifies the teams as high performers or not. In the last code, the employees were graded in three categories. Here it is binary: yes or no. Let us have a look at the main components of the code (prefix 0413).

- **Import libraries:** Libraries that are required are being loaded in this section. We have also used these libraries in earlier codes.
- **Customize:** Like the last code, we are providing values for the name of input data file, the features and target, and the name of the files to save the plot. Here is the section of the code with customizable parameters in italics, as usual.

```
# Customize parameters
my_input_file='0413 my_input.csv'
my_features = ['Avg_Project_Score', 'Avg_Training_Hours',
'Collaboration_Score', 'Turnover_Rate']
```

```
my_target = 'High_Performing_Team'
my_corr_plot = '0413 corr_plot.png'
my_feature_plot = '0413 feature_plot.png'
```

- **Load data and train classifier:** We start the section by loading the input data. We move on to creating a binary classification for performance level by providing benchmark values for each KPI. Have a look at the part of the code setting up the classification criterion.

```
conditions = (
    (data['Avg_Project_Score'] > 85) &
    (data['Collaboration_Score'] > 4.0) &
    (data['Turnover_Rate'] < 10)
)
```

  We specify the features and target for the `RandomForestClassifier` model. We split the input data into train and test components. We fit the model and use the fitted model to predict the score for a high-performing team.
- **Evaluate model:** Like the last code, we compute the classification table, confusion matrix, and feature importance. We continue to identify the high-performing teams based on the benchmarks specified. Against the high-performing teams, we displayed only the `Avg_Project_score` and the `Collaboration_Score`. If you want, you can add the other features in the code line `high_perf_teams = data.loc[model.predict(X) == 1, ['Team_ID', 'Avg_Project_Score', 'Collaboration_Score']]`.

The output of the code, as stated above, is the classification table, confusion matrix, and feature importance. The identification of the high-performance team is benchmark-based and self-explanatory.

Factors contributing to performance outcomes

It is essential to understand the factors that drive employee performance to design an effective development plan for the employees. ML techniques can be used to identify these factors through data-driven objective analysis.

There are various ways to approach performance factor analysis, including the following:

- **Feature importance ranking:** One of the approaches is to quantify the relative contribution of different factors to performance outcomes. These factors can range from technical skills to behavioral competencies.
- **Interaction effect detection:** Often, combinations of factors amplify or diminish performance beyond their individual effects. ML tools can identify these synergistic behaviors.

- **Contextual factor analysis:** Performance is not dependent on the competence of the individual alone. Environmental factors like team composition, leadership style, market conditions, and so on influence individual performance factors. ML tools can recognize these interactions and how they contribute to overall performance.
- **Temporal factor analysis:** Different performance factors evolve over an employee's tenure or career progression. They often explain why employee performance fluctuates over time. ML tools can recognize these temporal factors and integrate them into the performance prediction models.

Various ML tools help in understanding why certain employees perform better than others. This understanding is as important as predicting performance itself. ML tools, besides offering the capability to quantify feature importance, can extract interpretable rules that explain performance drivers.

Consider the case of a retail company that analyzes sales associate performance using a Random Forest Classifier. An analysis of feature importance may reveal that cross-training across product categories and regular attendance in weekly strategy meetings have the strongest influence on performance. This finding can be used to redesign training paths across all branches. While we have previously trained classifiers to predict performance, this case is about understanding the drivers of performance. Here we will interpret feature importance and identify patterns or relationships in the data that influence high performance. We have used these tools earlier, and the code is also similar, but lightweight. Additionally, we are using the output in management reporting. It is our end-use objective that is different. Let us have a quick look at the main components of the code (prefix 0414).

- **Import libraries:** By this time, you may know all the libraries that we are loading in this section. Though you will not need it here, just to remind you, if you do not have a library, you can always install it with the `pip` command. If you are executing the command from a notebook, it will be `! pip`.
- **Customize:** This code also needs similar inputs to be customized. That is the name of the input file, names of files to save plots to, a list of features and target, and the name of the file to save recommendations. Here is the code excerpt with the customizable parameters in italics.

```
# Customize parameters
my_input_file='0414 my_input.csv'
my_features = ['Project_Score', 'Training_Hours',
'Absenteeism_Rate', 'Peer_Feedback']
```

```
my_target = 'Performance_Level'
my_corr_plot = '0414 correl_plot.png'
my_feature_plot = '0414 feature_plot.png'
my_recommendation = '0414_hr_recommendations.csv'
```

- **Load data and train classifier:** Here, we have loaded the data into the system. We have classified the performance level into three groups: low (0), average (1), and high (3). We have defined the conditions for being classified in one of these three groups. You can always change the benchmark values in the code to change the classification criteria. The relevant section of the code is shown here.

```
conditions = [
   (data['Project_Score'] < 70) |
   (data['Peer_Feedback'] < 3.5),
   (data['Project_Score'].between(70, 85)) &
   (data['Peer_Feedback'] >= 3.5),
   (data['Project_Score'] > 85) &
   (data['Peer_Feedback'] >= 4.0)
]
```

We have split the data into train and test components. Subsequently, we have specified the features and target for the RandomForestClassifier model. The fitted model was used to extract feature importance; we have not made any predictions here.

- **Extract and visualize features:** We have extracted the feature importance from the fitted model and populated the correlation matrix from the input data. Both plots are also saved in specified files for future use. An executive summary is provided of the ranked features.
- **Management applications:** We are creating two functions that will use model output to assess promotion eligibility and training needs. The eligibility criteria are decided by the management and will be specified in the code. You will find the benchmark values stated in the code and can change those as per need. You can always include other criteria, too, but you will need to change the code to include those.
- **Management reports:** The functions defined in the earlier section are used to assess promotion eligibility and training needs. The top five results are displayed on screen as an extract. A summary report is also generated.
- **Save recommendations:** This section of the code creates a recommendation file with promotion eligibility and training needs stated against each employee. The file is saved in CSV format with a specified name. The short display of the top five entries is made as a sample.

The output from the code includes the feature importance plot and the correlation matrix. We have discussed these on earlier occasions. A short report of the ranked feature scores has also been displayed and is reproduced here.

```
Feature Ranking:
1.  Project_Score: 0.414
2.  Peer_Feedback: 0.403
3.  Absenteeism_Rate: 0.131
4.  Training_Hours: 0.053
```

A quick look at the results clarifies that the absenteeism rate and training hours do not contribute much to performance. So, our focus should be more on project score and peer feedback. This information can be used to identify performing employees as well as to spot potential. It may also lead to overhauling the attendance policy, as it is clear that though attendance is important, it does not contribute much to performance.

In addition, the output provides a report of promotional eligibility and training needs of each employee, along with their respective scores against each feature. A top-level summary of training needs against promotional eligibility is also presented. This summary shows the total number of employees requiring specific training against the promotional eligibility classifications. A management action summary is saved and partially displayed, showing the promotional eligibility and training needs against each employee ID.

Talent development and retention strategies

One of the most critical and expensive functions of the HR department includes targeted talent intervention. ML-augmented employee performance analysis provides powerful insights for HR teams to get the best return out of the investment. These insights would also help them to optimize the employee development plan and improve the retention of high-value employees.

ML tools help talent management in various ways, including the following:

- **Personalized development planning:** ML algorithms can recognize spheres where an employee needs support, keeping in mind the skill, competence, career path, and other features. This insight can be used to design customized development activities for each employee.

- **Retention risk prediction:** One of the major challenges that HR faces is employee retention and replacement. ML tools can reasonably identify employees at risk of leaving even before they actively begin job searching.
- **Development ROI optimization:** ML analysis can quantify the expected impact of different employee development activities. Though not accurate, the quantification can be used to optimize return from the limited resources allotted to employee development activities.
- **Team composition optimization:** It is a well-known fact that employee performance is often influenced by the team they are working in. ML algorithms can recommend team compositions based on skills, working styles, and performance patterns of employees.

ML tools can adopt various approaches depending on what the talent management system wants from them. These approaches would include developing a recommendation system, conducting survival analysis, identifying training needs, etc. One of the features that is often used in this application is the natural language processing ability of a system. The user can communicate with the system in a conversational style to get the output from the system.

The application of ML in HR is often layered. At a higher layer, ML outputs can directly support talent development, succession planning, or retention strategies. However, this outer layer needs support from an inner layer that is ready with the predictive models and performance drivers.

Let us look at a business case. Consider a financial services company building a system to predict performance levels and retention risk to identify training needs. The model outputs can be used to flag employees at various levels of performance potential and retention risk and prescribe targeted coaching for them. We did a similar exercise in the last section and are now proceeding with another business application of the same approach.

Let us have a look at the main components of the code (prefix 0415).

- **Import libraries:** As usual, all required libraries are imported here.
- **Customize:** We need to provide the names of the input file, the output report, and the features and target. Here is the relevant part of the code with the customizable values italicized.

```
# Customize parameters
my_input_file='0415 my_input.csv'
my_report_file='0415 hr_action.csv'
```

```
my_features = ['Project_Score', 'Training_Hours',
'Absenteeism_Rate', 'Peer_Feedback']
my_target = 'High_Potential'
my_pie_plot ='0415 recommendation_plot'
```

- **Load data and train model**: As earlier, we need to provide the number of classifications we need and the respective benchmarking parameters. Here we have created a binary classification labeled high potential. 1 denotes high potential, and 0 denotes any other classification but not high potential. The benchmark for being labeled as high potential is provided in this section of the code, and you may calibrate it as per the management policy.

```
conditions = (
   (data['Project_Score'] > 85) &
   (data['Peer_Feedback'] > 4.0) &
   (data['Training_Hours'] > 20)
)
```

  We feed the model with information on features and the target, following the protocol of splitting the input data into training and testing segments.
- **Fit model, predict potential, and check model performance**: We fit the model using the data and predict the potential of the employees from the entire data set. We have also tested model performance and reported the accuracy ratio, confusion matrix, and classification report on the screen. Note that we have not visualized the confusion matrix as a plot. You will find that wherever we have done that earlier, we have used the library `matplotlib, sklearn. and metrics.ConfusionMatrixDisplay` and `sklearn.metrics.confusion_matrix`. We have used text output here just as another way to see the matrix.
- **Flag retention risk and call to action**: The output of this section will be meaningful only when the model qualifies the evaluation criteria. We have defined retention risk as a binary output, 1 and 0 classified as having and not having retention risk, respectively. We have used benchmark values for the classification, and you can tweak the following code to align with your policy.

```
# Flag Retention Risk
   data['Retention_Risk'] = np.where(
   (data['Absenteeism_Rate'] > 4.0) &
   (data['Training_Hours'] < 10) &
   (data['Internal_Mobility'] == 0),
   1, 0
)
```

Table 4.2 Ruleset for action messages in code 0415

Potential	*Retention Risk*	*Action Returned*
1	1	"Prioritize for retention + leadership path"
1	0	"Recommend for development program"
0	1	"Alert: Retention intervention needed."
0	0	"Monitor regularly."

Once classified, we have created a function to generate action messages depending on the retention risk classification and predicted potential status. We have already predicted the potential status after fitting the model. Both these fields are binary, and we have created a ruleset to generate messages depending on various combinations of 1 and 0 values. Here is the ruleset that the code follows (Table 4.2).

We apply the rule to generate recommendations for each employee.

- **Generate output**: The output is displayed on the screen and saved in a CSV file under the specified name. This saves the rule-based recommendation against each employee ID. A pie chart showing the distribution of the recommendations is also presented and saved.

The output of the code comes in two parts. In the first part, the model evaluation metrics are presented. We have earlier discussed about confusion matrix and classification report. Here we have another parameter called Accuracy. This indicates how many predictions were correct out of all predictions made. Though it is easy to interpret, it is susceptible to unbalanced data. For example, if 90% of the employees are not high potential, the model is most likely to predict "not high potential," 90% of the time. This may be accurate from a modeling point of view, but it disregards the business reality. That is where the classification table and confusion matrix come into play.

The second part of the output is essentially a report of the recommendation. The management can filter the same and use it as an input to HR-related decisions like promotion, retention, succession, and allied. The pie chart gives a quick view of the recommendations made by the system.

Key takeaways

Performance is no longer restricted to financial numbers. Even the financial decision-makers are required to take note of performance measures that are essentially non-financial. ML can examine how various operational factors influence profit being a mere cost item. One can create a dashboard to display performance indicators in real time. These dashboards can also be customized to display parameters depending on the role selected by the user. In addition, ML tools can bring in insights to static data being displayed – all in real time. These dashboards can be hosted on local servers by the users themselves without much involvement of technical experts. Cluster analysis groups customers or products who behave in similar manner, thus enabling targeted interventions. Decision trees can explain the logic of segmentation or even a product purchase decision. Another interesting use of ML tools is in analysis of performance and identification of potential performers.

The financial decision-maker can use this information to better organizational performance.

Chapter 5

Strategic planning and decision support

Strategic decisions shape the long-term direction of an organization. In this chapter, we explore how ML tools can be applied to both quantitative and qualitative data to support such high-stake decisions. We demonstrate how we can make informed, forward-looking choices by integrating simulations, sentiment analysis, and predictive models.

Strategic financial decisions

Strategic decision-making involves making decisions with the future in mind.

It aims to achieve organizational goals by leveraging the dynamic environment. Strategic decision-making involves making choices that have a significant, long-term impact on an organization's direction, objectives, and performance. Unlike routine or operational decisions that focus on immediate concerns, strategic decisions are future-oriented and shape the overall direction of the business. Such decisions are usually characterized by the following:

- **Long-term focus**: These decisions look at the future, spanning years or even decades. They involve setting and continuously calibrating the organization's vision, mission, and strategic objectives.
- **Comprehensive analysis**: Strategic decisions require a thorough analysis of both internal and external environments. This typically involves analyzing strengths, weaknesses, opportunities, and threats (SWOT), market trends, competitive landscape, and resource availability. The decision-making seeks to optimize the organization's benefits within various constraints.
- **Resource commitment**: These decisions necessarily entail committing resources necessary to achieve goals. These resources would include time, financial, human, and technological commitments.

DOI: 10.4324/9781003619628-5

- **Risk and uncertainty:** Strategic decisions are made under conditions of uncertainty where outcomes are not guaranteed. They involve risk assessment, where the potential benefits are weighed against the potential downsides. Scenario planning and forecasting are used to view different combinations of future possibilities.
- **Stakeholder consideration:** Strategic decisions potentially affect multiple stakeholders, including shareholders, other investors, employees, customers, suppliers, and the community at large. Negotiating and balancing these interests is a key part of strategic decision-making.
- **Leadership and vision:** Strategic decisions require leadership that can visualize future possibilities, convince stakeholders, and guide the organization through change. It also requires the adaptability of all players to welcome and integrate change.

You can see that strategic decision-making is about making choices today that will define the organization's position tomorrow. It involves charting the course toward predefined goals, and navigating through uncertainty. This demands a blend of analytical skills, foresight, and leadership.

Strategic decision-making uses data-driven insights to improve the accuracy and effectiveness of these decisions. Advanced analytics, ML, and AI empower the organization to process vast amounts of data to uncover trends and forecast potential outcomes. These allow the decision-maker to identify opportunities and risks. After decision-making, these insights provide an evidence-based control tool that would realign the decisions based on real-time data.

Strategic decision-making processes and influencing factors

If you are engaged in the strategic decision-making process, one of your initial tasks would be to identify the key factors that could impact the decision's outcome. Additionally, it is important to recognize that there may be separate factors that influence how the decision-making process unfolds.

Let us have a look at how the process would generally work. Mind you, this is not a one-size-fits-all blueprint.

- **Define the objectives:** The first step is to decide what the entity wishes to achieve. Is it the best product, best customer service, fastest profit growth, best investor return, or others? There would also be a time frame within which these objectives should be attained.
- **Scan the environment:** The internal and external environment in which the business operates plays a critical role in decision-making. The external influencing factors would include, among others, market dynamics,

technological evolution, regulatory changes, and competitive pressure. The internal factors would include organizational capabilities, resource availability, corporate culture, and leadership vision. If the strategic objective is to become a market leader, it is essential to assess the competitive intensity within the industry. We would also need to evaluate whether necessary inputs such as raw material, skilled manpower, or production capacity are available and accessible. These become practical constraints that define what is achievable under current circumstances. Given the pace of change, strategic decisions must also account for uncertainty and remain adaptable. An effective strategy also considers the perspectives of key stakeholders, ensuring alignment between internal ambitions and external expectations.

- **Design alternatives**: Once the environmental scanning process is complete, one can generate different alternatives. To be a market leader, one can increase their share in the existing market, expand to a different market, launch a new product, or even decide to invest in a new product and seek to be a market leader with the new product.
- **Evaluate alternatives**: The strategic alternatives that have been developed now require thorough evaluation. To do this effectively and select the most appropriate option, we must first establish a set of evaluation criteria. These may include technical and economic feasibility, cost-effectiveness, alignment with organizational goals and values, risk exposure, and the organization's risk appetite. At this stage, it is also important to recognize the influence of psychological and behavioral factors. Cognitive biases and group dynamics can subtly shape the evaluation process, often steering decisions toward familiar or comfortable choices for the decision-makers. However, such options may not always represent the most optimal or strategic alternative. A conscious effort is needed to mitigate these biases and ensure a more objective assessment.
- **The selection**: Intertwined with the evaluation process is the selection from the alternatives. It is important to document the selection criteria along with the underlying assumptions, which may be useful during future realignment needs. The selection can be based on a simple hurdle rate, for example, highest profitability subject to a minimum value. It can have more complex criteria like a weighted evaluation where each criterion is assigned a weight, and the decision is based on the weighted score. We will discuss this in greater detail in the next section.
- **Implement, monitor, and realign**: Once selected, the chosen strategy is implemented. This involves deciding on the KPIs that will act as triggers for the control function. Monitoring will also include changes in the internal and external environment, which may force realigning the strategy with the revised reality.

There are numerous examples of how the process of strategic decision-making has influenced the future of an organization. Apple leveraged its competence to develop its silicon chips, giving it greater room for customization and consequently product differentiation. Netflix moved from DVD rentals to streaming services, capitalizing on the growth of handheld devices and customers' shifting preference for personal viewing space on a smaller screen. In contrast, Kodak, despite being an early innovator in digital photography, failed to pivot away from its traditional focus on film, ultimately losing its industry leadership. Microsoft's acquisition of Nokia's mobile business offers another cautionary tale. The company underestimated key factors such as customer operating system preferences, cultural differences in software design, and challenges of hardware integration. These oversights led to a $7.6 billion write-off, underscoring the high cost of strategic misalignment.

As these examples show, strategic decision-making is complex and multi-dimensional. Understanding the steps involved and the internal and external factors that influence each step is essential. This is where ML and AI can provide tremendous value. Not only can these tools support more data-driven, objective decision-making, but they can also help uncover hidden patterns and influencing variables that may not be immediately obvious through traditional analysis. For example, AI can be used to simulate strategic scenarios, assess risk exposure, or forecast customer behavior based on historical trends. ML models can identify leading indicators of market shifts or flag cognitive biases in past decisions, enabling organizations to learn and adapt.

In essence, the strategic use of AI/ML tools is not just about automating parts of the process, it is about enhancing the quality and foresight of decision-making itself. However, this requires a clear understanding of what needs to be solved and which tools are best suited for the job. After all, choosing the right AI tool itself is a strategic decision.

Making choices from among available alternatives

Identifying alternatives is one part of the strategic decision-making process. The other part, which is as important, involves choosing from the available alternatives. This process is further complicated by the fact that the decision is heavily influenced by the selection criteria. This is why the selection of the criteria becomes critical and draws heavily from domain expertise. We need to relate the criteria to the ultimate strategic objective. A well-designed choice framework will ensure that all alternatives have been properly evaluated without any bias. It will also set the foundation for using ML and AI-based tools. The decision criteria can be both quantitative and qualitative.

- **Quantitative decision-making:** These tools are objective and use a quantitative value for selecting among various options. A common criterion is an expected value analysis, where the expected value from each alternative is computed and the best among these is selected. There may even be minimum value criteria. A common application of this would be using the internal rate of return technique for investment decisions. One would select the alternative with the highest internal rate of return, subject to that being above a hurdle rate. The selection may be based on a single criterion or multiple criteria. Under multi-criteria decision-making, the decision is based on the values of different criteria. A final score may be obtained in the form of a simple or weighted average of the individual scores. A multi-criteria decision may include potential cost savings, increased market share, increase in investors' return, and similar. There may be cases where the multi-criteria decision model may include both quantitative and qualitative components.
- **Qualitative decision-making:** Not all selection criteria would be quantitative. Often, decisions involve behavioral aspects or perceptions that are difficult to quantify. This would include sentiments, views on strategic fit, or perceptions about changes in government policies. The value paid by Microsoft for the acquisition of LinkedIn or by Meta for the acquisition of WhatsApp was not solely because of quantitative criteria. The value also includes the perception of strategic fit and the evolution of social media as a revenue generator. Interestingly, there are tools available that can use these qualitative criteria as input to a decision-making model.

ML and AI-based tools are not only used to arrive at a decision. They can also be used to identify the criteria themselves. These tools can be applied to a historical data set to establish which factors are potentially influencing the outcome. The use of technology can narrow down the choices to a few, and this makes the selection process more structured and objective. Scenario analysis is an important tool that allows the decision-maker to visualize the impact of different scenarios on the strategic decision. For example, investment companies can use a Monte Carlo simulation to evaluate how asset allocation decisions will fare under various market conditions. Decision trees are diagrams that document the logical flow of a decision-making process, showing the alternatives that exist at each decision point. They are a great tool to visualize the impact of each alternative and to compute the expected value for each decision path. Cost-benefit analysis is one of the most used and time-tested tools to select among alternatives. We will be looking at some of these tools later in this section.

No matter what approach we take or what tools we use, we must identify the parameters that would be used to measure the performance of the strategic decision. For example, even in the relatively simple tool of cost-benefit analysis, we need to decide what counts as a benefit. Increased sales may lead to higher accounts receivable, thus questioning whether it can be viewed as an unqualified benefit. The abundance of alternative analytical tools often leads to decision paralysis, wherein we fail to decide in the face of varied results from different tools.

The abundance of data often leads to our anchoring the decision solely on the results of the analysis, overriding long-standing success factors. It is like changing an age-old logo solely based on better visual attributes, overlooking the brand association with the old logo. For example, a political party is split into two factions, each faction seeks to get the old party symbol, as the voters are familiar with the old symbol.

How simulation helps in making better strategic choices

Simulation involves building models to anticipate the outcomes of strategic decisions across various real-world scenarios. It also enables organizations to evaluate and compare the potential impact of alternative strategies. Strategic decisions try to prepare an organization for the future, more specifically, for future uncertainties.

Often, the decision-makers zero in on one or two possibilities and design the decision framework around them. This does not mean that they lack understanding of the other possibilities. This was often driven by the technical feasibility of considering multiple scenarios. In the bargain, the organization does not get a view of the impact of various scenarios, which may be unveiled in the future.

ML and AI-powered tools have enhanced the ability of financial decision-makers to use simulation techniques. These tools work by accepting a defined range of values for key inputs and assumptions. They then generate multiple combinations of these input values to simulate a variety of real-world scenarios. As a result, decision-makers can explore a wide spectrum of potential outcomes and better understand the risks and opportunities associated with different strategies.

Let us consider that your organization is launching a new product, and your projections indicate an 18% return on sales under normal circumstances. You decided to conduct a scenario analysis and use simulation as a tool to create these scenarios. You identified the sales volume, sales price, and cost of goods as three input variables. You have also provided a range of possible values for these three inputs and have specified that you need 50 possible values for each of the inputs. The tool will generate these values and combine them to create scenarios, that is, 125,000 scenarios in total (50 × 50 × 50). Assume that you found that 75 of these scenarios result in a loss. This would mean that there is a 0.06% probability of a loss from the new product. Now we have a better view of the future. We would go ahead with the launch if we were willing to accept a 0.06% probability of a loss against an expected gain of 18%.

The benefits of using simulation in the decision-making process would include the following:

- **Better risk management**: We get a better understanding of probabilities associated with different levels of return and corresponding risks.
- **Improved decision quality**: We can decide with greater clarity when we have an idea of the range of possible scenarios that may evolve in the future.
- **Better planning and adaptability**: With an idea of what is likely and what is not, we can allocate resources and maintain reserves for different situations.
- **Identification of key drivers and sensitivities**: It helps pinpoint which input variables have the greatest impact on outcomes. For example, sensitivity analysis may show that customer churn rate is the most critical driver of profitability in a subscription-based model.

Market trend analysis with sentiment analysis

Sentiment analysis is an important tool to assess public opinion, market sentiment, consumer behavior, and the like. This is a subfield of NLP focused on extracting and quantifying subjective information from text data. Most commonly, it classifies the tone of the content as negative, neutral, or positive. Sentiment analysis can have a dictionary-based approach or an ML-based approach.

- **Dictionary-based approach**: Under this approach, the object content is scanned against a dictionary of words that have been given a sentiment score ranging from positive to negative. For example, "satisfied" = +0.75, "disappointed" = (–) 0.6, and so on. The algorithm aggregates the sentiment scores of the words and determines the sentiment of a sentence. Though it is simple to use, it does not capture the context or creative usage.
- **ML-based approach**: Here, dictionaries are not used, and the system identifies the sentiment patterns from labeled training data. In labeled training data, texts come with sentiment labels. These tools use statistical features like frequency and different linguistic patterns to determine sentiment. The disadvantage of the approach is that this requires training data, and the quality of the output is defined by the accuracy of the labeling of the training data.

Sentiment analysis can be useful in predicting market trends, assessing brand image, measuring the success of a customer-centric program, and allied. Various tools can be used for sentiment analysis, and we will apply a few of those in the next section.

Assesses market sentiments that could impact strategic decisions

We have all noticed that the strategic decision-making process involves dealing with uncertainty. One of the major factors that contributes to the uncertainty is the market sentiment. The problem is aggravated because sentiment is subjective, and an output of a complex mental process is difficult to anticipate, let alone quantify. The sentiment analysis tools seek to quantify the sentiment. Once quantified, we can use those values to test whether they affect the strategic decision, and if they do, we can try to quantify the impact. For example, we can try to relate how much sales are affected if the customer sentiment score shifts by 5 points.

Sentiment analysis can be useful in various types of strategic decision-making, including the following.

- **Investment decisions:** These decisions are mostly taken using financial analysis techniques. However, sentiments often play a major role in investment decisions. Blending sentiment with traditional financial analysis can provide a layer of psychological insight into market behavior. While using sentiment analysis tools in investment decisions, we must note that it is difficult to assign causality between sentiment and investment decisions. Investment decision models using sentiments as an influencing factor must ensure a minimum level of consistent causal relation between these two.
- **Product launches:** Another common area of application of sentiment analysis is the timing of product launches. Companies often assess market sentiment to determine the optimal timing for introducing new products, aiming to maximize customer engagement and sales impact. For example, souvenir shops selling team merchandise may extend their operating hours to capitalize on the positive public mood after a home team defeats a traditional rival. Similarly, political leaders may time the launch of new campaigns or even the formation of new parties based on prevailing voter sentiment, using such insights to align with public opinion and enhance their appeal.
- **Regulatory compliance:** Industries that are highly regulated face public backlash in the event of non-compliance. If environmental agencies brand a company as non-compliant with environmental regulations, adverse public sentiments are likely to cause lower sales. These sentiments can be identified from comments on corporate websites, social

media postings, customer feedback, newspaper reports, and similar media.

There is no doubt that sentiments are a critical input variable. The challenge is how do we quantify them? Under the ML environment, we have libraries and functions that can be used for sentiment analysis. These tools are to be used with caution as they follow a specified approach to sentiment analysis. We need to keep in mind the approach adopted by our tool before we interpret and act upon the results.

Sentiment analysis on news articles and social media posts

Let us now see how ML tools are used for sentiment analysis. We will review two applications of the sentiment analysis tool. One for feedback in a CSV format, and another to analyze sentiment from a PDF document. One can use similar codes to query various websites and conduct sentiment analysis. However, we have not included those here as they may involve legal and copyright issues.

A note of caution on using ML tools for sentiment analysis. Sentiment analysis tools are designed to analyze texts to determine the sentiment expressed within them, generally classifying it as positive, negative, or neutral. These are very useful for quickly assessing the emotional tone behind large volumes of text. However, these tools also have their limitations. A major one is their dependency on predefined lexicons and rule-based systems. This may lead to inaccuracies when dealing with complex sentiments, satire, or irony that deviate from their training data. These tools also struggle with context-dependent meanings, sarcasm, and cultural nuances that humans naturally understand. This may lead to misinterpretations of the sentiment, especially in multicultural and multilingual settings. Have a look at the documentation of the tools before using them.

Sentiment analysis using a feedback file

In this section, we will conduct a sentiment analysis of feedback that is stored in a CSV file. The code is available at the repository (prefix 0501), and you can download the same. You can customize the code to your needs by changing a few values. The code is split into the following sections.

- **Import libraries**: In this section, the required libraries are being loaded. You will find we are loading `pandas`, `nltk`, `textblob`, and `matplotlib`. The library `nltk` is an NLP library. Within this library, "`stopwords`" provides a list of words that do not contribute to sentiment; "`word_tokenize`" splits text into individual words, and

`'SentimentIntensityAnalyzer'` is a sentiment analysis tool. The library `textblob` is another NLP library for sentiment analysis.

- **Download required data:** Here, the dataset required for Natural Language Toolkit (`NLTK`) is downloaded. These include `"stopwords,"` a list of common words to filter out; `"punkt,"` which is a tokenizer that helps break text into words; and `"vader_lexicon,"` which is a predefined dictionary for sentiment scoring. Once you have run this section, you do not need to download these files every time. You may mark the section as "Markdown" while checking it from time to time to check for updates.
- **Customize:** In this section, we will customize the names of our input and output files in CSV format,
  - o Name of the input file having the feedback
  - o Name of the output file where the sentiment scores will be stored
  - o Name of the column that stores the text response in the input file for feedback.

  The relevant lines of code with the values we need to provide are italicized below.

```
# customize your application

#name of the file where you have feedback data in CSV
format
myfile='0501 feedback.csv'

#name of the file to save sentiment score in CSV format
my_feedback='0501 feedback_with_sentiment.csv'

# name of the column where feedback is stored
feedback_column='text_column'
```

- **Load and preprocess data:** The code reads the file with the feedback report. The preprocessing involves various manipulations to make the input ready for analysis. For example, special characters and punctuation are removed, words are converted to lowercase, texts are split into words (tokenized), and stopwords like "is," "the," "and," and similar are removed.
- **Sentiment analysis using VADER and `TextBlob`:** In this section, the sentiment scores are computed after analyzing the cleaned text. Respective models are used to arrive at the sentiment scores. In the case of Valence Aware Dictionary and Sentiment Reasoner (VADER), sentiment scores are computed, and a compound score is arrived at. The score remains between –1.0 (most negative) and +1.0 (most positive). Neutral is designated by a score range of –0.5 to +0.5. VADER is lexicon-based and uses a predefined dictionary of words with sentiment scores. `TextBlob`

returns a polarity score where a score above zero is positive, a score below zero is negative, and scores close to zero are neutral. It uses an ML-based approach to sentiment analysis and relies on a pre-trained dataset to evaluate sentiment polarity. It can also award a subjectivity score ranging from 0 (objective) to 1 (subjective), though we have not used the feature here.

- **Identify negative feedback**: This section extracts feedback that VADER classified as strongly negative (score <–0.5) and displays the same.
- **Plot VADER/`TextBlob` sentiment score**: Creates a histogram showing how the customer feedback is distributed across sentiment scores. If the graph leans toward the left, the feedback is mostly negative, while a right-leaning graph shows predominantly positive feedback.
- **Save results in CSV file**: This section stores the original feedback with the VADER and `TextBlob` sentiment scores.

Sentiment analysis using a PDF file

There are times when we would want to conduct sentiment analysis from a file, for example, a PDF file. These files may be a press statement, an investment analysis, or even feedback. This code (prefix 0502), available in the repository, does exactly that. As mentioned earlier, you can change a few values to customize this to your needs. The code is divided into the following segments.

- **Import libraries**: As earlier, in this section, we will load the libraries necessary to conduct sentiment analysis. `PyPDF2` library extracts text from PDF files. We have used the other libraries in the earlier section.
- **Download required data**: We download the datasets required for `NLTK` as we have described in the earlier section. Hope you have noted that if you have run this section once, you do not need to run this code every time. You may mark the section as 'Markdown' and check from time to time for updates.
- **Customize**: In this section, we will customize the names of our input and output files in CSV format,
    - Name of the input file for sentiment analysis
    - Name of the output file where we will store the sentiment scores.

The following are the lines of the relevant section of the code, with the values we need to provide italicized.

```
#name of the PDF file you want to analyze
myfile='0502 prime-mmfs-onset-pandemic.pdf'

#name of the file to save sentiment score in CSV format
my_feedback='0502 pdf_feedback_with_sentiment.csv'
```

- **Read and extract text from a PDF file:** We are creating a function to be used to read a PDF file and extract text from all its pages. We have used `PyPDF2.PDFReader` to loop through all the pages and extract text.
- **Preprocess and split text:** This section removes special characters and numbers, converts text to lowercase for uniformity, tokenizes words using `word_tokenize()`, removes stopwords (common words like "the," "and," "in"), and finally splits the text into sentences for analysis. These split sentences are used for sentiment analysis, and you can see them in the final output saved as a CSV file.
- **Sentiment analysis with VADER and `TextBlob`:** In this section, the sentiment scores are computed for each of the split texts. We have already discussed how VADER and `TextBlob` work. Just to add on to what we have stated earlier, VADER is considered better for short texts, while TextBlob is for long texts.
- **Create a dataframe and display negative sentiments:** This section creates a dataframe to store the cleaned sentence, the VADER sentiment score, and the TextBlob sentiment score. The sentences marked as these with negative sentiment are displayed for a quick on-screen review.
- **Plot VADER and `TextBlob` sentiment scores:** The sentiment scores generated by VADER and `TextBlob` are plotted as a histogram. This will allow us to understand the frequency distribution of sentiment scores.
- **Save text and sentiment scores:** Finally, the split text and sentiment scores are saved in the specified CSV file.

A word of caution: Please ensure that you have permission to use the PDF file you select for sentiment analysis.

Sentiment scores and market movements

One very interesting application of sentiment score would be to examine the sentiment scores with major market movements. The influence of social media, news articles, and other textual data sources now extends to investment decisions. The ability to quantify sentiment and correlate it with market behavior can be a crucial tool for financial decision-makers.

We have seen in the earlier section that sentiment analysis involves processing textual data to extract emotional signals. In the context of financial markets, the volume of data increases significantly, and market sentiment may dictate future market movements. These signals can range from simple positive, negative, and neutral classifications to more nuanced emotional states like uncertainty, confidence, or fear.

Let us see how we can understand if there is any relation between sentiment and market movement. Please note that we are not suggesting that there is any causation; we are trying to see if their movements correspond and show any pattern of correlation.

In an earlier section, we used a feedback file as an import and computed sentiment score using VADER and `TextBlob`. We will use a similar file as input. The input file has five columns named date, headline, sentiment scores under VADER and `TextBlob`, and the price of the asset corresponding to the date. Table 5.1 shows the structure of the input file. All data used here is hypothetical.

As usual, the code (prefix 0503) is broken in the following sections:

- **Import Libraries:** The new library we have used here is `Seaborn`. This is built on top of `Matplotlib` to provide statistical visualizations. If it is not installed in your system, please install it.
- **Customize:** We will provide three values in the customization section, names of input and output files in CSV format, the number of days for price change computation, and the name of the graphics file to save the correlation heatmap. The following are the codes for customization with the input values italicized.

```
# Specify the input CSV file
file_path = "0503 feedback_sentiment.csv"

# Specify the number of days for price change computation
num_days = 5
```

Table 5.1 Structure of input file

Date	*Headline*	*vader_sentiment*	*textblob_sentiment*	*Close*
01-08-24	"Company beats earnings expectations"	0	0	14576
04-08-24	"New product launch receives critical acclaim"	−0.3182	0.068182	14567
05-08-24	"Minor operational issues reported"	0	−0.05	14567
06-08-24	"Company on track to meet yearly targets"	0	0	14568
07-08-24	"Market volatility impacts quarterly revenue"	0	0	14577
08-08-24	"Strong consumer demand for core product"	0.4215	0.433333	14641

```
# Specify the output CSV file
final_output_path ="0503 final_sentiment_market_data.csv"

# Specify the name of the graphics file to save the
heatmap
heatmap_path = "0503 correlation_heatmap.png"
```

- **Load and clean data:** This is a critical section of the code where we are loading the data and cleaning it for further processing. We are forcing the date to be in a uniform format, failing which the record is removed. We are forcing all values in the "Close" column to be numeric. We are then selecting only the date and numerical fields, as we cannot use text values for correlation computation. Further, if any row has a blank value in one of the columns, we are removing the row. Finally, we are computing the price change using the number of days provided and storing the data in the specified CSV file. The data can be used for various purposes and can also be used for auditing the code.
- **Compute price change and save file:** In this section, the price change has been computed over the period specified by you in the customization section. The data is then saved in a CSV file for external use and audit.
- **Compute correlation:** This is the computation engine that computes the correlation between three variables, two sentiment scores, and the price change. We will have nine correlations (3 × 3), however, do note that the correlation of a variable with itself is 1. Of the remaining six, three are mirror images of the other three. The correlation coefficient of the VADER score with the closing price and that between the closing price and VADER is the same.
- **Print and visualize correlation matrix:** In this section, we are displaying the correlation matrix on the screen. You can see all cells in the diagonal having a value of 1, and the sides above and below the diagonal are a mirror image. We are also displaying the heatmap for better visualization and saving the heatmap as a graphic, for subsequent use. You will see that the heatmap is color-coded, and the gradient of the color changes as the correlation changes.

A quick word on the correlation coefficient. The coefficient correlation quantifies the strength and direction of the linear relationship between two variables. In our context, this measures how closely sentiment scores align with actual market performance.

This metric ranges from –1 to +1, where –1 indicates a perfect negative correlation, +1 indicates a perfect positive correlation, and 0 suggests no linear relationship. Please note that correlation coefficients only capture linear relationships based on the data provided and do not imply causation.

A strong correlation between sentiment and price movements does not necessarily mean sentiment drives those changes.

Anticipates market shifts and adjusts strategies

In the last section, although we computed the correlation between sentiment scores and changes in asset price, we did not imply any causation. However, leveraging sentiment analysis from social media and press reports to anticipate market shifts has become a valuable tool in the hands of financial decision-makers. In other words, we are using market sentiment as a lead indicator. There are various ML tools that we have discussed and will discuss in subsequent sections to evaluate a model that uses sentiment scores as an influencer of market sentiment. In this context, we need to be careful about the sentiment triggers that we are using. For example, if we are trying to anticipate changes in the price of a single asset, we should reckon that this may be affected by specific asset-based sentiment, industry-based sentiment, and market-based sentiment. Our research should cover all the major possibilities and select the appropriate one. We must be open to the possibility that the best among the options examined may not be appropriate. This would simply mean that sentiment scores are not good lead indicators.

Considering that we find specific evidence of sentiment score, how do we adjust our investment strategies? Here are a few options:

- **Adjust the portfolio**: Financial decision-makers can rebalance their portfolio by adding investments that are showing stronger positive sentiment and reducing investments associated with reducing sentiment scores. Please note that this holds as well for product portfolios. A businessperson decides to stock materials having a favorable customer response, be it food items on the menu card, colors in the ready-made garment industry, or fuel that a car uses.
- **Sentiment-based risk management**: If sentiment scores are proven to be good lead indicators, they can be used to decide on hedging through derivatives or rebalancing assets.
- **Algorithmic trading or decision models**: Sentiment scores can become a major input to models that manage algorithmic trading or make a decision. A buy order may be triggered by a positive trend in sentiment scores and can be a useful input in a default prediction model.

However, one should consider the following while using sentiment scores as a factor in decision-making:

- **The weight**: One may find that different sentiment scores have different degrees of influence on the direction of the market. The price of an asset may be influenced by asset-based sentiment, industry-based sentiment, and market-based sentiment, though by different degrees.

- **Time window:** It is important to define what constitutes a change in sentiment. This would depend on the time frame. Movement between two successive days may not be a good indicator, while movement between seven days may be useful. You need to review the past data and identify the time frame that works best. You may change the period over which the return is being computed and find one that gives you the best results.
- **Correlation thresholds:** Another important parameter to be decided is the value of the correlation coefficient that we will consider significant. Should we consider 0.7 as significantly positive, or should that be 0.8 and above? We may need to experiment with various values to arrive at an acceptable value. Once we define what is significant, and depending on the approach adopted, we can either include it in the model or examine it for causality.

One of the ways to check if the sentiment scores have a future-looking property is to introduce a lag factor. We have altered the code used in the last section to bring in a lag between the change in the sentiment score and the closing price (prefix 0504).

We have added the following code in the customization section to specify the value.

```
#Specify the number of days lag between sentiment score and
price change

lag_day=1
```

Corresponding changes have also been made in the code section to compute price changes and save the file. You can use the code to see if there is any progress over the last results. You can also change the lag values to see the impact.

A quick reminder, we are only checking correlation and not causation. We can only comment on whether the sentiment score with lag has a better correlation with the price changes.

Investment appraisal using Monte Carlo simulations

One of the most critical decision-making processes in finance is investment appraisal. We can loosely categorize investments into two: one as capital assets and the other as monetary assets. Capital assets can be characterized as those assets that are used in the process of generating returns. This would include plant and machinery, real estate for rentals, intangible assets, and allied. They get consumed in the process. Monetary assets are those that generate income primarily because of market forces or a contract enforceable by law. Thus, the return comes in two ways: capital gains driven by market forces and regular returns driven by a contract.

In cases of investments in capital assets, we generally use techniques like internal rate of return (IRR), net present value (NPV), payback period, and others to identify investment-worthy opportunities. In our regular usage, we compute these values using a set of static assumptions when all investment parameters are fraught with uncertainty. These parameters include cash flow, time of cash flow, discounting rate, and allied.

In cases of monetary assets, we try to establish a relation between market forces and capital gain. The strength of these market forces is uncertain, and they will affect the return. Usually, we take a static proxy value and compute the expected return.

These parameters include inflation, interest rates, currency conversion rates, and values of alternative investments, among others.

Monte Carlo simulation is used to forecast uncertain returns by simulating a range of possible scenarios using a probability distribution. The name of the approach comes from the famous Monte Carlo casino, a place characterized by its reliance on randomness. Like in the casino, any value is possible from a range of values. In the simulation, a range of possible values is determined. This determination itself is a process that depends on the probability distribution. The users merely supply the data and define the extent of certainty they want. They cannot influence the process, and consequently, the values generated are random.

To conduct a basic Monte Carlo simulation, the user will have to go through at least these steps as described here:

- **Model setup:** At this stage, we will define the input variables. These are the variables that are likely to influence the return from the investment. One can use historical data or even expert judgment to identify these variables. Once these variables have been identified, a model will be developed based on the interplay of these variables. This will form the basis of the Monte Carlo simulation. We will also define the number of times the simulation function will run.
- **Model activation:** Once the simulation model is defined, we will activate the model. Upon activation, for every run, each parameter will assume different values from within a range. We will end up having the number of specified simulated scenarios, each having a unique set of values across the parameters. The total number of simulations, as we have seen earlier, will be the number of values each parameter can assume, raised to the power of the number of parameters. If we have seven parameters and each parameter can have five different values, the total number of scenarios possible is $5^7 = 78{,}125$. We may or may not use all possible combinations

and can specify a lesser number, say 25,000 scenarios. If we ask for more than 78,125 simulations, we will have some repeated combinations.
- **Interpretation**: The final step of the Monte Carlo simulation is interpretation. We can create a histogram from the simulated results to understand the likelihood of various returns. We can use percentiles like 5th, 50th, and 95th percentile values to understand the worst-case, normal-case, and best-case scenarios.

In any Monte Carlo simulation application, data quality and model complexity will play a major role in determining the accuracy and performance of the model. Once run properly, this is a great tool for risk quantification. The investment appraiser gets a better understanding of the risk-return trade-off possibilities.

Using ML tools to perform Monte Carlo simulations

Let us use two different ML tools to apply a Monte Carlo simulation with past returns from an investment and compute future returns. We will first perform a simple Monte Carlo simulation based on historical returns, and in the second, we will use a specialized tool for Monte Carlo simulation.

Simple Monte Carlo simulation

Here we use a simple stochastic model based on a normal distribution of returns. We obtain a database of quoted prices of an investment for a period and compute the periodic return for the investment. Using the distribution of the return, we simulate a large number of possible returns for the same period. When we apply the range of return to the closing value, we will get the range of possible future market prices of the investment. This distribution will allow us to find the probability of different market prices that the investment may achieve. Note that we are not considering any other factors that may influence the market prices of the assets invested. Let us now have a detailed look at the code (prefix 0505).

As usual, the code is divided into sections. By this time, you must have understood the purpose and functionalities of some of the sections, and we will be omitting discussing them. You can go to earlier chapters to have a look if needed.

- **Import libraries:** We have used two common libraries here, as we are using a downloaded file for this section. If you want to download data, you may use a library called `yfinance`. This library accesses financial data from Yahoo Finance. You may need to install it using the command `pip install yfinance`. You can use any other library of your choice. Just ensure that you know the data structure and change a few field names in the code, if they are different. You may also need to change the

Table 5.2 Format of data

Date	Close	High	Low	Open	Volume

code to download the data. As stated earlier, we have used a previously downloaded file. The structure of the file is given in Table 5.2, and if you provide new data in the same format, you will not need to change any code. We have only used the 'Close' data here and have retained the structure if you want to use some other price. This is also the most common format in which you will get the data.

- **Customize**: We can specify a few of the parameters of the code to customize it to our application. In this case, we will be customizing the following parameters.
  - Name of the files where we have the raw data, processed and cleaned data, and results of the simulation.
  - The number of days for which the return is to be computed. Keep in view the total number of days for which you have downloaded data.
  - The number of times you want to simulate return values.
  - The lower and upper confidence levels, which will be used to search for a price target for a level of probability.

The following are the lines of the relevant section of the code, with the values we need to provide italicized.

```
# Provide name of the CSV file to save/load the raw data
my_raw_data='0505 simulation_raw_data.csv'

# Provide name of the CSV file to save the clean data
my_clean_data= '0505 simulation_clean_data.csv'

# Provide name of the CSV file to save the clean data
my_simulated_data='0505 simulation_values.csv'

# Provide number of days over which return is to be
computed
return_days=10

# Provide the number of simulation runs
simulation_runs=10000

# Provide and lower and upper confidence levels
my_lower_limit=2.5
my_upper_limit=97.5
```

- **Load raw data and compute return:** In this section, the raw data file is loaded, whether downloaded presently or earlier. The periodic returns are also computed at this stage. The code uses "Close" values for computing return. In case your file has a different field name, please change it here. You can also decide how many days' return you want to compute, a one-day return, a ten-day return, or others. You can specify the same in the customization section. Another interesting aspect you may find is that we have used a log function while computing the return. Though we could have used a normal return, a log return has some advantages. One of the advantages is that in cases of large fluctuations, log returns are more symmetric and stable. Though we have not used it here, log returns are time-additive. If we have daily log returns, we can sum them to get monthly log returns. One of the greatest advantages is that log returns help in preventing negative forecast prices, as long as the previous price was positive.
- **Clean up and save data:** Once we compute the return, we will clean up the data for any missing values. While we may not have any missing values in the downloaded dataset, we will have missing values while computing the return. If we are computing for a one-day return, there will be no return for the first day. If we are computing a ten-day return, we will not have any return for the first ten days. In this section, we remove all data with any blank values. Once cleaned, we save the data in the specified CSV file. This file saves only date, adj close, and return values.
- **Load data and simulate:** We load the data from the saved file. Technically, we need not load the data from the saved file but have done so to maintain modularity. In case you have a file with returns computed, you can simply import the libraries and then run this module. This module uses the arithmetic mean and standard deviation of the return to simulate the number of specified values. Each of these values is generated randomly without any reference to the past value.
- **Compute simulated values:** Flowing from the earlier section, the simulated return values are applied to the latest price available to arrive at the range of possible future prices. You would see that since the returns were log returns, we have used an exponential function to get the price. Now we have the specified number of possible future values. Please note that these target values are linked to the period we specified while computing the return. Hence, the simulated prices represent possible values after the number of days specified while computing the return.
- **Save simulated values:** Here, we save the simulated return and simulated values in a CSV file for future use.
- **Print results:** This module prints the result of the simulation. It states the target values against a lower and upper range of probability. The lower level shows the probability of the price going lower than the stated

price. Similarly, the higher level shows the price which is unlikely to be bettered at the associated level of probability.

Library function for Monte Carlo simulation

We will now use a library called `QuantLib` to perform a Monte Carlo simulation. We will try to simulate and predict values for several days in the future. In the last case, we predicted different values for the same day. Now we will try to simulate different daily values over a period. For example, 1,000 different possible values for each of the next 100 days.

Let us have a quick look at the code, which you can find in the code repository (prefix 0506). As usual, we have broken the code into sections.

- **Import libraries**: The new library we have downloaded here is `QuantLib`. This library is designed for quantitative finance and provides a framework for pricing financial instruments, risk management, Monte Carlo simulations, and stochastic processes. You may need to install it using the command `pip install QuantLib`. There are other libraries too, and you may use them after making suitable changes to the code. We have earlier discussed `yfinance` and your freedom of using other libraries to download data. We have also imported another library, `matplotlib`. This library is used for displaying various kinds of plots.
- **Customize**: Here, we can specify the following parameters of the code to customize it to our application.
    - Names of the files with raw input data, one to save the results of the simulation, and another to save the histogram plot of simulated returns.
    - The number of days for which we will compute the return. Please do not lose sight of the total number of days for which you have data. You will also specify the number of working days in a year to annualize the computation.
    - We need to provide a rate of annual dividend or any such regular income for the asset, other than the increase in the price.
    - The number of times you want to simulate return values and the number of days in the future you wish to forecast prices using simulation.

  Here is the part of the customization code with the parameters that we will change italicized:

```
# Provide name of the CSV file to save/load the raw data
my_raw_data= '0506 quantlib_raw_data.csv'

# Provide name of the CSV file to save the simulated data
my_simulated_data= '0506 quantlib_simulated_data.csv'
```

```
# Provide name of the png file to save histogram
my_simulation_plot="0506 simulated_returns_histogram.png"

# Provide number of days to compute the return
return_days=10

# Number of days in a year to annualize the values
annual_working_days=252

# Provide the annual dividend rate (or income from asset
other than increase in price)
my_div=0.00

# Provide number of days to forecast
my_future_days=50

# Provide number of simulation runs
simulation_runs=10000
```

- **Load data and initial setup:** In this section, we load the data that had either been downloaded or that we already have with us. Please note that the closing price is stored in a field called "Close." You may need to change this depending on your data structure. You must have noted an evaluation date. This represents the current date from which all financial calculations, simulations, and pricing are performed. We have set this to the current system date.
- **Compute return and volatility:** In this section, the last value of the downloaded data is set as the basis for forecasting future values. Return is computed considering the days specified for return computation. In case there is not enough data, you will get a warning. Volatility is computed considering the number of working days specified in the customization section.
- **Setup parameters:** This section sets up parameters used by `QuantLib`. Though you do not need to change these, here is a quick explanation for those interested. You may consult the `QuantLib` official documentation to see other options available.
    - Market data setup: We are using a day count convention where a year has 365 days. We are also setting the New York Stock Exchange calendar as a computational basis.
    - Simulation Parameters: Here we have defined the horizon, which is the number of days to predict, along with the number of Monte Carlo runs. We have provided these values in customization.
    - `QuantLib` Market Data Objects:
        - spot_handle: Represents the current asset price.

  - flat_ts: Represents the risk-free rate curve. Here, the return over return_period_days is used instead of an annual risk-free rate.
  - div_yield: Represents the dividend yield or return from the asset, other than an increase in the market price. In cases of stocks, a higher dividend yield is often associated with slower stock price growth.
  - flat_vol_ts: Represents the constant volatility term structure using the historical volatility. Higher volatility is likely to cause more extreme price movements.
  - Stochastic Process: Defines a stochastic process using the parameters provided under the Black-Scholes-Merton framework.

- **Set up Monte Carlo simulation**: This section performs the core job of simulation execution. Here are some more details for those interested. Presented here are three major functions in the simulation process:

  - Random number generation: This generates uniform random numbers and then converts them into Gaussian (normal) distributed numbers.
  - Path generator: Simulates a random price path using the Black-Scholes-Merton stochastic process. The time horizon is divided by the annual working days.
  - Simulation execution: This section simulates for a specified number of times, extracting simulated values into an array.

- **Save simulated data**: The simulated data is saved in the specified CSV file. Each row in the table signifies a simulation, and the columns are the successive days of forecasting.
- **Plot histogram return for each simulation**: In this section, the code computes the return from the simulated data for every simulation run and plots a return histogram. The histogram will give the user an idea of the probability distribution being faced.
- **Confirm saving files**: This just displays a confirmation of completing the simulation run, saving the simulated results, and the histogram plot.

Surely you appreciate that this is a more sophisticated model than the previous one. You can select either depending on your requirements.

Models for various risk factors affecting investments

We know that various risk factors influence the ROI. Please note that when we speak of a portfolio of assets, they are not necessarily monetary assets. Most assets would have similar attributes, and the model can be used on them. Let us first discuss the underlying theory behind the computation of the investment return.

We have considered that the following four factors affect the ROI. We will provide these values in the computation of return.

- Market: Characterized by mean return and volatility
- Interest rate: This is broken into four parts: initial rate, long-term average, mean reversion period, and rate volatility
- Inflation rate: The average rate and volatility
- Credit spread: The average credit spread and volatility

To run the portfolio model, using the market-specific parameters provided, we will have to provide these investment-specific inputs:

- Initial investment: The amount we are investing
- Period: The investment horizon, in months
- Number of simulations: How many simulations do we want the model to run using the investment and market-specific values provided?

The model computes total return as market return + inflation impact – credit spread + interest rate contribution. The return is applied to the previous value to get the present value of the investment.

The model provides the following outputs:

- Key metrics:
  - Mean Final Value: The average portfolio value across all simulations
  - VaR (95%): The worst-case scenario at a 95% confidence level
  - Success Rate: Percentage of simulations where you end up with a gain
  - Maximum Drawdown: The largest peak-to-trough decline you might experience
- Visual Outputs
  - Blue Lines: Each represents one possible future path
  - Red Dashed Line: The average path across all simulations
  - Blue Shaded Area: Shows where 90% of outcomes fall
  - Histogram: Shows the distribution of final portfolio values

Let us now have a quick look at the code and its sections (prefix 0507).

- **Import libraries**: We are using one new library, which is `SciPy.Stats`. This library is used for statistical functions. If you need to install it, use the `pip install` command.
- **Customize**: In this section, you will provide two groups of values. The first set pertains to market variables, which will be used to compute the return from the investment. The second set would provide

details of the investment you intend to examine, along with the number of simulations you want to run. The customizable inputs are the following:

- Market returns-related: We are providing the average return from the market and the corresponding volatility. You can also use a return from an alternative if your investment so requires.
- Interest rate-related: Here we will provide the current interest rate, the average interest rate, interest rate volatility, and mean reversal speed. Mean reversal speed indicates how quickly the interest rate reaches the mean value.
- Inflation-related: In this code, we will provide the mean value and volatility of the inflation rate.
- Credit spread-related: Like others, we will provide the mean and volatility of the credit spread.
- Investment-related: We will provide information about the initial investment and the expected period of holding the investment in months.
- Simulation-related: This is the number of simulations we want the code to run. For example, we want 1,000 simulations.
- Save file: Name of the file where we will save all results and values at every simulation step.

Here is the excerpt of the code and the customizable values marked italicized.

```
# Section A: Provide details for the simulation model
#Market return
market_return_mean = 0.10
market_return_vol = 0.15

# About interest rate
Initial_rate = 0.03
rate_mean = 0.04
rate_speed = 0.15
rate_vol = 0.02

# Inflation details
inflation_mean = 0.025
inflation_vol = 0.01

# About credit spread
spread_mean = 0.02
spread_vol = 0.008

# Section B: Provide data on the investment
```

```
# Specify initial investment
my_investment= 100000

# Specify investment horizon
my_holding_period= 60

# Specify the number of simulations
my_iteration= 1000

# Specify the CSV file to save data
my_simulations='0507 portfolio_simulation.csv'
```

- **Prepare the computational module:** This is the heart of the code. This model can be initialized by providing three key data: initial investment, investment horizon, and number of simulations. The model then proceeds to simulate the values of the factors that influence the return from the investment. We have identified four such factors, which are, market return, interest rate, inflation rate, and credit spread. The code then proceeds to simulate the investment value using the simulated values of key factors. It also defines the parameters to store simulated values, display, and plot results. We have used 5% and 95% percentile levels to plot the results.
- **Load initial values for investment simulation:** The model now loads the initial values of investment to run the simulation.
- **Display simulation results:** In this section, the code saves the detailed values of each simulation run in the CSV file specified by you. The file saves the simulated market value of the investment along with the values of the underlying influencer for each day of the holding horizon, in separate columns. This means that if the holding horizon is 12 months, there will be 12 columns for each of the objects, market value, market return, interest rate, inflation rate, and credit spread. In addition, there will be rows for each simulation run. Thus, if we have twelve 12-month holding periods and 1,000 simulation runs, we will have 12 × 5 = 60 columns and 1,000 rows in the core report. You will find the data in the CSV file for further analysis and audit. In addition, it displays the key risk metrics and plots the Monte Carlo simulation value path and distribution of final portfolio values.

Let us take a quick look at the model output. As mentioned earlier, there will be a display of the key risk metrics and plots of the Monte Carlo simulation value path and distribution of final portfolio values. Let us see what they mean.

- **Mean final value:** This is the mean of the simulated portfolio values over the holding period. This represents the average expected return after factoring in market risk, interest rates, inflation, and credit spreads. Please note that this is not the expected value of the investment at the end of the holding period. This is the average of various possibilities, each of them having an associated probability.

- **VaR (95%)**: This is the value-at-risk at a 95% confidence level. This means that in the worst 5% of scenarios, the portfolio will lose at least this amount.
- **Success rate**: This represents the percentage of simulations where the final portfolio value exceeds the initial investment. A low success rate indicates that most simulated paths resulted in a loss.
- **Maximum drawdown**: This is the largest peak-to-trough drop in portfolio value, indicating the worst-case loss due to a market downturn.
- **Monte Carlo simulation value path**: The plot shows multiple possible future trajectories of the portfolio. If most paths trend upward, the portfolio is likely profitable. If many paths drop significantly, there is a high chance of large losses. The spread of the paths indicates volatility; a wider spread of lines means higher uncertainty. If most paths are above the initial investment, the strategy is profitable.
- **Distribution of final portfolio values (histogram)**: This is the distribution of final portfolio values after all simulations. VaR is given by the red line, and the mean return is shown by the green line. If the distribution is skewed to the left, the chances of losses are higher. A wider histogram would mean higher volatility.

Model to analyze the distribution of possible outcomes

You must have noticed that we saved all the results of the simulation in a CSV file. This was done to be able to do further analysis of the simulated results. A common use is to understand the distribution of the simulated results to get an idea of the probability associated with various outcomes. This will be useful for risk managers as they will know of the likely scenarios they may face.

We will use one of the output files from our earlier code to do a percentile analysis and visualize the data. The code (prefix 0508) is available on the repository and is divided into the following sections.

- **Import libraries**: We are loading the libraries necessary for the code.
- **Customize**: We are specifying the name of the input file and the fields we wish to analyze, along with the percentile values we want to compute. If you want to use only one field, name the other field "None." The percentile values should be comma-separated and between []. Here is the relevant part of the code with the variables italicized.

```
# Specify the file path and field names
file_path = '0505 simulation_values.csv'

# Specify the names of the field to analyze
# Change to 'None' to skip
field1 = 'Simulated Returns'
field2 = 'Simulated Index Values'

# Specify percentile values comma-separated and between
[]
quantiles = [0.10, 0.25, 0.50, 0.75, 0.90]
```

- **Define the function to analyze, plot, and save:** This is the heart of the code. A function is being defined here that will use the inputs provided to do a percentile analysis, plot the output, and save it as a graphic. The function computes and reports the values of the mean, maximum, minimum, and specified percentiles for each field. It plots a histogram and boxplot of the distribution of the values in the specified fields. It then saves the plots in a graphics file by the field name.
- **Run the function on input provided:** This section calls the functions using the input values and renders the output.

Let us quickly review what the boxplot does. A boxplot consists of five main parts:

- Minimum (Lower Whisker): This is the smallest data point, excluding outliers, and is defined as the lowest value within 1.5 × IQR (Interquartile Range) from the first quartile (Q1).
- First Quartile (Q1/25th percentile): It is the lower edge of the box. 25% of the data points fall below this value.
- Median (Q2/50th percentile): This is the middle line inside the box with 50% of data below and above this value.
- Third Quartile (Q3/75th percentile): This is the upper edge of the box with 75% of the data points falling below this value.
- Maximum (Upper Whisker): This is the largest data point excluding outliers and is defined as the highest value within 1.5 × IQR from the third quartile (Q3).
- Outliers (Points outside whiskers): Individual points beyond the whiskers are considered outliers (extreme values).

Feel free to use the code on any data you want to understand.

ML tools for strategic choices

We all appreciate that in finance, the ability to make quick and informed strategic choices often differentiates between success and failure. The greater the complexity of the decision-making process, the more difficult it is for the decision-maker to visualize the entire spectrum of options. This is where ML-based tools come in handy. It analyses past data to identify the inherent flow of the decision-making process and then uses the same process for future decision-making. An individual may not be able to visualize this intricate interplay among factors and may miss an important aspect of decision-making. For example, a borrower may have different degrees of aversion to being a defaulter in a housing loan, depending on whether the borrower stays in that house.

One of the popular tools used for strategic choices is a decision tree. A decision tree is a supervised ML algorithm used both for classification and regression tasks.

Classification teaches a machine to sort objects into categories by looking at examples that have been labeled. For example, we provided the machine with customer demographic details and marked them as "Defaulter" or "Non-Defaulter." The ML tool studies the data, and after learning, it can classify a new customer into these two classifications. The classification can be binary or multi class. We have spoken about regression earlier. You may remember that regression is another supervised learning technique that predicts a numerical value for the object based on one or more independent features. For example, we can predict the price of a house based on its location and size. The regression can be simple linear or multiple linear, reflecting the number of independent variables involved in the prediction.

Let us now have a look at how the decision tree works. It maps out the decision-making process in a tree-like structure. In the structure, each node represents a decision point or test of a specific attribute. Each branch represents the possible outcomes based on that decision, and leaf nodes represent the final answer.

Let us try to understand the intuition behind the decision tree using a simple example. We want to predict if a person prefers an expensive wearable gadget based on their age and income. An Indian female customer younger than 25 years or customers having annual earnings of more than INR 2.4 million may buy the gadget.

Step 1: Ask the root question (node) – Age: *Are you below 25 years of age?* This will give us two branches (groups). One aged below 25, the other aged 25 and above.

Step 2: First branch based on age (internal node). If the customer is below 25 years, ask: *Is the customer female?*

Step 3: Second branch based on income (internal node): If the annual income is above INR 2.4 million, the customer is likely to buy the gadget.

Before concluding that this looks like a decision flow chart, wait a while. Under an ML environment, we are not specifying the rule. We will provide a set of data of customers, each labeled with their age, gender, earnings, and past purchase preferences. The ML tool will find the decision tree for us. If we provide more labeled information, like marital status, we may even find another branch.

The following figure describes how the decision tree works. The legends A, B, C, D, E, and F are the objects of the study and are classified as the branches of the tree in Figure 5.1.

If you are interested in knowing how the ML tool does the prediction, read on for a simple explanation, based on the same example.

The decision tree works on the principle of improving classification power at each level. Let us award each response at every step described earlier.

Step 1: Ask the root question (node) – Age: *Are you below 25 years of age?* If yes, award +3, else award 1.

Step 2: First branch based on age (internal node). If the customer is female, award +1, else award –2.

Step 3: Second branch based on income (internal node): If the annual income is above INR 2.4 million, award +2, otherwise award –3.

If you follow the decision tree and the awards, you will find the following scenarios under each classification.

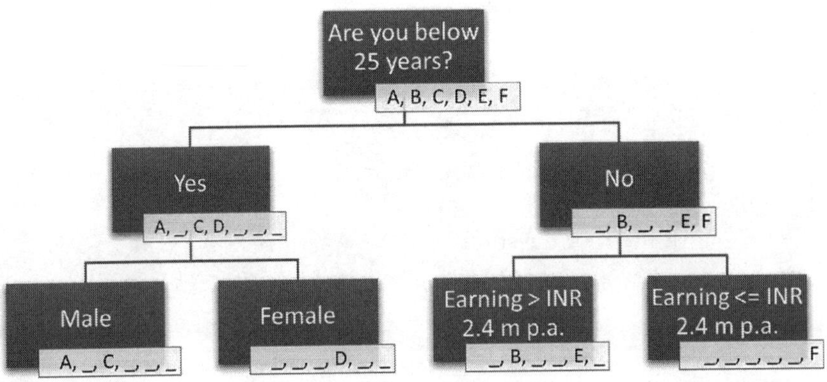

Figure 5.1 The decision tree and classification

Likely buyer:

Age below 25, Female, Annual earnings above INR 2.4 m: Score 3 + 1 + 2: 6
Age below 25, Female, Annual earnings below INR 2.4 m: Score 3 + 1 – 3: 1
Age below 25, Male, Annual earnings above INR 2.4 m: Score 3 – 2 + 2: 3
Age above 25, Female, Annual earnings above INR 2.4 m: Score 1 + 1 + 2: 4
Age above 25, Male, Annual earnings above INR 2.4 m: Score 1 – 2 + 2: 1

Unlikely buyer:

Age below 25, Male, Annual earnings below INR 2.4 m: Score 3 – 2 – 3: –2
Age above 25, Female, Annual earnings below INR 2.4 m: Score 1 + 1 – 3: –1
Age above 25, Male, Annual earnings below INR 2.4 m: Score 1 – 2 – 3: –4

You can see that in this classification, the unlikely buyers all have negative scores, while the likely buyers have positive scores. The algorithm tries to fit in such scores that would create clear non-overlapping classifications.

Utilize decision tree algorithms to map out strategic options

One of the major challenges in strategic decision-making is identifying all viable alternatives and understanding their interdependencies. Decision tree algorithms systematically map all possible options.

We will understand the application of decision trees using a case study. Consider a retailer that has a customer database containing their age, income, gender, and a field that shows their decision to buy or not to buy. The retailer wants to develop a model that will classify future customers between those who are likely to buy and those who are not likely to buy. The retailer is unsure about the reasons why the customers buy, or do not, but feels that the decision is influenced by their age, income, and gender of the customer. You can download the code (prefix 0509) from the repository. Let us examine the major components of the code.

- **Import libraries:** We have imported the `DecisionTreeClassifier` function. It makes decisions by learning simple decision rules inferred from the data features.
- **Customize:** In this section, we will provide the names of the input file containing data for training the model, the input file containing the new data, the output file where the results will be saved, the name of the text

file to save the decision rule, and the name of the graphics file to save the decision rule. Here is the relevant part of the code with the parameters in italics.

```
# Specify file names
past_data_path = '0509 Decision tree past data.csv'
new_data_path = '0509 Decision tree new data.csv'
tree_image_path = "0509 decision_tree.png"
rules_file_path = "0509 decision_rules.txt"
decision_file_path = '0509 decision.csv'
```

One component of the customization section specifies the fields that the retailer believes influence the purchase decision. It also specifies the field where the decision value is stored. Age and Income are numeric fields, while Gender and Purchase fields are binary. These two fields are also known as categorical variables as they categorize the record. In the Gender field, value 1 denotes male, and 0 denotes female. In the case of the Purchase field, the value 1 suggests the customer purchased from the retailer, while the value 0 suggests that the customer did not purchase. If your fields are different, you will have to change the name across the code, keeping the type of the field the same. You must have noticed we did not specify the Cust_id field since it does not play any role in the decision-making.

```
# Explicitly define features and target
features = ['Age', 'Income', 'Gender']
target = 'Purchase'
```

- **Load and clean past data:** In this section, the code loads the training data. This is data on past customer behavior that is available to the retailer. The code drops any unnamed columns from the database, converts Age and Income to numeric types (in case there was some formatting error), and encodes the categorical variable Gender. This is useful if the field values are Yes and No.
- **Train and save decision tree and decision rules:** This is where the model analyzes the past data and learns from it. It extracts features such as age, income, gender, and the target purchase. It uses the available data to train a `DecisionTreeClassifier` model from sklearn. This learning results in the creation of a decision rule. A decision tree is created and saved in the specified graphics file. A warning, if the tree is big and complex, the image may overlap and would be of no use. To counter this problem, the code exports the decision rule narrated in a specified text file. We will discuss this in detail later in this chapter. This code applies deep learning and may take some time. Keep an eye on the processing kernel to be sure that it is still processing. For large files, this can be resource-hungry.

- **Use decision tree on new data and print results:** This section applies the model to the new data to make predictions on likely purchase decisions to be made by the new customers. The customer database should have the same structure as the training file as far as the features are concerned, which are age, income, and gender, in this case. The code compares the availability of these fields and then conducts housekeeping in the same manner as it did with the training data. Finally, it predicts purchase behavior, displays, and saves the results in the specified file.

When you run the code, you will find some debugging information. The code will confirm if the necessary fields are present in the new data, and whether any rows were dropped from the new customer file because of inconsistency. The code mentions the file names that were saved during processing. It finally displays the results of the prediction and saves them in a CSV file for future use and audit. We will have the saved data display as in Table 5.3.

If you are wondering how a case study on purchase decisions can apply to other financial decisions, consider this: the same analytical approach can be used to validate budget forecasts, predict cash flows, and more. Furthermore, the underlying model or engine can be adapted for default prediction by modifying the input features and target variables.

Evaluates potential outcomes and associated probabilities

Hope you have found the last example interesting and useful. We successfully predicted whether a new customer is likely to make a buy decision or not. But we still do not know the associated probability of buying with each new customer. That would be critical information to have.

Table 5.3 Predicted decision extract

Cust_Id	*Age*	*Income*	*Gender*	*Purchase Decision*
1001	42	129,521	1	0
1002	39	89,277	0	1
1003	34	83,659	0	1
1004	56	188,839	0	0
1005	47	99,501	0	0
1006	43	126,594	1	1
1007	58	177,536	0	0
1008	39	92,203	1	1
1009	32	76,986	1	1
1010	23	66,757	1	0
1011	57	167,905	0	0

We will continue with the same case study we used in the last section about the retailer and the purchase possibilities. However, we will use another technique called Random Forest. We have earlier discussed this classifier, which is a learning method that combines multiple decision trees to improve accuracy and reduce overfitting.

Instead of relying on a single decision tree, it builds many trees and averages their predictions. We can also compute the associated probabilities. The processing is much faster than a decision tree, as we have limited individual tree complexity in the code. For the inquisitive, there is a line in the code:

```
RandomForestClassifier(n_estimators=100, random_state=42)
```

`n_estimators=100` means the random forest will create 100 decision trees. More trees generally improve accuracy but increase training time. You can change the same to higher values. `random_state=42` seeds the random number generation, ensuring that the same random splits and trees are created every time the code is run. If you remove this, each run may produce slightly different results.

The code remains the same except we import the `RandomForestClassifier` function and use the same in the training section. You can download the code (prefix 0510) from the repository. We have used the same input file for training and the new data. We have saved the prediction in a CSV file that you would specify in the customization section.

While classifying the new customers as prospective buyers or not, we have also computed the associated probability of purchase, displayed the same on the screen, and saved it for subsequent use. The output follows the structure in Table 5.4.

Table 5.4 Extract of predicted decision and associated probability

Cust_Id	*Age*	*Income*	*Gender*	*Purchase Decision*	*Purchase Probability*
1001	42	129,521	1	0	0.08
1002	39	89,277	0	1	0.8
1003	34	83,659	0	0	0.22
1004	56	188,839	0	0	0.38
1005	47	99,501	0	1	0.8
1006	43	126,594	1	1	0.71
1007	58	177,536	0	1	0.8
1008	39	92,203	1	0	0.25
1009	32	76,986	1	1	0.79
1010	23	66,757	1	0	0.4

Do not be surprised at the different predictions made by different models. This is where we test the suitability of the model. We will touch upon the same in the next section.

Decision paths and outcomes

Decision trees provide an intuitive graphical representation of decision paths and outcomes. A decision tree might illustrate the trade-offs between two strategic decisions, for example, between acquiring a startup versus developing similar capabilities internally. Such visualizations facilitate discussions and are useful as documentation for future reference. The example we used explained the characteristics in terms of age, income, and gender that make a customer a likely buyer.

The effectiveness of visualization will depend on the simplicity of the decision tree. If the nodes and branches are few, the decision tree can be visualized easily. In case of complex decisions, the image may overlap and become too complicated to understand. To understand the visualization, let us use the example from when we were demonstrating how a decision tree works. The example was based on whether an Indian female customer younger than 25 years old or customers having annual earnings of more than INR 2.4 million will buy a wearable gadget or not. We have created a database applying simple rules. The value of females in the database is 0.

We have truncated the code on the decision tree used earlier and removed the part where we make predictions using the new data and applied the decision rule to it. The code (prefix 0511) can be downloaded from the repository. The truncated code will now analyze data and draw the decision tree. We have used simplified data as input and obtained the decision path in a graphics file as well as in text (Figure 5.2).

The decision tree has summarized the customer behavior from the data provided and has found that the following rule is being applied.

1. High Income (>2.45) → Purchase
2. Low Income (≤2.45) and Gender > 0.5 → No Purchase
3. Low Income (≤2.45) and Gender ≤ 0.5 and Age ≤ 24.5 → Purchase
4. Low Income (≤2.45) and Gender ≤ 0.5 and Age > 24.5 → No Purchase

This is a slight variance from the rules we stated, but it has not violated the same. It has fine-tuned the model based on the data provided. Remember, we had mentioned that the decision tree algorithm uncovers the underlying rules. The algorithm has found that the income classifier is working at the value of 2.45. The gender classifier is set at 0.5. Lower than that is 0, representing "female." Each box in the decision tree has the following four

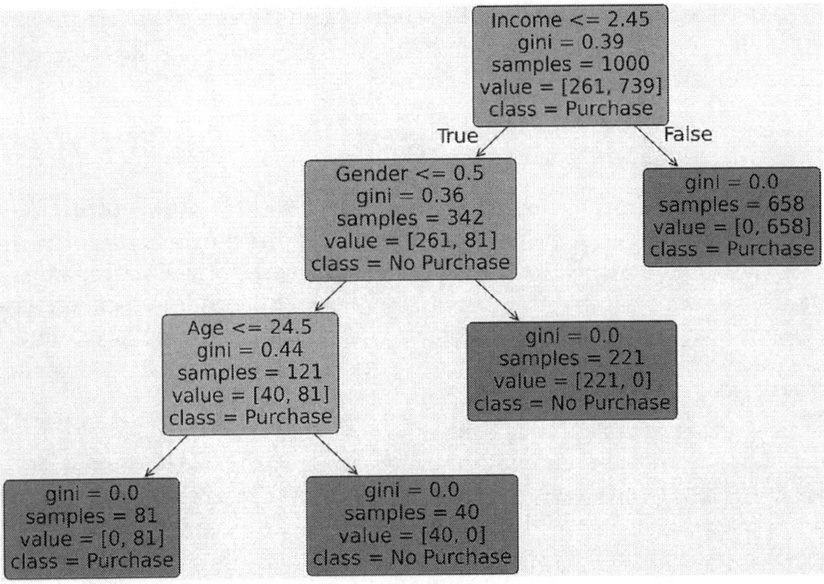

Figure 5.2 Decision tree path

common components. A fifth component depicting the classification question would appear in the decision boxes or decision nodes.

1. **Gini**: The Gini impurity measures how impure a node is, meaning how mixed the class like Purchase versus No Purchase is in that node. If Gini = 0, the node is pure, meaning all samples belong to the same class. As it goes higher, it means that the node is more mixed. A value close to 0.5 would mean that both classes are present in almost equal proportions.
2. **Samples**: The number of samples contained in the node after following the classification from the root node. If you sum up the number of samples inside all child nodes at any level, it equals the number of samples in the parent node from the immediately higher level.
3. **Value**: This represents the count of samples in each class at that node. The sum of values in a node represents the total samples at that node. These will be split into child nodes at the next level following the classification criteria.
4. **Class**: This is the predicted class representing the majority class at that node (that is, the predicted outcome at that stage). In this case, it is either "Purchase" or "No Purchase."

As a decision-maker, you are now equipped with a tool that can uncover the underlying reasoning behind a decision or classification. This would be particularly useful in scenarios where explicit rules are not provided, and we need to derive insights from available behavioral data.

Choosing strategies with optimal expected values

The goal of a strategic analysis is to identify the alternative that maximizes expected value. A decision tree identifies the best solution by integrating quantitative metrics with qualitative insights. Finance executives can simulate "what-if" scenarios, stress-test assumptions, and refine their strategies iteratively.

Expected value calculation is a core feature of ML-based decision tree analysis. The algorithms compute the expected value of each strategic option by combining the probability of different outcomes with their associated financial impacts. This quantitative approach promotes comparison between different strategies objectively and selects options that optimize expected returns while considering risk tolerance levels.

Here is an example of how it works in an inventory management scenario where we are deciding on a level of reorder. Let us consider a taco seller in Mexico City who is trying to find out the best reorder level. She has the following set of assumptions that will be useful in building the decision tree.

- Tourist inflow: There are three possibilities, which are low inflow, medium inflow, and high inflow. The chances of these three scenarios materializing are 20%, 40%, and 40%. In each of these cases, the sales volume will be 100 units, 150 units, and 200 units, respectively.
- Reorder size: She can order in batch sizes of 100 units, 150 units, or 200 units.
- Financials: The cost of each taco is N$10, while the unit sales price is N$20 per unit.
- Business arrangement: The trader has made a nice business arrangement with her supplier. In case she orders more, she can return the excess stock by paying a penalty of N$2 per unit. In case there is a stockout, her supplier will rush in the stock at an additional cost of N$5 per unit.

Considering this data the expected payoff for three different reorder levels at three different demand levels is given in the Table 5.5. Opportunity losses have not been considered.

ML tools can also be of help in issues like this. This code is custom-made for this example and can be used for similar cases. Let us have a look at

Table 5.5 Payoff at different levels of reorder

Reorder Quantity	*Tourist flow*	*Low Inflow*	*Medium Inflow*	*High Inflow*
	Probability	20%	40%	40%
	Units sold	100	150	200
100 Units	Sales (N$20)	2,000	3,000	4,000
	Cost (10)	1,000	1,500	2,000
	Stock out (N$5)	0	250	500
	Return (N$2)	0	0	0
	Profit/Loss: N$	1,000	1,250	1,500
	Expected value	(1,000 × 0.2) + (1,250 × 0.4) + (1,500 × 0.4): 1,300		
150 Units	Sales (N$20)	2,000	3,000	4,000
	Cost (N$10)	1,000	1,500	2,000
	Stock out (N$5)	0	0	250
	Return (N$2)	100	0	0
	Profit/Loss: N$	900	1,500	1,750
	Expected value	(900 × 0.2) + (1,500 × 0.4) + (1,750 × 0.4): 1,480		
200 Units	Sales (N$20)	2,000	3,000	4,000
	Cost (N$10)	1,000	1,500	2,000
	Stock out (N$5)	0	0	0
	Return (N$2)	200	100	0
	Profit/Loss:	800	1,400	2,000
	Expected value	(800 × 0.2) + (1,400 × 0.4) + (2,000 × 0.4): 1,520		

various components of the code. The code (prefix 0512) is available in the repository.

- **Import libraries:** As usual, the necessary libraries are loaded in this section. We have used these libraries several times earlier, except for `networkx`, which is used for building a decision tree visualization.
- **Customize:** This section uses variables for the specific problem structure. You can reuse the code for similar applications. We have not considered using table-based input, as the input would ideally come from various sources. One can always consider all input values stored on a table if the code is to be frequently used. The relevant section of the code that can be customized is shown below with the parameter values in italics.

```
# Specify output files
my_payoff= "0512 Detailed Payoff.csv"
my_decision_tree= "0512 Decision Tree.png"
```

```
# Define probabilities of tourist inflow scenarios tour-
ist_scenarios = "Low": 0.2, "Medium": 0.4, "High": 0.4}
sales_volume = "Low": 100, "Medium": 150, "High": 200}

# Define reorder sizes
reorder_sizes - [100, 150, 200]

# Define cost parameters
cost_per_unit = 10
price_per_unit = 20

# Penalty for excess stock returns
penalty_per_unit = 2

# Extra cost for stockouts
rush_cost_per_unit = 5
```

- **Create cost computation function:** This section creates the functions for computing revenue, cost, handling cost shortage or excess, and finally computing net profit. Please note that the business case assumes that the seller always ends up matching the demand, either by returning excess stocks ordered or by rushing stock, paying a premium. This cost computation function is designed to match the business case.
- **Adjust for probabilities**: In this section, each scenario is weighed by their respective probabilities. The results are appended to the file where the results were computed in the earlier section.
- **Display summary and save payoff table in CSV file**: This section displays and saves the payoff table in the specified file. The saved file can be useful for further understanding of each option and for an audit.
- **Create visualization**: The decision tree is displayed on the screen and saved in the specified file for use elsewhere. You can customize the way the tree is presented by altering the code pos = `nx.circular_layout(G)`. You have various options like `spring_layout`, `kamada_kawal_layout`, `spectral_layout`, `shell_layout`, and others. You can experiment with the formats to find the one that suits your use the best.
- **Draw decision tree**: Finally, the code displays the decision tree on the screen. A copy is also saved for subsequent use.

The final output from the code is a payoff table and a decision tree diagram. The payoff table includes the case-specific values like revenue, cost, cost of stock out and excess order, probability, and probability-weighted profit. The payoff table structure is provided in Table 5.6.

Table 5.6 Payoff table structure

Reorder Size	*Tourist Inflow*	*Demand*	*Revenue*	*Cost (for Demand)*	*Excess Stock*	*Penalty Cost*	*Stockout*	*Rush Cost*	*Net Profit*	*Probability*	*Weighted Profit*
100	Low	100	2,000	1,000	0	0	0	0	1,000	0.2	200
100	Medium	150	3,000	1,500	0	0	50	250	1,250	0.4	500
100	High	200	4,000	2,000	0	0	100	500	1,500	0.4	600
150	Low	100	2,000	1,000	50	100	0	0	900	0.2	180
150	Medium	150	3,000	1,500	0	0	0	0	1,500	0.4	600
150	High	200	4,000	2,000	0	0	50	250	1,750	0.4	700
200	Low	100	2,000	1,000	100	200	0	0	800	0.2	160
200	Medium	150	3,000	1,500	50	100	0	0	1,400	0.4	560
200	High	200	4,000	2,000	0	0	0	0	2,000	0.4	800

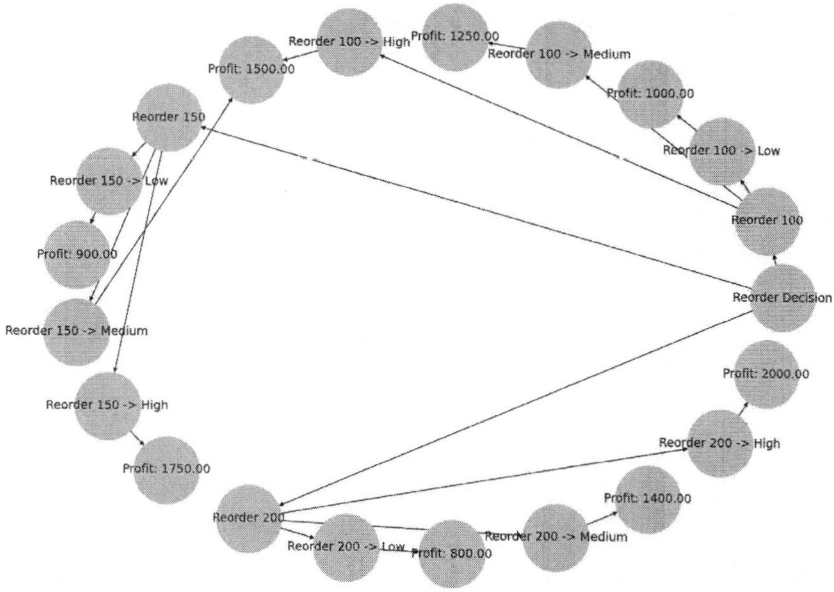

Figure 5.3 Decision tree

The decision tree will have the format defined by you. The format specified in the code generates the decision tree in a shell pattern (Figure 5.3). The root node is in the center of the right-hand margin of the diagram. Three arrows connect the three decision alternatives, which are the three reorder levels. Each of these nodes has three child nodes depicting the level of tourist inflow and the consequent profit. This graph helps you evaluate the expected profit trade-offs for different inventory reorder levels across different demand scenarios.

Key takeaways

In this chapter, we have explored the role of data-driven insights in strategic decision-making. We emphasized that an effective strategy requires a clear definition of objectives, thorough environmental scanning, careful evaluation of alternatives, and continuous realignment based on changing data and conditions. We used various AI and ML tools to aid financial decisions, including decision trees, simulation models, sentiment analysis, expected value, and others to enhance decision accuracy, manage uncertainty, and uncover hidden patterns. These tools supported both quantitative and qualitative decisions, making strategic planning more evidence- based and responsive.

Chapter 6

Inventory and supply chain management

Effective inventory and supply chain management is the key to running a smooth and profitable operation. In this chapter, we show you how the finance and operations teams can use ML tools to improve demand forecasting, optimize stock levels, and streamline logistics. Starting with the basics of inventory control, we slowly move into advanced techniques like time series analysis, network modeling, and inventory classification using clustering. With practical tools and clear examples, this chapter shows how data-driven decisions can reduce costs, prevent stock issues, and boost overall efficiency.

Understanding inventory management

Inventory management is a critical function of the management of any organization. Inventory affects a wide range of KPIs, ranging from profitability to working capital. Inventory management refers to the process of efficiently producing, ordering, storing, using, and selling a company's inventory. It deals with the management of raw materials, components, and finished products. Additionally, it also deals with warehousing and handling processes involved in maintaining optimal inventory levels.

Inventory is integral to the entire manufacturing/trading process in an organization. It plays a critical role in determining the operational efficiency and financial health of an organization. Inventory management directly influences customer satisfaction, cost control, cash flow, and profitability. If there is a shortage of raw material inventory, it would interrupt the entire production process. However, holding excess inventory would mean requiring additional working capital, obsolescence of unused items, and increased storage costs. It is therefore important to predict the optimal amount of inventory to be maintained to ensure smooth operation.

A shortage of finished goods would affect delivery to customers, reputation loss, and revenue loss. In turn, these may lead to stockouts, missed sales opportunities, lower customer satisfaction, and potential loss of

DOI: 10.4324/9781003619628-6

market share. These missed opportunities can be especially damaging in highly competitive markets or industries with volatile demand patterns. Ensuring the right amount of inventory at the right location to meet customer requirements increases satisfaction levels and customer loyalty, ensuring repeated business in the long run.

How inventory influences the overall performance of the company

Inventory is a component of current assets and an integral part of the working capital cycle. As such, it plays an important part in the company's operations and financial performance. With inventory, we are playing with a double-edged sword. On one hand, holding too much inventory could result in higher costs, reduced liquidity, and risk of obsolescence. On the other hand, holding a low inventory would result in stockouts, lost sales, and unhappy customers. Management of inventory is a balancing game aligning production, sales, and finance to enhance overall performance both financial and operational. It has the following impacts across a business.

- **Profitability:** When we think about impacts on financial performance, the first thought that comes to our mind is whether inventory holding would affect our profitability. Inventory is directly tied to the cost of goods sold (COGS). There are various methods of inventory valuation, such as first-in-first-out (FIFO), last-in- first-out (LIFO), or weighted average, which impacts gross profit. Efficient inventory turnover improves return on assets (ROA) and return on investments (ROI). The purchase of excess inventory directly draws out the liquidity of the organization. The increased cost of purchase, storage, ordering, insurance, depreciation, and impairment reduces profitability. Inventory write-downs due to obsolescence or damage also directly reduce profits. Insufficient inventory may lead to lost revenue and reduced customer satisfaction. Though these are not reflected in the financial statements, they surely influence performance in the long run.
- **Working capital and cash flow:** Inventory is a key component of working capital. Holding inventory requires funding, typically through a combination of internal cash or short-term financing. Even though inventory is a part of current assets, it may not convert into cash very quickly. Raw materials would need to move through the production process as work-in-progress to finished goods. These would then be sold and proceeds collected to finally get converted to cash. Excessive inventory holding, delays in production processes, and non-moving finished goods inventory all lead to the locking up of cash. These could have

been used for other business opportunities. Optimized inventory levels improve cash flow by reducing capital commitments while maintaining sales capability. The inventory turnover ratio measures how efficiently inventory is converted to sales. A low turnover may signal inefficiency. Efficient inventory management improves liquidity and cash flow.

- **Operational efficiency**: Adequate inventory of raw materials ensures smooth production processes. Shortages can halt operations, cause delays, and increase downtime costs. Proper inventory levels ensure product availability when customers want to purchase. Timely order fulfillment enhances customer loyalty. Stockouts lead to lost sales and potentially long-term customer loss. Excessive lead times due to inventory issues damage customer relationships. Especially in retail and FMCG, being "in stock" directly influences market share.
- **Supply chain efficiency**: Accurate inventory data allows better coordination with suppliers and distributors, reducing lead times and improving responsiveness. Inventory also serves as a safeguard against supply chain disruptions, price volatility, and sudden spikes in demand, ensuring business continuity in uncertain conditions. Disruptions can impact the availability of critical raw materials and finished goods. Maintaining adequate inventory levels helps mitigate these risks. They act as a cushion that allows operations to continue even when supply lines are temporarily compromised. The use of Just-In-Time (JIT) or Economic Order Quantity (EOQ) models can optimize ordering frequency and quantity. Optimal inventory holdings can help shield against price volatility risk. In essence, inventory serves as a strategic and operational risk management tool that supports business continuity and operational resilience.
- **Strategic implications**: Companies with superior inventory management can offer better service levels at lower costs, leading to a competitive advantage. Faster inventory turnovers allow quicker adaptation to market trends and changes. Lower inventory investment improves the ability to invest in growth opportunities. Inventory management techniques like JIT, or ABC, used along with inventory optimization algorithms help companies balance these factors to maximize overall performance while minimizing costs.
- **Risk management:** From the risk management perspective, having safety stock protects against supply disruptions. Holding inventory during inflation may be beneficial, but risky during deflation or technological upgrades. Sourcing inventory from multiple sources and locations reduces exposure to localized disruptions. Obsolescence and spoilage risks, especially for technology and perishable goods may lead to write-downs or losses.

Optimizing inventory holding

You would have seen from the above discussion that it is not desirable to have excessive or deficient inventory. They both involve a combination of actual and opportunity costs. But how do we decide on the optimal inventory level? There are three main determinants of that – the annual demand, cost of ordering, and cost of holding. The annual demand is self-explanatory and would hold for both raw materials and finished goods. The cost of ordering is related to every order placed or processed. This would include the cost of personnel, process, documentation, and all activities involved in the process. The greater the number of orders we place or process, the higher the total cost of ordering will be. The cost of holding or the carrying cost is linked with the volume of inventory we will carry on average between two orders. This cost will include the cost of storage, in-storage handling, records management, interest cost of the average inventory value carried, and allied. The traditional formula for computing the EOQ is the following:

$$\text{Economic ordering quantity} = \frac{\sqrt{2DK}}{H}$$

where,
D: Annual demand
K: Cost of placing each order
H: Holding cost

Though we have a formula to compute the EOQ in the real world, it would have limited application under dynamic conditions. In addition to the factors described, there would be many factors influencing inventory optimization. These factors will include the following:

- **Seasonality of demand and supply**: Many times the demand pattern is seasonal. This is very profound in the case of agricultural products. The material is essentially available at one time of the year. Similarly, the demand for a product could be seasonal depending on factors like weather or festivity. The traditional static formula of inventory optimization does not capture these impacts.
- **Quantity discount**: Many times, the price depends on the quantity ordered. Even if we find an EOQ, we may stand to gain more by ordering more to get a volume discount. This changes the total cost of procurement of inventory, a phenomenon that the static formula of inventory optimization fails to capture.

- **Annual purchase plan:** In the case of an annual purchase contract, the terms are frozen at the beginning of the year and supply is at the discretion of the buyer. Though this does not invalidate the EOQ but needs to alter the component of ordering cost. In this case, a large part of the ordering cost becomes fixed.

We will explore various dimensions of optimization of inventory-related costs in the following sections. We will also have a look at how ML tools can help us in creating a stochastic-based EOQ system.

Best practices in inventory management using ML

Inventory management best practices refer to proven strategies and techniques aimed at optimizing stock levels, minimizing costs, and enhancing operational efficiency. Good strategies focus on accurate forecasting, cost control, inventory levels and visibility, streamlining distribution processes, and timely decision-making. Using ML tools to implement these strategies improves accuracy, adaptability, and efficiency across inventory management and control. Let us take a look at some of the best practices in inventory management and how ML can enhance them.

- **Demand forecasting:** Forecasting customer demand is essential to inventory planning. Traditionally, businesses depend on factors like historical sales data, industry trends, and seasonality to forecast future demand. Using forecasted values, companies can plan production, inventory levels, and supply chain activities. ML algorithms like time series analysis, regression, or Long Short-Term Memory (LSTM) significantly improve this process. They are able to consider multiple complex factors, both internal and external. ML models continuously learn from real-time data which enables adjustments to suit changing market conditions.
- **Inventory optimization:** Maintaining optimal stock levels involves calculating EOQ, setting reorder points, and determining safety stock levels to protect against variability in demand and supply. Typically, these are calculated using historical data. ML improves this by dynamically adjusting reorder points and stock levels based on actual consumption patterns, supplier performance, and real-time demand volatility. Replenishment decisions are not based only on fixed schedules but are also informed by demand signals. This improves the overall efficiency of inventory management. ML classification models predict which items are at risk of becoming obsolete based on usage patterns and market trends. It can track real-time sales velocity and recommend adjustments to reorder frequencies and lot sizes.
- **ABC analysis:** ABC analysis allows companies to identify and prioritize resources and controls. Controls and review processes are based on

the relative importance of items. "A" category items are of high value though low in quantity, "B" category items have a moderate value and frequency, and "C" items are of low value though high in quantity. This classification is typically done using just one criterion, that is, annual monetary value (unit cost × annual usage). ML uses clustering techniques like K-means to segment inventory by value, sales velocity, and risk, beyond traditional rules.

- **Warehouse and distribution planning**: Efficient warehouse techniques include practices such as slotting, FIFO, RFID scanning, and space utilization. Distribution planning optimizes the delivery of goods by determining the necessary quantities and identifying the locations where the goods are most needed. It considers demands, current inventory levels, target safety stock, quantities, and replenishment lead times to ensure efficient and cost-effective distribution. ML enhances these functions by optimizing stock allocation across locations using real-time data. It helps in determining the most efficient routes and distribution networks, factoring in variables such as transit times, proximity to customers, and warehouse capacity. Further, ML and computer vision improve in-warehouse operations by optimizing shelf space, product placement, and routing within the warehouse.
- **Inventory visibility and anomaly detection**: Monitoring stock levels and movement is key to preventing running out of stock, overstocking, or data inaccuracies. This is usually done through periodic audits and manual cycle counts. ML automates anomaly detection by flagging unusual transactions, sudden inventory drops, or unplanned restocking. Through pattern recognition, it learns to highlight exceptions that may point to errors in the process, supplier issues, or theft. Such proactive monitoring helps in reducing manual oversight.
- **Performance monitoring and continuous improvement**: KPIs in inventory management are metrics that help to continuously monitor and track performance. KPIs influence financial decisions as they offer actionable insights into turnover, days of inventory outstanding, sales, order fulfillment rate, costs, process success, relationships, and ratios among others. ML can uncover hidden patterns in data and suggest corrective actions. For example, it can correlate lead time increases with supplier behavior or spot declining turnover trends before they seriously impact cash flow. Dashboards that provide real-time insights can also be designed, helping teams stay updated and responsive.

Inventory optimization – EOQ (stochastic model)

Here we have developed a stochastic model for EOQ. It is useful when demand and/or lead time are uncertain or variable. Unlike the traditional (deterministic) EOQ model, which assumes fixed demand and lead time, a stochastic EOQ model accounts for randomness, making inventory decisions more realistic and resilient.

We have included the codes for an EOQ model where we would simulate data to assess the range of inventory that would be optimal for the organization to order. Let us have a look at the main components of the code (prefix 0601).

- **Import libraries:** In this section, we would import the required libraries for our task. You are well acquainted with the libraries that we have used here.
- **Customize:** In this section, we will provide values for the customization parameters. This includes the base value for the computation of EOQ under static scenarios. We also provide a value for the number of simulations we want to run. We will also provide the variation level we expect the demand and the ordering cost to have besides the lower and upper bound of holding cost. The bin size for the creation of a histogram of simulated EOQ can be specified here. The names of files to store the simulation result and plot are also specified. The relevant part of the code with customizable parameters in italics is given here.

```
# Parameters for static EOQ
annual_demand = 10000
ordering_cost = 1200
holding_cost = 1250

# Parameters for stochastic EOQ
n_simulations = 10000
# Input values of variation in decimal
demand_fluctuation = 0.10
ordering_cost_fluctuation = 0.10
holding_cost_min = 1000
holding_cost_max= 1500
my_bin_size = 10

#save output
my_report="0601 Simulation_report.csv"
my_plot="0601 simulation_plot.png"
```

- **Computation of static EOQ:** This code block calculates the EOQ under a static (deterministic) model. We have provided the necessary input in the earlier section.
- **Simulation:** This is the core section for the stochastic EOQ. In this case, the key input variables (demand, ordering cost, holding cost) are not static but follow a probability distribution to reflect real-world

uncertainty. We have provided all necessary values in the customization section which includes the number of simulations run and information to create a range of values for annual demand, ordering, and holding cost. Seasonal trends, promotions, and macroeconomic changes may affect demand. Ordering costs may vary due to supply chain delays, rush orders, and others. Lead time may increase due to supplier backlogs, customs delays, weather, or geopolitical events, among others. Holding costs may vary due to storage rates, inflation, insurance, and spoilage. Perishable or seasonal items are likely to have high and volatile carrying costs. Real-world business environments are rarely predictable, and hence relying solely on fixed values can lead to suboptimal decisions, excess costs, or stockouts. We are now set to simulate random samples. We set a random seed so that simulations are reproducible. `np.random.seed(42)`. If we do not root the seed to a value, every time we run the simulation, we will have different results. That will make comparison difficult.

The demand, ordering, and holding costs are simulated using the number of simulations defined and considering the information provided for fluctuations. We have also built in a sanity check to ensure that no simulated demand or costs are less than one or negative, as negative values would make the EOQ calculation invalid.

- **Computation of stochastic EOQ:** We are now set to compute the EOQ using the simulated values of demand, ordering costs, and holding costs. The EOQ formula will be applied to each of the simulations we have generated. The results would each reflect a different simulated business condition. The EOQs form a distribution and not a single value. To understand this distribution and make decisions based on this distribution, we will next calculate summary statistics for 25th, 50th (median), 75th, 95th, and 99th percentile. We now know the most common (median) EOQ, and the EOQ in best-case (25th) or worst-case (99th) demand/cost scenarios. It helps decision-making under different risk appetites to choose the appropriate EOQ value based on their risk tolerance and business priorities. The 25th percentile EOQ is a conservative strategy, minimizing costs but having potential stockouts. The 75th percentile is slightly conservative with buffer and would result in fewer stockouts. The 99th percentile EOQ is considered for businesses with very low stockout tolerance.
- **EOQ range output and plotting:** In this section, we visualize the distribution of EOQ values obtained from a stochastic simulation in the form of a histogram. The histogram shows the frequency of simulated EOQ in each range. A frequency distribution table has also been generated. For the frequency table, we have specified the bin size in the customization section. The code generates a table displayed on the screen and a histogram plot which is also saved.

There are essentially four outputs of the code: EOQ report, EOQ frequency distribution table, histogram of simulated EOQ, and a CSV file with detailed results of the simulation. The EOQ Summary Statistics (Stochastic) displays a table as shown in Table 6.1.

This means that 25% of the simulated values are below or equal to 130.16, and 99% of the values did not exceed 170.02. If the company wants to minimize the risk of stockouts in high-demand scenarios or under high ordering costs, it may consider using an EOQ closer to the higher percentiles (like the 95th or 99th percentile). On the other hand, if cost control and average-case performance are more important, the median EOQ (50th percentile) may be a reasonable choice.

The second table displayed on the screen shows the EOQ frequency table, as is given in Table 6.2. It displays the frequency against specified ranges of EOQ.

In addition, the code generates a CSV file containing the results of the simulation. It stores values of simulated demand, simulated ordering cost, simulated holding cost, and the resultant EOQ. The file contains the number of simulations specified in the customization section.

Table 6.1 EOQ summary statistic (stochastic)

25th percentile:	130.16 units
50th percentile (median):	138.69 units
75th percentile:	147.61 units
95th percentile:	151.24 units
99th percentile:	170.02 units

Table 6.2 EOQ frequency distribution table

EOQ Range	Frequency
(97.379, 106.374)	24
(106.374, 115.281)	209
(115.281, 124.187)	978
(124.187, 133.094)	2,140
(133.094, 142.0)	2,662
(142.0, 150.907)	2,163
(150.907, 159.813)	1,227
(159.813, 168.72)	470
(168.72, 177.626)	108
(177.626, 186.533)	19

Demand forecasting with time series analysis

One of the major components of inventory management is demand. This influences a host of factors including purchasing decisions, storing decisions, funding decisions, production scheduling, and others. We have used ML tools for forecasting in earlier chapters. We will now see how such tools can be used in inventory management, specifically in demand forecasting.

Time series forecasting of demand

There are several ML libraries available for time series forecasting, and the one we will be using here is `Prophet`. We have seen during our earlier use that it is designed to handle time series data that have characteristics like seasonal patterns, holiday impacts, missing data points, and outliers that might distort conventional models.

Data preprocessing requirements are minimal as the tool automatically detects trends and seasonality. It also provides support for including holiday effects and requires minimal manual tuning. This makes it especially suitable for analysts and professionals without extensive background in statistical modeling. Users can also integrate confidence intervals when generating forecasts.

Consider a garments retailer that uses ML tools to forecast monthly demand. It then moves on to compute reorder points and safety stock levels using a confidence interval based on statistical normal distribution. Though we have not shown it here, this business case can be extended to procurement, distribution, and production planning.

The code (prefix 0602) is split into six sections as described hereunder:

- **Import libraries:** We have loaded `pandas`, `prophet`, `matplotlib`, `SciPy`, and `numpy` libraries. `Prophet` is the forecasting tool, `matplotlib` has been used to plot data and forecast results, and SciPy is used for statistical functions related to normal distribution.
- **Customize:** In this step, we have provided the parameters that need customization. This would include setting the confidence level, the number of months to forecast, the limit of the forecast period to historical data, files having input data and where the reports should be saved, and finally the names of files to save the plots. Here is the relevant part of the code with customizable parameters recognizable by italics and underlining.

```
# Parameter customization
confidence_level = 90 # e.g., 90 for 90% confidence
forecast_months = 6
forecast_limit = .25
```

```
my_transaction="0602 inventory_transaction.csv"
my_forecast_file='0602 Forecasted_demand.csv'
my_reorder_file='0602 Inventory_plan.csv'
my_forecast_plot="0602 Forecast.png"
my_reorder_plot="0602 Reorder_Forecast_Plot.png"
```

- **Load and preprocess data:** In this section, we are preparing the data for further processing. We ensure that the date field is indeed in date format and drop rows that are without any date. Similarly, we are ensuring that units sold are a numeric field and replacing any blank value with zero. Since this will be a time series operation, the date field is being set as an index. Forecasting too far beyond the available historical data makes the model unreliable, and the results may not be helpful for decision-making. We have limited this by providing that forecasts are limited to a specified percent of the total historical days. We have further derived a dataframe for monthly sales and renamed columns to match the requirement of `Prophet`. This removes noise from daily fluctuation and makes it easier to spot seasonality and trend components. `Prophet` allows this resampling even at a weekly level. To do it at the weekly level, you will have to change the code snippet .resample('MS') to

```
.resample('W'). This is the default for Sunday-based
weeks.
```

- **Fit and forecast demand and reorder level:** The Prophet forecasting model will now fit (trains) the model on our monthly aggregated sales data. This fitted model will then be used to forecast for the specified period capturing the trend and seasonality patterns. After forecasting, the code proceeds to compute the reorder level and safety stock under uncertainty. To factor in uncertainty, we assume a normal distribution and use a specified confidence level. For the statistical minded, we have computed the z-score. From the full forecast, we are extracting data corresponding to the period of forecast we had specified earlier. The dataset, apart from the forecast value, also contains the lower and upper bound of the forecast. The standard deviation of the projected value is computed by the code. The reorder value under uncertainty is computed using the forecast value, confidence interval provided, and standard deviation approximated. Similarly, the safety stock is computed.
- **Create plots:** In this section, we create two plots. The first plot shows the forecast, historical values, and prediction interval. The next plot overlays the reorder point on the forecasted demand. You can change the legends that appear on the chart by replacing them in the code with the one you prefer. Note that to provide a large picture for better clarity we have specified the size of the plot in the code `plt.figure(figsize=(10, 6)`. You can change the dimensions if you want. Both plots are displayed and saved.

- **Save data and plots:** This last section handles the exporting and display of results from the inventory forecasting and reorder point planning model. These are saved to a CSV file under names specified by you. The reorder plan for the forecast period is displayed on the screen.

The output of the code includes the plots and the CSV files apart from the display on the screen. The plot of the demand forecast (Figure 6.1) displays the forecast line along with historical data as a dot around the line. Intuitively, the closer the dots are to the forecast line, the better the model fit. The shaded area reflects the upper and lower bounds.

The next plot (Figure 6.2) shows the forecast demand and the reorder level. In this case as well, the shaded area shows the upper and lower bound of confidence level.

In addition to the plots, we have saved the forecast output (including lower/upper prediction bounds) to a CSV file. You may remember that ds is the date, yhat is the forecasted demand, yhat_lower is the lower bound of confidence interval and yhat_upper is the upper bound of confidence interval. The file content looks like Table 6.3.

We have also saved the reorder planning output (forecast, reorder point, safety stock) to a separate CSV called inventory plan, as shown in Table 6.4. It is created monthly and includes the reorder point and safety stock among others.

Another important area of focus that can influence our inventory decisions, among others, is the supply chain. In the next section, we will discuss how ML tools can be used in optimizing supply chains.

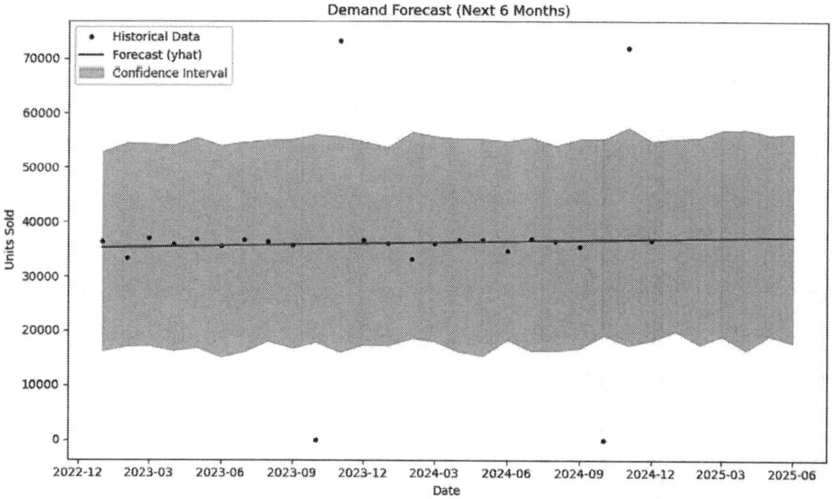

Figure 6.1 Demand forecast output

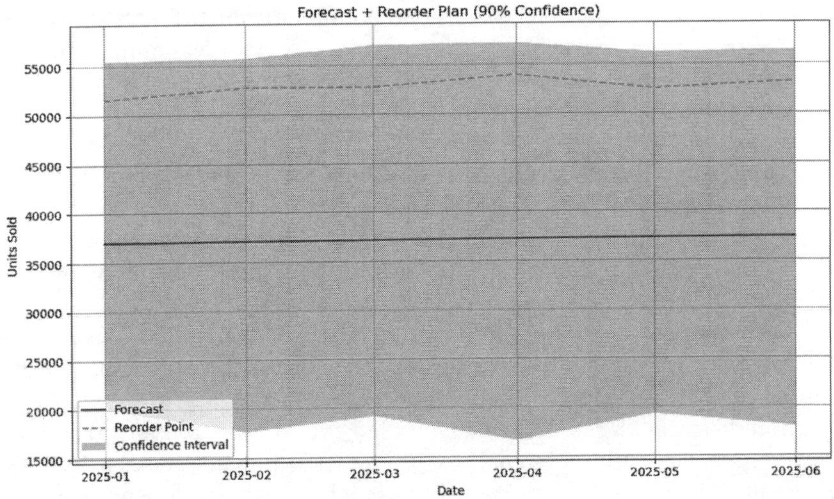

Figure 6.2 Forecast + Reorder plan output

Table 6.3 Forecast output table format

	ds	yhat	yhat_lower	yhat_upper
1				
2				

Table 6.4 Reorder planning output format

	ds	yhat	yhat_ lower	yhat_ upper	Reorder Point	SafetyStock
1						
2						

Supply chain optimization using network analysis

Efficient supply chain management is critical for maintaining competitiveness, reducing costs, and ensuring timely delivery of goods and services. Traditional supply chain strategies find it difficult to adapt to dynamic changes in demand or logistics. Supply chain management manages the end-to-end flow of goods, information, and finances across the entire value chain. It focuses on raw material sourcing to product delivery to end customers. Activities that result in the goods reaching the customers generate revenue. Similarly, activities that ensure raw materials reach the processing plant trigger the revenue generation capability. Both are important to financial decision-makers. If the efficiency of these activities is enhanced, it can increase revenue generation capability and can also optimize workflow to reduce costs.

Network analysis maps supplier relationships, distribution channels, and inventory flows as interconnected networks. The results of the analysis can be useful in identifying the bottlenecks that inflate working capital and pinpoint redundancies. This approach can improve cash conversion cycles through optimized inventory positioning and supplier payment terms.

Successful network optimization requires data support including capturing real-time flows across all supply chain nodes. We have seen elsewhere in the book how real-time data can be populated in a reporting dashboard. Network optimization can also reveal counterintuitive insights that challenge established supplier relationships and internal processes.

Let us study a scenario involving optimizing a supply network for cost and time efficiency. Consider a consumer goods company that operates a basic supply chain with one factory, two warehouses, and two retailers. The company wants to optimize the movement of goods through this network to minimize transportation costs from the factory to retailers. This will reduce delivery time to improve service levels. The company also wants to identify critical nodes in the network to ensure reliability and responsiveness. In case we have started thinking that these network optimization tools are useful only in the context of the movement of physical goods, let us get the context correct. Think of a typical cash conversion cycle or operating cycle. They also represent a network highlighted by process flow from one node to another with the corresponding time. Instead of goods, movement between the nodes signifies incremental creation of wealth. Instead of technology, management decisions like stock holding, credit period, and similar influence the time between these activity nodes. Network analysis is useful to optimize these conversion cycles.

Now back to our company. It ships products from its factory to retailers, passing through the warehouses. It can reach the retailer using any one of the warehouses. We have kept only one layer to keep the example simple, complexities in the form of intermediaries can be easily added. The company wants to determine the most cost-effective and time-efficient route from the factory to a specific retailer.

The supply network is modeled as a directed graph with nodes and edges. Nodes are the fundamental entities, points, or components in a network that represent a critical area of focus. These are also our decision centers as well as connection points. The nodes are factory, warehouse 1, warehouse 2, retailer 1, and retailer 2. Edges are permissible and feasible connections between nodes. The flow goes from factory to warehouse and then to retailer. In this case, six permissible edges connect the nodes. Every edge has two attributes: transportation cost and delivery time. In case you

Table 6.5 Edges with attributes

From	*To*	*Cost ($)*	*Time (hour)*
Factory	Warehouse 1	80	2
Factory	Warehouse 2	75	3
Warehouse 1	Retailer 1	55	1
Warehouse 1	Retailer 2	55	2
Warehouse 2	Retailer 2	45	3
Warehouse 2	Retailer 1	65	3

are getting confused between edges and connection, they are essentially the same thing. An edge is a formal representation of a connection in a graph, as given in Table 6.5.

The business wants to find the shortest path from the Factory to Retailer 2 under normal conditions. It will then consider a disruption when the route from the factory to Warehouse 2 is blocked.

The ML-based tool should be able to identify the shortest paths by cost and by time from factory to retailers. It should also be able to identify the centrality of nodes to understand which facilities are most critical to the flow of goods. To address these requirements, we will use ML tools. `NetworkX` library is an ML tool used to model, analyze, and optimize supply chain networks. Let us now have a look at the code (prefix 0603).

- **Import libraries:** In this section, we have loaded the necessary libraries. `NetworkX` library is a tool for creating, analyzing, and visualizing complex networks or graphs. While using this library for our case, the nodes would represent locations like suppliers, warehouses, stores, and others. The edges represent connections like transportation links, flow of goods, and similar. We can use it to compute the shortest paths between nodes to reduce delivery time or cost.
- **Customize:** We have specified the names of files to save the report and the plots. We have proceeded to define the nodes. Please note the use of square brackets, quotes, and commas. This will populate the directed network graph. The next part of customization involves defining the edges and their respective attributes in terms of cost and time. The first two elements are respectively the starting and terminal points of the edge. These must be one of the nodes that we have defined earlier. Subsequent items are the name and value of the parameters. The values may change for each edge, but the names of the attributes will have to be the same across all edges. The business case will decide what the feasible edges are. You can add nodes and edges depending on your business case. The last part of the code defines the source and target nodes. The

relevant part of the code with the customizable section in italics is provided here.

```
my_normal_report = "0603 Normal_Network_Report.csv"
my_disrupted_report = "0603 Disrupted_Network_Report.csv"
my_network_plot="0603 Supply_chain_network.png"
my_disrupted_plot="0603 Disrupted_Supply_chain_network.
png"

# Add supply chain nodes
nodes = ['Factory', 'Warehouse1', 'Warehouse2',
'Retailer1', 'Retailer2']

# Add edges with cost and time attributes edges = [
('Factory', 'Warehouse1', {'cost': 80, 'time': 2}),
('Factory', 'Warehouse2', {'cost': 75, 'time': 3}),
('Warehouse1', 'Retailer1', {'cost': 55, 'time': 1}),
('Warehouse2', 'Retailer2', {'cost': 45, 'time': 3}),
('Warehouse2', 'Retailer1', {'cost': 65, 'time': 3}),
('Warehouse1', 'Retailer2', {'cost': 55, 'time': 2})
]

my_source='Factory'
my_target='Retailer2'
# Under disruption scenario
disruption_source='Factory'
disruption_target='Warehouse2'
```

Just to be clear on how we are using the customization, here is a short summary of what we are doing here. We have nodes representing key supply chain entities which are one Factory, two Warehouses, and two Retailers.

These represent the starting point of goods, intermediary distribution points, and endpoints where goods are sold, respectively. Now the network graph knows the entities involved but has no connections yet. We define the edges to provide this information. Setting edges defines directed connections between nodes. We have defined the source and destination, and then for each connection we have provided the cost and time parameters.

- **Create the model**: In this section, we have invoked the model and provided information about the nodes and edges customized by us in the earlier section.
- **Analyze shortest path and centrality:** In this part, we compute the shortest path for the lowest cost and lowest time. Once these shortest paths are identified, we compute the cost of the shortest path with minimum cost and time for the shortest path with minimum cost. These two

shortest paths are more likely to be different than not. The selection will depend on the management objective – do we want to reach the fastest or cheapest? The code also calculates the centrality measures to identify critical nodes in the supply chain. Centrality helps us identify the most important or influential nodes in a network. It would play a key role in connecting various parts of the network. In our context, a "central" node might be a warehouse, factory, or retailer. There are different types of centralities, we will be using betweenness centrality. Betweenness centrality measures how often a node lies on the shortest paths between other nodes. Consider a road network. If most of the shortest routes from one city to another must pass through a particular city, that city is central, a critical connector. Centrality helps identify choke points, hubs, and optimization opportunities. `NetworkX` returns centrality scores as numbers between 0 and 1, 1 denoting that it is more central and 0 being a node that does not lie on any shortest path between factory and retailer. An interim self-explanatory report is presented on screen.

- **Simulate disruption:** In this step, we are going to simulate what happens when a specific connection (or route) is disrupted or removed, such as due to a logistics delay, natural disaster, or supplier issue. We are thus testing the network's resilience by simulating a failure on one edge of the supply chain graph. The program creates what-if scenarios multiple times and then recalculates the best new cost and time, on disruption. This is a practical tool in logistics and risk management. It tests the robustness of the business process network, identifies critical connections, and helps to plan backup routes and contingencies. An interim report reflecting the disrupted scenario is also presented on the screen.
- **Visualization; Plotting:** In this section, functions to create the network diagrams, display, and save them are being created. This is being done both for normal and disrupted networks. Please note that these are not being invoked here – that is the chart display or saving are not being done at this stage.
- **Visualization:** The functions defined in the earlier section are being called here and the network diagrams are rendered on screen. These are also being saved under the specified file name for subsequent use.
- **Compute network results:** The results of the normal and disrupted network are being computed by this section of the code. The descriptions after metric are customizable and you can change them to express yourself. However, the values are specific to this code and cannot be changed only here.
- **Data display and export to file:** In this step, we save the network results populated on the earlier section in the dataframe. These are then saved under specified CSV files. We provide a quick display of the network features, both under normal and disrupted scenarios. We have proceeded to

generate a summary report highlighting the difference in key parameters under normal and disrupted scenarios.

The output from the code includes on-screen reports, plots of normal and disrupted network diagrams, and key parameters of normal and disrupted networks saved in CSV format. The on-screen report after analysis of the disruption network also compares the criticality factor for each node. If you compare the two network diagrams, you will find that the disrupted edge has been removed from the network diagram. The final on-screen summary also shows the cost impact of the disruption.

The information provided will allow the financial decision-maker to assess how much disruption would cost. This information is useful for deciding on planning alternative management processes. Please note that in this case study we have focused primarily on the cost aspect.

Let us give a moment to think about how the tool can be used to optimize the cash conversion cycle. In that case, nodes will represent different stages of the business cycle like procurement, production, sales, collection, and related. Edges will represent the flow and transformation of value and wealth between these stages.

The flow will measure the incremental wealth creation rather than physical movement. Time will be the key optimization variable instead of distance or capacity. Time will be influenced by corresponding policies. Days inventory outstanding (DIO) is influenced by inventory management policies. Credit terms and collection efficiency will influence days sales outstanding (DSO). Days payable outstanding (DPO) will be determined by supplier payment strategies. Network optimization can suggest optimal time values for these activities after incorporating all associated costs and benefits. You can see that this tool can be used anywhere where there are sequential value-creating activities with measurable transitions between states.

We have been through tools to optimize inventory holding and supply chain management. However, to efficiently use these tools, we need to classify our inventory items and focus more on the critical items. In the next section, we will focus on how ML tools can help us identify critical items from the list of inventory.

Inventory classification with ML

Effective inventory management is essential for operational efficiency, cost control, and customer satisfaction. Traditional methods of inventory classification such as ABC and XYZ offer a foundational approach. ABC method categorizes inventory based on value or usage, while XYZ method categorizes using variability. ML tools help to perform ABC analysis automatically over a large volume of data. It can generate alerts to enable users to focus on areas identified as critical. However, the basis of classification is simple, and they may not capture underlying complexities.

However, with the growing volume and complexity of inventory data, ML provides a more dynamic and data-driven alternative for classification. This segment introduces the application of ML tools, particularly clustering algorithms like K-means, to classify inventory items for improved oversight and strategic decision-making. By analyzing attributes such as demand forecast and sales, turnover rates and profitability, our price, and competitors' pricing, ML techniques can uncover hidden patterns and segment inventory in ways that can lead to improved control.

ABC analysis integrated with a sales alert system

An ABC analysis segments inventory or sales items based on their value contribution. They typically classify items as the following:

- **A items:** High-value, low-quantity items, say 60%–70% of value
- **B items:** Moderate-value items, say next 15%–25% of value
- **C items:** Low-value, high-quantity items, say the bottom 10%–15% of value

ABC classification helps in prioritizing control and resource allocation. Similarly, an organization may have a sales alert system. This system can monitor item-level performance and trigger notifications when specific conditions are met. These two systems can be integrated to improve overall management control.

Let us investigate this code which does just that. Here are the main components of the code (prefix 0604).

- **Import libraries:** We have imported all libraries required for this code. All these libraries are known to us.
- **Customize:** In this section, we have specified the names of the CSV files containing input data and where details of ABC analysis and summary will be saved. We have also specified the names of files to save plots. In addition, we have set thresholds for cost alerts and for classifying inventory into A, B, and C classifications. Products are ranked by consumption value from highest to lowest. The top-consuming products that together account for the threshold for A, in this case 60%, of total consumption, are classified as "A" items. The thresholds are cumulative and not incremental. We have also specified the names of columns that will be used for ABC analysis. We have selected the item number, price, and usage data. The relevant part of the code with customizable parameters in italics is given here.

```
# Load Data
data = pd.read_csv('0604 Sales_data.csv')
my_detailed_report='0604_ABC_Details.csv'
my_summary_report='0604_ABC_Summary.csv'
my_cum_cost_plot='0604_ABC_Cumulative_Cost.png'
my_abc_per_sku='0604_ABC_Cost_per_SKU.png'
my_abc_class='0604_ABC_Class_Distribution.png'

# Sales Alert System
ALERT_THRESHOLD = 100000 # Adjust this value as needed

my_a_thresh=0.6
my_b_thresh=0.85

#Specify columns that will be used for ABC analysis
my_columns= ['SKU_number', 'PriceReg', 'ItemCount']
```

- **Preprocessing and classification:** In this section, we are performing three tasks. These are data preprocessing, creating cumulative totals, and creating a summary of categories. The code first creates a copy of the input data with three specified columns which are sourced from historical data. The total cost is computed as the price multiplied by the units sold. Next, we sorted all rows in descending order of total cost, so that the item with the highest cost comes at the top. The data is reindexed after sorting. We have also created a function that will classify the products into three categories depending on the threshold values. You can calibrate the classification thresholds during customization. Now the sorted list is used to create cumulative totals. This section of the code computes cumulative costs using the sorted list which leads to cumulative percentages. The cumulative percentage of total cost for each SKU determines whether an item falls into Class A, B, or C classification. Lastly, the summary table groups the data by Class (A, B, or C) and calculates the number of SKUs (line items) in each class and the corresponding total cost. A column converting the absolute cost numbers into percentages is added. Now the summary table shows what percentage of total cost is contributed by Class A, B, and C.

  So, here we have already got each sales transaction sorted by value, the cumulative distribution of cost, and SKUs categorized into A, B, or C classes. It also has a summary showing how many items are in each class, what cost each class contributes, and what percentage of the total each class represents.
- **Data output:** This section gives a quick screen output to the user. It provides the total number of items in each category with the corresponding total cost and percentage of total cost. The limit for A, B, and C classification is also provided as a ready reference.

- **Generating alerts:** This cost alert system is a powerful add-on to the ABC analysis. It creates a new column in the dataset called Alert. It applies the above-defined condition on each row of the specified class. You can change the target class by tweaking this part of the code - `np.where((data_sub['Class'] == 'A')`. You can change the value of A to B or C. The data is filtered to include only the rows where an alert has been triggered. If alerts are found, it prints a warning message mentioning the SKU number, the total cost, and item counts. Set the threshold carefully, as most items in the A classification are likely to have a high consumption. If there are no alerts, a positive confirmation message is printed.
- **Visualization and plot output:** This segment of the code displays and saves three plots. The first plot shows the number of items by each classification. The second chart displays the total cost per item. Note with a very large number of items, this chart may be difficult to comprehend. The third chart shows the total cost plotted against items along with the cutoff values for the three classifications.
- **Output data** to CSV file: In this section, we will export results to CSV files for reporting, auditing, and future analysis. We have exported both a detailed and a summary report. The files are saved in the name specified by the user.

The output from the code includes screen display, plot files, and CSV. The plot showing the number of items in each v=category is self-explanatory. The line chart visualizes the cost distribution across all items. We can visually identify outliers or extremely high-cost items. We also spot clusters, for example, a few items driving the most cost (Figure 6.3).

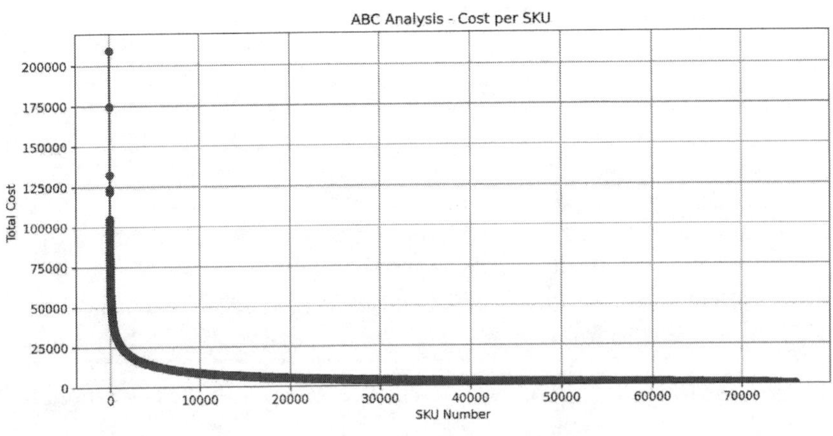

Figure 6.3 ABC analysis

Since the data in this chart is very compressed, you may want to visualize this by each classification. In that case, tweak the code. Just after the comment # Line Chart: TotalCost per SKU enter the following two lines of code.

```
class_filter = 'A' # or 'B' or 'C'
filtered_data = data_sub[data_sub['Class'] == class_filter]
```

Further, change the plt.plot(data_sub['TotalCost'] to

```
plt.plot(filtered_data['TotalCost']
```

The last chart plots cumulative costs with classification cutoffs. It is a key chart to visually validate ABC classification (Figure 6.4). This chart plots the cumulative percentage of cost for all items. Each point on the X-axis represents a ranked item, from the most expensive to the least. The Y-axis shows how much of the total cost has been covered up to that item. This chart shows how quickly cost accumulates. The steeper the curve at the beginning, the more dominant a few items are. The chart reinforces that a small number of items dominate the cost, justifying tight control on them.

The saved reports include various fields. In the detailed report, details of computation also include the running cost, the percentage that the cumulative cost bears to the total cost, the classification, and the alert (Table 6.6). This file will be very useful for further analysis and processing.

The summary report simply records the number of items, total cost, and percentage share of total against each classification.

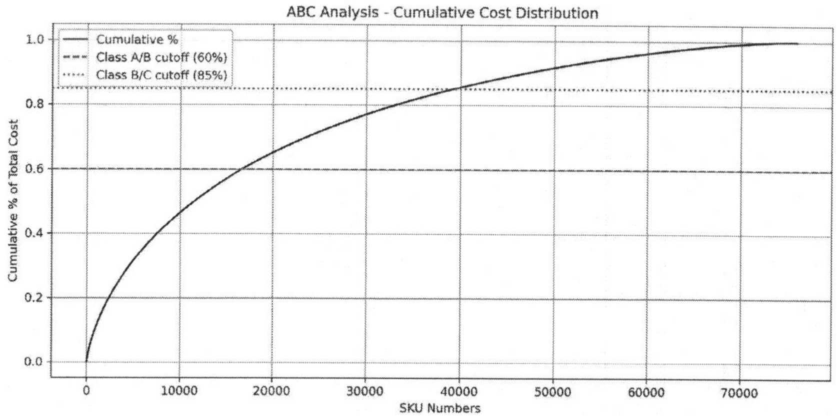

Figure 6.4 ABC analysis – cumulative distribution

Table 6.6 Detailed computation report

SKU_number	PriceReg	ItemCount	TotalCost	RunCumCost	RunPerc	Class	Alert

Though very useful and efficient, this application still follows the user intervention of defining the classifications. In the next section, we will use the power of ML tools to find its classification logic.

Clustering inventory items using clustering algorithms

Decision-makers can apply ML clustering techniques to segment inventory items based on key financial and operational attributes. These tools help businesses uncover actionable insights that can help them in making segment-specific decisions.

Let us consider the garment retailer who wants to get insight into how the market works. They want to review the data from the following three angles.

- **Price strategy segmentation:** Clustering based on item pricing, discounting, and competitor pricing. This will identify premium, competitive, and underpriced product groups.
- **Demand-seasonality segmentation:** Clustering based on units sold and forecasted demand with seasonal adjustment. This will be useful in detecting items with understocking, overstocking, or stable behavior.
- **Profitability and turnover segmentation:** Clustering based on profitability and turnover rate to highlight high-performing versus inefficient inventory items.

The code will process and analyze transactional inventory data using unsupervised learning techniques, specifically K-means clustering.

Let us now dive into the major components of the code (prefix 0605).

- **Import libraries:** Four libraries have been used in this code. They are loaded in this section.
- **Customize:** In this code, most of the customizable parameters have been defined in this section. They include the names of the input and output files and the files to save plots. Many of the files are application-specific and we need to be careful about the purpose while defining the name for the file. We have also defined a set of features for cluster analysis. We need to ensure that the features are all present in the data input file.

One of the unique parameters defined in this code is the color palette to be used for plotting the cluster diagram. We have created an option for black and white and color palettes. This may be useful if you are using the plots in black-and-white reports. Since we are using three clusters, three colors have been defined in the palette.

Apart from all these, we have some additional customization requirements during the code processing. These have been identified at their respective places. The relevant part of the code with the customizable sections in italics is given here.

```
# Customize parameters

my_inventory_input="0602 inventory_transaction.csv"
my_features = ['Inventory Level', 'Units Sold',
'Units Ordered', 'Demand Forecast', 'Price', 'Discount',
'Competitor Pricing']
my_price_competitor_cluster="0605 Price and Competitor.
png"
my_price_cluster="0605 Price_clusters.csv"
my_price_summary="0605 Price_summary.csv"
my_demand_forecast="0605 Demand_Forecast_units_sold.png"
my_demand_cluster="0605 Demand price_clusters.csv"
my_demand_summary="0605_Demand_summary.csv"
my_kmeans_cluster="0605 Clustering_KMeans_Output.csv"
my_cluster_profit="0605 Clustering_Profitability.png"

#Customize cluster markers. Set it to Set2 for color.
#Comment out the one not being used
my_palette='Set2'
#my_palette=['black', 'gray', 'lightgray']
```

- **Load data and preprocess:** We have loaded the input data at this point. At this stage, we are also incorporating encoded seasonality information. We have a categorical feature called seasonality which has four possible values – winter, spring, autumn, and summer. These are text values and are difficult to use in modeling. In the process of encoding, this feature is split into three columns say is_winter, is_spring, and is_autum. We can use these three columns to identify the season.

  One-hot encoding transforms non-numeric data into a form that clustering algorithms can use to detect season-driven behavior (Table 6.7). We combine these encoded fields with the features. Once combined, the model can cluster items by both supply chain dynamics and market behavior. Integration of seasonal influence with operational and pricing data will allow clustering to recognize patterns like high sales seasons, low inventory seasons, and similar. We also scaled the data to avoid

Table 6.7 One-hot encoding example

Season	*is_winter*	*is_spring*	*is_autumn*
Winter	1	0	0
Spring	0	1	0
Autumn	0	0	1
Summer	0	0	0

unnecessary weightage on high-value data. We are now ready with clean, standardized, multi-dimensional data, integrating seasonality, for use in our clustering algorithms.

- **Clustering based on price and competitor prices:** The first set of clustering is based on three features – price, competitor price, and discount. These are customizable values which you can tweak in this part of the code

```
features = df[['Price', 'Competitor Pricing', 'Dis-
count']]
```

  These features are then scaled as usual. We use K-means to create 3 clusters based on the features. We have discussed earlier that if you want more or a smaller number of clusters, you can do that by tweaking the code component n_clusters=3. We now have cluster membership information and plot the clusters. We also generate a summary of key features stating the units sold, price, competitor price, discount, and number of transactions in each of the three clusters. We save the plot along with the detailed and summary result of clustering.
- **Clustering for demand forecast and units sold:** In this section, we will apply K-means clustering on demand-related features. We have used codes similar to those used in the earlier section but with different features. Here we have used units sold and demand forecast as features and created a copy of the dataframe. We have appended the one-hot coded seasonality variables. The values are then normalized which factors in seasonality. The detailed and summary cluster information is saved along with the plot.
- **Clustering profitability and turnover rates:** This last section of clustering is based on profitability and turnover ratio. These two are critical performance metrics in inventory and financial analysis. The objective is to segment inventory items by how financially efficient they are, based on profitability and how fast they are sold. The turnover ratio measures how quickly the inventory moves. We have followed similar code but have used different features – turnover_rate and profitability. This is not information that is available directly from the input file and has been computed by the following code.

```
df['Turnover_Rate'] = df['Units Sold'] / df['Inventory
Level']
df['Profitability'] = (df['Price'] - df['Competitor
Pricing'] - df['Discount']) * df['Units Sold']
```

A high turnover indicates efficient stock movement; a low rate may indicate stagnation. Profitability measures the net profit contribution of each item after considering competitor pricing and discounts. It shows how much profit is being earned relative to the market and discounts applied. This does not show profitability from the accounting viewpoint.

We would need to scale and normalize data as turnover rate and profitability are likely to operate on different scales. This makes clustering fair and avoids dominance by larger numeric values. K-means clustering is applied with 3 clusters and each inventory item is assigned to a cluster labeled 0, 1, or 2.

The clusters are then plotted and a summary is displayed on screen. The plot and detailed and summary clustering results are saved in a file for future reference.

The outputs of the code are essentially of three types. On-screen display of summary results and clustering plots, graphics file saving the plot, and CSV files saving the detailed and summary result of clustering.

The first cluster is based on price and competitor price (Figure 6.5).

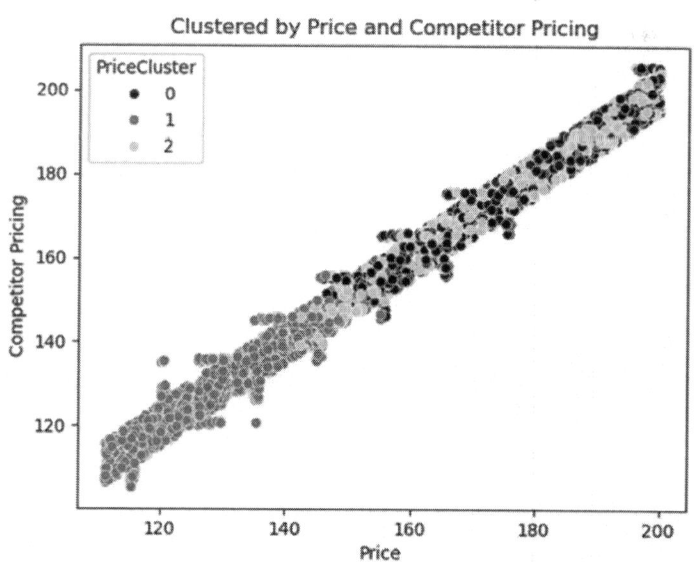

Figure 6.5 Price and competitor price based cluster

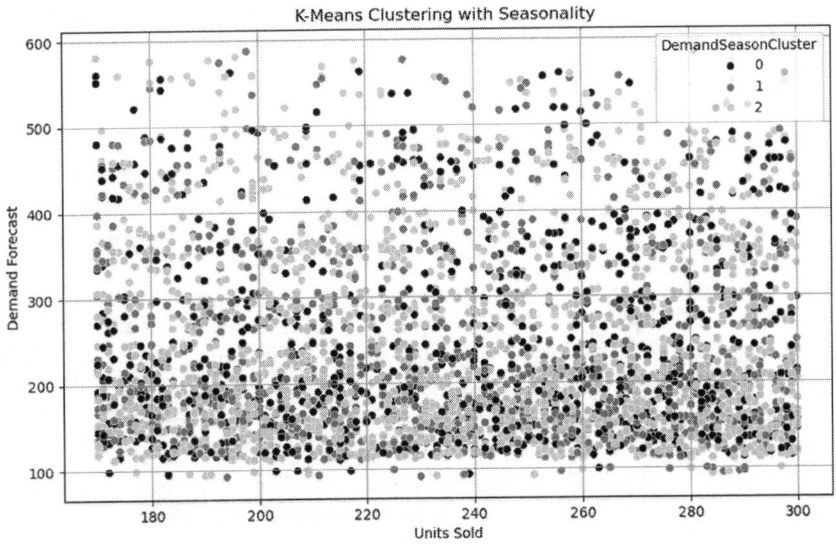

Figure 6.6 Demand forecast and actual sales-based cluster

The cluster plot suggests that cluster 0 is the premium segment, cluster 1 is the economy segment, and cluster 2 is the mid-market. You can also see the price of the retailer and that of their competitor follow a similar pattern across all segments.

There are some occasional minor outliers that can be investigated. The price strategy of the retailer seems to be well aligned with their competitor. Cluster 2, the mid-market, is quite dense, indicating a highly competitive segment. The on-screen summary results endorse this view.

The second cluster is based on demand forecast and units sold (Figure 6.6).

Interestingly, you can see that the segmentation is done primarily on demand forecasts rather than on actual units sold. The cluster boundaries are better defined against demand forecast. Actual sales show similar ranges across clusters indicating that forecasting accuracy varies significantly. We can say that cluster 0 is high demand forecast periods, cluster 1 is moderate demand forecast periods, and cluster 2 is low demand forecast periods. The vertical separation also indicates that seasonality is a major differentiating factor, besides forecasting. However, the impact of seasonality is built into the algorithm that has clustered the data. The forecast value itself is influenced by the seasonality.

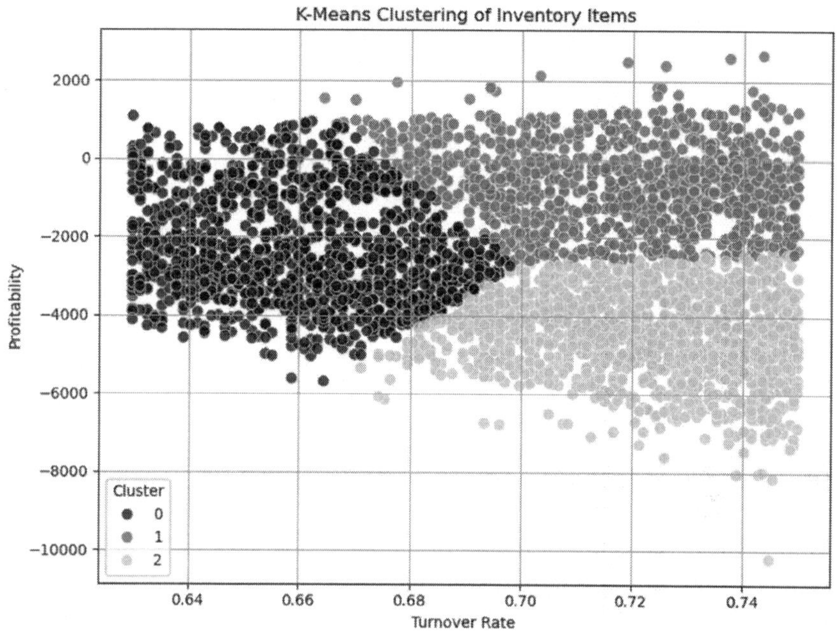

Figure 6.7 Turnover ratio and profitability-based clusters

The third cluster is based on profitability and turnover ratio (Figure 6.7). The clusters present a very interesting structure. Cluster 0 shows low-performance items. They are mostly underperforming with low turnover and though with a wide range of profitability, the majority of them are unprofitable from the viewpoint of competition. These would generally be low-moving items. Cluster 1 is moderately performing and operates over a wide range from mid to high values. The profitability is mixed but primarily in the middle range. This is likely to be the core business base highlighted by reliable products that generate steady business. There are a few exceptional performers with high profitability and a mixed turnover ratio. Cluster 2 is fast-moving with low profitability. These seem to be items that are competitively priced when compared with competition; most likely price-sensitive items. This explains their fast turnover.

You can clearly see the insight that ML tools generate over rule-driven classification tools discussed in the earlier section. Incorporating these insights into financial decision-making provides a more flexible and informed strategy.

Key takeaways

Inventory management is a strategic function that influences profit, performance, and customer experience. Integrating ML enhances forecast accuracy, automates replenishment, and improves classification. Clustering and simulation-based EOQ models provide data-driven insights for smarter inventory and procurement planning. Visualizations and decision support tools transform raw data into intelligence that can be used by cross-functional teams. Supply chain network optimization adds another dimension by simulating real-world complexities and provides a tool to understand the financial dimensions of supply line disruptions.

This chapter provides not just tools and techniques, but also a framework for thinking strategically about inventory. The availability of easy-to-use ML tools can make inventory management more efficient than ever earlier.

Chapter 7

Capital budgeting and investment analysis

Welcome to this chapter, where we explore the application of ML and AI tools in capital budgeting and investment analysis. We will automate techniques such as NPV and IRR using ML tools for quicker investment appraisals and dynamic capital budgeting analysis. This chapter will show us how to optimize investment portfolios using PyPortfolioOpt, and also use simulation techniques to value real options.

Building blocks of capital budgeting and investment analysis

Broadly speaking, capital budgeting refers to the evaluation of investments that lead to the acquisition of fixed assets recorded on the investor's balance sheet. In contrast, investment analysis typically focuses on decisions related to financial or monetary assets. Beyond the acquisition of new assets, the analysis framework can even be used for introducing a new product line. In essence, investment analysis tools prove highly valuable in any situation where a substantial, committed cash outflow leads to cash inflows spread over an extended period. These tools help businesses determine which long-term investments are worth pursuing. It involves evaluating potential projects or investments to see if they will generate sufficient returns in the future to justify the initial outlay of capital. Key components of investment analysis (or capital budgeting) include the following:

- **Cash flows**: The cash flows for investment analysis include cash inflows and outflows that arise as a direct result of the proposed investment.
- **Time value of money**: This centers around how much a sum of money would be worth tomorrow under purchasing power parity. There could be different ways of measuring the same.
- **Risk analysis**: This factors in the uncertainty and potential risks associated with a project. This includes risks of all kinds, including market risks, operational risks, and financial risks.

DOI: 10.4324/9781003619628-7

Investment is a multi-dimensional decision. Some of the key considerations would include the following:

- **Maximizing shareholder value**: The objective of any investment decision is to increase shareholder wealth. The wealth is measured in terms of potential realized cash, hence the importance of cash flow. The decision-making metrics will change depending on the objective of the investment.
- **Strategic alignment**: In addition to financial potential, a proposed investment should align with the company's long-term strategic goals. This includes considering long-term market trends, competitive dynamics, and technical and regulatory environments from a trajectory, transformation, and sustainability perspective. These also impact the cash flows and the risk exposure arising from the investment. A technical feasibility study is one of the input variables of the strategic alignment review process.
- **Financial feasibility**: The investment must make money over and above what is being spent after adjusting for the time value. In addition to assessing this primary criterion of investment, a financial feasibility study would also include evaluating whether the company has the financial resources to undertake the project. This involves evaluating the company's cash flows, debt levels, and access to financing. In addition to being financially feasible, the consequences should also be aligned with the strategic goals. For example, higher long-term borrowings will result in a higher gearing ratio, which the investor may not be comfortable with.
- **Risk management**: Evaluation of an investment proposal is commonly made considering a static environment. Risk management focuses on how environmental variations and consequent changes in the input assumptions affect the investment decision. We must note that the impact is to be considered after the mitigating measures have been put in place. This evaluation includes conducting a sensitivity analysis and scenario planning to understand how changes in key variables might affect the project's outcomes and whether the entity is willing to take that exposure.

Process of investment appraisal decisions and the time value of money

Investment appraisal decisions come at the end of an exhaustive process that involves several steps. Some of these steps include the following:

- **Investment objective**: An investment decision should start with deciding on the objective. Asking "Why is the investment necessary?" will define the subset of investment. It could be going into a new market, introducing a new product, supporting a higher dividend, or even utilizing idle funds. The opportunities that address the objective will be shortlisted for subsequent evaluation.

- **Investment alternatives**: Top-level criteria help define the broad set of available options. Second-level criteria, which include specific metrics, are then used to evaluate and select the most suitable option among them. It is at this stage that strategic alignment becomes a key consideration.
- **Evaluation metrics**: Once the investment alternatives are decided, the most popular evaluation criterion is wealth maximization. There may be other criteria also, and the selection of metrics will be driven by this objective. We will discuss these metrics in the following section. Exit options are often a critical criterion, as they determine the financial implications if investors need to withdraw from the investment. This may arise for different reasons, and unless there are clear exit routes, the extent of uncertainty associated with the project will increase. As the risk increases, so will the return associated with it.
- **Estimating cash flow**: In all cases, we will need to estimate the cash flows. This is a critical step, as the focus should be on identifying the actual cash flows for the acquisition, rather than relying solely on how they are reported in financial statements. Consider a manufacturing company diversifying into the hospitality industry was setting up a hotel near their factory in an industrial town. There were no other hotels nearby. The parent manufacturing company also used the facility for their employees and saved on the transport cost of hosting their employees in nearby places. These savings will not be reported anywhere as accounting records costs, and not savings. Further, the savings will be made by another company. However, for investment evaluation, we will consider all cash flows arising out of the investment irrespective of whether that is direct, viz., increased sales, or indirect, viz., cost savings, and wherever recorded.
- **Post-investment review**: Once the investment is made, the performance must be reviewed to ensure that it meets the expected return. We face an interesting challenge here. The evaluation of an investment opportunity is primarily driven by estimated cash inflows and outflows. In contrast, post-investment, accounting for the same is done under the accrual system. In addition, as we stated earlier, not all cash flow changes would be reported in the books of the investing entity. This poses a major challenge while measuring the post-investment performance of the project. The investing entity will have to design a reporting system should they want to review the performance of a project in the same way they evaluated it.

Investment entails cash outflow and inflow at different points in time. The change comes in terms of their purchasing power and not in terms of measurement. To make them somewhat comparable, we try to fair value the future cash flows to current prices. Theoretically, we can future value all cash flows to future periods also or anchor them anywhere. To relate present value to future value, we use a compounding factor, and the reverse relation is established using a discounting factor. We broadly describe this as the time value of money. The factors that affect the time value of money would include the following:

- **Consumer preference:** An investment also means deferring current consumption to a future period. The investee needs enough incentive to defer present consumption, and this is difficult to measure objectively. It would depend on many factors, including some that are being discussed here. Those that cannot be objectively determined bring into play behavioral factors like preference and bias. The investor uses a measurement proxy for these in evaluating the time value of money.
- **Opportunity cost:** One of the factors that influences the time value of money is what else the money can be invested in at the time of decision-making. However, this would not mean all the available opportunities. The benchmark would be chosen from the shortlisted alternatives, given the investment objective. The lowest of the available opportunities will form the basis of opportunity cost, and any investment must generate returns above that benchmark. However, we must note that the benchmark is established without considering the associated risk.
- **Inflation:** Another important factor that influences the time value of money is inflation. Inflation is the factor that erodes the purchasing power of money. For future cash flow to be comparable with present cash flow, it must at least compensate for inflation.

Choosing from various capital expense alternatives

Conceptually speaking, investment evaluation is a straightforward exercise. All we need to see is if our terminal wealth is greater than our invested wealth. So, the challenge lies in determining the amount of wealth and making that comparable across different time horizons. For short-term projects, investors may find the time value of money inconsequential, and they may focus on the period over which the investments will come back. All returns beyond the period are surplus. Some common techniques of investment evaluation is given in Table 7.1.

In these approaches, the underlying objective is wealth maximization. In some cases, we use a direct approach by making periodic cash flows equivalent and looking for surplus. In some cases, we use a proxy, selecting

Table 7.1 Common techniques of investment evaluation

Technique	*Computation*	*Selection Criteria*
Payback period	Adds up the cash inflow and outflow to arrive at the net cash flow. The period when the net cash flow turns positive is the payback period. If you discount the cash flows before aggregating, you will have a discounted payback period.	The project with the lowest payback period, subject to a qualifying benchmark, will be selected. For example, if the benchmark is 5 years, the project with the lowest payback period below 5 years will be selected.
Net Present Value (NPV)	Here, too, we add the cash inflow and outflow for every period to find the net cash flow for the period. These cash flows are then discounted back to the period when the initial investment is made. The aggregate of these discounted values is the NPV.	The project with the highest positive NPV, subject to a benchmark, is selected. The benchmark may be the level of investment or the rate of return computed by dividing the discounted cash inflow by the discounted cash outflow.
Internal rate of return (IRR)	Cash inflows from an investment may not occur evenly over its life. The IRR represents the annualized rate of return at which the present value of these inflows equals the initial investment outflow. In other words, it is the discount rate that makes the NPV of the investment zero. When cash inflows are discounted at the IRR, their total present value matches the original outlay.	The project with the highest internal rate of return, subject to a minimum benchmark, will be selected.

the project that recovers the initial investment the quickest, based on the intuition that it is generating returns at the fastest rate.

We must reiterate that the tools discussed here all serve the objective of wealth maximization. If the objectives change, so should the tools. In this context, we should recognize that even tools like NPV may not show us the true impact of a project. The cash flow from a project is not the

Table 7.2 Funding structure and investment details

	Unlevered Inc.		*Levered Inc.*	
Funding structure:				
Equity (Dividend 10%)	2,000		1,000	
Debt (Interest rate 6%)	1,000	3,000	2,000	3,000
Weighted average cost of capital		8.7%		7.3%
Cost of the proposed asset		1,000		1,000
Useful life		5		5
Salvage value		100		100
Depreciation	SLM	20%	WDV	27%

Table 7.3 Cash flow with NPV and IRR

Unlevered Inc.						*Levered Inc.*				
	1	2	3	4	5	1	2	3	4	5
Revenue	900	900	900	900	900	900	900	900	900	900
Production Cost	525	525	525	525	525	525	525	525	525	525
Depreciation	180	180	180	180	180	370	233	147	93	58
Interest	60	60	60	60	60	120	120	120	120	120
Profit before tax	135	135	135	135	135	−115	22	108	162	197
Tax @ 20%	27	27	27	27	27	0	0	22	32	39
Profit after tax	108	108	108	108	108	−115	22	86	130	158
Net cash flow	288	288	288	288	388	255	255	233	223	316
NPV					195.97					37.20
IRR					16%					9%

contribution of the operations alone, even the financing structure may have a role to play. A cash flow from an entity with a leveraged structure is likely to be different from the cash flow from another entity with an unlevered structure, even when the operating cash generation is the same. Even a differential rate of depreciation may cause an altered NPV or IRR.

Consider the example in Table 7.2 where all revenue and costs are received and paid immediately in cash, except pure noncash entries. We have considered that the residual value of the asset will be realized at the end of the useful life of the asset and that there is no loss carried over for tax computation.

Table 7.3 shows the cash flows from the proposed investment in the asset. You would have noticed that the operating cash flow is identical between the levered and unlevered entities.

This was the point we were discussing. The difference between these two cash flows is caused by differential depreciation policy and leverage.

The depreciation policy caused different amounts of depreciation charges. Though this is written back to compute the cash flow, it affects the pre-tax profit and the amount of taxes paid. Similarly, the leverage affects the amount of interest paid, and consequently, the cash flow. The result is that two projects having identical operating cash flows end up having different NPV and IRR because of accounting policies and leverage.

While using these metrics for investment appraisal, you must note that the selection based on NPV or IRR does not reflect inherent operating profitability from the asset being invested. The results are often influenced significantly by leverage and accounting policies. So, before discarding an option, check what is contributing to it.

Risk, return, and portfolio asset allocation optimization

Earlier, we spoke about using discounting rates to find the fair value of future cash flows. We also spoke about the time value of money. These two are separate but interlinked concepts. Discounting rates will account for the time value of money along with any other factors that may be relevant for making the investment decision. However, before we delve into these details, let us discuss two distinct schools of thought regarding the use of discounting rates.

One school of thought focuses on internal efficiency and uses the actual weighted average cost of capital or the specific cost of funding a project as the discounting rate. The argument is quite simple. The weighted average cost of capital includes the return that the suppliers of funds have either contractually agreed to or are happy with. If we use the weighted average cost of capital as the benchmark rate, all projects that qualify under this criterion are good to go. If using NPV as the criterion, as long as the value is positive after discounting, the project is good enough to satisfy suppliers of funds and is even increasing residual wealth after paying dividends and interest. This view has an accounting bias and tries to make a stronger balance sheet.

The other school of thought believes that a project must earn a fair rate of return. Fairness is determined not only by the fair cost of funds but also by other project-specific risk factors like financial risk, liquidity risk, technology risk, etc. The fair cost of the fund will take care of inflation and common economic factors, and we must explicitly factor in other variables. These factors are collectively referred to as the risk premium. The view is that we must evaluate a project based on the specific characteristics of the project and what the market visualizes as a fair return. This would increase the market value of the investment if the project return were higher than the fair rate of return, that is, positive NPV or IRR above the benchmark.

Let us quickly have a look at the views that the supporters of these two schools offer. The market rate supporters argue that using the weighted average cost of capital may potentially hide inefficient fund procurement. Two entities may be able to procure funds at the same time, at different rates. Project evaluation based on the weighted average cost of capital can support inefficiency, which will be discounted by the market. The accounting rate-based supporters point out that the rate at which the investors have agreed reflects their risk preference and the expected return for risk exposure. That is the very reason why two entities obtain funds at different rates. They counterargue that contractual requirements will define the minimum cash flow required, while the market rate is useful to determine fair value. Have a look at which one fits you better.

Adjusting for risk is one of the greatest challenges in deciding on discounting rates. This is where the market return from the industry comes in handy, as we can easily accept the same. The capital asset pricing model provides, among others, a framework to assess the appropriate risk-adjusted return.

However, there is another way of making the risk adjustment. Instead of adjusting the discounting rate, how about adjusting the cash flow? In an earlier section, we discussed the expected value. We derive the expected value by estimating different levels of cash flow and ascribing a probability to each level. Then we add the products of the individual cash flow estimates and corresponding probabilities.

Simply put, let us consider three business situations: optimist, normal, and pessimist, with corresponding probabilities of 30%, 50%, and 20%. The cash flows are \$10,000, \$6,000, and \$3,000, respectively. The expected cash flow will be (10,000 × 0.3) + (6,000 × 0.5) + (3,000 × 0.2) = \$6,600. If we adjust the cash flow for risk, we will not need to adjust the discounting rate.

Investment evaluation, apart from examining the feasibility of individual investment proposals, also focuses on portfolio optimization or asset allocation. While an individual opportunity may emerge as investment-worthy, we also need to review its impact on the overall investment portfolio. There are two common approaches to reviewing the same.

- **Cash flow-based:** This approach focuses on whether the total cash inflow exceeds the total cash outflow after being adjusted for the time value of money and other factors, including project-specific risks.
- **Risk-based:** This approach reviews any investment property from the viewpoint of the impact on overall risk that the investor will be facing. Since accounting focuses on the value of a transaction, cash flow inherits the same quality. However, a project, while being profitable and generating wealth, may alter the risk profile of the business. Consider a scenario

of two entities, one producing ice cream and the other fruit juice across various countries. They are presented with an opportunity to invest in a new ice cream flavor by taking over another entity. This new project has a positive NPV and is better than the benchmark IRR of both investing entities. This makes the new project acceptable to both. Now, note that investment in the new ice cream factory will increase the concentration risk of the entity producing ice cream. On the other hand, it will bring diversification benefits to the entity currently producing fruit juice.

The act of recognizing risk in investment appraisal leads us to asset allocation. The goal of asset allocation is to balance risk and reward by adjusting the percentage of each asset in the portfolio according to a different set of parameters. Asset allocation establishes the boundaries within which investment decisions based on NPV and IRR are made. These parameters are additional layers of decision criteria that should be satisfied by any investment. These parameters are aligned with, either directly or indirectly, the strategic objectives of the investing entity. Asset allocation is a strategy involving dividing an investment portfolio in a way that satisfies these parameters, besides being investment-worthy on its own. So, what could these parameters be? Let us look at a few of them.

- **Investment horizon**: An entity may consider the investment horizon a critical management objective. This would entail maintaining a mix of different maturity tenures within the asset holding. The underlying reasons may include liquidity management and economic cycle, among others.
- **Financial mandate**: An entity may have an internal or external mandate to maintain some financial parameters, like the leverage ratio and debt service coverage ratio. A project may be otherwise investible but may upset one of these mandates. These mandates are often imposed by lending institutions.
- **Diversification**: A part of the corporate strategy would be to ensure a diversified portfolio across industry, market, currency, and others. The evaluation of an investment proposal will have to adhere to these boundaries. This is often addressed by concentration risk management.
- **Rebalancing**: An existing portfolio may need to be rebalanced in response to changes in external conditions. For instance, if the market value of a particular investment increases significantly, it might exceed the prescribed cap for individual holdings within the overall portfolio. In such cases, even if the investment remains fundamentally sound, it may have to be reduced or removed to maintain portfolio discipline.
- **Strategic and tactical**: An entity would hold assets for both tactical and strategic reasons. Consider an entity investing in a cold chain that it hires

out to external parties in addition to using it for its products. If the entity divests itself of the product line that needs a cold chain, it may decide to dispose of the cold chain, as that was a tactical investment. The entity had never considered having a standalone cold chain business.

These parameters play a critical role in changing the problem of wealth maximization to that of optimization. Optimization may be loosely defined as maximization under constraints. This means that there would be multiple objectives to a problem, each having its own set of conditions. The wealth maximization objective will have to operate within the scope permitted by these limiting factors. We will be talking about the techniques used to achieve this later in this section.

Capital budgeting evaluators

We have discussed some of the common evaluators used in investment analysis. Traditional spreadsheet solutions have built-in functions to compute NPV, IRR, and other metrics. But there is certain inherent caution you should take while using these standard functions. Ensure that the version you are using is free from these possibilities. Let us have a look at the red flags for these two functions.

NPV-related

Please ensure whether these red flags exist in your version of the spreadsheet and the arrangement of data.

- **Row and time:** Each consecutive row is usually considered as a unit of time, which is also the basis for discounting rates. If you consider each consecutive row representing six months, please express your discounting rate as a six-month rate. If the intermittent periods are not uniform, there is a separate formula (XNPV) for computing the NPV.
- **Initial cash outflow:** When you use the NPV function, the cash outflow of the zero period does not get discounted. If the initial cash outflow is any time after the beginning of the project period, it should be discounted. The solution is to insert a dummy period before the initial cash flow with a cash flow of zero, and then compute the NPV.
- **Blank row:** If you do not have any cash flow in any of the periods, ensure that you have zero value there. The spreadsheet may ignore a blank row within the series of rows depicting cash flow while computing NPV. This will result in an incorrect NPV. IRR also suffers from this issue. We have described this problem in detail in the next section under IRR-related issues

IRR-related

Please check if these red flags exist in your version of the spreadsheet and the arrangement of data.

- **Row and time**: In the case of computation of IRR as well, each consecutive row is considered as a unit of time, which is also the periodicity for IRR. If the intermittent period is six months, then the IRR is also six months. You may need to convert it into an annual rate if you are reporting on an annual basis. In the case of a non-uniform intermittent period, use a separate formula (XIRR) for computing the IRR.
- **Cash flow-related:** One of the structural problems associated with IRR computation is that it requires all negative cash flows to come in a series. If there is a non-negative cash flow between negative cash flows, the IRR computation may yield multiple results. This is also referred to as the problem of multiple sign changes in net cash flow. Let us have a look at the example in Table 7.4.

  The cash flow above has multiple sign changes; that is, the negative cash flows are not consecutive. This has resulted in two values for IRR, 0% and 87.6%. Since NPV using IRR as a discounting factor is zero, we have computed the NPV of the cash flow using these two discounting rates. As you might have seen, the NPV in both cases is zero.
- **Blank row**: We have already discussed this problem in the earlier section. Let us now look at an example shown in Table 7.5.

  We have presented three variations of the cash flows of a project across its life. In Case I and Case II, we have four years of cash flow with no cash flow in the third year. In Case I, we have explicitly put zero in the cash flow, while in Case II, we have kept the cell blank. You can see how that has affected the NPV and IRR. Compare Case II and Case III. Case III has a lifespan of three years, and the NPV and IRR are the same as those of Case II. This proves that the blank cell in Case II

Table 7.4 Multiple IRR

Period	*Cash Flow*	*Discount Factor: 0%*	*Present Value @ 0%*	*Discount Factor: 87.6%*	*Present Value @ 87.6%*
Year 0	−1,000	1.00	−1,000	1.00	−1,000
Year 1	3,000	1.00	3,000	0.53	1,590
Year 2	−2,500	1.00	−2,500	0.28	−700
Year 3	1,000	1.00	1,000	0.15	150
Year 4	−500	1.00	−500	0.08	−40
		NPV	0		0

Table 7.5 Problem with blank rows

Discounting Factor			6%
Period	**Case I**	**Case II**	**Case III**
0	−10,000	−10,000	−10,000
1	4,000	4,000	4,000
2	4,000	4,000	4,000
3	0		4,000
4	4,000	4,000	
NPV	**502**	**692**	**692**
IRR	**8.36%**	**9.70%**	**9.70%**

is disregarded when computing NPV and IRR. Take care to see that if your spreadsheet suffers from the same weakness, you have not left any cell blank to signify zero.

In addition to these red flags, the standard metrics used for evaluating investments are often inefficient in the face of complex business environments. Evaluating a proposal for a new manufacturing facility is not just about construction costs and expected cash flows. It involves analyzing changing consumer preferences, environmental regulations, supply chain disruptions, technological advances, and competitive responses. Traditional spreadsheet functions cannot easily account for these interrelated factors or handle the vast amounts of data needed to make informed predictions.

This is where ML enters the picture. ML algorithms can process enormous amounts of historical data to identify patterns that humans might miss. They can analyze numerous similar past projects to better predict cost overruns, timeline delays, and revenue potential. These models can simultaneously consider market trends, economic indicators, and company-specific factors to provide better cash flow forecasts. These models can continuously learn and adapt to new data as soon as it becomes available.

Simulation is an important component of investment evaluation. While spreadsheets can run a few what-if scenarios, ML can simulate thousands of possible scenarios defined by various values of the model variables and their interactions. This capability helps the investor better understand project risks and opportunities, leading to more informed decisions.

You need to study the complexities of the business case and then decide whether to use spreadsheets or ML-based tools in investment evaluation.

We are all comfortable with calculating NPV and IRR using standard spreadsheet packages. They are simple to understand and easy to operate. We have already identified the red flags that we should keep an eye out for. Instead of replicating what we can already do with the spreadsheet, let us examine a few applications of ML tools that can complement the functionalities we already use.

Automate complex financial calculations for investment appraisal

Here is an interesting example of a code (prefix 0701) that can pick up specified keywords from a text description and carry out investment appraisal using NPV and IRR. In addition, it also creates a worksheet so that you can use it for further analysis. This tool can also be very useful in framing the worksheet. It would save you time from manually filling it up. You can create a worksheet from meeting notes or emails and proceed with further analysis. Before we proceed with the code functionality, please keep in mind that this code has been written to demonstrate the usage of ML tools to automate the computation. Unless these keywords are used, the code will not recognize the necessary input and will ask for it manually. You may like to improve upon the code by continuously adding more keywords. You can download the code from the repository; major components are described here:

- **Import libraries:** We are loading the libraries necessary for the code.
- **Customize:** We must specify the following parameters for the code to work with our data:
    - o Name of the file where the output will be saved for subsequent analysis.
    - o List of keywords that the code will search for and use in computation. These keywords are classified as keywords for asset value, asset life, asset residual, depreciation method, annual inflow, annual outflow, tax rate, and discounting rate. The higher the variations of specified keywords, the more powerful the code is. You must note that this code is rule-based, and it recognizes a key input based on the keyword. Be careful to maintain the syntax while adding a keyword.

  Here is the part of the code with the customizable parameters italicized.

```
# File names
my_output = "0701 cashflow_schedule.csv"

# User-defined keywords
ASSET_VALUE_KEYWORDS = ["cost of asset", "cost of
the asset", "cost of acquisition", "initial cost",
"purchase", "purchase price", "acquisition cost",
"acquisition"]
ASSET_LIFE_KEYWORDS = ["life", "useful"]
```

```
ASSET_RESIDUAL_KEYWORDS = ["residual", "terminal"]

DEPRECIATION_METHOD_STRAIGHT_KEYWORDS = ["straight line",
"slm"]
DEPRECIATION_METHOD_WRITTEN_DOWN_KEYWORDS = ["written
down", "wdv"]

DEPRECIATION_RATE_KEYWORDS = ["depreciated", "deprecia-
tion rate", "rate of depreciation"]

ANNUAL_INFLOW_KEYWORDS = ["inflow", "income", "revenue",
"revenues"]
ANNUAL_OUTFLOW_KEYWORDS = ["outflow", "cost", "expense",
"expenses"]

TAX_RATE_KEYWORDS = ["tax"]
DISCOUNT_RATE_KEYWORDS = ["discount", "discounting",
"cost of capital", "wacc"]
```

- **Create extraction functions:** In this section, the specified keywords are extracted from the text statement. These are then made ready for computation.
- **Create financial functions:** This section creates computation functions that will be used with the selected keywords.
- **Create functions for the main process:** This section contains the logic of using the keywords in the relevant financial functions. If the code identifies an error that makes computation impossible, it reports the same to the user.
- **Create user input interface:** This section provides for the text input by the user. Once you run the code, a window will open where you will be prompted to enter your input as shown in Figure 7.1. You may type the text or paste it from another place. For any monetary value like cost of asset, or annual outflow you must put a $ sign. Similarly, for anything that is given as a rate, you must put a % sign. Note that the input window may not pop up on your screen and you may need to access it by clicking on it in the taskbar.

The code then proceeds with the computation and provides the output. The output shows the input and the list of parameters extracted from the input. This serves the need for input verification. Subsequent output shows the cash flow schedule and financial metrics. The output also includes a spreadsheet where the cash flows are arranged, and metrics like NPV, IRR, and payback period are shown.

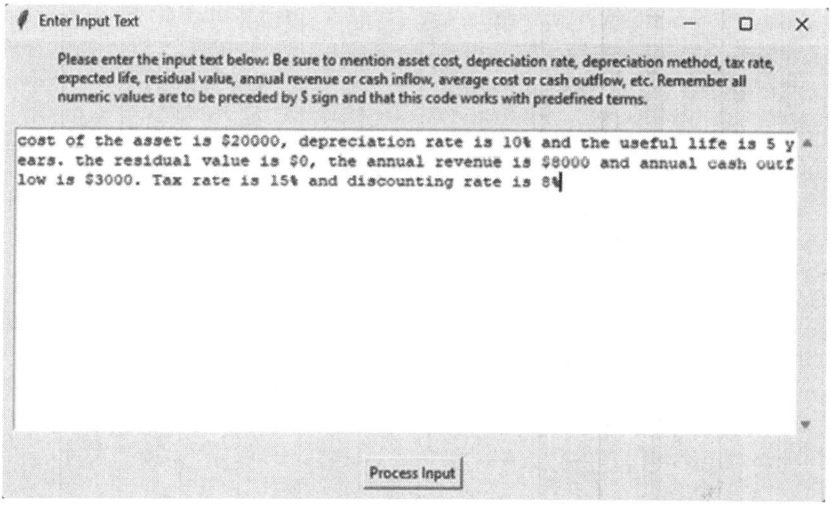

Figure 7.1 Window to enter input text

Create functions to compute NPV and IRR

In a standard spreadsheet, we use a standard formula to compute NPV, IRR, and others. We have also seen how financial leverage impacts NPV and IRR. The NPV or IRR we compute is usually either for levered or unlevered, depending on the input data. Though not through ML libraries, we can use code to separate the leverage and operating impact from basic data. This code uses primary inputs like leverage, discounting factor, and cash flow, and computes NPV and IRR under both leveraged and unleveraged conditions. But before we get into the codes, let us have a quick look at how leverage affects capital budgeting metrics.

Leverage impacts capital budgeting metrics like NPV and IRR in several significant ways:

- **Discount rate adjustment:** Leverage increases financial risk, which would usually raise the weighted average cost of capital (WACC) used as the discount rate. This would cause a lower NPV and a higher threshold for IRR-based investment decisions.
- **Tax shield benefits:** Interest payments on debt are tax-deductible, creating tax shields. These tax shields increase project cash flows and support both NPV and IRR.
- **Cash flow timing:** Leverage brings in debt service obligations. These obligations are likely to alter the timing and magnitude of cash flows, affecting both NPV and IRR calculations.

- **Magnification effect:** Leverage can amplify NPV and IRR when project returns exceed borrowing costs.
- **Financial risk:** The benchmark IRR may need adjustment to reflect enhanced financial risk from leverage. This would mostly cause a raised threshold IRR for accepting an investment proposal.

If a financial decision-maker is presented with NPV and IRR under both levered and unlevered conditions, it would be easy to view the impact of leverage. The decision-maker can decide on leverage, keeping in mind its impact on NPV and IRR.

Let us now look at the main components of the code (prefix 0702):

- **Import libraries:** We are loading the libraries necessary for the code. We have one new library being used in the code called `numpy_financial`. This library contains financial functions like NPV and IRR. Install it in your environment, if you have not already.
- **Customize:** This code requires multiple parameters to be specified. These parameters include the following:
    - o Name of the files where the computational steps and cash flows will be saved in the document in CSV format.
    - o Values of input parameters, including WACC, equity, debt, tax rate, interest rate, initial investment amount, project duration, levered cash flow, and reference currency.

  Here is the part of the code with customizable parameters in italics.

```
WACC = 0.12# Weighted average cost of capital
E = 50.0    # Equity in currency value
D = 50.0    # Debt in currency value
tax_rate = 0.20   # Tax Rate in decimal
interest_rate = 0.08     # Debt Interest Rate in decimal
initial_investment = 100.0     # Initial Investment in
currency value
n_years = 5# Project Duration in years input_levered_
cf = 30    # Levered CF in currency value

my_currency_unit="Million Dollars"
my_output_csv="0702 cash_flow_details.csv"
my_output_doc="0702 computational_details.txt"
```

- **Define functions:** This section of the code creates functions for computing the payback period with discounted and undiscounted cash flow.
- **Main computation module:** This is where all detailed computations are made. This includes the cash flow, NPV, IRR, payback period, and others.

- **Save cash flows:** The cash flows that have been computed earlier are saved into a specified CSV file. This would allow us to use them for further analysis and also as audit evidence.
- **Save computational steps:** This is an interesting module that saves all the detailed computational steps in a text file. This will be useful to understand the computation process and analyze any apparent error or inconsistency, besides serving the documentation needs.
- **Report results to console:** This module displays the results on the screen for the user. All data that is displayed here is also saved in the text file.

The output of the code is classified into two sections, unlevered analysis and levered analysis. It shows the NPV and IRR, along with discounted and undiscounted payback periods for both leveraged and unleveraged scenarios.

Analyze multiple projects efficiently

Let us now use an ML tool to recognize the deciding factors behind past successful investment appraisals. Not all projects that have qualified as an investible project succeed in the commercial world. It would be useful to further refine this analysis and find out if there is a pattern of such post-analysis failures and successes. We will use the decision tree to analyze past investments and then apply the lessons learned to classify new project opportunities. This is in addition to the criteria of NPV, IRR, and the like. This additional analysis will give an insight into the factors that can classify projects that qualified in the initial evaluation but were ultimately not successful.

The main components of the code (prefix 0703) are structured in a way we are now familiar with. These are the main modules of the code.

- **Import libraries:** All necessary libraries are loaded in this module.
- **Customize:** This code requires us to specify the input and output file names for the past data, the new data, the decision logic, and the prediction results with the new data. The input file contains details of the discounting factor, leverage, NPV, IRR, project life, and whether the project was successful or not. The test data is also presented in the same way, except for whether the project succeeded. If the field names change, the code will also have to be modified. The relevant code with the customizable parameters italicized is shown here.

```
my_train_data="0703 Train Data.csv"
my_new_cases="0703 New Cases.csv"
my_results="0703 predicted_new_cases.csv"
my_decision_rules="0703 decision_rules.txt"
```

- **Load and prepare the training data:** This module loads the past data into the system for training the decision tree model. In the code, there is a parameter "test_size=0.2". This means 80% of the data provided will be used to train the model, and 20% of the data will be used to test the model that has been trained. You may change these values if you want.
- **Train the decision tree model, evaluate, and predict:** In this module, the loaded data is used to train and test. It goes on to compute the accuracy of the trained model and then uses the data of the new cases to predict the likelihood of failure or success of these projects.
- **Save prediction:** We save the results of the prediction in a specified file for future reference, reporting, and analysis.
- **Extract decision tree and save decision rules:** This part of the module extracts the decision tree and saves it as a text file. One of the weaknesses of ML is that it is being used as a black box. Financial decision-makers are required to explain the logic behind their decision. The description of how the decision tree worked would be very useful to explain the predicted values.
- **Display prediction results:** This is the module that displays the results of the prediction on screen. These are the same data that were saved in the preceding section.

Support capital budgeting decisions with accurate metrics

A question may naturally come to mind as an extension of the last exercise. We have selected a project, but based on our experience, can we compute the project's probability of success? Random Forest is another powerful ML tool that can get this answer for us. We will use this tool to analyze the eventual performance of selected past projects and predict the probability of success of potential projects. In addition to the cash flow-driven metrics like NPV and IRR, we can now factor in past project experiences in the decision-making framework.

The code (prefix 0704) is structured in the usual way. Let us have a look at the major sections:

- **Import libraries:** All necessary libraries are loaded in this module.
- **Customize:** This code requires specifying the input and output file names for the past data, the new cases, and the prediction results. The input file contains the same details as in the preceding case. They are the discounting factor, leverage, NPV, IRR, project life, and probability of success and failure. The test data will also have the same structure. Any changes in the field name will require the code to be modified. The relevant code with the customizable parameters italicized is shown here.

```
input_file='0704 Train Data.csv'
test_file='0704 New Cases.csv'
output_file='0704_New_Cases_Results.csv'
```

- **Load data and train model:** This section loads the data and trains the Random Forest model. If the field names are different, you can specify the names of the fields you consider features of the model in this section. You may remember that features are the input columns that the model uses to make decisions.
- **Load new data and predict:** In this section, the model reads the new data from the specified file. Note that the features used in the training module must be the same in this module. It also computes the probability of success of each project.
- **Display the results:** This module displays the prediction results along with the computed probabilities. The results are also saved to a specified file for further analysis and as audit evidence. The output displays the values of investment, discounting factor, leverage, NPV, IRR, project life, prediction for the outcome, and probability of success and failure against each new project name or code.

Real options valuation using simulation

In the derivative market, options are rights, and not obligations. Real options are analogous to financial options but apply to real assets and investment projects. Here, the objective is the right to take certain actions in the future, such as expanding, contracting, or abandoning a project. These options allow financial decision-makers to adapt to new information and changing market conditions. Consequently, they are likely to have a financial value.

These options can be exercised under different circumstances defined by various states of the economy, project, and other influencing factors. The financial impact of exercising or not exercising the options under different circumstances would differ. Some of these situations would be more likely to occur than others. Thus, the valuation of the option becomes a dynamic exercise. This is where we can use simulation to visualize an array of possibilities and value the option accordingly.

Real options in capital projects

Consider a situation where the management of an entity is looking to acquire a machine for their production facility. They have a choice between two machines; a comparative analysis is given below:

Machine A has a capital cost of $500,000 and operates solely on fossil fuel. The operating cost directly depends on the fossil fuel price. On the other hand, machine B can operate on both fossil fuel and natural gas and comes with a capital cost of $600,000. Machine B enjoys fuel flexibility and would initially use fossil fuel, but the management can switch to natural gas if the price rises significantly. When fossil fuel prices exceed a 20% increase (from a baseline of $100 per unit to over $120 per unit), switching to natural gas would lead to significant operating cost savings. The cost of natural gas is expected to be $90 per unit at that time. Experience suggests that there is a 40% probability that the fossil fuel price will increase by more than 20%. In the event of such an increase, the operating cost of machine A will surge, while machine B can switch to natural gas, keeping its operating cost lower.

Apart from deciding on these machines independently, we may also need to examine whether it is justified to pay the additional money to get the option. We can do this by considering various scenarios where the fossil fuel price increases by different factors (for example, from 20% to 40%). For each scenario, we will calculate the operating costs for both machines and look for comparative savings. Since we are expecting the high-price scenario to happen 40% of the time, we will weigh the net benefit by 40% for cases where the net benefit is positive.

Let us have a look at the main components of the code (prefix 0705), which are available in the code repository.

- **Import libraries:** We are loading the necessary libraries in this module.
- **Customize:** This code requires specifying the input variables and the output file name for the output. The parameters that require customization include the following:
  - Capital costs for both machines, and the code will compute the price difference.
  - We specify the current cost of both kinds of fuel and the quantity of fuel expected to be used. We will also specify the probability that the price of fossil fuel will increase significantly (which is greater than 20% in this case), the lowest rate of probable increase, the highest rate of probable increase, and the number of instances within the lower and upper value of increase.
  - The file names to save the option values and the plot.

The relevant code with the customizable parameters italicized is shown here.

```
# Machine parameters
capital_cost_A = 500000
capital_cost_B = 600000
extra_capital_cost = capital_cost_B - capital_cost_A
```

```
# Fuel cost parameters
baseline_fossil_price = 100
natural_gas_price = 90
usage = 10000

# Parameters for increase (>20%) of price of fossil fuel
prob_high_price = 0.4
lowest_increase= 1.2
highest_increase= 1.5
number_of_cases = 5

#file names to save results
csv_filename = "0705 option_values.csv"
plot_image='0705 real_option_value.png'
```

- **Setup for scenario analysis:** This small section loads the values of different prices of fuel and stores the option values.
- **Compute and display results:** This section computes the expected benefits under a predesignated number of scenarios of an increase in fuel price. It also stores these values.
- **Save results in a file:** The various fuel price increase factors used and their corresponding operating benefits are saved in the specified CSV file.
- **Display results and save plot:** The value of the option against different levels of fuel price is displayed on the screen and then plotted in this section. The plot is also saved for future reference and use elsewhere.

The screen output of the code is the value of the option at different fuel price levels and the plot of the same. You would have noticed that as the price of the fuel increases, the value of the option also increases. This is natural as with the increase in the price of fossil fuel, machine B becomes more profitable to use. Consequently, the price difference between the machines widens.

Simulation techniques to value flexibility in investment decisions

We have discussed earlier how the value of an option varies with different scenarios. We will use simulation techniques to assess how these options might play out.

Simulation involves generating a great range of possible future scenarios by varying key inputs such as market demand, input costs, interest rates, etc. As we have seen earlier, this may involve considering multiple market scenarios, like normal, recession, and growth, instead of one static scenario as is normally used. In some simulated scenarios, the market might be booming, justifying an expansion plan. In some other simulations, the market might turn slow, delaying or abandoning the project's preferred outcome. By simulating multiple scenarios like these, we can estimate the likelihood and financial impact of various decisions. This would effectively cause assigning a monetary value to the managerial flexibility available in the project.

The code uses a Monte Carlo simulation to value a real option embedded in a project. In this example, the value of the project follows an uncertain path, and if the project value exceeds a certain threshold, we can "exercise" an option to expand, that is, add extra value. This extra value represents the managerial flexibility to grow the project when conditions are favorable. For those interested in understanding the uncertainties involved, this uncertain path is called a geometric Brownian motion, named after Robert Brown for his 1827 study of pollen particles suspended in water. In finance, Brownian motion is used to model the seemingly random movements of asset prices and interest rates over time. Geometric Brownian motion combines the elements of Brownian motion with the multiplicative property of geometric progression. This makes it suitable for modeling processes where values must remain positive even while exhibiting exponential growth or decay.

Say we have a project that has been assigned a valuation. The valuation of the project is likely to change in the future. One variant of the project has an option to expand if the project value increases beyond a threshold. If we expand, the project value will increase at an accelerated rate. Naturally, the entry value of the project with an option will be different from that without an option. The question is what the fair value of the option should be. In other words, how much more should we be willing to pay to have the options included in the project? In the example we have used, we have avoided the details such as earnings, cost, and taxes, and straightaway provided the project value.

In the example, we are calculating the project value after one year of initial investment. The distribution of outcomes can be wide due to volatility. Geometric Brownian motion helps simulate a spectrum of possible future values, capturing both upside and downside. This is critical for option valuation since options are valuable only under specific conditions. As stated earlier, geometric Brownian motion is a stochastic process commonly used in finance to model the evolution of asset prices (or project values, in our case) over time. It is called "geometric" because the value evolves multiplicatively and is always positive. We simulate several values for the project after one year of initial investment. Brownian motion models the randomness of how the project might evolve in that period. This enables a probabilistic valuation of the expansion option under uncertainty.

Let us now have a look at the main components of the code (prefix 0706):

- **Import libraries:** All necessary libraries are loaded in this module.
- **Customize:** We have to specify the information about the value and associated information necessary for computing the future value under geometric Brownian motion. We start by defining the number of simulations, the time horizon, the risk-free rate for discounting, and the initial project value. We also define the volatility of the project's value, a threshold above which the expansion option is available, and a multiplier that represents the extra value gained when the option is exercised. We will also specify the names of files to save the option values and the plot. The relevant portion of the code with the customizable parameters italicized is shown here.

```
# Set simulation parameters
N = 10000
T = 1
r = 0.05
V0 = 100
sigma = 0.2

# Define the real option
parameters threshold = 120
expansion_multiplier = 1.2

#file names to save results
csv_file='0706 real_option_simulation.csv'
plot_file='0706 real_option_value_distribution.png'
```

- **Simulating project values:** This section uses a geometric Brownian motion model to simulate the values of the project after one year. This is a standard way to simulate the evolution of asset values under uncertainty. The formula used incorporates the drift related to the risk-free rate and randomness through a normally distributed variable.
- **Calculate project values at different options:** This module uses the simulated project values, and if a simulated project value exceeds the threshold, the model adds extra value. This extra value is only applied in scenarios where the project is doing well, reflecting the value of having the flexibility to expand. Both the project values with and without the option are discounted back using the risk-free rate provided. The difference between the present values obtained from both scenarios is the value of the option.
- **Compute option values, save, and display:** In this section, the code calculates the average project values with and without the option and

prints the average value of the real option. It also generates and saves a histogram to show the distribution of the option values across all simulations.

The output of the code includes the average project value without the option, the average project value with the option, the average option value, and a histogram showing the distribution of the option values across all simulations. All these values and the histogram have been saved in specified files for future reference and use.

Modeling scenarios based on new information

A reason why we may prefer having an option is to be able to alter the course given a changed scenario. Dynamic allocation of assets is a powerful option to respond to changes in the external environment.

Consider a mid-sized enterprise that uses an AI-driven financial simulation model to guide its product mix decisions. The business has three product lines, each having a maximum supply capacity. Profitability of each product line is different, and there is a constraint on total supply across all product lines. The product mix strategy followed by the management is that no product should be greater than 50% and less than 30% of the aggregate supply. This, the management believes, balances their product mix. In light of changing product profitability, management has identified three potential scenarios, each of which will have a direct impact on the enterprise's overall profit.

We now examine how you can change the product mix in a dynamic environment. The code simulates the three possibilities for each of the three product lines and creates multiple scenarios, in this case, 27. The profit-maximizing mix is computed for each of the scenarios, and the report is presented in a CSV file. In addition, a histogram of different profit scenarios is also plotted to get an idea of what may unfold in the future.

We have a code to address a similar situation. Consider that at the start of the fiscal year, the company has allocated capital to three projects. Table 7.6 shows the initial investment and cash flows from the three projects.

The total supply capacity of the enterprise is 20,000 units, and there are three possibilities of profit fluctuation: down by 5%, no change, and up by 5%. Let us now discuss the main components of the code (prefix 0707).

- **Import libraries:** As usual, all necessary libraries are loaded in this module. You might have noticed a library named `itertools`. This is a standard library module in Python that provides fast, memory-efficient tools for working with iterators.

Table 7.6 Supply and profit data

Project	*Max. Supply*	*Unit Profit*
A	10,000	10
B	8,000	11
C	7,000	12

- **Customize**: This code customizes parameters in four distinct sections.
  - In the section where we define inputs, we provide data for the base profit and maximum supply for each of the three projects. In addition, we provide input for the total supply. We must be careful about formatting the parameters. Please note the curly brackets and use of single quotes in the input for base profit and maximum supply. The syntax associates the values with each project.
  - In the portfolio constraints section, we will specify the minimum and the maximum share of the total portfolio that each project can have.
  - We define the profit fluctuation scenario by providing the rates of change of profit in each scenario. Note the square brackets used.
  - The final section for customization specifies the names of files to save the results and histogram.

Here is the relevant part of the code with customizable parameters italicized.

```
# Define inputs
base_profits = {'A': 10, 'B': 11, 'C': 12}
max_supply = {'A': 10000, 'B': 8000, 'C': 7000}
total_supply = 20000

# Portfolio constraints
min_percentage = 0.30
max_percentage = 0.50

# Profit fluctuation scenarios (-10%, 0%, +10%)
fluctuations = [-0.10, 0, 0.10]
scenarios = list(product(fluctuations, repeat=3))

# Files to be saved
csv_file="0707 dynamic_allocation_results.csv"
plot_image="0707 Asset_allocation_histogram.png"
```

- **Create computation function**: This is the core computational engine of the code. It first creates the possible combinations of price fluctuations. It further creates the computational framework for optimizing profits within the constraints after making the first allocation based on profitability.

- **Compute initial and updated scenarios; Show management decision:** This section does the actual calculation using the functions created earlier. The code iterates over a list of profit fluctuation scenarios. Each scenario contains multipliers or changes for the profits of products A, B, and C.
- **Display and save results and histogram:** This section saves the detailed results for each combination of price fluctuation, corresponding revised price, allocation, total profit for each product, and aggregate profit. The results are also saved in the specified CSV file. The results are visualized as a histogram, and the plot is saved in the specified file for subsequent use. The output of the code includes a display of the results and a histogram of the same.

Incorporating option value into project evaluations

We have discussed and used ML-based tools for valuing options. Now, let us consider a scenario where we incorporate the option value into project evaluation. You are the financial adviser of a toy manufacturing firm planning to expand its production capacity. The base expansion project involves a significant investment in building a new production line, which is expected to increase revenue. Additionally, your firm can opt for an upgraded model of machinery that will provide a better finish to the toys. Customers' preference for quality varies, and the upgraded model will allow flexibility to cater to the demand for both standard and improved quality toys.

You may consider this expansion as a base project with its own set of cash flows. Traditional metrics like NPV and IRR can be used to evaluate cash flow. The upgrade can be treated as an independent investment requiring an additional cost of, say, $2 million. This upgrade is also expected to yield annual incremental cash flows of, say, $500,000 over five years. This option is being treated as a separate project, and we will calculate the incremental NPV and IRR to evaluate acceptability. If the incremental IRR is above the corporate benchmark or the incremental NPV is positive, the option is exercised. Otherwise, you may proceed with the base expansion alone without the upgraded feature.

This approach allows the firm to isolate the strategic value of the upgrade, ensuring that additional investment is made only if it substantially enhances overall project performance. Many times, the base project may be so strong that it overshadows the relatively inefficient upgrade module. This analysis thus provides a clear financial justification for incorporating managerial flexibility into capital budgeting decisions.

We have designed a code to explain the evaluation process. Table 7.7 shows all relevant information considering a 10% discounting rate.

The decision to implement the upgrade hinges on whether the incremental NPV (or its corresponding IRR) meets the firm's required return threshold. Consider that the benchmark IRR of the firm is 15%. In this example, both the base and upgraded option adds positive value, having positive NPV and above the benchmark IRR. However, if we do an incremental analysis, we will find that this incremental investment is generating less than the benchmark IRR. If this quality augmentation were a standalone project, we would not have accepted the same. But when this was bundled with the base project, this inefficiency conveniently got hidden.

Remember that this does not make the improved project non-investible; it makes it inefficient compared to the standard project. One may argue that instead of investing the additional 2 million in the improved product, if that is used to augment the standard project by 20%, that would create more end-period wealth.

However, this part of the task can also be performed easily with a standard spreadsheet package. ML tools provide additional capabilities and information, which we see in the code, that justify moving away from a spreadsheet. In case the incremental investment has an IRR below the hurdle rate, the code computes the amount of initial cash outflow that will yield the hurdle rate IRR. In addition to this, the code continues to compute the minimum probability of demand for the upgraded products for the incremental investment to make sense. The second component serves an interesting purpose. This example evaluates a base project alongside an optional feature enhancement, where the opportunity to shift to producing higher-quality toys remains uncertain. We calculate the minimum probability of demand for these improved toys that would justify the additional investment based on a risk-adjusted return analysis.

The approach adopted in the code allows the firm to separately assess the strategic value of managerial flexibility, independent of the base project.

Table 7.7 Incremental analysis

	Standard	*Improved*	*Incremental*
Year 0	–10,000,000	–12,000,000	–2,000,000
Year 1	3,000,000	3,400,000	400,000
Year 2	3,500,000	4,000,000	500,000
Year 3	4,000,000	4,600,000	600,000
Year 4	4,500,000	5,200,000	700,000
Year 5	5,000,000	5,800,000	800,000
NPV	4,803,261	5,005,756	202,495
IRR	26%	24%	13%

Let us have a look at the major components of the code (prefix 0708). Compared to other examples, this code is designed differently. This creates functions to perform various operations required for the business case and then calls the functions to produce output. You can always integrate the function logic into separate sections instead of creating functions and then calling them. We will leave that to the experts in coding.

- **Import libraries:** Only two libraries are used here. We could have used `NumPy` -financials to compute NPV and IRR, but decided to code it.
- **Customize:** This code customizes parameters for discount values, hurdle rates, project cash flows, and names of files to save results. Be careful while providing the cash flow. Note the square brackets and ensure that you have values for every year. The number of years in both projects does not need to be the same. However, ensure that there is a value for cash outflow, else the code will not proceed.

  Here is the relevant part of the code with customizable parameters italicized.

```
# provide parameters
my_discount_rate = 0.10
my_hurdle_rate = 0.15
my_new_project_cf = [-10000000, 3000000, 3500000,
4000000, 4500000, 5000000]
my_upgrade_project_cf = [-12000000, 3400000, 4000000,
4600000, 5200000, 5800000]
csv_file= '0708 project_evaluation_results.csv'
text_file= '0708 project_evaluation_results.txt'
```

- **Define functions:** This is the heart of the computation of the code. This defines various functions to compute, which are NPV, IRR, and discounted payback, saves results to a TXT and CSV file, computes investment metrics for a project individually and for incremental values, validates various business logic, and displays results on screen.
- **Run the main module:** The main module first validates if there is a negative cash flow in the projects. It will not proceed unless there is one. Once the rule is validated, it executes the main module, which runs all the functions described earlier.

The output of the code includes values for NPV, IRR, and discounted payback periods for all projects, including the incremental values. In case the metrics of incremental values do not match the hurdle rate, it will provide the maximum initial investment that the incremental project can bear. This, in an oblique way, is also the fair valuation of the real option to maintain the level of efficiency of the mother project. The code also computes the minimum probability necessary to have a positive NPV. If the probability of achieving the incremental values is lower than the computed value, the decision-maker needs to view it from the angle of risk management.

Portfolio optimization with ML tools

Selecting individual investments is an important area of financial decision-making. Another equally important area is understanding the impact of these individual selections on the overall investment portfolio. This is where we introduce portfolio optimization. Optimization, in this context, commonly refers to creating a portfolio that maximizes return for a given risk class or minimizes risk given a return class. Traditionally, financial professionals have relied on Modern Portfolio Theory (MPT) and various statistical models to construct and manage portfolios that balance risk and return. At the non-monetary asset level, there could be another angle that considers the business constraints. For example, in deciding on a product portfolio, a finance professional may have to recognize the importance of market presence while deciding on the most profitable profit mix. Driven by the constraint, the finance professional may have to include a low-profit product or market in the portfolio, as it is important to maintain a presence in all customer segments. Similarly, a lack of availability of raw materials may force one to accept a product mix that produces suboptimal profit.

This section explores how finance professionals can leverage ML tools to create and maintain optimized investment portfolios without extensive coding knowledge. There are Python libraries that offer a range of robust techniques to allocate assets efficiently, helping investors achieve their desired risk-return profiles. ML techniques can now process vast amounts of data, identify complex patterns, and adapt to changing market conditions. Finance professionals can use these tools to make more informed decisions.

By the end of this section, you will have a practical understanding of how to harness ML for more sophisticated portfolio management, even without extensive programming experience.

Optimizing investment portfolios to achieve desired risk-return profiles

The primary objective of a portfolio manager is to balance the risk-return trade-off. This is a fundamental goal in investment management, where investors seek to achieve the best risk-return combination that matches their risk appetite. Though MPT has laid out a framework to optimize the risk-return trade-off, it is often limited by the computational power available to the portfolio manager.

However, advancements in ML and computational finance have provided more sophisticated techniques to construct portfolios that maximize returns for a given level of risk while allowing for a dynamic scenario.

The risk-return trade-off is central to portfolio optimization. Portfolio managers decide on how much risk they are willing to tolerate for potential returns. Low-risk investments, such as government bonds, offer stability but lower returns. On the other hand, high-risk assets, like equities or emerging market funds, have greater return potential but increased volatility. Apart from the fact that the extent of risk that a manager will accept is a strategic decision, a manager needs to know if there are better combinations of assets that can improve the risk-return relation. This is where we require better computational power.

In the case of portfolios with two assets, the computational challenges are limited. We have two returns, two risk proxies, and one covariance. As the number of assets keeps increasing, the number of covariances increases at a quadratic rate following the formula n(n–1)/2, where n is the number of assets. So, with three assets we will have three covariances, four assets will get us six covariances, and five assets will have ten. Surely you can understand how quickly the combinations necessary for identifying an optimal portfolio can go beyond simple computational power.

This is an example of where simple tools like spreadsheets become inefficient in managing portfolios. Capital allocation to achieve the optimal risk-return mix uses historical correlations and covariance metrics as the two primary parameters.

Traditional portfolio optimization tools like variance-covariance assume a linear relation and normally distributed returns. ML algorithms can capture non-linear interactions and complex patterns in asset returns. For example, neural networks can identify subtle non-linear correlations between assets, economic indicators, or market sentiment.

ML techniques now allow us freedom from solely relying on standard deviation as a measure of risk; ML models can incorporate alternative risk metrics such as Conditional Value-at-Risk (CVaR), which focuses on the risk of extreme losses, known as the tail risk. It also allows us to focus only on downside deviation, which only considers negative returns as risk. These alternative risk measures often provide a more realistic representation of investor concerns than traditional volatility metrics. We can further integrate constraints like drawdown limitations, sector or geographic exposure caps, ESG criteria, liquidity requirements, tax considerations, and others, in our optimization modeling.

Let us start with a simple example (prefix 0709) and keep on adding challenges as we progress through the section.

- **Import libraries:** The necessary libraries are loaded into the system here.
- **Customize:** This code customizes parameters for the input file for closing prices, the number of working days in a year, the number of simulations to be run, the number of days for which return is to be computed, and the names of the files to save results. The number of working days is used to annualize the rate of return. The input data file comprises the date column and one column each for the closing price of each asset. The column head is also the asset ID, which the code uses for reporting. The relevant part of the code with customizable parameters italicized is given here.

```
# Provide customization parameters
my_data= '0709 Stock Close Price.csv'
my_working_days=252
my_simulation=5000
my_period=1
my_output_file= '0709 portfolio_simulations.csv'
my_optimal_file= '0709 optimal_portfolio.csv'
my_saved_chart= '0709 optimal_portfolio_pie_chart.png'
```

- **Load data and calculate return:** The input data is loaded in this section, and the daily return is computed while dropping cells with zero value. The periodic return is then annualized by using the mean and the number of specified working days. Annual covariance is also computed in this section.
- **Create functions and define constraints:** This section defines a function to compute the portfolio variance given the asset weights and the covariance matrix of asset returns. It specifies that the sum of all portfolio weights must equal 1. The last part of the module specifies that each weight is restricted between 0 and 1. This ensures that there is no short-selling (negative weights) and no leveraging (weights > 1).
- **Optimize:** This section starts by assigning equal weight to each asset and then optimizes the same, keeping the constraints in mind. The objective of optimization is to get the minimum variance irrespective of return. It runs an optimization algorithm – Sequential Least Squares Programming (SLSQP). The model has considered covariance between the assets while optimizing for the least variance portfolio. We have considered the variance-return optimization in a subsequent section. The final optimal weights are the portfolio composition that minimizes risk and are extracted from the optimization result.
- **Run simulation:** This module starts by computing the expected return and volatility from the optimized model. The module then generates many random portfolios to understand the broader landscape of

return-risk combinations. It stores the values for weights, returns, and volatility in a list. It uses the Monte Carlo simulation to explore all possible portfolios. This is very useful for understanding risk-return trade-offs. During the simulation, no minimum or target return, nor any upper limit on volatility or risk, is imposed. The objective is to explore the full feasible region of portfolios rather than to perform optimization. Every portfolio, no matter how poor its return or high its risk, is included in the simulation as long as the weights sum to 1.

- **Store and save results:** Results of the simulation are stored and saved in a CSV file. The weights optimized for the lowest variance are specifically added to the saved file. The weights for the optimized portfolio are saved in a separate CSV file.
- **Plot and print results:** Displays the optimized portfolio composition in a pie chart. The code also displays the weights, expected return, and volatility of the optimized portfolio on screen.

The output of the code includes files saved in CSV format, plots saved in PNG, and displays optimized weight, return, and variance on the screen. If you check the CSV file with the results of the simulation, you will find the weights for each asset with the corresponding volatility saved there. The values for the optimized portfolio are also stored and specifically labeled as "optimal." All other values are labeled as "simulation." You can check if the optimized values have the lowest variance, keeping in mind that when we save in CSV format, often numbers are not treated as being numeric. You may need to format them.

Employing an ML library to allocate assets efficiently

Various ML libraries can be used in Python to efficiently allocate assets. We will use a popular library named `Pypfopt` to understand how these libraries can be used to allocate assets efficiently. Please note that our examples and the choice of the library are designed for academic understanding and not investment advice. You need to select your own library and trading strategy. Even if you use the same library, please read the complete documentation to understand how the library works and what precautions you must take. In case you need to install the `Pypfopt` library, use this code:

```
!pip install PyPortfolioOpt
```

Pypfopt offers multiple methods for estimating expected returns and various approaches to risk modeling. The model offers a selection of optimization techniques like mean-variance optimization, minimum volatility portfolios, maximum Sharpe ratio portfolios, efficient risk (target return with minimum risk), and efficient return (target risk with maximum return), among others. It also allows specifying additional constraints like position size limits, exposure cap, transaction cost considerations, long-only or long-short allocations, among others. All these permit the financial decision-maker to optimize asset allocation even under complex situations.

Let us build on the example used in the earlier section. Here are the main components of the code (prefix 0710):

- **Import libraries:** The necessary libraries are loaded into the system here. You will see the library `Pypfopt` also being imported. In case you do not have it installed, please do that first.
- **Customize:** This section allows us to customize parameters for the input file for closing prices, total corpus or fund size, exposure limit for each asset vis-à-vis the total portfolio, and names of the files to save results. The input data file is the same one we have used in the last example. It has a date column and one column each for the closing price of each asset. The column head is also the asset ID, which the code uses for reporting. The relevant part of the code with customizable parameters italicized is given here.

```
# customization parameters
my_input_file="0709 Stock Close Price.csv"
total_corpus=1000000
my_limit=0.25
my_optimal_file="0710 optimal_portfolio.csv"
my_pie_chart="0710 optimal_portfolio_allocation.png"
```

- **Set up for optimization:** In this section, we will compute the expected return and covariance matrix depicting how returns from different assets move about each other. You may not find an explicit code to compute the return as we did in the earlier section. The library has an inbuilt function "mean_historical_return" to do the same, and we have used that. We are also specifying parameters for computing efficient frontiers and using exposure limits. We will work with the efficient frontier in the next section. This is the portfolio allocation that offers the highest expected return for a given level of risk.
- **Optimize portfolio:** This section assigns raw weight to the assets in the portfolio and then derives clean weight that maximizes the Sharpe ratio. The portfolio performance is computed based on the clean weights. The final allocation for each asset is then computed by using this computed weight, the latest price, and the corpus size. This will also compute the money that will remain unused after final allocation to each asset.
- **Save and display results:** The code goes on to save the optimal allocation results in a specified CSV graphics file.

The output of the code is the optimal allocation weights for each asset. This will change as we change the maximum exposure limit. The weight is displayed as a pie chart as well as in the number of shares. It further displays the amount of funds remaining unused, expected annual return, annual volatility from the optimal portfolio, and the Sharpe ratio.

Understanding modern portfolio theory principles

MPT provides the theoretical foundation for quantitative portfolio management. While the original theory has evolved significantly since Harry Markowitz's seminal work in the 1950s, its core understanding continues to influence how we approach portfolio construction. MPT began with Markowitz's insight that investors should take note that assets with imperfect correlations could reduce overall portfolio risk without necessarily sacrificing returns. This led to the concept of the efficient frontier: the set of portfolios that offer the highest expected return for a given level of risk.

Based on this foundation, more sophisticated models were developed in the following years. Some of the major ones include the following:

- **Capital Asset Pricing Model (CAPM)**: CAPM introduced the concepts of systematic and unsystematic risk, suggesting that only assets that can reduce systematic risk (beta) can charge a premium since unsystematic risk can be diversified away and mitigated.
- **Arbitrage Pricing Theory (APT)**: APT expanded CAPM by suggesting that asset returns are driven by multiple systematic risk factors, not just market risk. These factors might include macroeconomic indicators such as inflation, interest rates, industrial production, or exchange rates. APT does not rely on strict assumptions about investor behavior or market equilibrium, making it more adaptable to real-world applications.
- **Fama-French Factor Models**: These models identified specific factors, such as size and value, that help explain asset returns beyond market risk. For instance, smaller firms have often historically shown higher returns, suggesting a size premium. Similarly, companies trading at lower price-to-book ratios have often exhibited higher returns, reflecting a value premium. By incorporating these additional dimensions, multifactor models provide deeper insights into expected returns, unlike traditional models that solely use market risk.

Post-modern portfolio theory modified MPT by using downside risk measures instead of standard deviation, recognizing that investors are primarily concerned with losses rather than all deviations from the mean.

Let us take an example of drawing an efficient frontier following the classical MPT. The major components of the code (prefix 0711) are the following:

- **Import libraries**: We have imported the necessary libraries into the system here. One of the libraries imported is used for optimization.
- **Customize**: The customization parameters are primarily file names, input files for closing prices, and output files to save results. We are continuing with the same input data file used in the last example. It has a date column and one column each for the closing price of each asset. The column head shows the asset ID. In addition, we have provided the number of portfolios to be created for the recognition of the efficient frontier.
  The relevant part of the code with customizable parameters italicized is shown here.

```
# Customize the parameters
my_input_file="0709 Stock Close Price.csv"
num_portfolios = 10000
my_ef_weight="0711 efficient_frontier_weights.csv"
my_ef_plot="0711 efficient_frontier.png"
```

- **Prepare for optimization**: The section commences with the loading of stock data. It proceeds to the computation of daily returns and the covariance matrix.
- **Define portfolio optimization function**: A function to compute the return and volatility of a portfolio is developed in this section.
- **Compute and save efficient frontier**: In this section, we generate a specified number of portfolios and compute their corresponding return, volatility, and Sharpe ratio. This is necessary to identify the efficient frontier.
- **Plot and save efficient frontier**: The data generated in the preceding section is saved in a specified CSV file. The same dataset is then used to plot the efficient frontier, which is saved to a specified file. The screen displays a confirmation message after creating these files.

The efficient frontier is also plotted and displayed on the screen, in addition to being saved as a file. The outer boundary of the scatter plot, starting from the lowest volatility point on the left and curving upward to the right, represents the efficient frontier. All other portfolio combinations that fall below this frontier are inefficient, as they offer a lower return for the same or higher level of volatility.

Where on the frontier an investor chooses to operate depends on their individual risk preference, whether they are risk-averse or risk-seeking. The Sharpe ratio helps compare portfolios by measuring the return per unit of risk.

Adjusting portfolios in response to market changes

Portfolio optimization is an ongoing activity. It responds to changes in market conditions as well as changes in investment objectives. Traditionally, portfolio rebalancing was performed on fixed schedules or when asset allocations breached predetermined thresholds. Unscheduled rebalancing was done when the external environment witnessed major shifts or the internal investment objectives were changed. ML has introduced more sophisticated approaches to dynamic portfolio adjustments that can significantly enhance risk-adjusted returns. Let us have a look at a few such capabilities.

Detecting regime changes

Financial markets operate in distinct regimes. These regimes are periods usually characterized by specific correlation structures, volatility levels, and return patterns. Traditional portfolio optimization typically assumes a single regime and may underperform when the regime changes. ML techniques can identify regime shifts and adjust portfolios accordingly. Once a regime change is detected, the portfolio optimization process will use parameters calibrated to the new environment. For example, during a highly volatile market regime, the algorithm might increase allocations to defensive assets and reduce exposure to more volatile securities.

Several ML approaches are effective in regime detection. Here are a few examples of such models:

- **Hidden Markov Models (HMMs):** These models can identify hidden states in financial markets and estimate the probability of transitioning between different regimes.
- **Clustering Algorithms:** Techniques like K-means clustering or Gaussian mixture models can group market conditions into distinct regimes based on multiple factors.
- **Change Point Detection:** These algorithms identify structural breaks in time series data, signaling potential regime shifts that might require portfolio adjustments.

Adaptive risk management

ML enables more responsive risk management because of enhanced analytical capabilities. Some of these possibilities include the following:

- **Dynamic risk budgeting:** ML algorithms can continuously monitor risk contributions from different assets. It can adjust allocations to maintain target risk levels as volatilities and correlations change.

- **Tail risk forecasting:** Financial decision-makers keep worrying about tail risk events. Neural networks and extreme value theory can be combined to better predict potential extreme market movements and adjust portfolios to reduce tail risk exposure.
- **Stress testing with generative models:** There could be events that have not historically occurred but are theoretically possible. Because they have not happened, it becomes difficult to create a scenario reflecting the unseen. Generative adversarial networks (GANs) can simulate diverse market scenarios, allowing portfolios to be tested against conditions.

Tactical asset allocation

Beyond strategic allocation and risk management, ML can make tactical adjustments. The common tools that support tactical allocation include the following:

- **Factor Rotation:** ML models can identify which factor exposures, such as momentum, value, or quality, among others, are likely to perform well in current market conditions and adjust portfolio tilts accordingly.
- **Alternative Data Processing:** ML excels at extracting signals from non-traditional data sources, ranging from satellite imagery to social media sentiment, that might indicate emerging trends before they appear in traditional financial metrics.
- **Natural Language Processing (NLP):** NLP algorithms can analyze central bank communications, earnings calls, or news flow to gauge shifts in market sentiment that might warrant portfolio adjustments.

Implementation considerations

In addition to the adjustment scenarios discussed, several practical considerations are important. Frequent rebalancing causes higher transaction costs, and ML approaches can incorporate transaction costs in the model to ensure that adjustment benefits exceed implementation costs. There are tax implications, too. Often, longer-term holding leads to a lower tax burden, and the effective cost of rebalancing changes because of the holding period. The model can ensure that the benefit of rebalancing is not eaten up by a higher tax burden. Automated adjustment systems, including algorithmic trading, require clear governance frameworks. We need to distinguish between which changes can happen automatically and which ones should require human approval.

The most effective approaches to portfolio adjustment typically combine ML signals with human judgment. Let us use a case study.

XYZ Capital is a mid-sized asset management firm managing diversified portfolios for high-net-worth clients with varying risk tolerances. Recent market volatility has highlighted the need for a more adaptive approach to asset allocation that can anticipate changing market conditions rather than a simple reactive approach.

The investment committee at XYZ Capital has observed that traditional fixed-weight asset allocation strategies perform poorly during regime shifts in market volatility.

They want to develop a strategy that can predict future market volatility and dynamically adjust portfolio allocations based on these predictions. It should use a systematic, data-driven approach to tactical asset allocation.

The research team has assembled a dataset containing daily price information for the market index, bond index, and five individual stocks where the company invests, from Asset 1 to Asset 5. The dataset spans five years of daily prices, providing sufficient history to include multiple market regimes, including both low and high volatility periods.

The code begins by predicting daily market volatility using the previous day's values. Asset allocation strategies are manually defined for both high- and low-volatility scenarios. The change in market mood is deduced by following the movements in a primary asset and a secondary asset belonging to a contrasting asset class. For example, say the primary asset is equity. A contrasting asset class, such as bonds, would be used to measure the correlation between the primary asset and something fundamentally different. This is a way to model changing market dynamics. Under simple circumstances, equities and bonds are expected to move in the opposite direction because of their risk class. If equities and bonds start moving together, it may signal stress or loss of diversification. The code then compares the performance of the dynamic asset allocation strategy against a base static allocation. Finally, the code forecasts volatility for the next five days and recommends corresponding asset allocations. Let us take a look at the major components of the code (prefix 0712).

- **Import libraries:** All necessary libraries are imported into the system here. In case any one of the libraries is missing, install them first.
- **Customize:** The customization parameters are primarily file names, input files for closing prices, output files to save results and plots, and allocation ratios. Three allocation ratios are used. These are the ratios under high volatility, under low volatility, and the base allocation. Be careful to specify allocation ratios for each asset, ensure that the sum of the allocations is 100, and do not overlook the square brackets. Another important aspect is that the first column of the input data will be the date. The second column should be the market proxy, the primary asset. The third column should be the comparison asset, which will be used

to identify a regime change. A regime change refers to a structural shift in how the market behaves, often characterized by changes in volatility, shifts in correlation patterns between asset classes, or altered relationships between risk and return, among others.

The relevant part of the code with customizable parameters italicized is shown here.

```
# Customize parameters
my_input_data = "0712 market_data.csv"
my_area_chart = "0712 portfolio_weights_dynamic_area_
chart.png"
my_returns = "0712 risk_adjusted_returns.png"
my_output_csv = "0712 dynamic_risk_budgeting.csv"
my_high_allocation=[30, 50, 5, 5, 5, 2.5, 2.5]
my_low_allocation=[50, 20, 10, 10, 5, 2.5, 2.5]
my_base_allocation=[50, 20, 10, 10, 5, 2.5, 2.5]
```

- **Prepare data for processing:** In this section, we load the market data comprising dates and prices of assets. Daily simple and log returns are computed, followed by the computation of the volatility of the primary asset and correlation over rolling 30 days. In case you want to use some other period, you can change the value 30 to your preferred period in this part of the code, `rolling_window=30`. Volatility is measured by computing the standard deviation. Rows where volatility or correlation could not be computed are removed. These two derived features, volatility and correlation, are used as input to the ML model. High uncertainty in the market is indicated by high volatility, while high correlation indicates a potential loss of diversification opportunity.
- **Define features, target, and predict:** The code uses a Random Forest model to predict volatility. As discussed previously, we need to identify the features and targets for the model to work. This model learns from values of volatility and correlation of the last day (t–1) to estimate what the volatility will be on the current day (t). In this code, we have used 100 trees in the forest. You can change it to your preferred number by tweaking this part of the code: `n_estimators=100`. The code then adds a new column to the dataframe for storing predicted volatility. Please note that the prediction here is in-sample, that is, on the same data it was trained on. This makes it more suitable for back-testing over out-of-sample validation.
- **Allocate assets using prediction:** This section assigns different portfolio weightage based on the predicted level of volatility following the rule-based regime switching strategy. The model takes the predicted volatility and compares it with the average volatility to identify the volatility regime and switches to the corresponding allocation model. This

decision is made every day, forming the basis of a dynamic portfolio strategy. This allocation is driven by a dynamic risk allocation function developed for the purpose.

- **Storing results:** This section combines the model's predictions with the corresponding portfolio allocations and saves the result for review or further analysis. We get a dataset with predicted volatility, actual volatility, portfolio return, and allocation ratio for each asset for each date. This dataset is saved to the specified CSV file. The portfolio return is computed at the beginning of the module.
- **Back-testing using dynamic allocation:** In this section, we will compute the daily return from the portfolio under the dynamic asset allocation strategy and the base asset allocation strategy. This enables us to evaluate which strategy performs better under historical market conditions. Right at the outset, a function is defined to compute portfolio return. We load the values of the static allocation strategy and apply it to all dates. We proceed to compute the portfolio return from both strategies. The returns computed here are log returns.
- **Computing metrics:** We define a function that computes cumulative return, volatility, and the Sharpe ratio. We then apply the function to both dynamic and static portfolios. We will have comparative values for return, volatility, and the Sharpe ratio under both strategies.
- **Forecast volatility and allocation:** This section of the code predicts market volatility for the next five days. It then recommends asset allocation decisions for each of those days based on the predicted volatility. It starts with the latest date available in the input data and considers the market condition present on that date. The code uses the trained Random Forest model for prediction if the conditions remain the same. For each predicted value, it uses an appropriate allocation strategy.
- **Display results, store forecast, and save:** This section of the code visualizes portfolio allocations and risk-return relationships. It also prints back-tested performance comparisons and displays and saves predicted volatility and allocations for the next five days.

The output of the code includes a stacked area chart where each colored area represents the allocation to an asset over time, with time on the X-axis. This shows how the asset mix changed dynamically over time in response to predicted volatility regimes. The next chart is a scatterplot of actual returns from primary assets and predicted volatility. The color of the plot denotes actual observed volatility.

The next section displays comparative results for the static and dynamic strategies. This would allow us to decide which strategy is better suited. The forecast volatility and corresponding allocation for the next five days are also displayed on the screen. This result is also saved in a specified `CSV` file.

Key takeaways

This chapter has taken a comprehensive look at how traditional and machine learning-enhanced tools can be used for capital budgeting and investment appraisal. We saw that capital budgeting is not just about crunching numbers. It requires aligning investment choices with strategic priorities, managing risks, and ensuring financial viability. Understanding the time value of money is fundamental for comparing cash flows over time. While NPV and IRR remain central tools, they must be applied carefully, as results can be distorted by leverage, accounting policies, or spreadsheet issues. Risk analysis through sensitivity and scenario planning is essential for capturing uncertainty. ML adds value by automating complex analyses, improving forecasts, and identifying success patterns. The inclusion of real options introduces flexibility in decision-making, allowing adaptation to future scenarios. Finally, optimizing the overall investment portfolio ensures a better risk-return balance, supporting both financial goals and broader strategic constraints.

Chapter 8

Customer profitability and segmentation

Quantifying and leveraging customer relationships provides companies with a key competitive advantage. Traditional financial statements provide a snapshot of accounting metrics on a specific date or over a specified period. It does not provide information about the potential value customers have. They do not reveal a customer-level analysis, that is, which customers contribute most to profitability, which groups warrant greater investment, or which relationships are at risk of attrition. This chapter addresses the importance of customer analysis by leveraging AI-driven tools and techniques.

Treating customers as an asset

When talking about an asset, the statement of financial position is the first thing that comes to mind. This statement, also known as the balance sheet, captures a company's assets, liabilities, and equity at a specific point in time. The statements adhere to guidelines that are defined by various accounting standards, such as IFRS or GAAP. One of the most valuable components of a company's worth is its customer base, which remains conspicuously absent from these financial statements. This section examines the importance of treating customers as economic assets and why they are not recognized on financial statements.

Valuation and reporting of customer value

Economic assets are defined as resources that hold value and provide benefits to their economic owners over time. Customers are the fundamental drivers of a company's cash flow, contributing to the overall enterprise value, which makes them economic assets. In most industries, the viability of the business is directly tied to its ability to acquire, retain, and monetize its customers. To this effect, these industries often have a dedicated customer relationship manager.

DOI: 10.4324/9781003619628-8

Several frameworks have evolved to value customers. The most common one is CLV. CLV estimates the total revenue a company expects to generate from a customer throughout their entire lifetime. CLV helps guide decision-making to improve profitability, identify high-value customers, and optimize marketing spend. It is essential to identify the profitability of various customer segments, too.

Technically, CLV is of two types: historic CLV and predictive CLV. Historic CLV is very straightforward. Say you have purchased a $20 moisturizer from the same company thrice a year for the last ten years. Your historic CLV for the company is $600.

However, while this helps build the customer profile for the company, this alone is not useful for predicting future value. This is where predictive CLV comes in. Predictive CLV uses historical data and AI to predict how long a customer relationship will last and how much value it will generate for the company. CLV can be calculated at multiple levels:

- **Company level:** This is the most straightforward one. It is simply calculating the average CLV across all customers.
- **Customer segment level:** Calculating the CLV of individual segments within the customer base. We will discuss customer segmentation in detail in the next section.
- **Individual level:** Calculating the CLV of each customer.

There is no standard formula for calculating the CLV, and it varies with the company, industry, business model, customer behavior, and other similar factors. However, the foundational formula for calculating the CLV is:

CLV = Customer value * Average customer lifespan

Customer value captures the revenue-generating capacity of a customer over a fixed period. To calculate customer value, we need to multiply the average purchase value by the average purchase frequency. The average purchase value is simply the total revenue over a given period, divided by the number of purchases in the same period. The average purchase frequency is calculated by dividing the number of purchases by the number of unique customers who have made a purchase.

The second component, average customer lifespan, is the average duration (often in years) a customer continues buying from the business before churning or becoming inactive. It is computed as the sum of the customer lifespans divided by the number of customers. This formula gives a revenue-based CLV, which does not account for costs. If you want profit-based CLV, you would multiply the result by the gross margin percentage.

More sophisticated CLV models can have other variables too, such as Net Promoter Score (NPS) and Customer Satisfaction Score (CSAT). NPS measures customer loyalty by their likelihood to recommend the relevant business to others. Any time you have answered a question along the lines of "On a scale of 1–5, how likely are you to recommend this business to others in your circle, with 1 being not likely at all, and 5 being highly likely?", you have participated in measurement on NPS. CSAT, on the other hand, measures the satisfaction level of a customer. It is usually in the form of a survey asking customers to rate their experience in dealing with the company.

When incorporated into a predictive CLV model, both NPS and CSAT can enhance its accuracy.

CLV is primarily influenced by churn rate and brand loyalty. The churn rate is the rate at which customers stop buying products or services from a company they used to be loyal to. Although whether a churn rate will be categorized as good or bad depends on the industry, a high churn rate is generally considered bad. A continuous increase in churn rate may indicate a serious problem and will force the company to review its products and/or services. Brand loyalty plays a pivotal role in mitigating the churn rate. Investing in building and measuring brand loyalty will also help retain customers. Brand loyalty can be built in a variety of ways, like personalized interactions, outstanding after-sales service, loyalty programs, and building a strong brand identity, among others. Some customers are very loyal and are reluctant to switch over. Even when they have problems with the products, and there are a lot of other great options to switch to, they are incredibly forgiving and understanding.

Having loyal customers will eventually generate a high value over the lifetime of the company.

Despite the strong case for viewing customers as assets, accounting standards have strict asset recognition criteria that customer relationships fail to meet. This is to say that no doubt customers are being an asset, the question is if it fulfills the reporting criteria. There are three key requirements across most accounting standards that a customer relationship fails to satisfy. These are:

- **Control over assets:** The entities must have control over an asset. It must be able to obtain future economic benefits from it and control the use of the asset. Customers are independent entities. Customers represent a relationship, not a controllable resource. Moreover, unless explicitly laid out in a legal contract, companies cannot prevent customers from purchasing from others.
- **Probable future economic benefits:** It must be probable that an asset will generate future economic benefits for the company. Whether a customer

will keep generating future economic benefits and not churn unexpectedly is dependent on factors like pricing competition, customer satisfaction, and other market dynamics. This leads to the company not being able to reasonably assert that it will obtain future economic benefits from the customer.

- **Reliable measurement of cost**: An asset's cost or fair value must be reliably measurable. There are customer value models, such as CLV, which estimate customer worth. However, financial statements should be objective and verifiable, and the subjective nature of such models raises doubt about the reliability necessary for recognition as an asset.

While customers play a huge role in the overall value of a company, they do not meet the asset recognition requirements under accounting standards and thus cannot be reported on the financial statements. However, customers can form part of a company's Integrated Report (IR). An IR consists of reporting on an organization's business model, and six types of capital: financial, manufactured, intellectual, human, natural, social, and relationship. Customers form part of the social and relationship capital. Additionally, customers may also come under the business model section as key stakeholders whose needs drive value creation, influencing inputs, outputs, and long-term outcomes.

However, there is no doubt that the customers form the backbone of the revenue stream of a company. The financial decision-makers need to assess how stable this revenue stream is, and that is where valuing the customer becomes a major management control issue.

Customer segmentation and decision effectiveness

Customer segmentation is the process of dividing customers into separate groups based on common characteristics, such as demographics, behaviors, and preferences. There are many ways to segment customers, and the choice depends on various factors like the business model, the objective of segmentation, the industry, and similar factors. With segmentation, not only are companies able to create more personalized experiences and increase their customer engagement and loyalty, but it also improves the results of CLV modeling. Although customer segmentation is more commonly used as a marketing tool, it can also enhance decision effectiveness. Customer segmentation affects both financial and operational decision-making and effectiveness in the following ways:

- **Capital allocation efficiency**: Unsegmented customers may lead to inefficient capital deployment as it does not capture the differences in distinct groups. This may lead to companies misallocating their marketing investment. For example, if a bank allocated its acquisition budget evenly across all demographic segments, it would not be able to take advantage of demographic differences between the younger and older generations. Say, the younger generation has a higher product cross-sell rate and a lower cost to serve. This would result in a higher average CLV as compared to the older customer segment. Segmentation also enables marginal ROI optimization, where incremental capital could be redirected to segments with the highest return sensitivity.

- **Cost structure alignment**: Different customer segments would have different cost-to-serve structures. Segmentation allows companies to account for these differences by modeling cost structures that reflect segment behavior. ABC may be useful in determining the cost allocation in individual segments. Say, an equipment manufacturer discovered that while large clients generate higher revenue, they have extensive service requirements. They need dedicated account managers, custom installations, and extended credit terms. Compare this to smaller-sized clients, who, although they contribute less revenue, require minimal support. Based on this insight, the company can now redesign its service tiers by offering standardized solutions to lower- cost segments and reallocating the resources saved to the larger-sized clients. Further, they would also be able to avoid over-servicing unprofitable customers. They can also forecast departmental resource requirements by analyzing growth patterns across customer segments.
- **Working capital management**: Working capital decisions may be more effective when they recognize the behavioral and risk characteristics of customer segments. Cash on delivery (COD) purchases are very common in e-commerce transactions, create a longer receivables cycle, a higher chance of failed deliveries, and increased operational risk. By identifying COD users as a distinct segment, targeted efforts can be made either to migrate them to the pre-paid segment or charge a small fee to cover the additional cost. Likewise, inventory buffers may be adjusted based on the volatility of demand within each segment, ensuring that capital is not unnecessarily tied up in slow-moving stock. Even supplier arrangements may be structured to reflect the service expectations of each segment.
- **CLV modeling efficacy**: The efficacy of CLV models is completely dependent on the inputs and assumptions used. Segmenting customers before applying CLV models improves the precision of such models by reducing behavioral noise. Predictive models calibrated separately for high-frequency, low-margin retail buyers versus infrequent, high-margin retail customers yield different, and potentially better, results.
- **AI-driven decision frameworks**: Often, an important step in unsupervised learning algorithms, such as K-means clustering or decision

tree-based models, is the grouping of data. These models do not always produce conventional business groupings, as they are based on natural data patterns and groupings. Often, a primary business case-based segmentation during the data preprocessing stage may improve AI-driven segmentation. The output can then be used to implement strategies like personalized pricing, optimize service levels, and guide ML pipelines. On the same note, AI models that are trained and deployed on unsegmented customer data often suffer from average-performance bias, producing suboptimal recommendations.

In addition to the areas stated above, segmentation can also enhance risk management practices and long-term strategic planning. It is useful when evaluating market entry, designing credit policies, or devising product diversification strategies. To summarize, customer segmentation is critical in improving the quality and precision of financial decision-making, in addition to being an excellent marketing tool.

Customer lifetime cycle and segmentation

The customer lifecycle represents the entire journey of a customer's relationship with an organization. It starts from becoming a customer to not transacting with the company anymore. Customer lifecycles typically end with loyalty or advocacy from a marketing perspective. However, from a financial standpoint, the cycle ends when the customer no longer generates future economic value. The objectives of marketing and finance professionals are different; marketing departments view the lifecycle as a tool for customer engagement, and finance departments should view it as a driver of revenue realization, cost behavior, risk exposure, and customer-level profitability.

Each stage of the lifecycle carries different economic characteristics. The ability to measure and manage customers across these stages is fundamental in creating value in the long term. However, analyzing customer metrics over the entire customer base obscures underlying variations in behavior. This is where customer segmentation comes in. Integrating customer segmentation with customer lifecycle metrics provides a deeper understanding of the customers.

Although lifecycle specifics may differ across industries, the fundamental stages common to most sectors include the following:

- **Awareness and Acquisition**: The first stage in the lifecycle is where the customer becomes aware of the brand through marketing or referrals. It is shortly followed by acquisition, where they are converted into paying customers. This stage involves customer acquisition costs (CAC) and the early assessment of potential returns through conversion rates and initial engagement signals.

- **Onboarding and Engagement**: Onboarding is the initial experience of using the product or service. This includes setup, support, and first use. Onboarding is followed by engagement, where the customer begins using the product or service regularly. This stage is also where first impressions happen, which may translate into either early churn or long-term value.
- **Growth**: At the growth stage, customers deepen their relationship with the firm through increased usage, cross-product adoption, or higher transaction frequency. This represents a primary opportunity for revenue expansion.
- **Retention**: The retention stage involves keeping customers engaged and active over time, through offers, loyalty points, service outreach, and other techniques. This stage is crucial in realizing the full economic potential of a customer.
- **Loyalty and Advocacy**: At this stage, long-term loyal customers evolve into advocates. Not only do they exhibit brand preference, but they also refer to others. This generates secondary value through a lower acquisition cost per customer. Loyal customers are also more efficient to serve, more resistant to churn, and more likely to engage with premium offerings. This is the last stage of the customer lifecycle from a marketing perspective.
- **Churn/Exit**: This is the final stage of a customer lifecycle where the customer disengages from the brand, either passively or through active cancellation. This represents the end of realized CLV and offers an opportunity for an exit-stage analysis.

The role of segmentation in the customer lifecycle may be better understood through the following example. Consider a retail bank in an urban area. The bank may segment its customer base into the following behavioral segments based on historical data as presented in Table 8.1.

Recognition of different segments will be followed by designing appropriate strategies. Customer segmentation is vital for effective customer lifecycle management. The customer lifecycle provides a temporal view, and segmentation adds context. This combined approach improves capital allocation, refines cost management, and enhances CLV prediction.

CLV prediction

CLV helps us quantify the value a customer brings to an organization. There are multiple ways to predict CLV; however, in this section, we will predict CLV using regression models that identify high-value customers.

Table 8.1 Customer segmentation example

Segment	*Characteristics*	*Financial Implication*
Digital natives	• Comfortable with mobile apps, online onboarding, and digital customer service • Respond to in-app notifications, real-time alerts, and e-banking tools • Expect speed, transparency, and low friction when transacting • Often younger, but not exclusively	• Lower physical cost to serve, high technology cost to serve • High responsiveness to digital engagement • High scalability and cross-sell potential
Relationship seekers	• Prefer face-to-face onboarding, branch visits, and relationship managers • Prioritize stability, advice, and familiarity over rates or features • Tend to be older and comparatively financially stable • Located in communities with a strong branch presence	• Higher physical cost to serve • Lower churn rate • Suitable for premium products
Rate-sensitive shoppers	• Frequently switch based on promotions or changes in rates • Engage less with the brand and more with the financial terms • Often transitory in loyalty unless incentivized	• Low retention unless competitively priced • Volatile CLV • Low acquisition and retention costs

Predicting CLV to prioritize marketing efforts

Customer acquisition and retention may consume a significant amount of a company's marketing spending through advertising campaigns, loyalty programs, and so on. Companies invest substantial resources in these to attract and retain customers. CLV provides a handy tool to align the marketing needs and financial implications.

By allocating costs based on the future economic benefits a customer is expected to generate, companies can make marketing investments based on the potential financial value. CLV modeling allows the marketing function to be closely aligned with enterprise value creation. It directs acquisition, retention, and growth efforts toward customer segments with the highest projected ROI, also known as value-based targeting. CLV prediction shifts the focus from "how many customers?" to "which customers?" or from campaign performance to customer contribution.

CLV prediction enhances customer targeting within existing audiences. It helps in efficiently targeting discounts, reward programs, and retention efforts on customers whose future value justifies the cost. From a corporate governance perspective, predictive CLV adds a layer to marketing performance evaluation. Marketing ROI can be assessed by the profit generated over the full customer lifecycle. From a long-term view, it helps enable the company to build cohort-based financial forecasts and improve CLV-to-CAC ratios. Cohort-based forecasting is a method used to predict future trends in customer behavior based on historical data. It is a highly precise mechanism, but it provides the edge to remain competitive in an ever-changing market.

CLV ultimately strengthens the alignment between finance and marketing functions. CLV models can be used to validate marketing business cases, stress-test strategic assumptions like margin trajectories, and tie projected customer value to enterprise-level growth targets. Using CLV as a decision tool supports not just marketing execution but overall enterprise planning, investor confidence, valuation, and reputation.

Using regression models to estimate CLV

It is now time for a practical demonstration of CLV. Before getting to the code, let us discuss a few formulas that are used to calculate CLV. Each of these formulas serves a different type of business model, data availability, and analytical need.

Although these models differ from the basic CLV framework introduced in the prior section, they are built upon the same foundational concept.

Simplified deterministic CLV

$$CLV = Customer\ value \times Average\ customer\ lifespan$$

This CLV model is very simple and deterministic. It shows how much the average customer is expected to spend at the company over their lifetime. This works well for early-stage marketing analytics in businesses with stable and recurring purchases, like retail or e-commerce. However, it assumes consistent customer behavior and does not discount the future cash flows or allow for churn probability.

Retention-based CLV

$$CLV = m \times \left(\frac{r}{1 + d - r}\right)$$

where,
m is the gross margin over the expected lifespan
r is the retention rate per period
d is the discount rate

This CLV model is useful for subscription-based businesses, like telecommunication, SaaS, or streaming services. It incorporates the time value of money using the discount rate and further uses the retention rate to model customer survival. The retention rate is typically estimated from historical customer behavior.

Simplified discounted cash flow CLV

$$CLV = \sum_{t=0}^{T} a \frac{r^t}{(1+d)^t}$$

where,
a is the net cash flow per period (if alive)
r is the retention rate per period
d is the discount rate
T is the total time horizon
t is the current period

This model estimates CLV as the discounted sum of constant net margin across periods, adjusted by the retention rate. It is less granular than a fully probabilistic model, but it provides a simplified, time-structured view of customer value. It incorporates churn by using the retention rate raised to the power of time. Churn is effectively the inverse of retention and is mathematically baked into the model.

Fully discounted, probabilistic CLV

$$CLV = \sum_{t=1}^{T} \frac{(M_t - C_t) \times p^t}{(1+d)^t} - AC$$

where,
M_t is the margin produced in each period
C_t is the cost to serve the customer
p^t is the probability of the customer not churning within a year
d is the discount rate

T is the total time horizon
t is the current period
AC is the acquisition cost

This model is well-suited for most businesses as it dissects the CLV at a granular level. It incorporates most variables relevant to CLV modeling, such as individual customer margins, probability of churn, cost-to-serve, and acquisition costs. It also requires historical data. It may not always be feasible to use this model because of the complexity and the costs associated with implementing it.

A regression analysis predicts how changes in the independent variables impact the dependent variable. Regression analysis has been discussed in depth in Chapter 2. You may refer to it and refresh your knowledge. In our model, we have used three independent variables, which we assume capture customer behavior, and consequently predict CLV. These are the total number of purchases made by each customer, the time between their first and last purchase, and the number of days since their most recent purchase. We aim to see if these variables can predict CLV. Instead of using detailed business and economic parameters as stated above, we have simply assumed CLV to be the total amount the customer has spent in the company. We chose this approach to demonstrate how ML can be applied to predict CLV. However, do note that in real life, we should consider other factors as well. The model follows a train-test split and uses transaction data from the first nine months to train a linear regression model that attempts to predict annual CLV per customer.

For our case study, we are considering a fast-growing manufacturer of sweet snacks. It has developed a loyal customer following through its unique sweet treats. As it expands its operations and marketing efforts, understanding the long-term value of each customer has become crucial for strategic decision-making. The company has extracted the purchase data for each customer. This model is trained on historical data and then tests its accuracy in predicting CLV based on another set of historical data. The idea is to find, based on how this customer behaved in the first nine months, what the likely annual revenue (CLV) of the customer is at the end of the year.

Let us move on to the code (prefix 0801). The code is divided into the following five major sections:

- **Import libraries:** By now, you must have installed all the libraries we need to use for the regression analysis. However, in case you missed out on any, Python would throw a `ModuleNotFoundError`, and you can install the missing ones using pip. For example, `!pip install pandas` if you are installing them from a notebook cell.

- **Customize:** This section would allow you to customize certain input data. It is advised that you do not change the format of the CSV file where you provide your input. In this section, we are specifying the names of the input file, the output file, the names of the files to save the plot, and a list of features and targets. We will also provide the earliest date in the database and the date up to which we will use for training the model. You must enter both these dates in the format yyyy-mm-dd. In case your date format is different, please change it here. The code has been designed to stop if either of your dates is not present in the uploaded dataset. The relevant part of the code with the customizable section in italics is stated below.

```
input_path = "0801 Raw Data.csv"
# Don't include the extension for this file
output_path = "0801 CLV_Regression_Result"
image_path = "0801 CLV_Scatter.png"
start_date = pd.to_datetime("2024-01-01")
cutoff_date = pd.to_datetime("2024-09-30")
my_features=["ActivityPeriodDays", "TotalPurchases",
"DaysSinceLastPurchase"]
my_target='CLV'
```

- **Preprocess data:** In this section, read the input data and run a check to see whether the starting and cutoff dates are present. We also drop rows with blank invoice date or customer ID fields. We proceed with creating a dataframe grouped by customer ID. We truncate our original dataframe to contain transactions within the start and cutoff dates.
- **Extract behavior variables:** We extract the data of the first and last purchase date along with the count of total purchases. We further compute the total number of days the customer was active and the days of inactivity since the last purchase. All these data are stored in a new dataframe. If you are interested in seeing what the dataframe looks like at this stage, enter the following command after this section. It will only display the first and last few rows with ellipses in the middle.

```
print (full_df)
```

- **Run regression:** This is where the actual regression analysis takes place. We have used Linear Regression and provided the system with the list of features and the target. Once the model has been fit, we have run the model to predict values for the target using the same dataframe used to fit the model. We have not used the protocol of splitting the data into training and testing components. We then compute the metrics of model fit and store the values of slope and intercept as two variables.

- **Plot and save:** We have plotted the predicted and actual values of CLV to get a visual understanding of the fit of the model. The plot is saved to a file, and the data to both a CSV and an Excel file. The Excel file is saved with an _Excel suffix in the name. A plot of the predicted and actual CLV is displayed and saved for later use. In addition, the regression equation and the model fit metrics are displayed on screen.
- **Create formatted report (Optional):** This section includes codes used for formatting and saving in the Excel file. The first sheet saves the final dataframe to an Excel sheet, summarized by customer ID, with columns indicating the independent variables, actual CLV, and predicted CLV. The next sheet saves the scatter plot, along with the regression equation and a few ancillary information about general customer purchasing behavior. If you do not want to save the Excel file, you can disregard this section of the code. You can remove this cell or mark the cell as Markdown, and it will no longer run as code.

The output of the code includes the file with the predicted CLV. The major model for metrics and a plot of actual and predicted CLV is also displayed and stored. The predicted line is straight, as it is the output of a linear regression model. The regression equation and the model matrices are displayed after the plot.

Identifying high-value customers

To build on the CLV model developed earlier, we will now look at the importance of identifying characteristics that are commonly associated with high-value customers. We aim to understand what patterns of customer purchasing behavior can be linked to higher CLV. Businesses would want to identify customers who are most likely to generate substantial revenue and thus may prioritize marketing strategies toward them.

After running a regression model on the data, we see that the R^2 value is 0.79. This indicates that 79% of the variance in the CLV can be explained by the independent variables, that is, customer lifespan, frequency of purchase, and the time passed till the last purchase. The MAE and RMSE help understand the accuracy of the predictions and the amount of deviation from the actual values. As you can see in the worksheet, the CLV values range from a few hundred to a few thousand. An MAE of 581.76 means that, on average, the actual CLV is expected to lie within ±580 units in most cases, while an RMSE of 762.30 indicates that there are likely some outlier customers with larger deviations. For example, if a customer's predicted CLV is $2,500, the actual CLV is likely to fall within a range of ±580 to ±760 dollars. Whether this level of accuracy is acceptable or not is a strategic decision to be made by management. More importantly, the regression equation itself becomes a financial tool. If the management is happy with the R^2, RMSE, and MAE, they can apply the regression equation to current customer data to generate future estimates of CLV.

To estimate the CLV of any new or existing customer, we can insert the latest values for these three behavioral indicators in the regression equation. The regression equation in this case is:

$$CLV = 655.08 + (-2.89) \times ActivityPeriodDays + (126.23) \times TotalPurchases + (-5.08) * DaysSinceLast\ Purchase$$

Each coefficient in this equation explains how customer behavior influences lifetime value while holding all other variables constant. The coefficient for TotalPurchases is +126.23, indicating that each additional purchase made by a customer increases their CLV by approximately $126 units. This follows the intuitive understanding that frequent purchasers generate more value for the business.

`DaysSinceLastPurchase` has a coefficient of –5.08, indicating that for each day that passes since a customer's last purchase, their expected CLV decreases by approximately $5. Interestingly, the coefficient for `ActivityPeriodDays` is also negative (–2.89), which means that customers with a longer period between their first and last purchase tend to have lower CLV. This may seem counterintuitive, but that is what the data brings out – an insight that escapes normal overview. These various behavioral trends help us identify patterns that define high-value customers.

Once high-value potential customers have been identified, the next step is to act on such insights. The focus then shifts from measurement to management. This can be through either increasing revenue per customer, such as targeted cross-selling, upselling, price optimization, or by improving the quality of service provided. Beyond revenue and cost adjustments, CLV analysis also enables strategic portfolio management. Finance teams can use these insights to prioritize acquisition efforts toward high-value profiles, discourage persistently unprofitable behaviors, and consider exiting or repricing segments that dilute overall contribution margins. The use of predictive CLV models enables differentiated financial treatment of different customer groups. This would help organizations manage contribution margin, customer-level ROI, and long-term value realization by customer segments.

Identifying high-value customers is important for financial decision-making. However, you may have a question. Regression can also be achieved in Excel, so why do I need ML tools to do this? In Excel, each new customer or transaction batch would require the equation to be reworked.

Using ML tools, the model can be built once and applied automatically across all customers in real time without any time spent to build the model and predict future values. Though we have not followed the protocol here, splitting the data between training and testing is likely to give us a more robust model. Finally, for the Excel experts, the model output is being provided in CSV for any additional Excel-based analysis that you may want to do.

Customer clustering

You might have noticed that our discussion on customer segmentation earlier in the chapter overlapped with the development of CLV-based strategies to enhance profitability. This is because CLV and customer segmentation are inherently linked. In this section, we will explore customer segmentation more closely. We will look at how to use unsupervised learning techniques, specifically, K-means clustering, to segment customers based on behavior and demographics. We will use indicators such as purchase frequency, income, age, gender, and spending habits. Unlike in regression, we will not assume any cause-and-effect relation.

Segmenting customers

From a financial decision-making perspective, the advantage of customer segmentation lies in recognizing potential economic differences among groups of customers. Take our example of the bank from earlier. The different segments of customers were worth different values to the bank. There is no one right way to segment customers; they can be divided into different segments in a multitude of ways. The underlying factor is grouping customers with common characteristics. Let us look at the five most common categories to segment customers:

- **Demographic:** Demographic segmentation segments people based on attributes like age, gender, income, occupation, education, marital status, ethnicity, and the like. It is assumed that customers belonging to similar demographics have similar purchasing habits. For example, a café near a university is likely to experience different customer behavior from one in a shopping mall. At the same time, all cafés near a University are likely to experience similar customer behavior.
- **Behavioral:** Behavioral segmentation segments customers based on their purchasing behaviors and interactions with the business. They explain how customers perceive, interact with, and buy and use from a particular business. Behavioral patterns can evolve, with changes in demographic data. For example, a clothing store may target frequent shoppers with

early access to sales, while offering first-time buyers a welcome discount to incentivize them to make a purchase.

- **Geographic**: Geographic segmentation segments customers based on their region. This not only includes their city or country, but also climate, language, culture, or anything region-specific. Geographic data is a part of demographic data, but they are treated differently because they serve different purposes. Geographic segmentation focuses on where the customer is situated, while demographic segmentation focuses on who the customer is. Consider a fast food chain. Geographic segmentation may demonstrate that vegetarian and vegan options are more popular in certain areas, irrespective of demographic data such as age or income. Fast food chains often have different menus in different countries to suit the region-specific tastes.
- **Psychographic**: Psychographic segmentation groups customers based on psychological variables, such as interests, opinions, lifestyle, social status, and hobbies. It is more complex than the other forms of segmentation, as it requires intense research, data collection, analysis, and interpretation. For example, a brand that sells eco-friendly products will target environmentally conscious consumers who place importance on sustainability.
- **Value-based**: Value-based segmentation segments customers according to the economic value that they bring to a business. In other words, segmenting customers based on their CLV. For example, a streaming service may offer premium subscribers more features such as better audio and video quality, ad-free viewing, and the ability to add multiple profiles and devices. On the other hand, the basic subscribers may receive limited access, such as single-device streaming with ads.

There is a possibility that intuitive segmentation may be influenced by personal biases. This is where ML tools such as K-means clustering come in. Not only is it useful in identifying obscure patterns that may escape us, but it also prevents any form of bias in segmentation, as it is purely data-driven. In the next section, we will look at the application of ML tools in customer segmentation.

Grouping customers using ML tools

Let us consider a company that is an up-and-coming online health and beauty retailer. It has grown its customer base rapidly through aggressive marketing campaigns. To sustain their growth, the finance and marketing departments are now looking at how they can do targeted marketing for better returns. They have customer-level demographic and behavioral data obtained through data mining and surveys. The demographic information is age, gender, and income. Income is given in thousands per year. The behavioral data includes spending score and purchase frequency. Both these variables are scores given to the customers based on their purchasing habits. The spending score is on a scale of 1–100, where 1 is the least and 100 is the most. The purchase frequency is on a scale of 1–20, where 1 is the least and 20 is the most.

In this study, we will use an unsupervised ML algorithm known as K-means clustering. Unlike supervised learning, unsupervised learning models do not require predefined labels to group data. It groups data based on observed underlying similarities and patterns. A good thing about K-means clustering is that you do not need any specific format for the data. It is typically applied to numerical data, and all you need for your dataset is for it to have a header row and the values filled in. You would also need to specify in the code which columns you wish to apply K-means clustering to, the features.

Clustering will help us answer what type of customers we serve, how their behaviors differ within different segments, and which segments are worth higher marketing investment. The entire code is available for you at the repository (prefix 0802). The code is divided into the following sections:

- **Import libraries:** In this section, you import all of the libraries you require to run this code.
- **Customize:** This is the only section where you are required to make any changes. We are providing the names of input and output files, the names of files to save the plot, and a list of features. The customizable portion has been italicized.

```
dataset_path = "0802 Customer Segmentation Dataset.csv"
elbow_plot_path = "0802 Elbow_Plot.png"
pca_plot_path = "0802 PCA_Plot.png"

my_report = '0802 cluster_report.csv'
my_cluster='0802 cluster_summary.csv'
my_corr_file='0802 corr_matrix.csv'
my_loadings ='0802 feature_loadings.csv'
my_features = ['Age', 'Gender', 'Annual Income',
'Spending Score', 'Purchase Frequency']

#Customize cluster markers. Set it to Set2 for color.
#Comment out the one not being used.
#my_palette='Set2'
my_palette=['black', 'gray', 'lightgray']
```

- **Read and normalize data:** This section prepares the data for clustering. K-means clustering is applied to numerical data, but gender has text labels (Male, Female). We need to change this into numerical values, and we do it in the following way:

```
df['Gender'] = df['Gender'].map({'Male': 0, 'Female': 1})
```

Since in this case, the input data is binary, we just assign 0 and 1. Avoid assigning numerical values if the categorical variables are multinomial, like Directions – North, South, East, and West. We can use one-hot encoding, which is discussed elsewhere in the book. Assigning values like (0,1,2,3,4, . . .) to categorical variables will assume a false numerical relationship between them.

Finally, we apply standardization to the data using StandardScalar. This step ensures that features with larger values, such as income, do not dominate those with smaller values, such as age or gender.

- **Use K-means, define clusters, and create an elbow plot:** This section of the code identifies and visualizes various customer segments. The elbow method plots the inertia against a range of clusters. Inertia, as discussed earlier, also essentially measures how compact each cluster is. As the number of clusters increases, inertia decreases. The elbow method is a graph used to determine the optimal number of clusters. We calculate the inertia for a range of clusters b by specifying K_range = range(1, 11)

  When calculating the optimal number of clusters using the elbow method, you will also encounter this variable in the code, random_state=42. This is the seed number for the random decisions made by K-means clustering, and we have seen this in many other models. K-means makes clusters by assigning the observations to a cluster's center. However, if this center is chosen randomly, and this is the starting point where clustering starts, each time the program is run, the results may differ. Setting random_state to a fixed number is simply telling the code to use the same starting point every time you run the code. As a result, the results are reproducible and consistent. You can set the random_state variable to any number you want.

  We can determine the optimal number of clusters based on where the "elbow" is plotted, that is, where the sharpest break in the curve is. We then set the number of clusters in the code to optimal_k = 3.

  In this case, we instruct the model to form three distinct clusters. This is because we observed the "elbow" at around three clusters. We can always create more clusters; however, it only provides a marginal improvement in inertia.
- **Identify PCA and plot**: Since the data has multiple variables, we use Principal Component Analysis (PCA) to reduce the data to two dimensions for ease of visualization. It works by reducing the number of dimensions into its two principal components while preserving as much

variability as possible. PCA reduces the five dimensions (age, gender, income, spending score, and purchasing frequency) into two new features (PCA1 and PCA2). It is important to note that PCA is not used for clustering itself, but just for the visualization of the high-dimensional data. In addition to the plot, we have generated two reports in this section. The first one states the percentage of variance explained by the two principal components. The second report is a table that shows the loadings against each feature. This output is also saved in a CSV file.
- **Save CSV and plot files:** In this section, we have saved all reports in CSV format along with the plots. The names of these files were specified in the customization section.

The output from the code is the two sets of reports and two plots. The two plots are the elbow plot and the plot showing customer segmentation by PCA. The first set of reports is the cluster summary, correlation matrix, and the main report showing the assignment of clusters to all customers. These have been saved in CSV format. The second set of reports focuses on PCA. The first report, which is displayed on the screen, shows the percentage of variance explained by each principal component. The current report reads the following:

```
Variance explained by PCA [0.38343977 0.21644177]
```

This means that the principal component 1 captured 38.34% of the variance in the original data while the principal component 2 captured 21.64%. Together, they have explained almost 60% of the total variance in the original data.

Let us now move on to the next report on feature loading. Table 8.2 shows the weight the two principal components have given to each of the features. This would help us in recognizing the two features that are represented by the two principal components. Each value in the table tells us how much a feature contributes to a principal component. These are the coefficients in the linear combination used to compute each PCA axis.

Table 8.2 PCA weights assigned to features

Feature Loading	*PCA 1*	*PCA 2*
Age	0.704192	0.051297
Gender	0.059748	-0.58497
Annual Income	0.132724	0.526217
Spending Score	-0.68982	0.027981
Purchase Frequency	-0.08417	0.614406

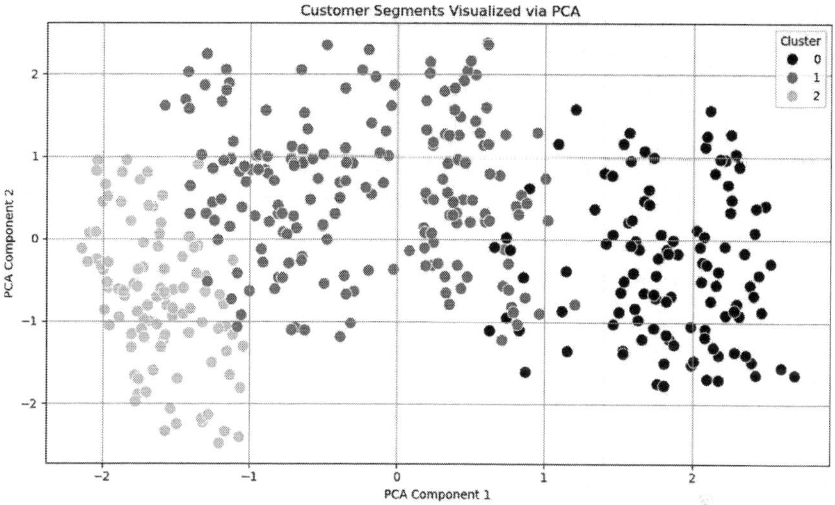

Figure 8.1 Customer segment clustering

Values closer to +1 or −1 indicate a strong contribution, while values closer to 0 indicate a weak contribution. In this table, Age has a strong positive loading (0.704), suggesting that older customers tend to have higher PCA1 scores. Spending score has a strong negative loading (−0.690), suggesting that customers with higher spending scores have lower PCA1 scores. Similarly, for PCA2, purchase frequency has a strong positive loading, and gender has a strong negative loading. PCA1 seems to capture a contrast between older, lower-spending customers and younger, higher-spending customers. PCA2 appears to distinguish between high-income, frequent purchasers of one gender and customers of the opposite gender with different purchasing patterns.

Thus, PCA has reduced the five-dimensional customer data into two main patterns. One captures an age–spending relationship (PCA1) and the other captures a gender–income–frequency relationship (PCA2). Let us now have a look at the customer segment visualization as given in Figure 8.1.

Here are the three clusters:

Cluster 0 (Right Side) has high PCA1 values (positive) and mixed PCA2 values. Based on our loadings, PCA1 customers have high age (0.704) and low spending score (−0.690). PCA2 customers have varied gender, income, and purchase frequency patterns. Typical customers in this segment will be older, conservative spenders.

Cluster 1 (Center/Upper) shows mixed to slightly negative PCA1 and high PCA2 values. This would translate to PCA1 customers of moderate age with moderate to higher spending scores. PCA2 customers have high purchase frequency, high annual income (0.526), and a specific gender pattern. A typical customer in this segment will have a high income and be a frequent buyer.

Cluster 2 (Left/Lower) has negative values for both PCA1 and PCA2. This would refer to young customers with a high spending score in PCA1. In PCA2, they would have lower purchase frequency, different gender patterns, and potentially lower income. So, a typical customer is likely to be young and a high spender.

You can see that PCA-based scatterplot is providing deeper insight than the feature-based scatterplots.

Segmentation-driven customization

Now that we have identified distinct customer segments using K-means clustering, the next step is to use this data to tailor marketing strategies and product offerings for each segment. Not all customers have the same purchasing patterns, and they will not respond to marketing communication uniformly either. Customization would allow a company to deliver more relevant messages, increase conversion rates, build loyalty, and reduce churn. For a business that operates in the online health and beauty space, aligning communication, product development, and delivery with customer behavior can significantly impact profitability. Let us now summarize the three clusters identified in the analysis in Table 8.3. We have used our legends to describe income and purchase frequency scores.

By analyzing behavioral and demographic differences across segments, the company can move beyond generic marketing and instead engage each group with strategies that match their profile. This not only improves customer experience, leading to better retention, but it also maximizes return on marketing investment. We have seen in previous chapters that management action can also be automated using the output of the clustering.

Once marketing strategies have been tailored to customer segments, the next step for the company is to improve customer relationships. While

Table 8.3 Cluster data

Cluster feature	*Average age*	*Gender mix*	*Income*	*Spending score*	*Purchase frequency*
0	59	Slightly more females	Moderate	Low (21/100)	Low
1	37	Quite balanced	High	Moderate–High (69/100)	Moderate
2	22	Balanced	Low	Very high (85/100)	Moderate

personalized offerings attract customers, satisfaction and loyalty are built through consistent value delivery, service excellence, and emotional connection with the brand.

Customer loyalty is extremely valuable in any business, and brand trust has a huge impact on buying decisions. Loyal customers purchase more frequently and are more likely to try other products. They are also more likely to recommend the brand to others, reducing CAC for the company. The goal is not only to get the customer to purchase something but also to ensure that customers are happy with their experience and have a reason to return. This brings us into our next segment on churn analysis and retention strategies.

Churn analysis using classification models

From a financial perspective, churn represents the loss of potential future revenue. With each customer lost, current sales are reduced. It also increases the CAC. Churn also compromises any long-term financial projections associated with CLV. While some level of customer attrition is natural for any business, being proactive in predicting churn helps businesses intervene early to protect high-value relationships. It also helps with allocating resources toward the most at risk, yet recoverable, customers. This section demonstrates how ML tools like Random Forests can be used as predictive tools for churn management.

Predicting churn

In accounting, the prudence concept says that all losses should be provided for, but profits can only be accounted for when realized. Planning for churn is an application of the prudence concept. As discussed earlier, churn is the rate at which customers stop transacting with a company. Monitoring and mitigating customer attrition directly impacts organizational sustainability and its growth potential. It helps businesses analyze the lifecycle of the customer and offers opportunities to improve. It is an important business metric that is not only valuable in a marketing context but has far-reaching financial implications.

The finance department can use churn prediction to improve financial planning, resource allocation, and strategic decision-making. Unanticipated churn affects revenue forecasts by overstating projected customer inflows, cost planning, working capital, inventory, and valuation models. Experiencing unexpected churn of key clients would result in them not meeting their projections. Further, usually the cost of acquiring a new customer is higher than retaining an existing one. The ability to predict which customers are likely to churn can help businesses maintain their profit. Churn analysis also adds another layer to the IR.

Once churn probabilities are assigned to each customer, they can be translated into actionable business insights through the financial applications of churn modeling.

Revenue at risk (RAR) is one such application. It refers to any potential situation that could reduce the company's future revenue. RAR can be calculated by multiplying churn probability by CLV to estimate potential financial loss. Churn rates can also be calculated broadly across segments to anticipate financial performance. Churn can also be used to discount projected cash flows in predictive CLV modeling, as demonstrated in earlier sections. Integrating churn modeling into financial dashboards would allow for real-time monitoring of customer health and proactive financial planning.

Churn analysis can be done through various classification and regression algorithms. These algorithms use historical customer data to identify underlying patterns in customer behavior before they churn. We are going to use an ML tool called Random Forest for predictive churn modeling. Random Forests also help us understand the driving factors behind customer attrition.

ML models to predict churn

For our case study, we will analyze the churn at a gym. The gym wishes to predict churn to improve its costing strategies. It analyses the following features, such as age, gender, days since the customer last visited the gym, how close is their house or workplace to the gym, whether they work at a partner company, whether they signed up during a promotion, the average number of times a month they come to the gym, whether they attend group classes, and finally whether they have been referred by a friend. All these factors are considered to have an impact on churn. Let us now get to the code, which is available to you at the repository (prefix 0803). The code has the following major sections:

- **Importing libraries**: You simply import all of the libraries you need for the code to run smoothly.
- **Customization**: The following code may be customized to include your relevant files. These parameters include names of input and output files, names of files to save plots, feature fields, and a separate list of the categorical features along with the target. Note that all categorical features, like gender, or whether they work at a partner company, need to be entered under both `my_categories` and `my_features`. The relevant part of the code is given here with the customizable portion italicized.

```
input_path = "0803 Gym Dataset.csv"
cust_data = "0803 Churn_Customer_Data.csv"
churn_risk = "0803 Churn_Risk.csv"
conf_matrix_img = "0803 confusion_matrix.png"
class_report_img = "0803 classification_report.png"
feature_importance_img = "0803
feature_importance_plot.png"
pie_chart_img = "0803 churn_risk_pie_chart.png"
churn_avg_img = "0803 churn_feature_averages.png"
my_categories= ['gender', 'distance_from_gym',
'works_at_partner_company', 'discounted_signup',
'attends_group_classes', 'referred_by_friend']
my_features= ['age', 'gender',
'days_since_last_signed_in', 'distance_from_gym',
'works_at_partner_company', 'discounted_signup',
'avg_monthly_visits', 'attends_group_classes',
'referred_by_friend']
my_target='churned'
```

- **Read and preprocess data:** In this section, Python will read and preprocess the data. We will identify the categorical variables and the features and target we want the model to consider. The categorical data will be encoded by the library, making those usable by the model. We will also define a target for the model.

  One of the critical parts of the code is to encode categorical variables. Some of the categorical data would already have numerical labels in the dataset.

  However, variables such as gender and distance from the gym do not have numerical labels. What encoding does is assign 0 for male, 1 for female, 0 for <2 miles, 1 for 2–4 miles, and 2 for > 4 miles. The numerical values assigned should also be able to capture the relative importance of the options with the variable. For example, if 1 represents the distance from the house being less than 1 km and 2 represents that being 2 km, that makes intuitive sense. The second value is greater than the first, and so is the distance. A mismatch there may cause a wrong interpretation by the model.
- **Fit model, make predictions, assign churn risk scores:** This section bears the bulk of the analysis. The data is split into training (80%) and testing (20%) using the code.

```
X_train, X_test, y_train, y_test = train_test_split(X, y,
test_size=0.2, random_state=42)
```

The test_size is customizable and controls the split ratio. You may increase or decrease it depending on whether you want more or less data for testing.

The rest of the code initializes and trains a Random Forest Classifier, which is an ensemble learning method. We fit the model and use the fitted model to predict the churn probability of the test component of the data. We assign a rule-based churn risk score to the model. You can tweak the rule from the code.

```
def assign_risk(prob):
     if prob < 0.33:
           return 1
     elif prob < 0.66:
          return 2
     else:
          return 3
```

We also have a section that advises the management on what action to take, depending on the group assigned by the rules just discussed. This is also rule-based, and you can tweak the code to suit your needs.

```
def interpret_risk(score): mapping = {
          1: "No action needed",
          2: "Monitor regularly",
          3: "Needs immediate intervention"
}
return mapping[score]
```

Note that if you change the risk response to 1, 2, or 3 here, you must change it in the previous section and vice versa.

- **Generate dataframe, display data, and save results**: This section generates a detailed CSV file consisting of the input data, the predicted churn, and churn probability. Another CSV file is created, which records the churn risk and specifies the management action required. It also creates a confusion matrix, a classification report, and a feature importance bar chart. A pie chart summarizes the total customer churn, and a table shows the average of the most relevant churn features. It both displays and saves this data to our computer.

The output of the code includes the report containing the complete data for each customer with the computed churn probability. The churn risk report comprises the management action plan for each customer. In addition, we have the confusion matrix, classification report, and feature importance plot, all being displayed and saved for subsequent use. A report with the executive view of the churn has also been displayed. It shows the average values of days since last signed in, age, and average monthly visits for both churn classifications. We have discussed the implications of these values in earlier chapters and will review a few of them here.

For the gym in our case, 0 stands for no churn, and 1 stands for churn. In the confusion matrix, out of the 1,000 data points tested, there are 795 true negatives, which means that these are the customers who did not churn and were correctly predicted as such. There are 19 false positives, which indicates that they were predicted to churn, but did not. There are 50 false negatives, which are customers who churned but were predicted not to. Finally, there are 136 true positives, which are customers who were predicted to churn and have churned. The false negatives suggest that the current features do not predict all possible churners, therefore, additional features may be required if catching every possible churner is critical. To better interpret the confusion matrix, we need to look at it with the classification report.

The classification report includes the following key performance percentages:

- **Accuracy score**: This is a useful metric in measuring how well the model is working overall. This model correctly predicted churn or no churn for 93% of the customers, which indicates a very well-fitted model.
- **Precision**: This tells us how accurate the positive predictions are. Looking at the output, we can say that of all the customers the model predicted would churn, 88% did, while 94% of the customers who were predicted not to churn did not.
- **Recall**: This measures the sensitivity of the model, that is, out of all the customers who churned, what percentage the model correctly identified. The model is very accurate in identifying non-churners, capturing 98% of them. It is slightly less accurate in capturing churners, 73%, however, it is not a bad recall rate.
- **F1-score**: This metric balances precision and recall. It is useful in imbalanced datasets, where the values of one variable (non-churn) are significantly different from the other (churn). It has a good overall balance of 80%, indicating that the model misses some churners.
- **Support**: This is simply the actual number of occurrences of each class in the test.

Other than these, we have the following visualizations:

- **Feature importance**: This is a bar chart to help us visualize the features by their relative importance in predicting churn, as determined by the Random Forest model. Higher scores indicate the feature played a more significant role in customer churning. We see that the most important features are the days since the customer last visited the gym, their age, and the number of times they used to visit the gym on average over their lifetime.

- **Churn risk distribution:** This is a pie chart that illustrates the total percentage of low-risk churners, medium-risk churners, and high-risk churners. It gives us a holistic view of churn, and we can see that the model predicted most people are at a low risk of churning.
- **Churn feature averages:** This shows the average value of the top contributing features across churned and non-churned customers. In our output, the average number of days since the customers' last visit to the gym is 29. This makes intuitive sense as well; if you have not gone to the gym in a long time, you are likely to leave. We also see that the average age of people who churned is higher than people who did not churn.

These results suggest that the churn prediction model is performing well, with an overall accuracy score of 93%. The model shows strong reliability in identifying customers who will not churn and performs decently in detecting the customers who will. It also reveals meaningful behavioral patterns such as customers who have not visited recently, are older, or show lower gym engagement are more likely to churn. This model can now be run on an active customer base every month using the latest customer data. We have seen in an earlier chapter how we can save a model and use it later on a new database.

Utilizing churn analysis

The feature importance analysis is the key document that brings out the contribution of factors to churn. The diagram suggests that the days since last purchase is the most critical factor that influences churn, followed by age. Feature importance value in tree-based models is computed by measuring how much each feature contributes to decreasing impurity. Please note that this does not mean that these features have the highest influence in reducing churn. Feature importance tells us which features are most useful for distinguishing between churners and non-churners. It tells us about the predictive power of each feature, but not the direction of influence (positive or negative effect). This also means that it plays a significant role in predicting churn but does not necessarily influence churn. So, we may not know what causes churn, but we can know the features that are predictors of churn.

Once we have predicted churn, the next step is to act on those insights. After all, the objective of churn analysis is not only prediction, it is also to implement preventive measures. For the gym, in our case, knowing the at-risk customers will let us step in before they leave.

We have shown in the code how intervention strategies can be automated along with ML-based predictive tools. We have assigned a rule-based management intervention plan that uses the probability of churn as a trigger.

We may fine-tune this analysis by conducting another analysis to see the empirical relation between churn probability and actual churn.

We can further integrate churn prediction with the budget forecast to factor in revenue drain. We can create a churn dashboard and even initiate scenario planning to develop various scenario-based intervention plans.

Churn costs money. Apart from the revenue drain, it also triggers CAC. Financial decision-makers need to factor in this aspect in their financial strategic planning. It was difficult to quantify earlier, but thanks to these ML tools, operational issues like these can now be factored into financial decision-making.

Key takeaways

This chapter has demonstrated how finance professionals can move beyond traditional financial statements and better understand customer behavior. By viewing customers as economic assets, businesses gain a clearer picture of what drives long-term value. Tools like CLV help companies understand how much each customer can potentially contribute to future cash inflows. Customer segmentation, on the other hand, helps management make better decisions. We have also used a few ML tools, such as regression analysis, K-means clustering, and Random Forests, to analyze our customers better and align financial goals with customer needs.

Helping customers increase their perceived value ultimately helps the business remain profitable in the long term.

Chapter 9

Risk management and compliance

In today's rapidly evolving business landscape, effective risk management and regulatory compliance have become more critical than ever. This chapter explores how financial professionals can use ML tools to better understand, predict, and respond to risks. We will look at practical applications of AI, from building credit risk models and detecting fraud, to compliance monitoring using NLP. By using tools like NLTK, compliance teams can work faster and reduce manual checks. We demonstrate how finance teams can play a central role in making risk management smarter and more proactive.

Risk management for sustainable performance

Uncertainty reduction is necessary for sustainability, but as we all know, it is not easy to guess the future. We may be able to reduce the uncertainty, but we cannot completely remove it. So, what is the second-best solution? To guess the probable range of possibilities and keep a plan ready for them. This is where risk management tools come in useful. It is one of the ways a potential threat can be turned into a competitive advantage.

Risk management has various dimensions in an organization. However, a financial decision-maker is primarily concerned about financial risks. These risks can significantly affect an organization's performance, reputation, and sustainability. The most common types of financial risks include the following:

- **Credit Risk**: This is the risk of a borrower defaulting on their obligations under a credit contract. This can adversely impact cash flows and profitability before leading to a loss of assets. AI-driven credit risk models assess borrower profiles, predict default probabilities, and enable financial institutions to make better lending decisions.
- **Market Risk**: This involves changes in various market-determined factors. Fluctuations in interest rates, currency values, and stock prices

DOI: 10.4324/9781003619628-9

can affect an organization's financial health. They impact profitability, cash flow, and asset holding. ML algorithms can analyze historical market data and provide predictive analytics to hedge against market volatility.

- **Operational Risk**: These risks stem from internal processes, system failures, or human errors, and all industries are exposed to them. However, in the case of banks and other financial institutions, regulators have defined specific frameworks for operational risk. AI-powered anomaly detection can assist in the identification of inefficiencies, fraud, and compliance breaches before they escalate.
- **Liquidity Risk**: Defined roughly, this is the inability of an entity to meet short-term obligations. This is distinct from solvency risk, which measures whether the entity can honor all its liabilities in the long run. AI models can analyze cash flow trends and optimize liquidity management strategies.
- **Regulatory Risk**: Non-compliance with laws and regulations can result in fines and reputational damage. NLP techniques can help organizations monitor regulatory requirements and ensure compliance.

One of the interesting developments in the world of risk management is an alteration of its scope inside the organization. Moving away from being a concern of a dedicated risk department, it has become the onus of every department and person in the organization. The risk management culture has progressively integrated itself with various functions of the entity, becoming a business issue in the process. Risk management practices enable an organization to be better prepared to, among others, achieve the following:

- **Preserve capital and ensure liquidity**: By identifying potential financial losses that can arise from a risk event materializing, organizations can maintain adequate capital buffers and liquidity positions. This advanced preparedness would ensure business continuity and resilience.
- **Optimize resource allocation**: Understanding risk-adjusted returns allows for smarter deployment of capital toward ventures that potentially maximize value creation while maintaining acceptable risk levels. We have seen these tools in action in earlier modules.
- **Enhance decision-making agility**: Organizations with robust risk frameworks can navigate uncertainties with greater confidence. Advanced preparedness augments faster and more informed decisions when opportunities or threats emerge.
- **Foster innovation**: Good risk management enables innovation by creating safe spaces for experimentation, while establishing guardrails against failures that may come in the process.

Much as the entities, investors also stand to gain by understanding the risk management capabilities across various dimensions, including the following:

- **Governance structures:** Do clear lines of accountability exist? Is there appropriate board-level oversight?
- **Risk culture:** Does the organization promote transparency and escalation of potential issues? Often, management finds short-term incentives to hide an emerging issue, hoping that it will settle on its own.
- **Risk identification processes:** How comprehensive and forward-looking are the organization's risk assessment methodologies? At this stage, the investor should seek to distinguish between compliance-driven risk management practices and business-driven ones.
- **Response capabilities:** Can the organization pivot quickly when risks materialize? This would invariably call for advanced preparedness through simulations and stress tests.
- **Technology infrastructure:** Are appropriate tools deployed to monitor and manage risks? This is an area that has progressed not only in capabilities but also in terms of expanded reach.

At the heart of modern risk management capabilities lies computational power. The phenomenal rise in computational abilities has made advanced tools accessible and affordable. Many of them no longer require extensive training and can be used after basic user training. The focus has moved from computation to interpretation.

The ultimate measure of effective risk management is not the sophistication of the models that are being used. It lies in how seamlessly those models integrate with day-to-day financial decision-making. This integration occurs across multiple levels, including the following:

- **Strategic planning:** Risk models are used to measure and communicate the organization's risk appetite and strategic direction.
- **Portfolio construction:** Risk insights guide asset allocation and position sizing. The integrated system also monitors and rebalances the allocation on a dynamic basis.
- **Product development:** Risk assessments shape product features and pricing. The ML tools give a better understanding of customer preferences, reducing the chances of failure of new products.
- **Operational processes:** Risk controls become embedded in routine workflows. These controls can range from technological interfaces to better management reporting.

As prudent financial decision-makers, we need to recognize that ML tools do not merely provide insights into traditional process and product-oriented risk management. The new tools cover a greater scope, allowing us not only to monitor performance but also to use past experiences in future decision-making. As events that we have seen in the past form a basis of decision-making, the horizon of the unknown diminishes. This results in more sustainable performance by reducing uncertainty and minimizing the risks associated with the unknown.

In this section, we will discuss how the risk models are designed, how they work, and finally, how they expose us to new kinds of risk. We will also see some of the practical applications of ML tools in the world of risk management.

Risk modeling and developing application-specific models

Risk modeling involves a delicate balance between mathematical rigor and practical business judgment. Risk modeling, conventionally, is the process of using quantitative methods to forecast potential losses, identify vulnerabilities, and support decision-making under uncertainty. In addition, some models employing qualitative methods have evolved and are well developed today. Effective risk models enable organizations to proactively mitigate threats, allocate resources efficiently, and maintain financial stability.

Risk models range from simple deterministic ones to those using complex stochastic simulations. Though the degree of complexity in underlying computations may differ, financial risk models may be broadly grouped as follows:

- **Statistical models**: These models leverage historical data to identify patterns and relationships, often using regression techniques to estimate the probability of adverse events. Arguably, this type of model is used most.
- **Structural models**: Structural models are mathematical models that describe the relationships between different variables based on underlying theoretical assumptions. These are based on theoretical frameworks that model the underlying mechanics of risk events, such as Merton's model for credit risk.
- **ML models**: These data-driven approaches can capture complex, non-linear relationships without requiring explicit theoretical structures. We have already been introduced to such models in earlier sections.
- **Scenario-based models**: These simulate specific "what-if" scenarios to assess potential outcomes under different conditions. These models allow an entity to visualize a range of possibilities and be prepared for those that are more likely to happen than others. Hope you have noticed that we have stated "more likely"; we are still dealing with probability.

- **Hybrid models**: Combining elements from multiple approaches to leverage their respective strengths. For example, we can combine a structural model and an ML model to create a credit risk assessment tool.

Over the years, general-purpose models have given way to application-specific models. Earlier, we would have used a statistical package to develop a credit risk model, now, we have specific models for credit risk. These application-specific models use a selection of tools that are relevant to the application. Application-specific risk models, when properly developed and implemented, serve as powerful tools that support decisions. They transform uncertainty into quantifiable metrics that enable more consistent and transparent risk management.

Risk models need to adapt quickly to the evolution of business and the emergence of new data sources. Models are not to be treated as static tools but as living systems that require ongoing refinement. This adaptability is particularly crucial in the face of emerging risks like climate change, cyber threats, and pandemic disruptions, where historical data may provide limited guidance.

To develop application-specific models, we may follow a typical path stated here.

- **Define the model objectives precisely**: It is not easy to define what we want the model to do. Many models fail to deliver because we have failed to articulate our precise needs. When we are looking for a credit model, we must specify whether it is a probability of default that we are looking to compute, or if we wish to find out whether a loan will default or not. We also need to understand what type of loans we are talking about. A mortgage loan would have different characteristics from a credit card exposure.
- **Identify and source relevant data**: In addition to the deliverables and selection of models, it is critical to define model inputs and confirm their availability. These inputs greatly influence the selection of models. We need to particularly focus on data quality and representativeness. Historical data may not reflect emerging risks or changing market conditions. We may also need to supplement the quantitative data with qualitative insights from domain experts. Overreliance on quantitative data may lead to blind spots in the model's performance.
- **Structure the model architecture**: The model structure needs to balance complexity and interpretability. There are no fixed rules that define an ideal balance, and it is a business decision made by the entity. Complex models are more likely to capture subtle relationships but are prone to overfitting and a lack of transparency. On the other hand, simpler

models may miss important interactions between variables but may offer greater clarity and ease of implementation.

- **Calibrate and validate:** Model calibration involves tuning parameters to optimize performance against historical data. However, a good historical fit does not ensure future performance. It requires further validation. One of the major components of validation is testing the model using data that was not used for model development. It also involves back-testing using historical scenarios and comparing the model results with the actuals. Stress testing shows the predictive ability of the model under extreme situations where the input data represents the rarest of the rare scenarios. Sensitivity testing measures the impact of a new parameter on the overall model performance and is another important aspect of validation. Another important validation technique is the "challenger model." Alternative models using different approaches are used to see if they yield similar results. Significant divergences may indicate conceptual weaknesses in your primary model. Common performance metrics for model validation include the following:
    - Accuracy and Precision: How well the model classifies risk classes or predicts risk events.
    - Confusion Matrix: Measuring false positives and false negatives. This essentially focuses on whether the predictions made by the model were accurate and the extent to which the model predicted what happened. We will discuss these in detail later in the section.
    - Receiver Operating Characteristic–Area Under the Curves (ROC-AUC) Score: Determining how effectively the model distinguishes between risky and non-risky entities.
- **Implementation with operational controls:** One of the critical areas of failure of risk models is implementation. There must be clear procedures for model monitoring and periodic recalibration. Provisions for override protocols are necessary for situations when models produce counterintuitive results. It is also important to document model limitations explicitly to prevent misapplication and to maintain the model.

By its very nature, risk modeling faces numerous challenges, ranging from computational to psychological. Some of the most common challenges include the following:

- **Data quality issues:** Poor or incomplete data can lead to inaccurate or underperforming models.
- **Model risk:** Incorrect assumptions or overfitting can make models unreliable. We will be discussing it in detail a little later.

- **Regulatory compliance**: Models used in financial decision-making must comply with various regulatory guidelines. The problem that arises is that regulatory requirements may not align with business objectives, and the modeler faces a stiff challenge balancing these often-divergent objectives.
- **Evolving risks**: The financial landscape is dynamic, and risk models must adapt to new economic, technological, and geopolitical changes. This, at times, becomes difficult as the structure of a model may not be adept at incorporating new challenges.

Appreciating how computational models work

Risk management decisions are usually backed up by a decisional model, mostly run by systems. In cases where the model is using ML tools, to untrained eyes, this may appear to be a "black box"; no one knows how the input data is being transformed into output. However, to have proper implementation, interpretation, and governance, one needs to understand how these models work. Let us have a quick look at the common anatomical structure of these models.

- **Input variables**: The first component is the raw data elements that feed into the model. These data may be of different types, such as market prices, economic indicators, customer attributes, transaction patterns, and even communications.
- **Transformation functions**: The input variable often goes through these transformation functions. These are mathematical operations that convert, normalize, or combine raw inputs into more useful features. This is a critical step that converts data to potential information. The transformation prepares the data to be processed by core algorithms.
- **Core algorithms**: These are the central mathematical techniques that identify patterns, estimate relationships, or simulate outcomes. For the uninitiated, this is the center of the black box. However, each model follows a logical process, and our expectations and consequent interpretation may be misplaced if we do not understand this algorithm. Every algorithm, coming to us in the form of a module, is accompanied by documentation and a robust theoretical justification. We need to understand the same before trying to use and interpret the model output.
- **Output calibration**: This section governs the output from the model that the end user will work on. These are mechanisms to translate algorithmic results into meaningful risk metrics like probability of default, value-at-risk, or fraud scores. In addition to the knowledge of the capabilities of the algorithm, sound domain knowledge is necessary for the proper interpretation of these outputs.

- **Decision thresholds:** A little away from the computational framework lies this important management control aspect of model use. These are the cutoff points that convert continuous risk measures into discrete actions or decisions. The management has to decide a tolerance level beyond which corrective action will kick in.

Some of the common characteristics of computational models include the following:

- **Probabilistic:** Most risk models have a probabilistic foundation, underlying a key feature of decision-making, as certainty is rarely achievable. These models deliver the next best alternative, that is, they express outcomes in terms of probabilities, confidence intervals, or distributional properties. The probabilistic nature of risk models does not eliminate uncertainty; they quantify and structure it. This distinction is crucial for decision-makers who might otherwise misinterpret model outputs as deterministic predictions rather than probabilistic estimates. So, instead of stating whether a borrower will default or not, a probabilistic model assigns a probability of default based on class characteristics.
- **Causation and correlation:** Many models, particularly those built on statistical or ML approaches, identify correlations between variables. That does not necessarily establish causal relationships between them. It is found that credit card customers who make frequent small-value transactions default the least. This insight may be very useful in predicting the default rate, but it does not mean that frequent transactions would lead to financial stability. The real reason could be underlying factors like income level or financial discipline, data that were overlooked by the model. Acting based on correlation may not produce expected results; focusing on the causal drivers would.
- **Simulation:** Many computational models leverage simulation techniques to explore the full distribution of possible outcomes rather than producing single-point estimates. These approaches generate thousands or millions of scenarios by randomly sampling from probability distributions for key risk factors. This technique often helps in overcoming the lack of enough data to build a model by providing data that is possible, though might not have been observed till that point in time. Simulation approaches are particularly valuable for stress testing. It allows entities to assess resilience under extreme but plausible scenarios that may not exist in historical data. They provide a structured way to ask "what-if" questions that challenge assumptions and reveal hidden vulnerabilities.
- **Ensemble:** Another great feature of many modern computational models is that they often do not rely on a single model. Instead, they employ

ensemble methods, that is, combining multiple models to improve accuracy, robustness, and insight. These ensembles might include models that are built using different statistical techniques, trained on different subsets of data, and incorporate different assumptions. This aggregation achieved under ensemble approaches mitigates the weaknesses of individual models. It is also likely to reduce the risk of overfitting to historical patterns that may not persist in the future.

- **Explainability**: Models must not only have computational accuracy and transparency, but they should also explain why they make the specific prediction. Various techniques transform computational models from an algorithmic marvel to a decision support tool. These would include explaining the contribution of each variable in the decision-making process, explaining how inputs would need to change to produce different outcomes, and similar.

Understanding how risk models work, their components, assumptions, strengths, and limitations, is not a matter of concern only for modeling specialists. It is essential knowledge for anyone involved in financial decision-making operating in a model-driven world. The common areas of concern for the user would include the following:

- **Data quality:** Poor data quality, including incomplete records, outdated information, or biased datasets, can lead to inaccurate predictions. Entities using models for decision-making need to invest in robust data management practices to ensure data quality.
- **Overfitting and underfitting:** A model that is too complex may perform exceptionally well on training data but fail in real-world scenarios (overfitting).

  Conversely, a model that is too simplistic may not capture key risk factors (underfitting). Balancing model complexity with generalizability is crucial for the successful implementation of the model.
- **Interpretability and transparency:** As identified earlier, many modern models, especially those involving deep learning, often operate in a black box. In addition to adhering to regulatory transparency requirements that may exist, transparency is essential for a user to be able to properly understand and interpret the results.
- **Adapting to a changing risk environment:** Risks evolve due to internal and external changes. These may include changes in strategy, focus, market conditions, economic policies, regulatory requirements, and others. A model trained on past data may become obsolete if it fails to adapt to new conditions. Regular model retraining and updates are necessary to maintain accuracy and should be a part of the overall model management framework.

Integrating model outputs with financial decision-making

Often, there is a disconnect between the developers of a model and the users, which results in technically sound models not serving the business purpose. In business, models must give a competitive advantage to the model owner. The desired level of precision of a model should be defined by the business requirement and not solely by the theoretical foundation of the model. Models need to be integrated with the decision-making process of the entity. This integration process requires thoughtful design, clear communication channels, and an organizational culture that balances quantitative insights with human judgment.

Risk models typically generate numerical outputs like probabilities, scores, expected losses, and so on. These quantitative results must be translated into concrete actions that business stakeholders can implement. This translation process involves several critical steps:

- **Establishing a decision framework:** Model outputs and follow-up actions should be linked to each other to the extent possible. It is also important to define the model override parameters in the framework.
- **Contextualizing results:** Results from the model need to be interpreted in the correct context. They may be analyzed in the context of past values, industry norms, or confidence metrics of the model. Such contextualization will result in abstract values providing actionable insight.
- **Establishing risk threshold and decision rules:** Model outputs often come as a quantified measure, like the probability of default. To translate these values into decisions, the user entity should establish predefined risk thresholds. For example, if the probability of default is less than 2%, grant the loan, and if the probability of default is above 5%, refuse the loan application. Between 2% and 5%, additional information may be necessary to decide.
- **Embedding models in the business workflow:** To best utilize the output from the model, implementing entities may need to decide how to integrate the model outputs into the business workflow. This may involve creating a front-end application to view model output or drilling down to the root cause. One can even have automated workflows driven by the model's output, like in the case of algorithmic trading.
- **Balancing models and judgment:** Unless specified by regulatory requirements, models must not be designed as the final word. Models derive their output based on specific assumptions and bases. It is prudent to have mechanisms that ensure inappropriate decisions do not pass through the models to the workflow. When unexpected results are produced, consequent feedback would create opportunities to learn continuously.
- **Continuous model monitoring and feedback loops:** The environments in which decisions are made and models are developed are susceptible

to continuous change. This may make models inappropriate and even erroneous. Any entity using the model should establish a regular model maintenance schedule. There should also be a functioning feedback loop to promote continuous learning by the model.
- **Cultural challenge:** While the functioning of a model may be rule-driven, there is a strong human dimension of model integration that should not be overlooked. Quantitative insights are respected but not deified. The decision-makers must understand both the capabilities and limitations of risk models. It is also important to ensure that the model development team gets business insight from various departments.

As financial decisions become increasingly data-driven, the ability to effectively integrate risk models into decision-making processes has evolved from a technical challenge to a strategic imperative. The management of an entity should initiate the integration process from the top and consider how computational power can be used in strategic decision-making.

Knowing about model risk

Ironically, the very tools designed to measure and mitigate risks can themselves become sources of risk. This meta-risk, known as the model risk, has emerged as a critical concern for financial institutions, regulators, and stakeholders. Model risk can be defined as the potential for adverse consequences from decisions based on incorrect or inappropriate model outputs. The first type of error refers to errors in the output caused by a faulty model design, wrong iteration specification, or even poor implementation. The second type of error arises when the model is computationally perfect and conceptually sound but is being used for purposes outside its competence. For example, a model may be computing correlation perfectly, but the user may be interpreting it as causation.

Model risk may lead to incorrect predictions, regulatory non-compliance, reputational damage, and other issues. Understanding and managing model risk has become a fundamental component of sound risk governance. Let us get a quick understanding of the common sources of model risk. Model risk may arise at different points of the model lifecycle. Model outputs and follow-up actions should be linked to each other to the extent possible.

- **Data limitation:** This is one of the most common sources of model risk. Data limitations include incomplete data, biased sample data, inaccuracies during data collection, and relying on the false notion that historical data would persist in the future.
- **Specification errors:** Models seek to simplify reality to arrive at an implementable solution. This process may lead to material errors in different

forms, including omitted variables, incorrect specification of the relation between variables, inappropriate assumptions, and overparameterization that leads to fitting in noise rather than signals.

- **Implementation flaws:** Even when data and specifications are correct, there may be errors in implementation. These would include errors in coding and data processing, integration failures, and others. An interesting error observed during implementation is the truncation error. Often, numeric values are approximated, and that may affect results. It is important to assess the sensitivity of the results to truncation.
- **Governance weakness:** Weak oversight and internal controls are a breeding ground for model risk. These may include inadequate validation, poor documentation, inefficient change management systems, and others. Poor governance is also an impediment to the development of an organizational culture of using models.
- **Interpretation errors:** Though not directly related to model efficiency and design, the wrong interpretation of model output is a risk that arises out of the use of models. Decision-makers may misinterpret model outputs or overextend their applicability.

How does one manage model risk? Effective model risk management requires a comprehensive approach that addresses risks throughout the model lifecycle. This would cover various aspects of the model ecosystem, including the following:

- **Robust model development:** A strong development practice is the first line of defense against model risk. The purpose and intended use of the model should be clearly defined. There must be a system to ensure data quality, specifying the data cleaning and validation norms, wherever possible. All key assumptions should also be documented to prevent misuse of model output. Another good practice is to test multiple model specifications to assess sensitivity before selecting an optimal specification.
- **Independent validation:** Model validators should be independent of the model developer, and preferably, even the model user group. The validation process should not be restricted only to the verification of computational soundness and logical consistency. The testing should review model performance against historical data and alternative models. The behavior of the model under stress and extreme scenarios should also be tested. The validator must ensure that the user team is aware of the conceptual framework and limitations of the model. Lack of knowledge of limitations potentially leads to misuse of model output.
- **Effective governance:** The governance framework should establish clear responsibilities and control over various aspects of the use of models.

This would include maintaining model inventory and specifying review requirements. A formal approval process for model deployment should be in place. Another critical aspect of governance is defining clear ownership for model design and performance. The stakeholders of the model universe must be aware of their respective roles and responsibilities.

- **Prudent usage practice:** Training model users is as important as the model development process. The users need to understand the model's capabilities and limitations. There should ideally be a control system that will prevent misapplication. Chances of model failure should be recognized, and a contingency plan designed to face the situation. Another area of critical importance is to encourage professional skepticism of model output. If the output does not seem right, it must be investigated before being used.

Model risk represents the unavoidable flip side of model benefits. To harness the true potential of model usage, organizations should focus on implementing comprehensive governance, validation, and usage frameworks. As we progress with model usage, we should always keep the principles of model risk management in mind. It is the way to ensure that the inherent weaknesses of models do not prevent us from leveraging models to get a competitive advantage.

Let us now move into a specific application of ML-based tools in the domain of risk management.

Credit risk modeling using logistic regression

Credit risk is the risk of loss arising from borrowers failing to honor their credit commitments, primarily related to repayment. This risk is perhaps one of the most common forms of financial risk. The ability to accurately assess the likelihood of default impacts the profitability, capital requirements, and long-term sustainability of an entity.

Traditionally, credit decisions relied heavily on expert judgment, manual underwriting processes, and relatively simple scoring systems. Though these approaches have served organizations well, they often suffered from inconsistency, had scalability limitations, and were prone to bias. In addition, regulators started demanding the use of models that generate more precise output and have a robust foundation. Further, all data related to finance is being gradually digitized, ushering in more sophisticated approaches that harness the power of data and predictive analytics. ML-based techniques are increasingly more accessible, and computational power to process a large volume of data sourced from diverse sources is now gradually available at a cheaper cost. The complexities of business and the availability of resources have gradually increased reliance on model-based credit decisions.

Among these modern techniques, logistic regression has emerged as a popular methodology for credit risk assessment. Despite the advent of more complex and arguably robust ML algorithms, logistic regression maintains its prominence for several compelling reasons. It produces easily interpretable risk scores, provides transparent insights into key risk drivers, serves regulatory expectations for model explainability well, and performs efficiently across diverse lending contexts. In this section, we will focus on the process of building and implementing credit risk models using logistic regression. Though we will be using a specific Python library, our focus will remain on the business applications and decision-making implications rather than coding details.

Credit risk models help address critical business issues, including the following:

- **Accurate risk assessment**: Models identify patterns in borrower characteristics that a human analyst might miss. This is likely to lead to better default prediction.
- **Consistent decision-making**: Standardized scoring approaches ensure that similar applications receive similar credit assessments. This reduces the variability experienced in manual processing.
- **Efficient resource allocation**: A standardized risk assessment system promotes risk-based pricing and resource allocation. The entity can strike a balance between risk and return across various segments of its credit portfolio.
- **Regulatory compliance**: Model-driven credit assessment approaches are more adept at satisfying various regulatory expectations for systematic, documentable credit assessment processes.

As financial decision-makers, we will focus on the interpretation of model outputs and integrate the model's insight into a broader risk management strategy.

The need for assessing creditworthiness

Before we start building a model to assess creditworthiness, let us address the need for the same. Predicting whether a credit deal will be successfully closed has been one of the oldest challenges of business. The criticality of a credit decision arises for three reasons.

- **Earning impact**: A credit engagement is essentially justified by earnings. If it is based on borrowing, it is the interest earned that takes care of the risk. If it is by way of credit-driven products and services, the price is likely to include the cost of the funds involved. A failed credit commitment either delays the earnings flow or denies it completely. This would also have an impact on liquidity.

- **Profit impact:** In addition to being deprived of an earning, a failed credit commitment often leads to fear of not being able to recover the funds blocked in the transaction. Accounting standards require that such possible losses be recognized in the form of a provision and charged against the income of the current year. Thus, not only are we deprived of income, but we may incur an actual charge against the profit.
- **Balance sheet impact:** If the credit engagement turns bad and recovery is not possible, the unrecoverable amount is to be written off from the balance sheet. Since a provision is likely to have already been built, there will not be an impact on the profit statement unless the provision is inadequate.

In addition to the impact of the credit deal going bad, the assessment of creditworthiness serves a few critical business purposes, including the following:

- **Customer segmentation:** The credit assessment models assign risk scores to the credit proposals. These scores, often computed in the form of the probability of default, allow the entity to classify the credit applicants into different groups. These homogenous groups would have unique characteristics, and the lender can design specific management plans for each group. One critical area that the lending entity focuses on is the transition of a lender from one classification to another.
- **Risk-based pricing:** Once classified, the lending entity can then charge risk premiums that are calibrated to each group. Groups with higher risk will be charged higher risk premiums and vice versa. In addition to pricing, each of these classifications faces a different expected credit loss profile. This leads to different rates of provisions being charged against each classification.

When we develop a model for credit risk assessment, we need to keep in mind the end use of the model output. Though the computational framework may be the same, the model output should align with the end use to avoid any misunderstanding. For example, if the model objective is borrower classification, the model output should classify a prospective credit counterparty. If the objective is to assign a probability of default, then that should be the model output.

Building logistic regression models to predict default probabilities

Logistic regression is a powerful tool that can help the decision-maker to make credit decisions accurately and consistently. Though we have discussed logistic regression earlier, let us have a quick recap of the major features.

Logistic regression predicts the probability of a binary outcome. In our case, this is whether the counterparty of a credit transaction will default or not. While many models draw a straight line between good and bad, logistic regression recognizes that credit risk exists on a probability spectrum. The name "logistic" comes from the S-shaped curve (called a logistic function) that transforms raw data into probability values between 0 and 1.

We start with data that includes factors that we believe contribute to the borrowing being repaid. The model is then trained on the historical data to identify patterns that correlate with loan repayment or default. Once the model is optimized and considered good to use, it will be used to calculate a score for a new application based on the data provided. This score will then be transformed into the probability of default using the logistic function. Based on the risk appetite of the entity, a threshold probability of default will be established to decide on granting a credit facility.

Let us now use code (prefix 0901) to see how the tool can be used. Please note that this code is divided into two parts, A and B. In part A, we will compute the probability of default, and in part B, we will check the goodness of the model. Part B will use some of the outputs of part A and hence has been kept together. Here are the major components of part A of the code.

- **Import libraries:** As usual, all libraries necessary for the code are imported in this section.
- **Customize:** In this section, we have specified the name of the input file and output files where the model will be saved for subsequent use. The features of the model are also specified. Please note the square brackets and the quotes while specifying the features. You may remember that features are the factors that influence prediction. The input file must have these features as columns, along with the outcome. The outcome is binary: defaulted or not defaulted. Here is the part of the code with customizable parameters italicized.

```
# Customize parameters
my_credit_data = "0901 Credit_data.csv"
my_features = ['Income', 'Credit_Score', 'Loan', 'Age']
# part of the data to be used for testing
my_test_size=0.3
# names of the output models
my_logit="0901 logistic_credit_model.joblib"
my_scaler="0901 credit_scaler.joblib"
```

- **Load and prepare the dataset:** We have loaded the features here and identified the dependent variable Y, which is "default" in our case. As mentioned earlier, this is a binary field, 1 and 0, designating default and non-default. One important part of the code is standardization. This part is very important for mathematical stability and accuracy. StandardScaler() adjusts the values so that all features are on the same scale, viz., age and income, and loan amount. The average of each column becomes 0, and with a standard deviation of 1, that is, the range is balanced. Say the age range is 21–65, income is between 20,000 and 200,000, and credit history may be 0 or 1. If we use the values as they stand, there is a possibility that large numbers, like income, will overpower the small numbers, like credit history. Standardizing ensures fairness by equal weighting of the features. At the end of this operation, we have standardized borrower details, the scaled features.

- **Train and save model**: We train the model using the historical data provided, after reserving a part of the data for testing the model. We would not like to test the model on the same data we used for training it. That would potentially cause overfitting, where the model will do well with the data it knows but not with unknown data. We can specify the part of the historical database reserved for testing. Another important aspect of the code is the random seed, a starting point for Python to randomly split the data consistently every time you run the code. You can use any value for it, and every time you run the code, the split will be identical. A non-identical split may cause different values for regression each time you run the code. The code goes on to train the model and compute the regression equation. The equation is displayed on the screen. This equation is then used to compute scores, which are then converted into the probability of default. The logit and scaler models are saved for subsequent use with new values. Once saved, we will not have to train the model till such time we witness a changed behavior of the borrowers.

The outputs of the code are the saved models and screen display of the equation to compute the probability of default using the computed values of intercept and slopes of features derived from the logistic regression.

Evaluating model accuracy and implementing risk thresholds

A credit risk model is good only if it can distinguish between those who are likely to default and those who are not. We develop a model on past data and test the model on another set of past data. This gives us the ability to comment on how accurate the prediction of model is. We will examine techniques like the Receiver Operating Characteristic (ROC) curve, the Gini coefficient, and the Kolmogorov-Smirnov test.

These tools quantify a model's ability to rate borrowers by their default risk. It is to be noted that we are checking the fit of the model based on its use of the test data and not on a new dataset.

Before we move to the code, let us talk about these metrics. The performance of predictive models in finance can be evaluated using these statistical measures. They are particularly useful in assessing credit scoring and risk assessment. Here is a concise overview of the three key metrics used in this chapter.

Receiver Operating Characteristic (ROC) curve

One of the key reasons we use models is their ability to discriminate between two groups of observations. For example, it can classify customers into those who are likely to default and those who are not. The ROC curve graphically illustrates a classification model's discriminative power. It plots the true positive rate (sensitivity) against the false-positive rate (1 – specificity) at various threshold settings. Let us understand these two words, sensitivity and specificity.

Sensitivity is a statistical measure that evaluates how well a binary classification model identifies positive cases. It is also known as the true positive rate or recall. Sensitivity = True Positives / (True Positives + False Negatives). This metric answers the question: "When the actual condition is positive, how often does the test correctly predict positive?" In a credit risk model, true positives would be borrowers correctly identified as defaulters, and false negatives would be defaulters incorrectly classified as good borrowers. High sensitivity (close to 1 or 100%) indicates that the model captures most of the positive cases. A perfectly sensitive model would identify all positive cases without missing any.

High sensitivity is critical in finance when the cost of missing a positive case is significant. It is important to correctly predict potential market crashes, as missing signals of downturns can be devastating.

The ROC curve represents the trade-off between sensitivity and specificity at various threshold settings of the model. Threshold settings are the cutoff values that decide the classification.

Specificity is a statistical measure used to evaluate the performance of binary classification models. It measures the proportion of actual negatives that are correctly identified as such. Thus, specificity = True Negatives / (True Negatives + False Positives). This metric answers the question: "When the actual condition is negative, how often does the test predict negative?" (1 – specificity) is the false-positive rate (FPR) in a binary classification model. It represents the proportion of actual negative cases that are incorrectly classified as positive. This metric answers the question: "When the actual condition is negative, how often does the test incorrectly predict positive?" For credit risk models, the ROC curve represents how well the model distinguishes between good and bad borrowers.

Gini coefficient

The Gini coefficient, widely used in credit scoring, measures the model's ability to separate populations. It is derived from the ROC curve. But to derive this value, we need to compute the AUC. AUC refers to the area under the ROC curve. It measures the performance of a binary classification model across all threshold settings.

Mathematically, AUC is calculated by finding the area underneath the ROC curve in the unit square. The value ranges from 0.5 (random guessing, represented by the diagonal line) to 1.0 (perfect classification). If AUC = 0.5, the model has no discriminative ability and is as good as random guessing. Values above 0.7 are considered acceptable for financial applications.

Mathematically, AUC is the integral of the ROC curve function from $x = 0$ to $x = 1$. However, the ML tools compute the same for us. Now, coming to Gini.

$$\text{Gini} = 2 \times \text{AUC} - 1$$

This transformation rescales the AUC to range from 0, signifying a random model, to 1, signifying a perfect model.

Kolmogorov-Smirnov (KS) test

The KS test measures the maximum difference between the cumulative distribution functions of two populations. In finance, it quantifies the greatest separation between the distributions of two groups, say, defaulters and non-defaulters.

The KS statistic ranges from 0 to 1, with higher values indicating better discriminatory power. While the ROC curve and Gini coefficient evaluate overall model performance, the KS test identifies the specific threshold at which maximum separation occurs. This thus provides actionable insights into setting cutoff points in lending decisions. A KS value close to 1 (or 100%) indicates a strong model that separates the two classes. The threshold is the score cutoff, for example, the probability at which the KS statistic reaches its maximum value. This is where the model achieves the best class separation. In practice, this threshold may be used to classify an observation as a defaulter or not.

If your KS test report states KS statistic: 0.690890 at Threshold = 0.3321, this is what it means:

- **KS statistic:** The model has a high value, signifying that it separates the defaulters and non-defaulters very well. Remember, 0 is no discrimination, and 1 is the best fit.
- **Threshold:** This is the cutoff where the KS statistic reaches the highest value. This means that if the predicted probability is greater than 0.3321, the borrower is likely to default.

Let us now have a look at the major components of part B of the code introduced in the last section. This section requires part A of the code to be processed.

- **Import libraries:** As usual, we have loaded the required libraries in this section of the code. You would have noted that we have loaded modules specific to ROC, AUC, classification, and confusion matrix.
- **Customize:** In this section, we have defined the name of the file to store the output report in .pdf format, the confusion matrix, and the ROC curve in .png format.
- **Predict probabilities and compute validation metrics:** The predicted class level of test data based on the probability of default is computed in this section. It also computes a confusion matrix, classification report, AUC score, Gini coefficient, and KS statistic.
- **Display results on screen and save files:** The metrics computed are displayed on the screen and saved as specified files.

The output from this section includes a classification report, values of AUC, Gini, and KS statistic, ROC curve, and confusion matrix. Though we have discussed the classification reports and confusion matrices earlier, let us have a quick recap.

- **Classification report:** This is a summary of key performance metrics used to evaluate the quality of predictions made by a classification model, such as logistic regression. We can see how the report looks after running the code in Table 9.1.

  Here is an explanation of the components of the report:

  - **Precision:** The proportion of predicted positives that were positive.
  - **Recall (Sensitivity):** The proportion of actual positives that were correctly predicted.
  - **F1 score:** This is the harmonic mean of precision and recall. It balances both metrics and is particularly useful when classes are imbalanced,

Table 9.1 Classification report components

	precision	recall	f1 score	support
0	0.968804	1.000000	0.984155	1118
1	1.000000	0.560976	0.718750	82
accuracy			0.970000	1200
macro avg	0.984402	0.780488	0.851452	1200
weighted avg	0.970936	0.970000	0.966019	1200

like many repaid loans and few defaults. The harmonic mean is used instead of the arithmetic mean as it gives more weight to lower values. So, if either precision or recall is low, the F1 score will also be low. This discourages a model that performs well on one metric but poorly on the other.

- **Support:** The number of true instances for each class in the dataset.
- **Accuracy:** Overall, how many predictions were correct?
- **Macro average:** Average of the metrics treating all classes equally.
- **Weighted average:** Average weighted by the number of instances in each class.

- **Confusion matrix:** This is a summary table used to evaluate the performance of a classification model. It compares the predicted values with the actual values in the test data and presents the same in a 2 × 2 matrix.

There is no defined threshold for these metrics for the underlying model to be accepted. It would depend on the use case, for example, fraud detection, credit scoring, compliance, risk appetite of the institution, class imbalance, regulatory or business constraints, etc.

Integrating models into credit approval processes

Once we are comfortable using a model, we will integrate the model with the business decision process. We have earlier discussed some of these features and will incorporate them in the model that we have developed so far. We will now provide the model with new cases and predict whether they are likely to default or not.

However, before we run this code, we should have with us an approved logistic regression and scaler model. These models were trained in the earlier section.

Let us have a look at the main components of the code (prefix 0902).

- **Import libraries:** All libraries necessary for the code are imported in this section. You would have noticed a library named `joblib`. This is a tool for efficient serialization and parallel processing. This is commonly used for saving and loading ML models and datasets.

- **Customize**: In this section, we have specified the name of the saved models and provided the input values for a new applicant. These input values pertain to income, credit score, loan amount, and age of the applicant. There is also a value for the decision threshold, which is the cutoff value for classifying between potential and non-potential. One can also provide these values in a file for batch processing. Here is the part of the code with customizable parameters italicized.

```
# Customize parameters
my_logit="0901 logistic_credit_model.joblib"
my_scaler="0901 credit_scaler.joblib"
decision_threshold=0.5
new_income = 50000
new_credit_score = 620
new_loan = 15000
new_age = 40
```

- **Use model on a new credit application**: The models are loaded into the system to process the data provided for the new applicant. The logistic regression model provides the weights assigned to individual features. The scaler model transforms new input data in the same way the training data was transformed. The threshold value provided is used to decide on the acceptance or rejection of the application.
- **Generate output**: This section displays the input values, the computed probability of default, and the credit decision.

The output of the code is displayed on the screen. The credit decision is made based on the probability of default computed and the decision threshold.

Fraud detection with anomaly detection techniques

Fraud represents one of the most persistent and evolving threats to organizational stability, customer trust, and regulatory compliance. Beyond direct financial costs, fraud incidents divert significant resources toward efforts to rebuild trust. Financial fraud can be defined as the intentional deception or misrepresentation carried out by individuals or entities to secure unauthorized financial gain, commonly at the expense of another party. Fraud encompasses a broad spectrum of illicit activities. It would include payment fraud, identity theft, insurance scams, money laundering, insider trading, and even loan fraud. The common feature across these diverse schemes is the element of deliberate deception designed to circumvent controls, exploit vulnerabilities, or manipulate systems.

Traditional rule-based approaches to fraud detection have served the industry well in the past. However, over time, the nature and the methodology of fraud have evolved. Static thresholds and predefined patterns that worked effectively in the past now struggle against current adaptive tactics. Further, rules-based systems are usually conservative, tending to generate high false-positive rates that frustrate customers and overwhelm investigation teams.

This is where anomaly detection techniques powered by advanced ML approaches come into play. These techniques establish a baseline of "normal" activity across millions of transactions and then identify statistical outliers that deviate significantly from that norm. This is a major shift from relying exclusively on predefined patterns of fraudulent behavior. This shift assists in the detection of both known fraud scenarios and emerging patterns that have not previously been observed. The focus is on deviation from normal and not merely on following a pattern.

The core premise of anomaly detection is that legitimate financial behavior tends to follow certain patterns. Fraudulent activities are likely to exhibit subtle but detectable deviations from these patterns. A credit card customer's transaction might show consistent patterns regarding timing, location, merchant categories, and amount ranges. When transactions suddenly violate these established patterns, they are flagged for closer scrutiny, even if they do not trigger traditional rules.

In this section, we will explore how financial institutions can harness anomaly detection techniques to support their fraud defense systems. Financial decision-makers need to understand these techniques conceptually without necessarily mastering their technical implementation details. In this section, as earlier, we will explain the tools using tool-specific case studies.

Train and test models for fraud detection

Financial transaction data is the lifeblood of anomaly detection systems in fraud detection. However, raw data is not often ready for training a model, and transforming it into a useful form is the first challenge that a decision-maker is likely to face. We, as financial decision-makers, need to understand these challenges to ensure our models have reliable fraud detection capabilities.

Datasets of financial transactions typically contain a rich but messy array of information. It may include timestamps, monetary values, merchant details, location data, device identifiers, product codes, customer information, and allied data. Much as this diversity offers the potential for powerful pattern recognition, it also creates substantial data preparation challenges. Let us have a quick look at some of the challenges that we are likely to face with the raw input data.

Temporal complexities

Transaction timestamps are not mere simple chronological markers. They may hold crucial behavioral patterns. However, several challenges emerge:

- **Date-time format inconsistencies**: Timestamps may appear in various formats (MM/DD/YYYY, DD/MM/YYYY, UNIX timestamps), requiring standardization.
- **Time zone disparities**: Global transactions may be recorded in different time zones, requiring normalization to avoid artificial patterns.
- **Temporal feature extraction**: Raw timestamps must be transformed into meaningful features like day-of-week, hour-of-day, time-since-last-transaction, or transaction velocity to reveal behavioral patterns.

Without addressing these temporal complexities, models may miss important anomalies tied to unusual timing or sequence.

Categorical data challenges

Categorical fields like merchant names, transaction types, or location data may also present unique challenges like the following:

- **High cardinality**: Fields like the name of the city can have numerous unique values, creating sparse representation challenges.
- **Hierarchical categories**: Merchant categories often have hierarchical relationships, for example, "Electronics > Computers > Laptops", which models must understand. Anomalies may be detectable at a certain level but not at all levels. Another risk is that errors or anomalies at lower hierarchical levels might propagate upward, misleading the anomaly detection at higher levels, or vice versa.
- **Novel categories**: New merchants or categories appearing in production data but absent from training data can trigger false positives.

Effective encoding strategies, such as frequency encoding, target encoding, or embedding techniques, are necessary to transform categorical data into useful numeric formats, making it understandable by ML models. It is also critical to ensure that the predictive power of the data is not compromised during transformation.

Numerical data pitfalls

Even seemingly straightforward numerical fields require scrutiny:

- **Data type inconsistencies**: Monetary values sometimes appear as strings with currency symbols or commas, requiring cleaning and conversion.

- **Scale variations:** Transaction amounts vary dramatically across different types of purchases, potentially overwhelming other signals.
- **Regional differences:** Amount patterns differ across regions due to currency value differences and spending norms.

Standardization, normalization, or log transformations are often necessary to make numerical features comparable and prevent high-value transactions from dominating the model's attention.

Feature relevance and noise

Not all data elements contribute meaningfully to fraud detection. Including irrelevant features can introduce noise and decrease model performance:

- **Unique identifiers:** Transaction IDs, reference numbers, or similar fields hold no predictive value and should be excluded.
- **Leakage fields:** Some fields might inadvertently "leak" information about fraud status. For example, chargeback status may create misleading patterns if included while detecting fraud.
- **Static customer attributes:** While demographic data may have some relevance, exclusively static attributes often have limited value in detecting behavioral anomalies.

In some cases, derived features capture behavioral patterns. Examples include deviation from customer spending patterns, frequency of merchant visits, or variation in transaction locations. These features may often prove more valuable than raw transaction attributes.

Class imbalance: The fundamental challenge

Perhaps the most significant challenge in fraud detection datasets is extreme class imbalance. Genuine fraudulent transactions typically represent a very low percentage of all transactions. This creates several complications:

- **Biased performance metrics:** Accuracy becomes meaningless if a model achieves 99.9% accuracy by simply predicting "not fraud" for every transaction.
- **Learning difficulties:** Models struggle to learn patterns from extremely rare examples, potentially ignoring minority class features.
- **Threshold sensitivity:** With such an imbalance, small changes in decision thresholds can dramatically affect false-positive and false-negative rates.

Addressing this imbalance requires specialized approaches, such as sampling techniques like under-sampling the majority class or over-sampling the minority class. One can also resort to synthetic data generation methods like Synthetic Minority Over-sampling Technique (SMOTE) or algorithm modifications to assign higher weights to minority class examples.

Train-test consistency requirements

Maintaining consistency between training and production data is critical for anomaly detection models. This would include the following:

- **Feature consistency**: All features used during training must be available in the same format during testing as well as in production.
- **Preprocessing alignment**: Transformations applied during training, like scaling or encoding, must be identically applied to new data.
- **Data drift monitoring**: Transaction patterns evolve due to changing customer behavior, seasonal effects, economic conditions, and similar factors. These movements require monitoring for any drift between training, test, and production data.

Data pipelines should ensure consistent preprocessing across all environments. There should also be a system of monitoring to detect when models may need retraining due to evolving patterns.

Production considerations for new data

The use of raw data is not restricted to training and testing. When deploying anomaly detection models to production environments, we also use raw data. Several additional considerations, like the following, may arise at this stage.

- **Missing data handling**: Production systems must handle missing values consistently with training procedures.
- **Latency requirements**: Transaction approval decisions often require near-real-time processing, limiting the complexity of feature engineering. For example, credit card transaction approval happens in real time. This limits the use of a complex model, which may be more data-intensive and would take a longer time.
- **Unexpected inputs**: Production systems must handle unexpected inputs like new merchant categories or unusual value ranges.
- **Explainability needs**: For investigation purposes, the model should indicate which features contributed most to flagging a transaction as anomalous.

Moreover, effective anomaly detection requires a feedback loop. Confirmed fraud cases and false positives are used to populate the loop to continuously refine and retrain the model. This ensures that the model adapts quickly to evolving fraud tactics.

In subsequent sections, we will see how these are put into real-life use.

Tackling financial fraud by identifying unusual transaction patterns

The frequency of financial fraud is low, and they are committed to a clear collateral objective of hiding their tracks. Fraudsters also know the likely identifiers of fraud, and they seek to commit the fraud in a way that does not trigger the same. This makes the detection of financial fraud a challenge. One effective approach to tackling fraud involves analyzing transaction data to detect patterns that deviate from typical behaviors.

The foundation of pattern-based fraud detection techniques is the premise that legitimate financial behavior usually exhibits consistency. ML models, particularly anomaly detection techniques, systematically identify these deviations. The tool analyzes historical transaction data to discern what constitutes "normal" behavior. Once a deviation from the established norms is detected, the fraud alarm is sounded. These deviations usually take place in the following ways:

- **Behavioral anomalies:** When a customer's transaction patterns suddenly change. This may include unusual purchase timing, atypical merchant categories, unexpected geographic locations, etc. These changes may signal account compromise.
- **Contextual anomalies:** When transactions seem unusual within specific contexts, even if they appear normal in isolation. For example, a high-value purchase might be completely normal for a customer in their home country. Similar transactions become suspicious when they occur at odd hours in a foreign country that the customer has never visited before.
- **Collective anomalies:** When a series of transactions, each appearing legitimate individually, form suspicious patterns collectively. For instance, a series of escalating small purchases is followed by a large transaction. These independently are normal transactions, but collectively may indicate fraudsters testing the validity of a stolen credit card before cleaning out the limit.

ML tools are effective at detecting these multi-dimensional patterns by learning from historical transaction data. ML algorithms can discover subtle anomalies that human analysts might overlook. They can incorporate hundreds of features simultaneously, detect non-linear relationships, and adapt to evolving patterns over time. Pattern-based fraud detection usually follows this workflow:

- **Feature engineering:** Transforming raw transaction data into meaningful features representing customer behavior. Some of the common features are calculating transaction velocities, understanding spending patterns by merchant category, geographic dispersion of activities, temporal usage patterns, etc.
- **Profile building:** This stage involves establishing baseline behavior profiles for individual customers, customer segments, or specific transaction types. These profiles represent "normal" behavior against which new activities are compared to identify anomalies. You can appreciate that the chances of observing an anomaly depend largely on how these profiles are defined.
- **Anomaly scoring:** Deviation scores that quantify how much a new transaction differs from expected patterns based on established profiles are calculated. A threshold value to define deviation is to be established for flagging a transaction as anomalous.
- **Decision-making:** The model converts anomaly scores into actionable decisions based on risk thresholds. These decisions are likely to have different levels of intervention based on the severity of the anomaly.

Let us use an example to see how the codes work. The major components of the code (prefix 0903) used are the following:

- **Import libraries:** We have imported all necessary libraries in this section of the code.
- **Customize:** In this section, we have provided the name of the input file, the name of the file to save the resultant plot and anomalous transactions, and the cutoff percentage. If the value is within this percentage, it will be considered non-anomalous. In addition, the number of clusters we want the data to be classified into is also provided. In this case, we have provided a value of 2, as we want classification into anomalous and non-anomalous. The extract of the code with the customizable parameters is italicized, and provided here. Besides these, there are a few other customizable values which we have marked along with the subsequent code section.

```
# Customize parameters
my_file_path = "0903 Transaction_data.csv"
my_anomaly_file = "0903 anomalous_transactions.csv"
my_plot_file = "0903 anomaly_detection_plot.png"
no_of_clusters=2
my_normal_percentage=98
```

- **Prepare data:** This is a critical section where the input data is made ready for processing. In this example, we have three fields in the input file: zip, TransactionAmount, and TransactionHour. In this section, we have marked all non-numeric data as "None" and dropped them. This is necessary, as clustering can be performed only with numeric data. The code cleans the data by ensuring two features are numeric: Transaction-Amount and TransactionHour. You may customize this section should you have different field names. The code then standardizes the numeric features to ensure fair clustering. We have seen how scalar operations standardized unbalanced data.
- **Apply K-means clustering:** In this section of the code, K-means clustering is applied with a specified number of clusters. It assumes transactions are either normal or anomalous. In K-means clustering, every data point is assigned to the nearest cluster center, called the centroid. The distance between a point and its assigned centroid is a measure of how typical or atypical that point is within its cluster. Upon computation of the distance, it flags the top specified percent as potential anomalies based on the percentage defined as normal. If a transaction is close to the centroid, it behaves similarly to many other transactions in that cluster and is likely normal. If a transaction is far away from the centroid, it is unusual compared to other points and possibly is anomalous.
- **Save and display results:** This section plots the transactions with color-coded anomalies. It also saves the plot and the anomalous transactions to individual specified files.

The output of the code is the cluster plot and a file containing transactions deemed anomalous based on the specified threshold. The output file contains the input file fields, that is, zip, TransactionAmount, and TransactionHour. In addition, it contains three additional fields, which are Cluster, DistanceToCenter, and PredictedAnomaly.

The axes of the scatter plot represent transaction hour and transaction amount, as was identified in the model. The predicted anomalies are presented in a different color from the predicted non-anomalies. Please note that if we change the anomaly threshold (my_normal_percentage), the distribution patterns of anomalies and non-anomalies on the scatterplot will also change.

Implementing anomaly detection algorithms such as Isolation Forests

While various ML algorithms can detect anomalies, certain techniques have proven particularly effective for financial fraud detection. We have seen an example of such in the earlier section. Among the available algorithms, Isolation Forests stand out for their efficiency, effectiveness with imbalanced datasets, and intuitive approach to identifying outliers.

Anomaly detection algorithms, such as Isolation Forests, are particularly effective for financial fraud detection due to their capacity to efficiently identify outliers without needing labeled datasets. The Isolation Forest algorithm operates on a simple principle; anomalous transactions are easier to "isolate" than normal ones. The Isolation Forest algorithm operates by randomly selecting features and splitting values to isolate data points. Points requiring fewer splits to isolate are considered anomalies, indicating potentially fraudulent transactions.

Let us consider an example of a dataset of financial transactions. The algorithm might randomly select the feature "transaction amount" and then randomly choose a split value, say $5,000. Transactions are separated into groups based on whether they exceed this value or not. Further splits on other randomly selected features, like transaction frequency or location, continue until each transaction is isolated into its leaf node. Transactions that end up isolated quickly in fewer splits are classified as anomalies, signaling potentially suspicious activities.

Isolation Forests use decision trees to partition data, creating isolated branches for anomalous data points. Since anomalies typically represent a small percentage of all transactions, this method effectively and rapidly flags suspicious transactions.

Isolation Forests work well with imbalanced data. Since the incidence of fraud is far less than that of a normal transaction, Isolation Forest emerges as a good tool for fraud detection. In addition, the algorithm naturally focuses on features that effectively separate anomalies. This reduces the impact of irrelevant or noisy variables that might be present in transaction data. Importantly, Isolation Forest does not require a specific statistical distribution or extensive parameter tuning. These advantages make it a popular tool for fraud detection.

The implementation of Isolation Forests typically follows these steps:

- **Training**: The algorithm builds multiple isolation trees using random subsamples of the data and features. Each tree partitions the data space by randomly selecting features and split points until all observations are isolated.
- **Path length calculation**: For each observation, the algorithm calculates the average path length. This is the number of splits required to isolate that observation across all trees in the forest.
- **Anomaly scoring**: Observations with shorter average path lengths receive higher anomaly scores, as they are easier to isolate from the general population. This is a central requirement for isolation.

- **Threshold setting:** A decision benchmark is established to classify transactions as normal or potentially fraudulent based on their anomaly scores. Those marked as anomalous are flagged for special treatment.

Let us understand the operation with the help of a code (prefix 0904). Here are the main components of the code:

- **Import libraries:** All necessary libraries are loaded in this section of the code
- **Customize:** Here, we have provided the name of the input file and the name of the output file to save the plot and anomalous transactions. We have provided values for n_estimators and contamination. n_estimators is the number of trees in the Isolation Forest. Each tree is built by randomly splitting features to isolate points. The more trees, the more stable and reliable the anomaly scores are, but it will take longer processing times. Contamination is our estimate of the proportion of anomalies in the data. The Isolation Forest does not automatically know how many anomalies are in our data. It ranks all data by how isolated they are and then marks the top specified estimate as outliers. We have further provided the names of the numeric and categorical features we have decided to work with. In the last section, you may remember we provided this directly when we were running the model. Isolation Forest can work well with both numeric and categorical features, unlike K-means clustering, which is best used with only numeric features. The relevant section of the code with the customizable parameters italicized is given here.

```
# Customize parameters
my_input_data="0904 Transaction_data.csv"
my_output_file="0904 isolation_forest_anomalies.csv"
my_plot_file="0904 isolation_forest_plot.png"
my_n_estimator=100
my_contamination=0.2
# Specify which features to use
numeric_features = ["TransactionAmount", "TransactionHour"]
categorical_features = ["MerchantCategory", "DeviceID"]
# 'Country' was dropped
```

- **Prepare data:** In this section, we start by loading the dataset that contains, at a minimum, the features we have defined in the last section. We then create a preprocessing pipeline to standardize the numeric features using the StandardScaler function as we did earlier. For categorical features, we use OneHotEncoder, which converts strings to binary vectors. Let us understand what this does. Consider there is a categorical feature named Country, and there are three options: USA, UAE, and India. One-hot encoding will convert this categorical variable into three to represent the value. The new fields may be called Country_USA, Country_UAE, and Country_India. If the country is the USA, only that field will have a value of "1," and the other two will have a value of "0." In the code, we have used drop="first"; one of the categories will be dropped. Consider that Country_USA is dropped. In that case, if the country is the USA, we will have 0 as the value for Country_UAE and Country _India. This automatically means that the country is the USA. For the curious, pipeline is a tool provided by some libraries that allows you to bundle together multiple steps, such as preprocessing and model training, into a single, streamlined process. We have also created an Isolation Forest pipeline, which combines preprocessing and modeling.

- **Fit model and generate scores**: This part of the code trains the pipeline on the full dataset after preprocessing. An anomaly score, ranging from –1 to 1, is predicted for each transaction. Lower value means more anomalous. For easier filtering, this score is converted to a Boolean value, either True or False.
- **Save results and visualize**: All anomalous transactions are saved to a specified file. A scatter plot of transactions is also displayed and saved.

The output of the code is a scatter plot and a file containing anomalous transactions. The data file would have two additional columns over the input data, Anomaly Score and Predicted Anomaly. The latter contains the Boolean value of either true or false. The axes of the scatterplot are Transaction Hour and Transaction Amount. The color of the plots denotes the predicted anomaly.

Since Isolation Forest classification is based on the provided value of contamination, it is important to find an appropriate value. Apart from using domain knowledge and past experience, you can also measure precision, recall, and F1-score against different values of contamination. This will allow you to select the value that results in the best-performing model.

In the last section, we did a similar exercise using K-means clustering. Are we likely to have different results when we use the Isolation Forest? Yes, most likely because of the way these two tools work. Clustering assumes normal transactions form tight clusters, and outliers lie farther from cluster centroids. It also works best with numeric features. Isolation Forest builds random trees and isolates points quickly if they are anomalies. It flags anomalies based on the average path length required for isolation. It can use both categorical and numerical features.

Setting up alerts for potentially fraudulent activities

Detecting anomalies is the first step in an effective fraud prevention system. This should be followed by transforming anomaly scores into actionable alerts and routing those alerts to appropriate response channels. This requires deciding on the extent of residual risk that we are willing to accept. A relaxed threshold would potentially increase the risks of fraud loss, while a rigid threshold would be disruptive for customers. The challenge is to implement a fraud detection system that balances operational efficiency and customer experience.

An effective alert system for fraud detection typically incorporates several key components:

- **Multi-tiered thresholds**: It may make more business sense to have multiple threshold levels that trigger different responses instead of using a single threshold for all alerts. For example, low-risk anomalies might simply be logged for pattern analysis, while medium-risk anomalies might trigger additional authentication steps. On the other hand, extremely high-risk anomalies might block transactions pending investigation.
- **Contextual prioritization**: Alert systems can incorporate contextual factors to prioritize responses. For instance, a stricter threshold may be defined for high-value transactions or those in high-fraud channels. On the other hand, a lenient threshold may be established for trusted customer segments.
- **Explanatory context**: Effective alerts should not stop at just flagging anomalous transactions. They should provide investigators with context explaining why the transaction was flagged. This might include details of features that contributed most to the anomaly score, for example, an explanation of how the transaction deviated from expected patterns.
- **Feedback mechanisms**: Any good alert system should have a mechanism to capture investigation outcomes. These outcomes should be reviewed and feedback provided to the anomaly detection system for continuous improvement.

Delivery of these alerts through different channels may involve coding beyond that of pure data science. We are not moving into that sphere. The code (prefix 0905) used in this section will explain how these alerts can be generated while using the anomaly detection tools. Let us have a look at the major components of the code.

- **Import libraries**: As earlier, we have loaded all necessary libraries in this section of the code.
- **Customize**: Here, we have provided the name of the input file and the name of the output file to save the plot and alerts. The amount corresponding to

high- and mid-level alerts has also been specified. In addition, we have used a few more customizable parameters while using the model. The section of the code with the customizable parameters in italics is given here.

```
# Customize parameters
my_input_file="0904 Transaction_data.csv"
my_plot_file="0905 alert_scatter_plot.png"
my_output_file="0905 alert_transactions.csv"
my_high_alert_amount=1000
my_mid_alert_amount=500
```

- **Prepare data and inline customization:** We loaded the input file and cleaned up the numeric field. Subsequently, we have identified the numerical and categorical features and preprocessed them. We have standardized the numeric features and one-hot encoded the categorical features. We have also inserted a transaction ID if not already present. This ID will help us identify the transactions associated with an alert.
- **Use Isolation Forest:** In this section, we have defined the pipelines for preprocessing and applying the Isolation Forest model. We will generate a predicted score for an anomaly and use it to create a true/false flag.
- **Create business-defined alert levels:** In this section, we have combined the anomaly flag and transaction amount to assign an alert level. High alert is accorded for flagged anomalies and high amounts. Medium alert is given for moderate amounts, and low alert for any other anomaly. No alert is given for normal transactions.
- **Visualize and save:** To visualize distinctly, the code assigns different colors for plotting different alert levels. Gray denotes normal transactions, blue denotes low alert, orange stands for medium alert, and red stands for high alert. A scatter plot with anomaly score and transaction amount as axes is displayed and saved. The alert-triggering transactions are also saved in a specified file.

The output of the code includes a scatterplot and a file containing the alert-triggering transactions. The saved file for alert-generating transactions also includes the base fields of the input file. It adds transaction ID, anomaly score, predicted anomaly, alert level, and alert label fields. This file can be used for subsequent analysis and audit reference.

Compliance monitoring using NLP

Most corporate entities face an ever-expanding universe of compliance requirements. Financial institutions, arguably, are the most affected entities.

These requirements include revenue regulations, financial reporting, governance reporting, anti-money laundering regulations, consumer protection laws, privacy standards, emission reporting, stock exchange listing obligations, and many more. The compliance burden has grown exponentially, and so has the volume of text-based information that must be monitored. Emails, chat logs, contracts, policies, marketing materials, and many others have grown beyond what manual review processes can effectively handle within the compliance dates.

NLP offers a compelling solution to the problem created by the convergence of regulatory complexity and information overload. NLP is a branch of AI focused on understanding human language. The tools transform compliance monitoring by enabling computers to analyze large volumes of text while identifying potential issues for human review. Modern NLP goes far beyond simple keyword matching to deliver sophisticated capabilities, including the following:

- **Context understanding:** NLP recognizes the meaning of communications in the given context rather than focusing on individual words. For example, the word "chips" would have different meanings in a restaurant, an electronics factory, and a casino.
- **Entity identification:** NLP applications automatically detect and categorize references to people, organizations, and other elements.
- **Pattern recognition:** Problematic language patterns that might indicate compliance risks can be identified by NLP tools.
- **Relationship mapping:** NLP tools can discover connections between entities mentioned in communications.
- **Sentiment analysis:** An NLP method that assesses the emotional tone behind texts, identifying potential unethical behavior or internal conflicts.
- **Classification:** ML algorithms such as SVM, Random Forests, and Neural Networks can classify documents, prioritize reviews, and flag those that merit further investigation.

These capabilities are delivered through powerful NLP libraries such as NLTK. The library provides pre-built components that financial decision-makers can leverage to build tailored compliance monitoring systems. NLP technologies enable, among others, the following:

- **Communications surveillance:** Monitoring employee emails, chats, and call transcripts to identify inappropriate conduct, insider trading, collusion, or harassment.
- **Contract and document review:** Analyzing legal agreements to identify problematic clauses, regulatory conflicts, or inconsistencies with

institutional policies. These advanced applications need careful training with the tools.

- **Policy alignment**: Comparing internal policies against regulatory requirements to identify gaps or contradictions.
- **Customer complaint analysis**: Examining customer feedback to detect potential compliance issues in products, services, or sales practices.
- **Regulatory change management**: Assessing new regulations to determine their impact on existing processes and requirements.

NLP offers powerful capabilities for compliance monitoring. However, successful implementation requires addressing several key considerations, like the following:

- **Domain adaptation**: Legal and technical terminology often requires specialized NLP models trained on domain-specific data.
- **Explainability**: Compliance systems must provide transparent explanations for why specific content was flagged as problematic. The output should allow the analyst to understand the context of the flagging.
- **False-positive management**: Systems must balance comprehensiveness with precision to avoid burdening analysts and managers with irrelevant alerts. The threshold calibration, besides legal requirements, needs a clear understanding of risk tolerance.
- **Integration**: Ultimately, NLP tools must fit seamlessly into existing compliance workflows and case management systems. This may involve skills that are outside the domain of pure data science.

Utilizing NLP to analyze textual data

The first critical step in compliance monitoring involves gathering textual data from various sources, including contracts, internal emails, communications, regulatory reports, and policies. Optical Character Recognition (OCR) technology is used for digitizing printed or handwritten texts. Once texts are digitized, they undergo preprocessing to enhance quality and prepare for analysis. Preprocessing activities typically include various activities like the following:

- **Tokenization:** Tokenize means splitting text into smaller pieces. This involves breaking text into words or phrases. When we tokenize by words, we break a sentence into a list of words. If we tokenize by sentences, we split a paragraph into individual sentences. For example, the sentence "Compliance monitoring is crucial" is tokenized into ['Compliance', 'monitoring', 'is', 'crucial'].

- **Stemming or lemmatization**: This step reduces words to their base forms. For example, "complies," "compliance," and "complying" could all be reduced to "comply."
- **Stop-word removal**: Common words that add little meaning are eliminated. Examples of stopwords include "is", "the", "at", and "on". The sentence "Monitoring compliance is vital" could become ['Monitoring', 'compliance', 'vital'] after stop-word removal.
- **Part-of-speech tagging**: Words are categorized into their grammatical roles, like nouns, verbs, adjectives, and so on. For example, in the sentence "Compliance monitoring helps institutions," the tagging could be [('Compliance', 'NN'), ('monitoring', 'NN'), ('helps', 'VBZ'), ('institutions', 'NNS')].

Leveraging ML libraries to process and interpret language data

NLP libraries, for example, NLTK, provide powerful tools to process, analyze, and interpret large volumes of language data. NLTK is well known for its extensive modules and tools for tokenization, parsing, stemming, and semantic reasoning. This power allows compliance teams to develop customized text-processing solutions.

For instance, NLTK can tokenize contractual clauses, extract critical terms, and identify discrepancies or anomalies against standard regulatory requirements. Entities are real-world things mentioned in the text. This would include person, organization, date, place, amount, and so on. This is part of a process called Named Entity Recognition (NER), which will be performed. We will be using this library in our code.

Another NLP library is spaCy. It excels with speed and ease of use, particularly with its built-in pre-trained models. These models are optimized for NER, dependency parsing, and linguistic annotation. Compliance monitoring often involves analyzing substantial volumes of textual data rapidly. spaCy allows quick identification and tagging of compliance-critical entities and facilitates near real-time monitoring.

Let us now get the code (prefix 0906) from the repository and review the main components.

- **Import libraries**: As usual, in this section, we load the libraries we will use in the code. You might have noticed a few new libraries being used. Here is what they do. NLTK is used for text preprocessing. This involves tokenizing, stop-word removal, and lemmatization. Stopwords are common words like "the", "is", "at", "which", and "on", which do not contribute much to the meaning of a sentence. Lemmatization means reducing a word to its dictionary form (root form). It uses vocabulary and grammar rules to find the correct root. For example, the word "better" is rooted in the word "good," "cleaning" is rooted in "clean," and so on. Docx is used to read and manipulate .docx files. SequenceMatcher calculates text similarity between policy clauses and regulatory requirements.

- **Download data file (one time):** This section is to be run only once. Even if this has been run for some other code, we do not need to run it here. The modules are loading tokenizer models, a common stopwords list, and a word database for lemmatization. Though we have stated that these are to be run only once, it is good practice to run this once in a while to have the updated version.
- **Customize:** This is the section where we provide values for customizable parameters. In this section, we will provide the value of the similarity threshold, a list of policy and regulatory clauses, and the name of the file to store the report. The similarity threshold measures the similarity between policy and regulation. If the similarity value exceeds 0.6, it is considered a match. The model reviews the policy clauses, evaluates them against the regulatory requirements, and comments on compliance. A list of red flags has also been provided. Red flags here are phrases that may indicate a compliance risk. When each policy clause is processed, the code checks each clause for the presence of any red flags. Please note the use of quotes and square brackets while providing values for red flags, policy, and regulatory clauses.
- **Load model and data:** In this section, we will load models and feed them with the policy and regulatory clauses.
- **Prepare and run model:** In this section, we will define functions to be used in assessing similarity and identifying red flags. We calculate a similarity score (0 to 1) between two sentences using SequenceMatcher. The red flags are loaded at this stage.
- **Run analysis, prepare, and save the report:** This section of the code starts with setting up the Word document to create a report. It then moves to the main processing loop. Here, for each policy clause, the code displays and records the clause text and adds it to a Word file. The preprocessing code tokenizes, removes stopwords, and lemmatizes. It then extracts and displays entities using NER. The processed data is subjected to red flag detection and is highlighted in the report if found. Similarity check compares policy clauses to every regulatory clause. If similarity > 0.6, it is considered matching; else, a review is recommended. The results from each procedure are stored in a specified file.

The output from the code includes a compliance report. This shows the original text, extracted tokens, named entities identified, and red flags detected. A summary of the observation is also reported.

Automating the detection of regulatory breaches or policy violations

The primary benefit of NLP-powered compliance monitoring lies in its ability to automatically detect potential violations across massive document collections. This automated detection is possible only if the models that are constructed understand both explicit and implicit regulatory concerns. Key approaches include:

- Rule-based systems that encode specific compliance requirements.
- Classification models that identify high-risk content based on historical examples.
- Entity-relationship extraction that maps connections between related parties or events.

Effective detection systems often combine these approaches with domain-specific features like regulatory terminology dictionaries, prohibited phrase lists, and contextual risk indicators. The automation of this detection process transforms compliance monitoring from a reactive, sample-based approach to a comprehensive, proactive system that can flag potential issues in near-real-time.

A major feature of NLP-driven compliance monitoring is automation. This enables organizations to rapidly detect regulatory breaches or policy violations. NLP-based automation driven by rules and ML models trained on historical data, flags anomalies or suspicious language patterns promptly. This proactive approach minimizes manual intervention and accelerates the compliance response process.

Let us look at a code (prefix 0907) that builds an automated compliance breach detection system using ML (Logistic Regression), rule-based checking using specific red-flag phrases, and NER. The main components of the code are the following:

- **Import libraries:** All libraries required to run this code are imported in this section. Just in case you do not have one installed on your system, please do that before you run the code.
- **Download NLTK resources (one time):** As with the earlier section, we download the resources for stopwords, tokenization, and lemmatization. If you have already run this on your system, you do not need to download it again. But keep updating it once in a while to take advantage of the latest version.
- **Customize:** In the customization section, we specify the name for the output file, provide the messages labeled as non-compliant, provide a list of keywords that indicate violation, and the text messages that are

our input. The labeled messages are the primary resource for training the logistics regression model. Please note the syntax of the labeled message; each message is followed by a label, 0 or 1, indicating the status of the violation. Of course, you would have noticed the use of quotes and square brackets in all cases involving the provision of text. The relevant part of the text with the customizable portion is italicized.

```
# Customize parameters
my_output_report="0907 Compliance_Automation_Report.docx"
# These are internal messages labeled as 1 = non- compli-
ant, 0 = compliant
my_labeled_messages = [
("The transaction was approved by the manager after the
cut-off time.", 1),
("We reported all client data transfers to the compliance
desk.", 0),
("Funds were moved without notifying compliance.", 1),
("Customer complaints were logged and forwarded.", 0),
("Executive approval was bypassed for this urgent
request.", 1),
("Quarterly audit data submitted as per guidelines.", 0),
("There was no report submitted for the flagged transac-
tion.", 1),
("New compliance rules were implemented by the team.", 0),
("The request was executed even though review was pend-
ing.", 1),
("The report was checked and signed off.", 0)
]
# Define a list of phrases known to indicate violations
my_flags=[
"without notifying", "bypassed", "no report", "review was
pending", "unreported", "not informed"
]

my_text_messages=[
"Transaction was completed without notifying the compli-
ance team.",
"Audit report submitted to the risk committee.",
"The review was pending, but funds were already moved.",
"Customer concerns were documented and handled.", "Policy
update approved by Director Smith on April 3rd."
]
```

- **Load models and preprocess data:** In this section, we prepare the text for being used by the model. The labeled messages are separated into texts and corresponding labels for ML.

- **Preprocess function:** A text cleaning function is being defined for use in the next section. The function tokenizes, converts to lowercase, removes stop-words, and lemmatizes. The function is used on texts provided as needed.
- **Train a logistics regression model:** This is one of the key steps where we train the logistics regression model. The model uses the labels (1,0) as the target variable and the corresponding text as the input values. You might have noticed that the texts are vectorized. Vectorization means converting text into numbers since ML models cannot understand text directly. Logistic regression needs numeric input, like arrays of numbers. The conversion method used here is TF-IDF vectorization. TF stands for Term Frequency, signifying how often a word appears in a document. IDF stands for Inverse Document Frequency, measuring how unique that word is across all documents. It gives higher weight to words that occur frequently in the document but rarely across all documents. So common words end up getting a low score.
- **Define detection rules:** In this section, we load the defined flags. A function is defined to process an input text to identify the presence of the flags.
- **Entity extraction:** Code in this small section extracts entities using the values loaded earlier.
- **Analyze, write, and save the report:** The final section of the code starts by creating a document to store the findings of the analysis. All input messages are read and preprocessed. They are converted to TF-IDF vectors, and prediction is made as to their likely compliance and non-compliance using the trained logistic regression model. This value is then converted into a probability. The messages are also flagged for the presence of red-flag phrases and analyzed for entity extraction. The report is then saved as a specified file.

The output of the code is displayed on the screen as well as saved in a file. The report file contains the message text, ML prediction and confidence, rule-based alerts, and named entities. The computed probability is reported as confidence.

Supporting compliance officers in monitoring and reporting

The usefulness of even the most sophisticated NLP model depends on how well the insights are effectively communicated to compliance officers for appropriate action. These systems can generate alerts, compile detailed reports, and maintain comprehensive documentation. All these will significantly simplify monitoring and reporting tasks. A well-designed compliance monitoring system would prioritize the human–computer interface. It would ideally provide dashboards highlighting potential violations, explaining detection rationale, and supporting efficient workflow management.

Contextual reference will permit compliance officers to quickly evaluate potential issues while minimizing false positives that waste valuable time.

The reporting capabilities should support both operational needs and regulatory requirements. Operational needs will include case management and investigation tracking. Regulatory needs would include documentation of monitoring activities, audit trails of decisions, and evidence of comprehensive compliance coverage.

Let us consider a scenario where the system has flagged specific messages, providing details such as their source, the prediction made by the ML tool, the associated confidence score, and whether a predefined rule was triggered during the flagging process. Based on this information, the system should prescribe the next course of action. Let us look at the main components of the code (prefix 0908):

- **Import libraries**: As usual, in this section, we have loaded the necessary libraries.
- **Download NLTK data (one time)**: We need to download this data only once in an environment. We have discussed their usage in earlier sections. Just to remind you, if you are running it for the first time, please remove the # sign ahead of the code and run it. It is a good idea to run these codes periodically to get the latest update.
- **Customize**: In this section, we will provide the values for the customizable parameters. We will specify the file names to save the report and the plots. The critical components of the customization are the list of messages flagged by the system as non-compliance, the source of the message like email, or office notes, the predicted state of the message (1,0), the confidence scores which were the basis of the prediction, and finally whether the rule-based logic was triggered. The trigger is dependent on the confidence scores. The relevant part of the code with the customizable parts is italicized. Note the use of square brackets and double quotes in case of text values. Also, confirm that you have provided the same number of values for every parameter. If you have provided ten messages, you should also provide metadata for all ten of them.

```
# Customize parameters
my_case_report="0908 Compliance_Case_Report.docx"
my_csv_report="0908 Compliance_Case_Report.csv"
my_risk_level_plot="0908 risk_level_distribution.png"
my_message_source_plot="0908 source_distribution.png"
my_entity_plot="0908 entity_frequency_chart.png"

my_flagged_messages=[
"Transaction was processed without notifying the compli-
ance officer.",
```

```
"Audit report was completed and emailed to the external
auditor.",
"The request was executed while the internal review was
still pending.",
"Policy update was approved by Director John Smith on
March 5th.",
"Customer complaint was not logged due to verbal
communication.",
"All cash deposits above threshold were reported as
required.",
"Account access was granted to an unauthorized third
party.",
"Client data backup was delayed without proper
documentation.",
"Risk control policy was acknowledged and filed.", "Funds
were transferred after hours with no approval."
]

# Metadata for each message
sources = ["Email", "Chat", "Log", "Memo", "Email",
"Log", "Chat", "Email", "Log", "Chat"]
ml_predictions = [1, 0, 1, 0, 1, 0, 1, 1, 0, 1]
ml_confidences = [0.92, 0.15, 0.87, 0.20, 0.90, 0.05,
0.95, 0.89, 0.08, 0.93]
rule_triggers = [True, False, True, False, True, False,
True, True, False, True]
```

- **Load model and data:** In this section, we are loading the flagged messages. We have also generated an arbitrary timestamp. This is not necessary to understand the functionality, but is often useful for a document trail. Consider a system where numerous messages are generated every minute. In such cases, the timestamp comes in handy for easy recall and identification. We used this timestamp later during report generation. In real life, the time stamp is likely to be available with the message.
- **Helper function:** This section creates functions for various purposes. The preprocess function cleans and lemmatizes text for ML processing. The extraction function extracts named entities like names, dates, and organizations. The risk assignment section combines rule-based and ML flags to assign one of four risk levels: high, medium, low, and none. The "recommend" section returns actions like "Immediate Review" or "Archive" based on the risk. The last function simulates the status of whether a case is pending, escalated, reviewed, or closed. This part is loosely rule-based; higher-risk cases are still in process or under scrutiny and are marked "pending" or "escalated." Lower-risk cases are considered handled and marked "reviewed" or "closed."

- **Analyze and generate reports**: The code loops through each flagged message, and for each message, it does the following. It also displays a summary report for each case on-screen.
    - Extracts metadata and timestamp,
    - Assigns risk and recommends action,
    - Extracts named entities,
    - Tracks counts for summary plots (risk levels, sources, entities), and
    - Writes details into a Word document and prepares rows for export to a CSV file.
- **Generate and save reports and visualizations**: This section of the code saves the Word document and CSV file. It also plots risk levels (High, Medium, Low, None), source types (email, Chat, Log), and the five most mentioned named entities.

The output primarily generates the plots and displays the report. It plots several cases by risk levels as a bar chart and by sources as a pie chart. It also gives a bar chart for the top-named entities.

Words like "March" may be flagged as entities because, in NER systems such as NLTK, they often match patterns linked to dates or time expressions. Pre-trained models are built on large text corpora where "March" commonly appears as a month, leading the system to classify it as a DATE entity.

To summarize, this code is designed to use the output from an ML tool that flags text messages as non-compliant. We have seen examples of these in the earlier section. These messages are now being processed for further action. This is done using rule-based logic and a standard library of keywords.

Key takeaways

The chapter emphasizes the need for an integrated approach where risk awareness permeates all organizational levels and functions. AI and ML models have enhanced capabilities in assessing credit, market, operational, and fraud-related risks. We also saw the use of ML in probability of default computation, default detection, anomaly detection, and applied NLP tools to aid compliances.

To maximize benefits from all these models, they need to be clearly defined, validated, understood, and regularly updated to remain effective. The risk of misusing models, model risk, highlighted the importance of robust governance, transparency, and user training. Moreover, successful model integration requires contextual interpretation, appropriate decision thresholds, and alignment with organizational workflows.

Chapter 10

Conclusion

As we wrap up, this chapter looks ahead to what is next. By now, you already know AI and ML's potential in improving financial decision-making. In this chapter, you will know the future we can hope to look forward to. You will also find guidance on how to build a data-driven culture that supports these tools in your business. Whether you are just getting started or ready to go further, this chapter encourages you to embrace innovation, stay curious, and lead the way in shaping the future of finance.

The future of AI/ML in financial decision-making

We have been exploring the use of AI and ML applications for financial decision-making. We stand at an evolutionary point in the finance profession. This department, which had predominantly depended on professionals to make inferences based on data provided by the computing system, is now looking forward to inferences made by the system. Throughout this book, we have demonstrated how Lo-code ML tools are transforming traditional financial decision-making processes. This has been achieved by making sophisticated data science tools accessible to finance professionals without programming backgrounds. Though this makes decision-making more scientific, it also challenges the finance professional to remain relevant.

The accessibility to AI/ML tools that we have witnessed so far is just the beginning. The convergence of financial expertise with data science capabilities will reshape the landscape of decision-making by creating more application-specific tools. Reliance on historical data and intuition will be replaced with predictive algorithms, NLP, and automated optimization techniques. All these will lead to even more informed, forward-looking decisions. Most importantly, it will remove subjectivity from decision-making.

Where would this go from here? Though it is impossible to predict the future of technology because of the rate at which it is changing, let us at least be aware of emerging trends. These trends are likely to define the next

DOI: 10.4324/9781003619628-10

wave of innovation in financial decision-making. Technologies like generative AI (GenAI), automated machine learning (AutoML), and embedded analytics are poised to further transform the finance function. However, there will be a broader implication of these technological advances for organizations. There will be changes in skill requirements for finance professionals and a potential conflict between human judgment and algorithmic recommendations.

The real difficulty may not come from the technology front alone. We need to consider the challenges and responsibilities that come with the use of increasingly powerful analytical tools. Do we use technology to replace human decision-makers or to create new decision-making models using advanced computational capabilities?

Let us reminisce about the journey we have made so far, try to peek into the future, and consider how we can leverage the same.

The journey so far

Throughout this book, we have explored how Lo-code AI/ML tools are revolutionizing financial decision-making across numerous domains. We saw how powerful time series capabilities can transform our approach to financial forecasting. We reviewed clustering algorithms, revealing hidden patterns in customer behavior. These usages demonstrated that sophisticated data science tools have now become friendly enough to be used by professionals other than data scientists. The journey from spreadsheet-based analysis to implementing Monte Carlo simulations for investment appraisal represents a phenomenal shift in how financial professionals approach uncertainty and risk.

We have discussed the integration of ML into ABC and resource optimization. This enables a level of cost precision and operational efficiency previously unattainable with traditional methods. Similarly, our exploration of sentiment analysis showed how unstructured data from news and social media can now directly influence strategic financial decisions. This helps us bridge the gap between market perceptions and financial planning. These usages put to rest the notion that data analytics require advanced coding skills or specialized computing infrastructure. This is not to deny that advanced analytics is resource-hungry. At the same time, a large number of financial decisions can be made using ML tools on standard IT infrastructure.

Cases from fraud detection techniques and compliance monitoring systems demonstrated how AI can simultaneously enhance both operational efficiency and risk management. Traditionally, these two were considered competing priorities. This has been made possible by the ability to process vast quantities of transaction data to identify anomalies. The ability to scan and check documents for compliance issues using NLP enables financial professionals to uphold organizational values.

These tools have transformed the finance professional's role from a reactive reporter to a strategic adviser.

The journey ahead

The advantage of looking into the future is that you are correct until you get there! Beyond the tools we have explored, a new wave of emerging technologies can potentially transform financial decision-making processes. GenAI systems are rapidly evolving beyond simple language processing to solve financial problems. It will be able to create sophisticated financial narratives, automate financial reporting, and even generate alternative scenarios for strategic planning. These systems can now synthesize insights from vast document repositories and extract patterns from unstructured financial data. It can then communicate complex financial concepts in accessible language.

GenAI has made rapid strides in producing financial narratives, drafting reports, and summarizing regulatory content. These tools are increasingly being embedded in business intelligence platforms and ERP systems. It has also achieved a reasonable level of maturity, making it a good technology candidate for adoption.

Edge computing and real-time analytics platforms are bringing computational power directly to data sources. Edge computing processes data locally, at the "edge" of the network. This will enable instantaneous financial analysis at the point of transaction. This has a high rate of adoption in the manufacturing and logistics industry as compared to the finance industry, where there is selective adoption. Treasury functions are being reimagined with systems that continuously optimize cash positions using real-time market conditions. You can imagine the improvement in decision-making compared to when the optimization was done in periodic reporting cycles.

Quantum computing, though still in its early stages, promises to revolutionize optimization problems by offering tremendous computational power. They will have tremendous applications in portfolio management, risk assessment, and algorithmic trading. However, this is still at a research level and its potential is more conceptual than demonstrable. We have purposely not spoken about the computational power of quantum computing, fearing that the data may become outdated by the time this book hits the press. We always remind ourselves of the computing power of the Apollo Guidance Computer (AGC) onboard the Apollo spacecraft. AGC was designed specifically for spaceflight and was crucial for navigation, guidance, and control of the spacecraft. The AGC had 4KB of RAM, 72KB of

ROM, and a processor speed of about 1 MHz. Mind checking the power of your smartphone! The future can surprise all except the imaginative. We leave you to imagine what quantum computing can do.

AutoML platforms would make access to sophisticated analytics even easier. These systems automate the entire ML workflow, starting from data preparation and feature selection to model training, validation, and deployment. This will allow finance professionals to create custom predictive models with minimal technical expertise. The integration of embedded analytics into everyday financial systems would make advanced predictions and insights available within the existing applications.

Shaping the future of financial decision-making

The convergence of these technological trends will reshape the very foundation of the financial decision-making process. We will see a truly continuous planning and forecasting cycle. This will potentially replace traditional periodic budgeting with dynamic, AI-driven models that constantly adjust to changing conditions. The concept and methodology of variance analysis will have to be changed. Financial plans will evolve from static documents to living systems that automatically recalibrate as new data becomes available. This will allow financial decision-makers to respond to opportunities and threats with unprecedented agility, and most likely, with greater appropriateness.

The role of financial professionals will undergo significant transformation. They will shift from data gathering and processing toward generating insights and providing strategic guidance. AI systems will increasingly handle routine analytical tasks.

Financial decision-makers can then focus more on asking the right questions and interpreting model outputs in a business context. They will use their domain expertise to translate analytical insights into strategic action. This evolution will require a hybrid skill set combining financial expertise with data science literacy. The financial experts will be expected to be comfortable with algorithmic thinking and be able to explain complex model-driven recommendations to non-technical stakeholders. Since you are reading the last chapter, we do not doubt that you are ready with these skills.

The most exciting possibility is the emergence of augmented decision-making frameworks. Here, human judgment and machine intelligence will work in complementary ways. The systems will bring in algorithms with great computational power and pattern recognition ability. Human expertise will be used for contextual understanding, ethical considerations, and creative problem-solving. Organizations need to balance algorithmic efficiency with human wisdom and create governance structures to maximize the strengths of both. Financial decision-making will not be about choosing between human or machine approaches; it will be about designing integrated systems to enhance the combined capabilities.

Building a data-driven culture

In the face of the continuously evolving technical capability of AI/ML, a question arises. Is technology alone sufficient to drive transformation in the way financial decisions are taken? The advanced algorithms and Lo-code tools will yield limited value unless complemented by contextual interpretation and the right organizational culture. Building a data-driven culture remains a formidable challenge and a crucial element in the journey toward AI-enhanced financial decision-making.

Investment in AI/ML technologies and data infrastructure alone is likely to result in low adoption rates and limited impact. The key factor that is likely to make a difference is often cultural. This represents the collective mindsets, behaviors, and values that define the approach to decisions. Finance professionals may adopt or resist data analytics. The implementation of technology is arguably straightforward compared to the task of cultural transformation.

Let us explore strategies for fostering an organizational culture that is open to data-driven financial decision-making. We need to overcome common resistance points and develop data literacy across finance teams. The work does not end here. We will have to create governance frameworks that balance innovation with appropriate oversight. What we are discussing here is to be understood in the context of the technical knowledge presented throughout the book. It addresses the human elements that ultimately determine whether AI/ML tools will transform financial practice or merely add technical complexity.

The journey toward a data-driven culture is not one where financial decision-makers will walk alone. It requires thoughtful leadership, patience, and recognition that change does not happen overnight. While guiding their organizations through digital transformation, financial decision-makers will need to maintain a delicate balance between the excitement of technological possibilities and concern for the workflows affected by these changes. This balance will define the road to success. Let us explore how to navigate this challenging yet rewarding transition.

Importance of organizational culture in leveraging AI/ML tools

The technological infrastructure for AI/ML implementation is only what meets our eye. This financial transformation would stand on the complex foundation of organizational culture. The simplest of the Lo-code tools we have explored in this book will also falter without a supportive cultural environment. Cultural barriers, not technical limitations, are the primary threat to the successful implementation of AI initiatives. If finance teams find comfort in legacy processes or view data-driven approaches with skepticism, even well-designed algorithms will remain underutilized.

Cultural transformation does not mean approving technology investment. It begins with leadership commitment to actively encourage data-driven decision-making. By grounding their decision in advanced analytical insights, finance leadership can set the tone from the top. They need to demonstrate that evidence-based decision-making is valued more than intuitive ones. Senior leaders need to champion the data-driven mindset, celebrate every success, and accommodate the gradually rising learning curve. At the same time, the leadership must acknowledge and provide for setbacks, as not all initiatives may succeed. The reasons may range from lack of employee support to ineffective models.

The transition to a data-driven culture also requires the finance function to shift its identity from being reactive record-keepers to forward-looking strategic advisers. This evolution can be threatening to professionals who have built careers on traditional financial expertise. They need to be convinced of how AI/ML tools enhance rather than replace human judgment. It must be understood that the benefits of technology are amplified by human expertise, which has so far not been replicated by systems.

Fostering data literacy among accounting professionals

Data literacy involves the ability to read, understand, work with, analyze, and communicate with data. This is the fundamental building block of a data-driven financial culture. The challenge is profound, as traditional finance education has emphasized compliance over data-driven thinking and data science. We must systematically develop data literacy through structured learning pathways starting with basic concepts and progressing toward sophisticated analytical skills. These pathways should be set within financial contexts. As we have stated at the beginning of the book, the aim is not to make financial professionals data scientists. The aim is to get data support and analytics for decisions in the fields of budgeting, costing, investment analysis, and others.

Peer learning networks have been particularly effective in developing data literacy among finance professionals. Team members are encouraged when their colleagues successfully apply Lo-code ML tools to solve real business problems. We need to create formal mechanisms for knowledge sharing. One of the popular ways is to host an "analytics spotlight" where finance team members demonstrate practical applications of tools. You will find a host of them discussed in this book. These showcases make use of data science in everyday financial work as a normal phenomenon while building a repository of internal use cases that others can adapt.

Immersive learning through applied projects accelerates data literacy more than theoretical training alone. We need to identify low-risk opportunities for finance professionals to apply AI/ML tools to actual business challenges. These efforts should be supplemented by coaching and technical support throughout the process. These projects should start small before expanding into more complex applications. One may start with simple forecasting and gradually reach the stage of default prediction. The hands-on knowledge gained through these projects will build both technical competence and confidence. A positive feedback loop will further drive exploration and learning.

Change management techniques for technology adoption

Technology transition has both rational and emotional aspects. Recognition of both in the formal change management framework is necessary for the successful adoption of AI/ML. A popular change management model is the ADKAR model. This model combines the main pillars of change management. These are awareness, desire, knowledge, ability, and reinforcement. It provides a useful structure for guiding finance teams on this journey. We should begin by creating awareness of the specific pain points that AI/ML tools can address. These could be forecasting accuracy, variance analysis efficiency, risk detection capabilities, simulation, and others. This will focus on the "why," creating a stage for introducing the "how" of new technologies and approaches.

Resistance to data-driven approaches is likely to arise from legitimate concerns about job security, skill relevance, and decision authority. These need to be addressed and not dismissed as irrelevant. Effective change management would address them directly through transparent communication about how roles will evolve. It is imperative to recognize that we will need new skill sets, and at the same time, some of the old skill sets will become redundant. The acquisition of hybrid financial-analytical skills should be rewarded while providing opportunities to acquire the same. Data science should be positioned as a skill that enhances career prospects. Involving finance professionals in tool selection and implementation design will build ownership and reduce resistance to change.

New technology adoption should not be limited to critical issues alone, as that would make it seem restrictive. Sustainable adoption will require mainstream applications extending to everyday workflows and performance expectations. We may need to revise standard operating procedures to incorporate data-driven methods. Outputs from AI/ML systems should be integrated into regular management reporting.

Performance metrics may be changed to recognize the adoption of an analytical approach. Another important component of the change management process will be training. Training should focus beyond the technical functionality of the tool. It should include contextual judgment of when to apply which analytical technique and how to interpret results. It is easy to prove the technical competence of the tool; it is necessary to embed it within career progression.

Next steps for practitioners

We have seen some exciting tools and discussed adoption challenges. The question follows: "Where do we go from here?" What we have discussed in this book represents a starting point rather than a destination. This is a foundation upon which we can continue our journey by exploring the greater potential of these tools. Given the pace at which AI in finance continues to evolve, it is difficult to set a destination. As technology will bring new capabilities, we will shape best practices to adopt them. Implementing the tools that you have been introduced to requires both your conviction and a thoughtful strategy for organizational adoption. Your knowledge of finance holds the key to realizing the immense potential of these technologies.

In this final section, we will talk about continuing our learning journey beyond these pages. We will search for ways to implement AI/ML tools in ways that create lasting value for our organization. Our goal is to devise a roadmap that connects our existing knowledge of finance, the conceptual understanding acquired by reading this book, and the real-world impact we aspire to create. This may be broken into the following four steps, discussed later in this section.

- Identify low-risk use cases
- Form cross-functional teams
- Pilot projects and evaluate impact
- Refine and scale

All these will lead us to be at the forefront of a transformation that is redefining the finance profession.

Implementing the tools and techniques learned

It is often tempting to implement AI/ML tools across the complete spectrum of financial decision-making. However, following a strategic incremental approach is likely to lead to better absorption in the organization. We can start by identifying specific "pain points" where data-driven approaches could create immediate value. We need to carefully select issues that require the use of a simple tool. These targeted applications will provide quick wins to build acceptance and learning opportunities with low-risk exposures. For example, instead of applying ML tools to the entire budgeting process, we can start by applying ML tools to a single revenue stream with sufficient historical data and clear seasonal patterns.

One mistake to avoid is recognizing the importance of cross-functional collaboration beyond the finance department in creating a data-driven decision culture. It is important to create small, diverse teams that combine financial domain expertise with technical knowledge. The team members may be drawn from in-house data scientists or analytically minded finance professionals. You, having developed skills with the Lo-code tools discussed in this book, are a good candidate for such a team. The team should be able to address concerns of IT, business, and executive leadership. The IT department will look after infrastructure and security considerations, business units will provide operational context, and executive leadership will ensure strategic alignment. Insightful input from these perspectives will help in anticipating challenges and ensuring that AI solutions will solve critical business problems.

Much as it is important to implement data-driven solutions to business problems, it is equally important to develop evaluation frameworks. The impact of AI/ML implementations must be measured against clearly established baseline metrics. We need to document current performance levels for various processes, which would include forecasting accuracy, time spent on analysis, error rates, precision, and allied. We need to track these metrics as we implement new tools to quantify improvements and decide on further investment. This evidence-based approach will establish accountability and build organizational support by demonstrating tangible value. A note of caution here. No modes can guarantee precise forecasts; they merely reduce uncertainties around them. On top of it, initial models rarely perform satisfactorily, let alone perfectly. While establishing benchmarks, we need to include elbow room for improvement cycles to refine approaches based on performance feedback and the changing business environment.

Another important aspect of designing the implementation strategy is to encourage innovation. The technology supporting data-driven financial decision-making will continue evolving rapidly. This will not only lead to the emergence of improved tools but can also create space for new decision-making approaches. It would pay to establish formal mechanisms for ongoing exploration. These may include periodic "innovation harvesting," where the team will experiment with new tools or new areas of application. These structured innovation opportunities will make use of analytical tools dynamically and will continually expand decision-making capabilities.

Further learning and professional development

We have maintained throughout the book that our objective is not to make a finance professional a coding expert. However, we do want the finance professional to be comfortable with the available tools and techniques to arrive at better financial decisions. This process is continuous. We have admitted in the first chapter that the used libraries keep on evolving, including new libraries replacing old ones. This may require the code to be updated. The foundational knowledge provided in this book can be useful in adapting to most of the changes. You are aware of the resources available for finance professionals to enhance their finance skills. Similarly, there are resources available in the public domain to remain updated about the developments in technology. You can get financial datasets to apply techniques from this book and perfect your application skills. Whenever in doubt, consult the original documentation sites for the tools we have used. You may even find examples of financial applications in the documentation. Open-source learning communities provide valuable resources for ongoing skill development. These communities are particularly valuable for staying current with emerging best practices as the field rapidly evolves.

You may benefit from creating personalized learning pathways by focusing on a specific tool within a business context. Identify key tools or techniques that are relevant to your role and explore them in-depth. For example, if you work in management accounting, you might focus on mastering regression models for cost driver analysis. If you are an investment planner, you may focus on Monte Carlo simulations for risk assessment. You may gain from case studies of successful AI implementations in finance that can inspire your applications.

Between the time we started authoring this book and the time we have reached this page, much has changed in the AI landscape. These improvements have made our conviction of being able to use Lo-code tools even stronger. GenAI tools have shown tremendous improvement in the field of coding. We have used those tools to validate and even modify some of the code we have used in the book and have found them useful. We encourage you to consider using them while experimenting with new applications or when the libraries we have used are replaced with better ones. Be clear about what you want while prompting the GenAI tools. This includes defining the business problem, the nature of input data, and any specific tools you want to use. You can ask GenAI tools to modify the code to use a new library, replacing the one being used. Wherever possible, explain to the engine the computational steps involved. Once the output comes, verify the same outside the code. Do remember to specify to the GenAI tool what you need from the code and not the numeric or textual answer to the problem. In case of high-risk applications, have your IT team vouch for and modify the code. Also note that your organization may have some coding protocols and predefined structures, particularly about security and regulatory compliance. Include them in your prompt to the GenAI but have them verified by your IT team. In short, use the technologies available, but be wary of their limitations.

Continuous learning, innovation, and adaptation

A word of caution before we end. Please maintain perspective on the ultimate purpose of these technological advances. The book is focused on enhancing human decision-making rather than on replacing it. Migrate to a tool only when it improves financial decisions and creates organizational value. Do not succumb to the technical charm of a tool unless the one you are using is inefficient or outdated. There must be a balance between automating routine tasks and strengthening strategic decision-making.

Let us put this across for one last time. We have approached AI as a complement to financial expertise rather than a substitute for it. Navigate this evolving landscape with both innovation and wisdom. Adapt to the advancement of new technology, but do not lose sight of the fundamental purpose of financial decision-making: create sustainable organizational value.

We welcome you to the world of data-driven financial decision-makers.

Index

Made in the USA
Monee, IL
20 December 2025

39674078R00188